AF746794

Hinterlands and Commodities

European Expansion and Indigenous Response

Editor-in-Chief

George Bryan Souza (*University of Texas, San Antonio*)

Editorial Board

Cátia Antunes (*Leiden University*)
João Paulo Oliveira e Costa (*CHAM, Universidade Nova de Lisboa*)
Frank Dutra (*University of California, Santa Barbara*)
Kris Lane (*Tulane University*)
Pedro Machado (*Indiana University, Bloomington*)
Malyn Newitt (*King's College, London*)
Michael Pearson (*University of New South Wales*)

VOLUME 14

The titles published in this series are listed at *brill.com/euro*

Hinterlands and Commodities

Place, Space, Time and the Political Economic Development of Asia over the Long Eighteenth Century

Edited by

Tsukasa Mizushima
George Bryan Souza
Dennis O. Flynn

TUTA SUB AEGIDE PALLAS · 1683 ·

BRILL

LEIDEN | BOSTON

Cover illustration: Marie Anna Lee, 2013. Partially adapted from original illustrations by *Song Yingxing* in "Tian gong kai wu" manuscript, *1637*. Copyright of images by Song Yingxing: Max Planck Institute for the History of Science License: CC-BY-SA. See also *About the Cover Illustration.*

This publication has been typeset in the multilingual "Brill" typeface. With over 5,100 characters covering Latin, IPA, Greek, and Cyrillic, this typeface is especially suitable for use in the humanities.
For more information, please see www.brill.com/brill-typeface.

ISSN 1873-8974
ISBN 978-90-04-28388-6 (hardback)
ISBN 978-90-04-28390-9 (e-book)

Copyright 2015 by Koninklijke Brill NV, Leiden, The Netherlands.
Koninklijke Brill NV incorporates the imprints Brill, Brill Nijhoff and Hotei Publishing.
All rights reserved. No part of this publication may be reproduced, translated, stored in a retrieval system, or transmitted in any form or by any means, electronic, mechanical, photocopying, recording or otherwise, without prior written permission from the publisher.
Authorization to photocopy items for internal or personal use is granted by Koninklijke Brill NV provided that the appropriate fees are paid directly to The Copyright Clearance Center, 222 Rosewood Drive, Suite 910, Danvers, MA 01923, USA.
Fees are subject to change.

This book is printed on acid-free paper.

FSC www.fsc.org MIX Paper from responsible sources FSC® C109576

Printed by Printforce, the Netherlands

Contents

General Editor's Foreword

Over the past half millennium, from ca. 1450 until the last third or so of the twentieth century, much of the world's history has been influenced in great part by one general dynamic and complex historical process known as European expansion. Defined as the opening up, unfolding, or increasing the extent, number, volumes or scope of the space, size, or participants belonging to a defined people or group, location or geographical region, Europe's expansion initially emerged and emanated physically, intellectually, and politically in general in southern Europe and specifically on the Iberian peninsula in the fifteenth century and developed rapidly to include all of Europe's maritime and, subsequently, most of its continental states and peoples. Most commonly associated with events described as the discovery of America and of a passage to the East Indies (Asia) by rounding the Cape of Good Hope (Africa), during the early modern and modern periods, European expansion and encounters with the rest of the world multiplied and morphed into several ancillary historical processes including colonization, imperialism, capitalism, and globalization and dealt with themes, amongst others, that relate to contacts, ..."connections and exchanges peoples, ideas and products, especially through the medium of trading companies; the exchange of religions and traditions; the transfer of technologies; and the development of new forms of political, social and economic policy, as well as identity formation." (from the series' original objectives and mission statement) In consequence of its intrinsic importance, extensive research has been performed and much has been written about this field and the diverse topics that embody this subject over this entire period.

With the first volume published in 2009, Brill launched the European Expansion and Indigenous Response book series at the initiative of a well-known scholar and respected historian, Glenn J. Ames, who prior to his untimely passing was the founding editor and guided the first seven volumes of the series to publication. George Bryan Souza, who was one of the early members of the series' editorial board, was appointed the series' second General Editor. The series' founding objectives were and are to focus on publications "that understand and deal with the process of European expansion, interchange and connectivity in a global context in the early modern and modern period" and to "provide a forum for a variety of types of scholarly work with a wider disciplinary approach that moves beyond the traditional isolated and nation bound historiographical emphases of this field, encouraging whenever possible non-European perspectives"..."that seek to understand this indigenous transformative process and period in autonomous as well as interrelated cultural, economic, social, and ideological terms." (from the series' original objectives and mission statement)

The history of European expansion is a field that is challenging and interest in it, which is high is likely to continue, if not grow, in spite or perhaps, because of it being so polemical. The heightened dispute about the field has centered primarily on tropes conceived and written in the past by Europeans, primarily, concerning their early reflections, claims, and contestation about the transcendental historical nature of this process and its emergence and importance in the creation of an early modern global economy and society.

One of the most persistent complaints about the field is that it is "Eurocentric," which is a complaint about the perennial difficulty in introducing and balancing different historical perspectives, when one of the actors to some degree is neither European nor Europeanized – a conundrum that is alluded to in an African proverb, which states: "Until the lion tells his tale the hunt will always glorify the hunter." Another and, perhaps, an even more important and growing historiographical issue is that with the re-emergence of historical millennial societies (China and India, for example) and the emergence of other non-Western European societies successfully competing competitively politically, economically and intellectually on the global scene vis-à-vis Europe, the seminal nature of European expansion is being subjected to greater scrutiny, debate, and comparison with other historical alternatives.

Despite and, perhaps, because of these new directions and stimulating sources of existing and emerging debating points or lines of dispute about the field of history of European expansion, Souza and the editorial board of the series will continue with the original objectives and mission statement of the series and vigorously "...seek out studies that employ diverse forms of analysis from all scholarly disciplines, including anthropology, archaeology, art history, history, (including the history of science), linguistics, literature, music, philosophy, and religious studies." In addition, we shall seek to stimulate, locate, incorporate, and publish the most important and exciting scholarship in the field.

Towards that purpose, I am pleased to introduce volume 14 of Brill's EURO series, entitled: *Hinterlands and Commodities: Place, Space, Time and the Political Economic Development of Asia over the Long Eighteenth Century*. This group of scholars was assembled under the aegis of Professor Shigeru Akita of Osaka University, Japan to re-visit a quintessential, recurring and a constricted but perpetual research question, which is how to situate a place and its spatial relationship within its physical environments. These nine essays from ten contributors present new and stimulating theoretical conceptualizations and visualizations of place, space, and time relative to hinterlands, commodities, agency, and political economic development. Despite the diversity in the range in the topical and geographical coverage of the research presented in this volume, by focusing on hinterlands and commodities in the history of Asia's political economic development over the long eighteenth century, they deliver sophisticated, nuanced, and novel approaches towards the examination of early modern societies in general and those influenced and impacted in particular via their encounters with European expansion. These essays are case studies based on empirical research that is both exceptionally extensive and theoretically and conceptually well-grounded. And I, as the General Editor of this series and one of the editors of this volume, share the aspiration and conviction that this volume should provoke fresh thinking and debate on roles of hinterlands and commodities in place, space, time and the political economic development in Asian and Global history and the history of early modern and modern European expansion.

George Bryan Souza

Preface and Acknowledgements

Hinterlands and Commodities: Place, Space, Time and the Political Economic Development of Asia over the Long Eighteenth Century is a collection of essays that were prepared and presented by a group of American, Indian, and Japanese scholars at a session entitled: "Maritime Trade and Hinterland in Eighteenth Century Asia" at the XVth World Economic History Congress held in Utrecht, The Netherlands, in 2009. We, the editors, are grateful for the valuable comments from the floor and wish to thank in particular three session discussants: Professors Osamu Saito, Om Prakash, and Dennis O. Flynn for their observations.

Organization of the panel and of this volume, however, originated as part of a larger collaborative research project aimed at developing the field of Global History in Japan, one that profiles contributions from Asian perspectives under the leadership of Professor Shigeru Akita,[1] whose national joint-research team of prominent economic and social historians is headquartered at Osaka University. This initiative, with strong international academic connections, began joint-research activities in September 2003 and has already organized several international conferences, thirty-seven seminars and ten workshops.

This research grant's Global History seminar maintains a special academic connection with the Global Economic History Network (GEHN), an international collaboration of four universities (and key organizers): LSE (Patrick K. O'Brien), University of California, Irvine (Kenneth Pomeranz, now University of Chicago), University of Leiden (Peer Vries, now University of Vienna), and Osaka University (Kaoru Sugihara, now National Graduate Institute for Policy Studies: GRIPS, Tokyo). It endeavors to integrate excellent work in area studies, especially Asian studies, with which most participants are familiar with the comparative advantage of multi-archival research capability in multiple Asian languages. It has examined interactions among South Asian studies, Northeast Asian studies and Global History. Aims of this Japanese-originated project are twofold: first, to attempt to overcome academic barriers among three conventional divisions of departmental and research fields in Japanese historical studies: that is, Japanese history, Oriental history and Western history. The second aim is to accelerate academic dialogue and discussion with foreign

1 See Shigeru Akita, "Creating Global History from Asian Perspectives," in Patrick Manning (ed.), *Global Practice in World History: Advances Worldwide* (Princeton: Markus Wiener Publishers, 2008), chapter 4, pp. 57–68.

scholars in diverse fields of study, and to propagate the excellent work of Japanese scholars to the wider world.

Activities have been financially supported by grant-in-aids for scientific research from the Japan Society for the Promotion of Science (JSPS), as well as subsidies from the Suntory Foundation (Osaka) and the 21st Century COE (Center for Excellence) Programme<Interface Humanities>, Osaka University. This support has permitted Japan's Global History seminar to organize a wide range of activities, including "Cross-regional Chains in Global History: Europe-Asia Interface through Commodity and Information Flows" (December 2008 in Osaka), organization of participation in the XVth World Economic History Congress, and preparation of these essays for publication. The editors and all contributors gratefully acknowledge support for these efforts.

Shigeru Akita and the Editors

List of Contributors

Bhaswati Bhattacharya
is affiliated with the Centre for Modern Indian Studies, Göttingen as a senior fellow and with the International Institute of Social History, Amsterdam as an honorary fellow. She is the author of *The Indian Coffee House: A Social History*, (New Delhi, Social Science Press, 2014); *Distant Neighbours: the Armenian networks in the Indian Ocean and India, 1700–1947*, (Delhi: Primus, 2014) and articles in peer reviewed journals

George Bryan Souza
is affiliated with the University of Texas, San Antonio and, recently, a Mercator Guest Professor at Eberhard Karls Universität Tübingen. He is the author of *The Survival of Empire: Portuguese Trade and Society in China and the South China Sea, 1630–1754*, (Cambridge University Press, 1986 and 2004) and *Portuguese, Dutch and Chinese in Maritime Asia, c. 1585–1800: Merchants, Commodities and Commerce*, (Aldershot: Ashgate/Variorum, 2014).

Dennis O. Flynn
has been Alexander R. Heron Distinguished Professor of Economics, University of the Pacific, since 1998, and Director, Pacific World History Institute, since 2000. He is author/editor of eleven previous volumes, and co-General Editor (with Arturo Giráldez) of a seventeen-volume series, *The Pacific World: Lands, Peoples, and History of the Pacific, 1500–1900*, (Aldershot: Ashgate/Variorum, 2001–2014).

Tomotaka Kawamura
is a research fellow of the University of Tokyo, Japan. He is the author of several major articles: "British Business and Empire in Asia: The Eastern Exchange Banks, 1851–63," in David Bates and Kazuhiko Kondo eds. *Migration and Identity in British History: Proceedings of the 5th Anglo-Japanese Conference of Historians*, Tokyo, pp. 193–207, November 2006 and "Maritime Trade and Economic Development of Penang, c. 1786–1830," in Loh Wei Leng, T.N. Harper and Sunil S. Amrith eds., *Penang and the Indian Ocean: Proceedings of the Penang Indian Ocean Conference 2011*, Malaysia, pp. 52–59, November 2012.

Marie A. Lee
is Assistant Professor of Graphic Design, University of the Pacific. She focuses on communication design with emphasis on community-based design, cultural

sustainability and interdisciplinary collaboration. She heads a Kam Minority Heritage Project (China) that received 2013 and 2014 SEED (Social Economic Environmental Design) Award honorable mentions.

Tsukasa Mizushima
is a Professor in the Department of Oriental History at the University of Tokyo. His interests include Indian rural development, Pan-Asian GIS-based historical studies, and global history from an Asian perspective. He is the author of *Nattar and the Socio-Economic Change in South India in the 18th-19th Centuries*, (ILCAA, Tokyo University of Foreign Studies, 1986) and others.

Ei Murakami
is an Associate Professor at the Institute for Research in Humanities, Kyoto University. He is the author of *Umi no Kindai Chūgoku: Fukkenjin no katsudō to Igisiru/Shinchō* [Maritime History of Modern China: Local Fujian actors and British and Chinese Empires], (Nagoya: University of Nagoya Press, 2013), and his main academic interest is socio-economic history of modern China.

Ghulam A. Nadri
is an Assistant Professor of History at Georgia State University, USA. He is the author of *Eighteenth-Century Gujarat: The Dynamics of Its Political Economy, 1750–1800* (Leiden: Brill, 2009) and has published a number of journal articles and book chapters on the aspects of merchants and maritime trade of Surat and Gujarat in the early modern period.

Atsushi Ota
is an Associate Professor in the Graduate School of Letters at the Hiroshima University. He is the author of *Changes of Regime and Social Dynamics in West Java: Society, State, and the Outer World of Banten, 1750–1830*, (Leiden: Brill, 2006) and other articles.

Ryuto Shimada
is an Associate Professor in the Graduate School of Humanities and Sociology at the University of Tokyo. He has published several articles and a book on maritime Asian history including his doctoral thesis at Leiden University in 2005: *The Intra-Asian Trade in Japanese Copper by the Dutch East India Company during the Eighteenth Century* (Leiden: Brill, 2006).

About the Cover Illustration

Nine panels on the cover of this volume graphically represent elements of porcelain's commodity chain production system, including depiction of transportation overland of items from hinterland fabrication to a regional port, continuing on to distant port facilities. Upon arrival overseas, some porcelain objects settle within port cities themselves, while other items migrate to urban and rural areas connected via waterways and land routes. Retail end-market purchase by a Japanese customer – resident of an urban environment, a hinterland, or somewhere in between – is depicted in the final panel.

Panels reflect the underlying theme of this collection of essays: linkages among/between hinterlands, port cities, and urban areas. Metamorphosis from raw materials to end products is emphasized, as is relocation of products from place to place, across space, over time, to diverse end-market destinations. This volume presents theoretical constructs and case-studies with the collective goal of improved comprehension of interconnections among hinterlands and urban concentrations in context of powerful regional and global forces.

List of Figures, Maps and Tables

Figures

Maps

Tables

Introduction

Tsukasa Mizushima, George Bryan Souza and Dennis O. Flynn

Hinterlands and Commodities: Place, Space, Time and the Political Economic Development of Asia over the Long Eighteenth Century is a collection of essays that examine questions concerning temporal and spatial relationships among central places (such as cities, trading centers or ports),[1] hinterlands (a term to be defined and elaborated below), commodities, and political economic developments in Asia and the Global economy over the long eighteenth century. Editors of this volume decided to assemble a group of economic historians of Asia for the purpose of discussing those topics in context of inter-connections among and between local, regional and global economies. With that objective in mind, a session on these issues was organized for the World Economic History Congress (WEHC) in Utrecht, the Netherlands, in August 2009.

A talented group of senior and emerging scholars of early modern Asian and Global History – five from Japan, two from India, and two from the United States of America – contributed. They include historians and an economist who have written and produced major works and articles that are empirically-driven and theoretically and conceptually sound. Contributors possess wide-ranging linguistic skills. Some are well versed in use of European (in particular Dutch-language documents in archives of the Dutch East India Company) and Asian primary sources, including some sources either not previously utilized or not readily accessible.

This collection of essays is timely and important, since scholarly interest in hinterlands and commodities continues and there is renewed interest in novel foci that clarify impacts of maritime trade connected to Asia and their importance

1 Walter Christaller, a German geographer, developed central place theory (a set of ideas that explain the spacing and function of settlement patterns) in 1933 after he began work on the economic relationships between cities and their hinterlands, see the English translation of his original work, *Die zentralen Orte in Süddeutschland* (1933), Walter Christaller, *Central places in southern Germany*, trans. Carlisle W. Baskin (Englewood Cliffs, N.J.: Prentice-Hall, 1966). G. William Skinner, the American anthropologist, emerged as a leading proponent of its incorporation and application to Chinese history in the latter half of the twentieth century; see G. William Skinner, "Presidential Address: The Structure of Chinese History," *The Journal of Asian Studies* 44, no. 2 (1985). and "Marketing and Social Structure in Rural China: Part I, Part II, and Part III," *The Journal of Asian Studies* 24, no. 1 (1964): 3–43; 24, no. 2 (1965), pp. 195–228; and 24, no. 3 (1965), pp. 363–399. We are arguing that it may and should be incorporated and applied to all Asian history.

© KONINKLIJKE BRILL NV, LEIDEN, 2015 | DOI 10.1163/9789004283909_002

for political economic development of place, space, and time across regions in the eighteenth century. This volume also fits well in context of current discourse on Asian economic history, in which much attention is devoted to indigenous entrepreneurial activity. Interesting concrete examples illustrate instances whereby local indigenous merchant's controlled distant trading relations. These essays contribute substantially to an Asia-centered approach to early modern trade history that stretches from the Indian Ocean to the East China Sea, a region that experienced increasingly intense interactions among Asian merchant communities and European commercial powers over the period.

The central theme of this volume deals with historical relationships between Asian hinterlands, commodities, and port cities over the long eighteenth century. While this statement is accurate, essays by Souza and Flynn/Lee, two explicitly conceptual and theoretical contributions, lead off by offering and developing the following additional sub-themes. One, they observe that in historiographic terms there is generalized disconnect or disjuncture between work by historians who focus on maritime issues vis-à-vis work by others who deal exclusively with land-based or terrestrial pursuits and activities. This means that specialists in maritime history (i.e. experts who investigate organization, handling, transport, and commercialization of goods, services, and ideas via water) pay scant attention to work by specialists who focus on terrestrial issues. The same is true for terrestrial (social, cultural, and political economic) historians, who fail to address or acknowledge linkages with contributions by maritime historians. Mechanisms to remedy this artificial maritime-terrestrial disjuncture are offered.

Second, meaningful progress requires new conceptualizations and models that permit visualization of how hinterlands – as productive, commercial and end-market spatial units of analysis – integrated and inter-connected via ports and maritime routes to productive, commercial and end-markets in nearby, regional and global locations, including dis-contiguous, distant hinterlands. Theoretical constructs offered herein define, examine, and model individual behaviors of objects, services, or ideas (i.e. every "thing" that may be commoditized) such that inter-dependent or symbiotic linkages across place, space, and time can be visualized. Taken together, these complementary models expose the powerful transformational nature of commodities in terms of their dynamic interconnections to power, wealth, knowledge and meaning,[2] along with interactions with epidemiological and ecological forces.

2 For an introduction to three of these four concepts and their relationship to civilizational analysis, see Jóhann Páll Árnason, *Civilizations in dispute: historical questions and theoreticaltraditions* (Leiden; Boston: Brill, 2003). While Mercator Guest Professor at Tübingen

Third, hinterlands need to be examined in terms of (what has been described as) "time compression." Namely, when, how and why did places and spaces change over time? Rates of change accelerate and intensify to a degree that compressed time, in a manner that significantly impacted hinterlands, cities, and polities throughout the globe. Think of the impact of maritime technology during a few hundred years prior to the eighteenth century. Global warming at the end of the last Ice Age – more than 10,000 years ago – raised oceans worldwide by over three hundred feet, thereby isolating Eastern and Western Hemispheres. Atlantic and Pacific Oceans became such formidable barriers to interaction that humans were mutually unaware that another hemisphere even existed. Establishment of trans-Atlantic and trans-Pacific linkages in the late-15th and 16th centuries, respectively, resulted in ecological and social transformations so profound that Crosby depicts the post-fifteenth century exchange of flora, fauna and diseases as "a revolution more extreme than any seen on this planet since the extinction at the end of the Pleistocene."[3] Worldwide reconnection of the Americas with the rest of the world marked the birth of globalization – an epochal sea-change in economic, epidemiological, ecological, demographic and cultural history.[4] Our aim here is not to revisit birth-of-globalization debates, of course, but rather to focus upon time compression.

Time required for Atlantic and Pacific crossing was essentially infinite prior to the late-15th century. These aquatic barriers were quickly transformed into "liquid highways" during the sixteenth and seventeenth centuries, on the other hand, once passage (while difficult) could be routinely completed within months. Mountainous and desert barriers remained relatively formidable in terms of land travel, while oceanic routes experienced phase transition from barriers into maritime freeways. Speed of maritime travel accelerated further during the eighteenth century, as turn-around times shrank and efficiency of cargo handling improved dramatically (for instance, through development of warehousing). In the context of global history, in other words, today's ubiquitous containerized freight systems represent but recent developments in a

---

University in 2010–2011, Souza and his colleague, Hans Ulrich Vogel, in an as yet unpublished article are responsible for modifying Árnason's civilizational analysis and ideas of worldmaking by dividing his idea of knowledge into and advocating the addition of meaning as a fourth component to the analysis.

3 Alfred W. Crosby Jr., *Ecological imperialism: the biological expansion of Europe, 900–1900* (Cambridge; New York: Cambridge University Press, 1986). p. 271.

4 For example, see Dennis O. Flynn and Arturo Giráldez, *China and the birth of globalization in the 16th century* (Farnham: Ashgate/Variorum, 2010).

five-century evolutionary process of efficiency gains in cargo-handling. For purposes of this discussion, the key point is that significant transportation efficiencies emerged during the eighteenth century.

While physical environments for the handling of goods at ports and instruments and capital to finance long-distance commercial and colonial exchanges improved, modifications in ship design and building technologies not only kept pace but grew at an even faster rate over time in comparison with some other efficiencies.[5] Search for speed under sail, which had been well underway during the eighteenth century, would reach its apogee with clipper ship design and building technology toward the middle of the nineteenth century.[6] With surprising rapidity induced by an "industrious" era being replaced by the "industrial" age, steamship design and construction emerged to liberate movement of goods over water from its previous dependence upon wind power.[7] In sum, our intention in alluding to these over-arching transformative trends that occurred during our period and continued and intensified after is, in the first instance, to stress that time compressed, and time continues to compress in the sense that places and spaces worldwide – including hinterlands – experience intensified interaction in fundamental respects that beckon for historical context. In the second instance, articulating and examining time compression and its connection with hinterlands is of fundamental importance. And, third, articulation of this theme with study of hinterlands in general, and Asian hinterlands in particular, must engage global history.

Taken individually or together, these themes permit us to direct attention, reflecting transition from economic systems organized for maintenance of local societies (in some instances) to systems geared for market economies linked to the outside world. The shift was further facilitated by great inflows of specific types of bullion and specie from the other side of the world, which exchanged for Asian commodities via ports. Bullion inflows throughout Asia also prompted intra-Asian transactions among ports and hinterlands.

---

5 For an introduction to the arguments that we are alluding to see the following articles: Jan Lucassen and Richard W. Unger, "Shipping, Productivity and Economic Growth"; Paul A. Van Dyke, "Operational Efficiencies and the Decline of the Chinese Junk Trade in the Eighteenth and Nineteenth Centuries: The Connection"; Richard W. Unger, "Ship Design and Energy Use, 1350–1875"; and Jan Lucassen, "Work on the Docks: Sailors' Labour Productivity and the Organization of Loading and Unloading," in Richard W. Unger, ed. *Shipping and economic growth, 1350–1850* (Leiden; Boston: Brill, 2011). pp. 3–44; 223–246; 249–267 and 269–278.

6 See the classic study on this topic, Howard Irving Chapelle, *The search for speed under sail, 1700–1855* (New York: Norton, 1967).

7 Jan De Vries, *The industrious revolution: consumer behavior and the household economy, 1650 to the present* (Cambridge; New York Cambridge University Press, 2008).

Increasing monetary and commodity transactions throughout the eighteenth century propelled Asian societies through a phase transition that fundamentally altered relations among ports and hinterlands, and redirected Asian societal paths.

These essays discuss how transformations experienced in different regions of Asia were shaped through different prisms, such as European and Asian expansions, colonial administration, diaspora activities, and local control over political economic development. By marshalling information on population trends, land usage, productivity, prices, division of labor and other basic building blocks, they aim to clarify the nature and extent of changing economic structures in diverse regions of Asia. Many analyze hinterland relationships among port cities and emerging markets. Some discuss the importance of intra-regional maritime trade in general, and volumes and composition of exchanges in particular, by focusing upon evolving experiences of producers and society in one particular place and space during a particularly crucial period of time in the emerging history of Asia and the Global economy.

Place: Situating Asian Hinterlands

For historians and other social scientists engaged in research on general, broad topics, themes, locations, and time frames mentioned above, the issue of situating a specific central place and its relationship to physical surroundings is of paramount interest. In other words, in our specific case, the perennial question is: did Asian central places create hinterlands? Or did Asian hinterlands create central places? And to what extent is the relationship between the two over time dynamic and evolving? Situating a place in spatial relationship to its environment is a quintessential, recurring and perpetual research question.

In this volume, we chose to re-visit the question of importance of hinterlands in Asian history.[8] "Hinterland" comes from German and literally translates as "behind land." Synonyms for the term are environs, surroundings, vicinity, and neighborhood; one antonym is heartland. Academics – geographers, historians, and other social scientists – have extensively discussed and employed the term. Nevertheless, there has been controversy over its definition, which to some degree remains. Consider the following definition: "the region lying behind the coast district; hence, a region remote from cities and

8 For a not so recent but excellent example of scholarship that deals with hinterlands in the making of Asian society, see Kenneth Pomeranz, *The making of a hinterland: state, society, and economy in inland North China, 1853–1937* (Berkeley: University of California Press, 1993).

towns."[9] Historians and other social scientists have long held that this dictionary definition is *de facto* too vague and imprecise to be applicable to the types of historical processes that are the focus of this volume.

While generally acknowledging this dictionary definition of a hinterland, historians have tightened it by focusing and delimiting the spatial relationship between a central place, such as a port city involved in maritime trade, and areas immediately contiguous, known to geographers as "*umland*."[10] Furthermore, they have generated additional concepts related to physical proximity of hinterlands through application of the terms "continuous" and "discontinuous." By emphasizing hinterland-port relations, rather than focusing solely on relations among ports, we strive to elucidate interconnections among hinterland-port networks as well as reorganize studies to explicitly recognize and address current imbalances between maritime versus land-based or terrestrial histories in this volume. Also, we embrace the port and colonial-port paradigm[11] and its articulation vis-à-vis hinterlands.

Two important aspects about Asia should be noted before turning to specific features of the eighteenth century. First, Asia was environmentally and economically diverse (and evolving) throughout the eighteenth century, as were relations among ports and hinterlands. India and China manufactured great varieties of commodities for world markets. Many areas in Southeast Asia were thinly populated, yet rich due to exportation of spices and other natural products. Some areas concentrated production on distinct commodity exports to diverse end-markets in exchange for an array of imports necessary for sustenance of local economies. Distant trade networks were essential for maintenance of diverse and dispersed economies.

The second aspect concerns the role of merchant intermediaries in construction and maintenance of commercial networks, since markets were too scattered for producers to conduct trade by themselves. Considerable numbers of intermediaries specialized in trade. Statistics for an area in South India, for instance, indicate that trading communities comprised around six percent of total population in the late eighteenth century.[12] Southeast Asia also contained

---

9 Noah Webster, *New Collegiate dictionary. A Merriam-Webster* (Springfield, Mass.: G. & C. Merriam Co., 1959). p. 391.

10 Eugene van Cleef, "Hinterland and Umland," *Geographical Review* 31, no. 2 (1941).

11 There exists an extensive and growing literature of works on this paradigm, see, for example, Frank Broeze, ed. *Brides of the sea: port cities of Asia from the 16th–20th centuries* (Honolulu: University of Hawaii Press, 1989); *Gateways of Asia: port cities of Asia in the 13th–20th centuries* (London; New York: Kegan Paul International, 1997).

12 J.K. Bajaj and M.D. Srinivas, "Indian Economy and Polity in the Eighteenth Century: The Chengalpattu Survey: 1767–74," *Indian Economy and Polity* (1995).

prominent trading groups such as the Chams and the Bugis, as did South China.

Space and Time: Economic Developments in Asia over the Long Eighteenth Century[13]

Indigenous economic developments in Asia met ever-increasing activities of European commercial powers during the eighteenth century, when the balance between Asia and Europe started to lean toward the latter, and when different regions within Asia came to be further integrated due to movement of people and commodities. The century may also be defined as the period when Asia headed towards "modernization," while at the same time beginning colonization under European powers. As locations of Asian and European contacts, early modern Asian ports have been widely studied by historians over the past few decades.

Widely-observed Asian port activity was one expression of market-economy development in its hinterlands. Commodities transacted ranged from high-skill textiles to spices, sugar, sea-cucumber, and others, some with intimate links to global markets. Asians migrated across rivers, mountains, seas, and oceans, transforming areas by opening fields and mines in response to dynamic markets, after having already experienced vigorous trade activities among ports and hinterlands long before arrival of maritime Europeans. Some new economic fields were indeed opened upon entry of Europeans, but the general sphere had long been dominated by Asians. The power balance between Asians and Europeans shifted during the eighteenth century, however, as European maritime powers gradually extended their control from ports to hinterlands in many parts of Asia. Multifaceted processes observed in this historical phase have attracted considerable attention by historians, but the main focus of this book is mutual relations among port and hinterland developments during this critical period.

Ports were spheres where dynamic interactions with hinterlands are observable. They served multiple functions. First, Asian ports acted as gateways for commodity exchange between hinterlands and overseas markets. The preponderance of the value of European exports and re-exports to Asia consisted

13 See Leonard Blussé and Femme S. Gaastra, eds., *On the eighteenth century as a category of Asian history: Van Leur in retrospect* (Brookfield, Vt.: Ashgate, 1998), and Robert Travers, "The Eighteenth Century in Indian History: A Review Essay," *Eighteenth-Century Studies* 40, no. 3 (2007).

overwhelmingly of American silver, specie, base metals (iron and lead), broad cloth, and a relatively limited number of other items.[14] Conversely, categories of Asian exports to Europe were far more numerous and diverse, including agricultural products (e.g. spices and teas), minerals and metals (e.g. copper and zinc), sea shells (e.g. cowries from the Maldives and Mozambique),[15] and a host of raw and manufactured cotton and silk textiles and other manufactures (e.g. porcelain). While Europe-Asia trade was vibrant and expanding, significantly larger volumes of the same and other sets of goods from diverse parts of Asia were involved in intra-Asian commerce that was executed by both Asian and European merchants. European companies benefited from participation in intra-Asian commerce, although both groups were active during the eighteenth century. Toward the end of the century, European state-sponsored company activities waned, while private European and American merchant activities grew to dominate Eurasian-American and intra-Asian trade.

Second, ports served as distribution centers for imported items, as *entrepôts* that channeled products to various locations, including hinterlands. Ports also were centers of production in their own right. Major ports in India, for example, contained textile manufacturing and warehouse facilities necessary for overseas export as well as inland distribution.

Third, in addition to their *entrepôt* function, ports also served as end-markets for commodities brought both from internal hinterlands and overseas.

14 For recent scholarship that documents the narrow range and composition of trading items from Europe that were involved on the Cape route, see Jan De Vries, "Connecting Europe and Asia: A Quantitative Analysis of the Cape-route Trade, 1497–1795," in *Global Connections and Monetary HIstory, 1470–1800*, ed. Dennis O. Flynn, Arturo Giráldez, and Richard Von Glahn (Burlington, VT Ashgate, 2003); Jan De Vries, "The limits of globalization in the early modern world," *The Economic History Review* 63, no. 3 (2010).

15 For the classic study dealing with cowries, see Jan S. Hogendorn and Marion Johnson, *The shell money of the slave trade* (Cambridge; New York: Cambridge University Press, 1986). For recent work based on Portuguese sources that document significant collection and incorporation of cowries from Mozambique in Indian and Atlantic Ocean commercialization networks over the eighteenth century, see George Bryan Souza, "The Portuguese Crown and Brazil: Tobacco Cultivation, the African Slave Trade, and the Atlantic and Global Economy c.1674 to 1776," *Revista da Cultura* 25(2008); "Cowries and Commerce: Mozambique, the Portuguese, and Afro-Asian-American exchanges in the emerging Global economy" in *Monies for ordinary people: neither precious nor national* (Institute of Oriental Culture, University of Tokyo, Tokyo, Japan unpublished conference presentation 2009).

Since ports, especially major colonial port cities in Asia attracted more and more people during our period, they increasingly functioned as end-markets. Investments in built environment and infrastructure expanded in order to accommodate burgeoning volumes of grains and other daily consumables as well as manufactured goods.

Fourth, ports were places of interaction among migrants from hinterlands and immigrants. Missionaries, merchants, soldiers, and communities of various beliefs (Buddhist, Christian, Hindu, Taoists and other religious traditions), and diverse origins and ethnicities came together to inhabit dynamic ports and colonial port cities. New views and attitudes toward religion, life styles, and the world evolved in response to proximity and intimacy among inhabitants of central places.

Last, colonial port cities emerged as military, political, and economic bases used to penetrate and control hinterlands. During the latter half of the eighteenth century most of Asia, with the exception of East Asia, faced major political unrest and conflict. European powers possessed relatively small, well-equipped and well-organized armies comprised of European as well as locally recruited and trained Asian soldiers, which contributed substantially to their military supremacy. With their success, indigenous inhabitants increasingly sought to settle disputes via intermediation of local authorities in colonial port cities. In addition, indigenous rulers began to gradually transfer local resources, via cession of land and tax authority to Europeans, thereby facilitating and strengthening colonial rule.

Asian port and colonial port cities participated in one or more of the functional roles mentioned above. Ports and hinterlands evolved out of mutual interaction, although not every Asian central place experienced the same rate or level of growth and development over the eighteenth century. Many of these central places still play important roles in Asia, including some that remain or emerged as state capitals or provincial centers. Over this period, interaction between Asian central places in general (and port and colonial port cities in particular) with their hinterlands was dynamic – not passive. Individual central places demonstrated a variety and range of complicity and density in urban-commercial and political growth and development. At the same time, respective hinterlands to which these central places were (and in some cases still are) connected experienced distinctive indigenous economic developments which affected and influenced the central places to which they were articulated. In sum, mirror-like recursive relationships between hinterland and central spaces are quintessential features of eighteenth-century Asian history and development.

Organization and Presentation

Nine individual case studies address the nature of place, space, and time at local through regional to global levels. Some questions asked and answered extend beyond nation state treatments, leading to reinterpretation of pre-colonial and colonial Asian and European commercial (especially maritime) connections during a time of historic inter-regional connections. Case studies in this volume are organized and presented in two parts. Although the first two case studies (Souza and Flynn/Lee) are intentionally and explicitly theoretical and conceptual, all essays are based upon empirically driven research and interpretation of myriad archival and secondary source literatures.

The geographical range and distribution of these empirical case studies are distributed from East Africa to East Asia. The western most case study (Flynn/Lee) deals with connections between Gujarat, Mozambique and attending hinterlands. Three others (Bhattacharya, Mizushima, and Nadri) focus primarily on human agency topics associated with central-place-hinterlands India and transnational inter-connections with Southeast and East Asia. Three additional case studies (Kawamura, Ota, and Shimada) focus on topics dealing primarily with production and distribution dynamics within Southeast Asia and beyond. Two case studies (Murakami and Souza) deal with topics that study cases focusing primarily on (1) the internal Chinese economy and hinterland environment; and (2) an examination of southern Chinese sugar's commodity chain from production through commercialization throughout Asia (primarily, Japan).

In Chapter 1, "Hinterlands, Commodity Chains and Monetary Circuits in Asian History: Sugar in Qing China and Tokugawa Japan," Souza discusses the continued conceptual and theoretical importance of hinterlands that is emerging for commodity chains, and production, commercial and currency circuits. He examines crucial issues and questions dealing with place, space, and time relationships among production, commercial expansion and economic development in Asia in the early modern period, especially over the long eighteenth century. He asks and provides preliminary answers to questions: what are hinterlands, commodity chains, production, commercial and currency circuits? How are they interconnected? And why are they important in the history of production, commercial expansion and economic development in early modern Asia? He uses the well-known and well-studied case of expansion of sugarcane production in South China over the long eighteenth century and its general and specific roles in China's internal and external economy, via China's maritime trade and exports to Japan, to elucidate, analyze, develop and visualize his arguments. By using commodity chain analysis and linking expansion of hinterland cash-crop production circuits with commercial and currency circuits, he shows that it is possible to estimate the volume and the utilization of single or multiple monies or media of exchange paid to producers by merchants. He advocates linking historical individual commodity chain analysis with production, commercial and currency circuits of individual and categories of commodities in general and in Asia in particular. Commodity chain analysis offers an important conceptual and theoretical tool for connecting maritime trade and internal economies in Asia. It is of fundamental importance in articulating and examining the role of maritime trade and exchange with the history of economic development of state or imperial formations and their hinterlands.

In Chapter 2, "Hydraulic Metaphor: A Model of Global and Local Connectivity," Flynn and Lee argue that the history of hinterlands in part demonstrates conceptual and theoretical inadequacies inherent at the building-blocks-foundation level of conventional supply and demand concepts. Consequently, they offer an intuitive, visual representation of hinterlands in local, regional, and global contexts via a Hydraulic Metaphor that is based upon an unconventional model of supply and demand; it is more comprehensive than the standard supply and demand model and is designed for non-economists to comprehend. They incorporate Pedro Machado's archival research on eighteenth-century textile trade between West India and East Africa as an example for development and illustration of their model. Machado's research describes large-scale international trade that depended fundamentally upon hinterland end-markets in Africa as well as hinterland production centers in India. Not only was there no direct interaction between residents of Indian hinterlands and African hinterlands, Banyan merchants who coordinated distant overseas markets also had no direct contact with residents of any hinterland group. The Hydraulic Metaphor describes explicit mechanisms that enlarge or deplete inventory stocks (i.e. populations, or holdings of items), and thereby determine the precise quantity of a good – monetary or non-monetary – destined to remain in inventory (i.e. to populate) each distinct market area throughout the world. The Hydraulic Metaphor helps to expose the logic of market connections across local as well as distant spaces. It also depicts economics as a physical science – in addition to a social science – that corresponds more accurately with historical evidence than is possible using conventional supply–demand models.

In Chapter 3, "Changing Dynamics of Port-Hinterland Relationships in Eighteenth-Century Gujarat," Nadri argues that relationships between ports and their hinterlands involved interdependence and complementarities, and depended upon complex sets of factors such as production and consumption capacity, strength of commercial entrepreneurs, volume and value of maritime trade, and policies and orientation of states/rulers. According to Nadri, these factors experienced major transformation in the eighteenth century as a consequence of political and economic developments, and he examines changing dynamics of port-hinterland relationships in Gujarat. His article highlights major reconfigurations that took place in coastal structures with regard to relative importance of ports and analyzes their impacts on the society, economy and people of the region that constituted the hinterland.

In Chapter 4, "Ports, Hinterlands and Merchant Networks: Armenians in Bengal in the Eighteenth Century," Bhattacharya focuses on intermediaries who actively operated during the concerned period. She examines Armenian merchants in Bengal in the eighteenth century, demonstrating how spatially-separated members of a merchant community (such as Armenians) operated in different capacities at distinct locations, key linkages that connected ports with their hinterlands and beyond. Examination of wills of Armenian merchants operating in Bengal brings to light mechanisms underlying this network. According to her, for instance, the area streching from inland places like Dacca, Patna and Saidabad were connected to ports like Calcutta, Madras, Bombay and Basra via extremely flexible mechanisms that on the one hand yielded lesser Armenian merchants distinct autonomy, by allowing them to act on their own, while on the other hand, they could enter into long-standing credit relationship with merchants across religious boundaries. Her case study clearly exhibits inter-linages among various networks operating in the region.

In Chapter 5, "Linking Hinterlands with Colonial Port Towns: Madras and Pondicherry in Early Modern India," Mizushima assesses the impact of development of colonial port towns upon indigenous structures in the interior. He examines various aspects of indigenous structures in the interior, including occupational structure, rural–urban grain trade, and social order, to clarify the process of how the latter's position toward urban centers in general and colonial port towns in particular and their hinterlands were transformed. He concludes that establishment of colonial port towns as colonial capitals with political, economic, and social hegemony over hinterlands progressed in parallel with formation of extremely unbalanced relations between rulers and ruled in the colonial economy, and also that the relational change between port and hinterland itself constitutes colonial history.

In Chapter 6, "Maritime Asian Trade and Colonization of Penang, c. 1786–1830," Kawamura investigates maritime trade, population, urban development, and colonial formation of Penang between the late eighteenth and early nineteenth centuries. He examines correlation of economic development of

Penang's hinterland with expansion of maritime trade, and the extent to which the "Chinese century" influenced socio-economic development of Penang and its hinterland. Unlike previous studies, his essay attempts to direct attention more heavily toward the Indian world of Penang, which acted as a regional port for the Bay of Bengal as well as for the eastern part of the Straits of Malacca.

In Chapter 7, "Toward a Transborder, Market-Oriented Society: Changes in the Hinterlands of Banten, c. 1760–1790," Ota challenges the conventional view that Banten, West Java, was in constant decline in the eighteenth century, while presenting complex features of the area's development. He shows that *ponggawa* elite began to exert stronger influence over cultivators in hinterlands of Banten as cultivators came to settle in one place longer than before because of promotion of pepper cultivation by the Dutch East India Company. Pepper cultivation itself was not very successful, but important local impacts stemmed from formation of an increasingly market-oriented society, as people became more and more involved with cash income obtained via crop markets. When withdraw from pepper production began, some ponggawa switched instead to cultivation of rice for outside markets. Other cultivators grew coffee. Some migrated to the eastern part of Banten hinterland for wage work in the sugar industry, which had developed there because of sugar's shift away from the *ommelanden* (environs) of Batavia. The east Banten hinterland also attracted increasing numbers of Chinese and Sundanese migrants, who were engaged in "clandestine" trade networks of opium and other items linked to Chinese, Southeast Asian, and British traders. These factors facilitated transformation of East Banten into a multi-ethnic borderland society. Development of this hinterland area contrasts sharply with the waning state-controlled trade-and-commerce image portrayed in previous studies.

In Chapter 8, "South-East Asian Tin Production and its Export Trade in the Eighteenth Century," Shimada engages one of the most important products in Southeast Asia, tin, as a case study that reveals a close relationship between indigenous development of local industry and the ever-growing global economy in the period. His essay demonstrates that the eighteenth century was the key age for extensive development of the tin industry around the Malay Peninsula, thanks to growing intra-regional market demand, particularly in China. His survey of tin production history in Thailand, Malaysia and Indonesia clarifies the practical present-day combination of Chinese immigrant laborers and mining techniques, as well as the role of foreign traders such as the Dutch East India Company.

In "Trade and Crisis: China's Hinterlands in the Eighteenth Century": Chapter 9 and the final essay of this volume, Murakami discusses the relationship between (a) development of China's hinterlands led by trade expansion, and (b) the economic and social crisis that occurred later in the 19th century. After summarizing the Ming–Qing transition and features of the Qing system, he investigates development of trade and population expansion in the hinterlands from the late-seventeenth century to the late-eighteenth century, including problems accumulating in the hinterlands. Through analysis of political, social, and economic institutions related to the crisis, he concludes that trade fluctuations and disasters in these remote areas from the late-eighteenth century to the mid-nineteenth century resulted directly from the type of economic development that previously occurred in the hinterlands.

In conclusion, this collection of essays seeks to stimulate new theoretical conceptualizations and visualizations of place, space, and time relative to hinterlands and political economic development in Asian history. Despite, and perhaps because of, diversity of individual contributor foci and interpretation in this volume, we hope to encourage historians and other social scientists to perennially re-envisage and recreate historical images of place, space, and time, and to beware of interpretations that diminish or reduce actual complexity and diversity to one-dimensional foci that falsify reality. We believe that understanding is enhanced via fine-grained case studies that are theoretically and conceptually well-grounded. Case studies in this volume aspire to provoke fresh thinking and debate on roles of hinterlands in place, space, and time in Asian and Global history.

CHAPTER 1

Hinterlands, Commodity Chains, and Circuits in Early Modern Asian History

Sugar in Qing China and Tokugawa Japan

*George Bryan Souza**

Introduction

This essay (re-)examines a well-known and well-studied example of an Asian hinterland: the case of cash-crop production of sugar in South China over the long eighteenth century.[1] It pays particular attention to this commodity's importance in China's (internal and external) economy. It overviews expansion of production in Liangnan and on Taiwan and documents how sugar emerged as one of China's primary exports in regional and intra-regional Asian maritime trade. Sugar in Qing China and Tokugawa Japan is examined as an example of a (generic) commodity and its commodity chain (i.e. how sugar was productively, commercially and culturally employed) in order to elucidate, analyze, and develop my arguments concerning the conceptual and theoretical importance of hinterlands, commodity chains, and production, commercial and currency circuits in place, space, and time relationships in Asia in the early modern period. It argues that individual commodities and their chains must be examined and integrated into an analysis of networks of commodity chains and production, commercial, and currency circuits in order to develop an essential methodological tool for visualizing and understanding the evolution and dynamism of commercial expansion and the history of economic development.

* I wish to thank Professors David Anthony Bello, Mark Elvin, Jane Kate Leonard and Hans Ulrich Vogel, students in several seminars and workshops while a Mercator Guest Professor in Germany, and two ayonomous referees for helpful suggestions to earlier drafts of this essay.

1 For the general case of sugar, see Sidney Wilfred Mintz, *Sweetness and Power: The Place of Sugar in Modern History* (New York: Viking, 1985). For the specific case of sugar in China, see Christian Daniels, *Science and Civilisation in China, Vol. 6. Biology and Biological Technology. Pt. 3. Agro-Industries and Forestry: Sugarcane Technology* (Cambridge; New York: Cambridge University Press, 1996); and Sucheta Mazumdar, *Sugar and Society in China: Peasants, Technology, and the World Market* (Cambridge, Mass.: Harvard University Asia Center, 1998).

© KONINKLIJKE BRILL NV, LEIDEN, 2015 | DOI 10.1163/9789004283909_003

It is based primarily upon published Japanese[2] and Dutch[3] archival materials and pertinent secondary literature and organized into five sections: First: "Introduction"; Second: "Hinterlands, Commodity Chains, and Circuits"; Third: "Chinese Sugar in Qing China and Tokugawa Japan"; Fourth: "Hinterlands, Commodities, Commercialization and Monies in Early Modern Asian History"; and Fifth: "Conclusions."

Hinterlands, Commodity Chains, and Circuits

The following questions are answered in this section: what are hinterlands, commodity chains, production, commercial and currency circuits? How and why are they interconnected? Why are they important in the history of production, commercial expansion and economic development in early modern Asia?

2 For statistics primarily from Japanese sources on numbers and cargo lists dealing with trade in sugar from China (and Southeast Asia) to Japan by Chinese junks and Dutch East India Company (VOC) shipping over our period, see Anon. *Tōban Kamotsu-Chō* [*唐蛮貨物帳*] [the Cargo List of Chinese and European Ships] 2 vols. (Tokyo: Naikaku bunko, 1970); Yōko Nagazumi, ed. *Tōsen Yushutsunyūhin Sūryō Ichiran – 1637~1833 Nen Fukugen Tōsen Kamotsu Aratamechō, Kihan Nimotsu Kaiwatashichō* [*唐船輸出入品数量一覧: 1637~1833年 復元唐船貨物改帳・帰帆荷物買渡帳*] [Statistical Lists of Import–export Goods by Chinese Ships for the Years 1637–1833: Reconstruction of *Tōsen Kamotsu Aratamechō* (Control List of Chinese Cargo) and *Kihan Nimotsu Kaiwatashichō* (List of Japanese Goods Sold to Ships Returning to China) Using Dutch Records] (Tokyo: Sōbunsha, 1987); and Yoneo Ishii, *The Junk Trade from Southeast Asia: Translations from the Tôsen Fusetsu-Gaki, 1674–1723* (Singapore: Institute of Southeast Asian Studies, 1998).

3 For statistics primarily from Dutch East India Company (VOC) sources on numbers and cargo lists dealing with trade in sugar from China, Taiwan (and Southeast Asia) to Japan primarily by VOC shipping over our period, see Leonard Blussé, et. al. (eds.) *De Dagregisters van het Kasteel Zeelandia, Taiwan, 1629–1662*. 4 vols. (s-Gravenhage: M. Nijhoff, 1986–2000); Cynthia Viallé and Leonard Blussé, (eds.) *The Deshima Dagregisters*. 12 vols. (Leiden: Institute for the History of European Expansion, 1986–2005); H.T. Colenbrander, et. al. (eds.) *Daghregister Gehouden int Casteel Batavia vant Passerende daer ter Plaetse als over Geheel Nederlandts-India*. 31 vols. ('s-Gravenhage; Batavia: Martinus Nijhoff; Landsdrukkerii, 1887–1931); Willem Philippus Coolhaas, et. al. (eds.) *Generale Missiven van Gouverneurs-General en Raden aan Heren XVII der Verenigde Oostindische Compagnie*. 14 vols. ('s-Gravenhage: M. Nijhoff, 1960–2008); and Pieter van Dam [Frederik Willem Stapel and Carel Wessel Theodorus van Boetzelaer van Asperen en Dubbeldam, eds.] *Beschrijvinge van de Oostindische Compagnie*. 7 vols. ('s-Gravenhage: Nijhoff, 1927–1954).

"Hinterland," as already discussed in the Introduction to this volume, comes from the German words for "behind" and "land" and may be defined as a remote country region, which is distant from cities or their cultural influence; and land adjacent to water, which lies next to coastline or a river. Some of the synonyms for the term are environs, surroundings, vicinity, and neighborhood and one antonym is heartland. Academics, from geographers, historians, and other social scientists have extensively discussed and employed the term.[4] Proponents of the port and colonial port paradigm[5] have narrowed and made its definition very precise. Hinterlands, for them, are lands that lie near or next to coastline or a river that are articulated to central places (port and colonial port cities). They also recognize that the physical proximity of hinterlands to ports may be continuous or discontinuous and remote, distant areas from cities or their cultural influence may also be considered hinterlands.[6] We follow the port and colonial port paradigm definition of hinterlands in this essay.

Thing(s)[7] is a term that can be used to refer in an approximate way to an object or to a particular set of objects. Both, things or objects, can be objectified or treated as inanimate, with no feelings, opinions or rights of their own. Goods and chattels[8] are things that one may own other than land and buildings. A commodity is a substance, material, or product (produced by an industrial process or, less commonly, something that is grown or obtained through farming) with particular physical characteristics from which things or objects have been or can be made. It is also a substance or product with a quality or

4 See, for example, Kenneth Pomeranz, *The Making of a Hinterland: State, Society, and Economy in Inland North China, 1853–1937* (Berkeley: University of California Press, 1993).

5 For examples of the port and colonial port paradigm and hinterland relationships with maritime trade, see Frank Broeze, (ed.) *Brides of sea: Port Cities of Asia from the 16th-20th Centuries* (New South Wales: University Press, 1989); Frank Broeze, (ed.) *Gateways of Asia: Port Cities of Asia in the 13th-20th Centuries* (London; New York: Kegan Paul International, 1997); Dilip K. Basu, (ed.) *The Rise and Growth of the Colonial Port Cities in Asia* (Lanham: University Press of America, 1985); Indu Banga, (ed.) *Ports and Their Hinterlands in India, 1700–1950* (New Delhi: Manohar Publications, 1992); and Rudrangshu Mukherjee and Lakshmi Subramanian, (eds.) *Politics and Trade in the Indian Ocean World: Essays in Honour of Ashin Das Gupta* (Delhi; New York: Oxford University Press, 1998).

6 Jeremy Adelman and Stephen Aron, "From Borderlands to Borders: Empires, Nation-States, and the Peoples in between in North American History," *American Historical Review* 10:3–4 (1999).

7 Arjun Appadurai, "Commodities and the Politics of Value" in Arjun Appadurai (ed.) *The Social Life of Things: Commodities in Cultural Perspective* (Cambridge; New York: Cambridge University Press, 1986).

8 Commodification, regrettably, also includes human beings via enslavement as indicated by our use of chattels in this definition.

value that can be traded, bought or sold. Commodities are, generally, objectified and, logically, commoditized. "Commodity chains" begin with synonyms: things or objects, which can be seen or touched but are not usually a living animal, plant or person.

A commodity chain or chains refers to factors, processes, technology, logistics, distribution and commercialization networks, consumption patterns, and demand for one or more substances, materials, or products with particular physical characteristics which things or objects have been or can be made that are of a quality and value, which are traded, bought or sold by society. A typical generic representation of a commodity chain is shown in Figure 1.1. As a general proposition, it begins with a commoditized object that is identified, defined, and situated by its particular physical characteristics and its subsequent use, value, and demand within society. While described as a chain, operationally it is more circular and screw-like in function as the commodity moves or flows through place(s), space(s) and time(s). Temporally, it is a dynamic historical process that is subject to change, evolution, contraction, cessation, growth, and progression over time. Spatially, it is also an inclusive analytical tool, since it captures either a moment or large segments in time that encompasses all factors of production, commercialization, and consumption of a commodity over space. And it captures the actions of multiple agents and their agencies in this process. Since individual commodities and their chains share symbiotic production and marketing networks with other commodity chains, this analytical tool is even more dynamic, because it interfaces relationships

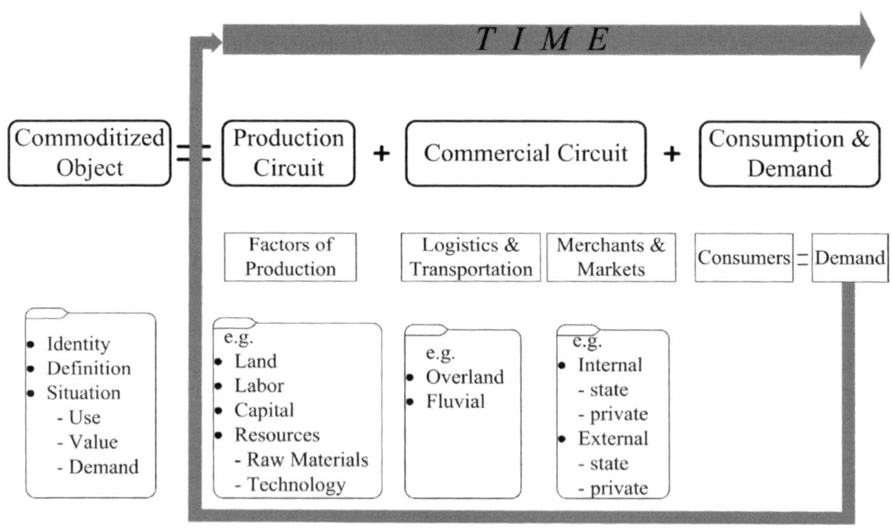

FIGURE 1.1 *A generic commodity chain: Characteristics and components*

between one commodity chain and others, one example being production of raw cotton or silk and multiple natural dyes with handicraft textile production, and another example being mining of copper and zinc for minting of coin and metallurgical production of brass.[9]

A production circuit is in general a finite geographically delimited area where a commoditized object is obligatorily produced. If the object is dependent upon elaboration or process of transformation, its production circuit is likewise where those modifications are performed. It is also an area that may contain the initial or primary market(s) in which the commodity is sold. The term circuit is employed in this case to suggest some regularity in production and some geographically fixed location(s) or site(s) of production. A commercial circuit(s) is/are the area(s) in which the produced commodity is introduced into its final or end-market, commercialized, and, generally, consumed. The term circuit is employed in this case to suggest some geographically fixed or localizable site(s) of some regularity and volume in commercialization and consumption of the commodity. Depending upon the commodity and by focusing on the trajectory and acceptance of a commodity in individual and multiple commercial circuit(s), it is possible to capture and visualize the overland and maritime flows of commodities, in this case, within and from China to Japan and identify catchments areas where commodities such as Chinese sugars were consumed not only in their internal, regional but also global end-markets. Furthermore, the flow of credit and debt and related documents (as distinct from specie and coins, see currency circuit below) and related documents are considered in our model as components found and integrated within production and commercial circuits. Although they share in some functions and behavior as near or semi- currency, we have chosen not to raise credit and debt to a level or degree of consideration as a circuit.

Finally, the term currency circuit has been employed, primarily by economic historians specializing in the history of types and flows of monies and commodity monies.[10] The term circuit is employed in this case to suggest (1) a finite but, more generally, a broad geographically delimited area, region, or state, where money or monies, as media of exchange, circulated for purposes of

---

9 See for example, the doctoral dissertation by Hailian Chen, "Zinc for Coin and Brass: Bureaucrats, Merchants, and Laborers in Qing China, c.1684–1835," Ph.D. dissertation, Eberhard Karls Universität Tübingen, forthcoming: 2014.

10 Akinobu Kuroda, "Another Monetary Economy: The Case of Traditional China." in A.J.H. Latham and Heita Kawakatsu (eds.). *Asia Pacific Dynamism, 1550–2000* (London; New York: Routledge, 2000), pp. 187–198; and Akinobu Kuroda, "Concurrent but Non-Integrable Currency Circuits: Complementary Relationships among Monies in Modern China and Other Regions." *Financial History Review* 15:1 (2008), pp. 7–15.

payments of goods, services, and obligations such as taxes or debts; or (2) a more explicit and much less broadly defined finite geographically delimited area, where one money, as a medium exchange, was preferred over all others by one group, normally producers of one commodity, and preferentially circulated for purposes of payment to those producers for their production of a specific commodity. For example, in the first case in Qing China, over the period under examination, two metals, un-minted silver and copper coin were in circulation and the accepted media of exchange for larger and smaller transaction purposes in payments for goods, services, and obligations such as taxes or debts.[11] In the second case in Qing China, still in the period under examination, tea producers in the Fujian highlands, for example, developed a preference from the very late eighteenth and into the early nineteenth century to receive payment for their tea production in a foreign minted silver coin, the Carolus peso or dollar, because of its reliability in touch and purity of silver content over the usual and here-to-fore commonly accepted un-minted silver and copper coin in circulation.[12] It is critically important to observe that in this second example both production and the currency circuits shared the same space.

Chinese Sugar in Qing China and Tokugawa Japan

Based upon our definitions presented above, the historical example of sugar in Qing China and Tokugawa Japan is examined in this section to elucidate, analyze, and develop my arguments concerning the conceptual and theoretical importance of hinterlands, commodity chains, and production, commercial and currency circuits in place, space, and time relationships in Asia in the early modern period.

Why sugar? First, it is a well-studied and examined historical example of a (generic) commodity that was embroiled on a significant scale as a cash-crop in the expansion of agricultural production, commerce and economic development in South China. Second, although sugar's commercial and cultural trajectory as a commodity made it a fundamentally important object in trade and daily life, its basic characteristics are shared with all other commoditized objects. And, any number of other famous (e.g. tea, cotton, silk), infamous (e.g. opium), little known (e.g. zinc, mercury), seemingly innocuous or

11 See Richard Von Glahn, *Fountain of Fortune, Money and Monetary Policy in China, 1000–1700* (Berkeley: University of California Press, 1996).

12 See Kuroda, "Another Monetary Economy."

exotic (e.g. safflower, saffron, tumeric) commoditized objects could have been chosen for this same process of examination and evaluation. Third, its selection and examination also permits us to develop a simplified methodological model that explicates and provides a "how to" situate a commodity spatially (vis-a-viz hinterlands and central places), physically, and meta-physically within its chain of production to consumption and articulate that commodity and those chain-linked relationships within the circuits in which the commodity is produced, commercialized, consumed and demanded.

Sugar's salient characteristics as a commodity and the components of its commodity chain may be outlined by inserting, following or flowing sugar as the commodity that is being refered to in Figure 1.1. Sugar, as a commoditized object in general and in particular in China, has as already cited been identified, defined, and situated by Mintz, Daniels, and Mazumdar. They focused initially on sugar's particular physical characteristics, its subsequent use, value, and demand within society. Sugar's use as a sweetener and a source of energy, value, and demand within Chinese society paralleled its use elsewhere. However, there was a significant difference – sugar in China was not employed as in many other societies in drinking or consuming tea nor in chocolate or coffee, the latter not being introduced or widely accepted in China as in other parts of the world at this time.

Because of the cultivar's requirements in regards to climatic, elevation, soil, and temperature conditions, sugar production in China was dramatically concentrated in the south, southeast, Taiwan, and Sichuan. In this essay, we shall concentrate our examination on those areas of production that are quintessentially and incontestably hinterlands –land found next to coastlines, adjacent to water, and out-laying or some distance from central place locations (e.g. cities and port cities) in Liangnan in Guangdong in the south, Fujian in the southeast, and offshore Taiwan. These areas possessed significantly large tracts of land suitable for growing sugar-cane and producing sugar and they were found in the macro-region of China that was most directly and intensely involved in the internal and external commercialization of sugar over this period.

There are several reasons why it was decided to exclude an examination of the history of Sichuan's sugar production in this essay. First, the history of sugar cultivation, production, and commercialization in this part of China is less well-known by this author, which impedes inclusion and competent treatment. Second, regardless or in part because of Sichuan's location in the southwest, its incorporation by Skinner into one of the macro-regions of China, and may be considered remote from Ming-Qing China's political centers, it is a region that resists facile typification as a hinterland.[13] However, within the macro-region in which Sichuan is situated, it is obvious that sugar-cane cultivation and sugar production was located in rural areas that were distant from central places (i.e. its hinterlands) and sugar's internal and external commercialization was controlled primarily by merchants in its central places.

Skinner used drainage basins of principal river systems to define and align the geographical and spatial categorization of macro-regions of China.[14] (See Map 1.1) Sugar was produced in regions of Liangnan, primarily in Guangdong, in the Southeast Coast, primarily in Fujian, and offshore on Taiwan, the latter being treated by Skinner as a physiographic subsystem and not a macro-region. He found core areas, essentially sub-regional spaces with nested markets and centers of population within all of China's macro-regions. Core areas in regions of Liangnan, primarily in Guangdong, and in the Southeast Coast, primarily in Fujian, interestingly enough, share identically the same space as hinterlands of those regions where sugarcane could be and was produced.[15]

---

13 Although located some distance from most of China's major cities, to designate Sichuan as "a remote country region" and to suggest that it was a hinterland in relation to other parts of China is highly problematic. Sichuan, as Professor Elvin in personal correspondence has reminded me, was the center of a distinctive bronze-working art very roughly contemporaneous with the Shang and Chengdu was considered one of China's finest cities. It was one of the three main centers of trade and taxation during the Song dynasty, and arguably the original home of Chinese paper money (whether or not depends on the precise definition adopted). And its population in Qing times was larger than that of most (possibly all) European states. See Cao Shuji 曹樹基 in Ge Jianxiong 葛劍雄 ed. *Zhongguo renkou shi* 國人口史 [History of the Population of China] volume 5 (Fudan University Publishing, 2001), p. 691.

14 For a description of the macro-region concept, see G. William Skinner, "Presidential Address: The Structure of Chinese History." *The Journal of Asian Studies* 44:2 (1985). And for an effective critique of it, see Carolyn Cartier, "Origins and Evolution of a Geographical Idea: The Macroregion in China," *Modern China* 28:1 (2002).

15 Harold Adams Innis, a Canadian political economist and a contemporary of Skinner, made numerous general contributions and in particular to the study of economic geography and history, communications theory, and regional development in the latter half of the twentieth century. In his work on economic settlements and markets, he was preoccupied with the effects of a vast new land area on Europe (long before "ghost acres" came into vogue), the importance of staple products in development and the political implications of unused capacity in frontier economies. To my knowledge, during their lifetimes, Innis' work was not directly linked to scholarly discussion of either Skinner's macro-regions, Liangnan and Taiwan as frontiers, or sugar as a staple crop in commerce and economic development of Liangnan and China. This is regrettable since the commerce and political economic development of the hinterlands and the central places in one of Skinner's macro-regions of China: Liangnan (and Taiwan) may also be viewed and framed

MAP 1.1 *China: Skinner's macro-regions*

MAP 1.2 *Sugar in China: Elevation*

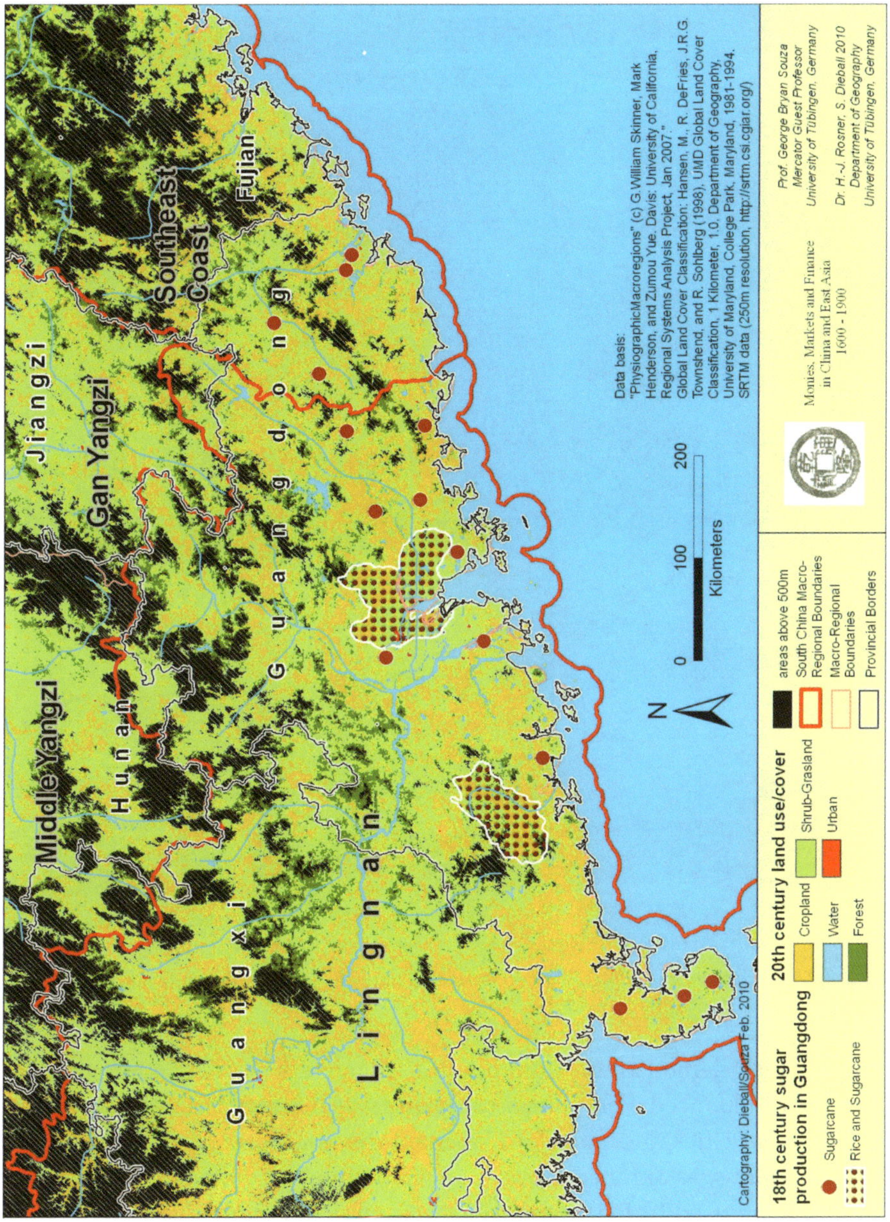

MAP 1.3 *Sugar in China: Land use*

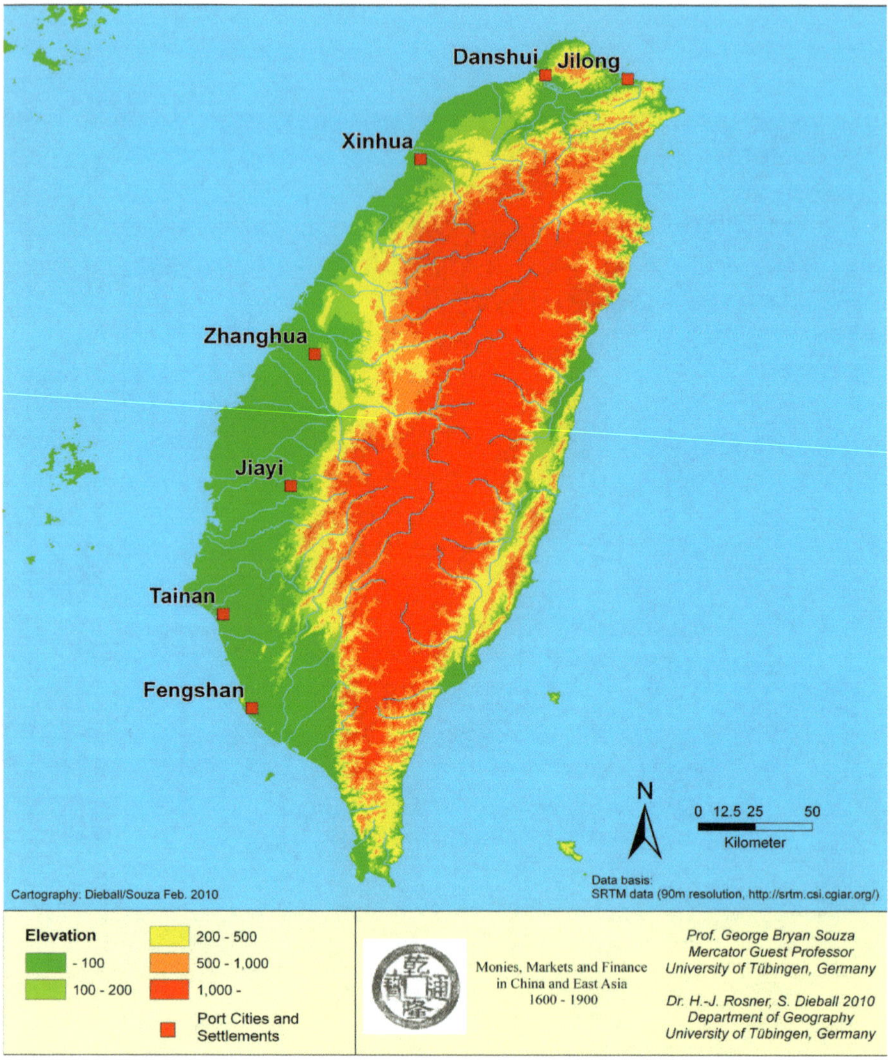

MAP 1.4 *Taiwan: Elevation*

Maps 1.2–1.5 demonstrate some physical characteristics (elevation and land use) that influenced where sugar could and was produced as well as locations of principal cities and ports of Liangnan, the Southeast Coast, and Taiwan. Macro-regions, as Skinner shows, may be defined by drainage basins, which may also be used to locate and separate physical boundaries in space. It is within those macro-regions in which a network of geographical, ecological, geological, and physiological chararcteristics emerge that favor or dis-favor resource exploitation and contribute to the creation of a productive regional

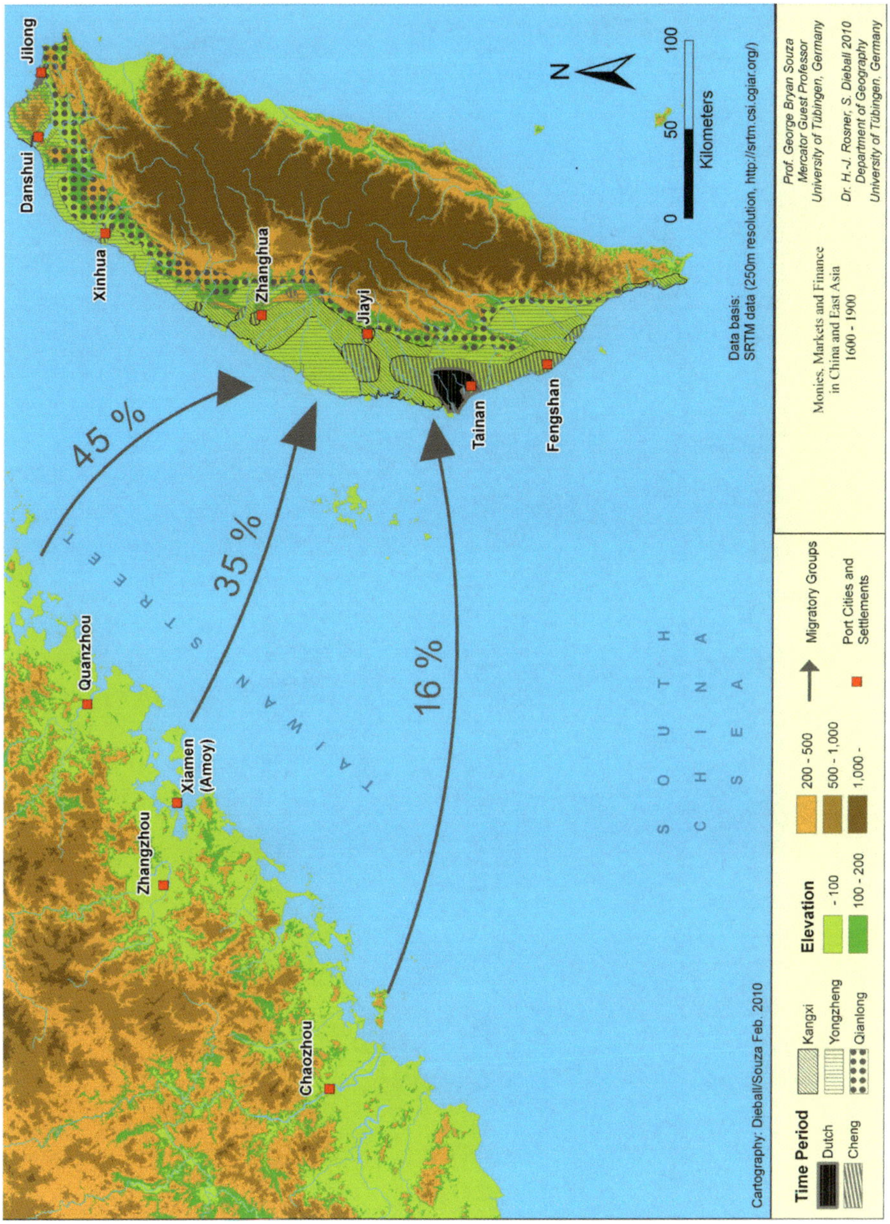

MAP 1.5 *Migration and sugar expansion on Taiwan, ca. 1620–1796*

MAP 1.6 *China's sugar: Commodity chain, circuits, commerce, and consumption*

identity, such as in our case sugar-cane cultivation and production in South China.[16]

During our period, sugar production was organized by peasants whose economy was oriented toward production of subsistence crops, rice primarily, and sugar as the major cash crop on rather small plots of land. Population in both of these regions was relatively dense and was more acute in Fujian, which resulted in both internal and external migration. Map 1.5 indicates migratory flows from Fujian to Taiwan and areas on the island, which they brought into rice and sugar cultivation at different times over the period.

Map 1.6 shows China's macro-regions, their sub-regional cores, population centers, and areas of sugar production, and ports from which junks and other ships sailed with the export commodity to Japan, India, Persia, and elsewhere.

Our specific focus as alluded to above is to examine the case of Chinese sugar to provide a background and a framework of analysis for comparing and examining all other cases of commercial production of cash-crops (including subsistence crops, rice in particular, whose surplus also emerged and entered market economies), metals, and handicrafts in Asia and interconnecting their internal and external market relationships, via maritime and overland trade, with general and spatially specific internal monetary flows and economic developments. Pomeranz[17] developed a series of important observations and arguments about sugar in *The Great Divergence* (2000) that focused on the relative strength of China's production, commercialization, and its comparatively high levels of per-capita consumption vis-à-vis Europe.[18]

---

as being frontiers and almost completely dependent historically upon mono-cultural production of a cash- or staple crop for its development. For Innis' works that support this observation, see, for example, the first two chapters (The Importance of Staple Products in Canadian Development and The Political Implications of Unused Capacity in Frontier Economies) in Harold Adams Innis, *Staples, Markets, and Cultural Change: Selected Essays* (Montreal: McGill-Queen's University Press, 1995), pp. 1–34.

16 For a thorough discussion of natural resource exploitation, see Edward B. Barbier, *Scarcity and Frontiers: How Economies Have Developed through Natural Resource Exploitation* (Cambridge; New York: Cambridge University Press, 2011).

17 See Kenneth Pomeranz, *The Great Divergence: China, Europe, and the Making of the Modern World Economy* (Princeton; Oxford: Princeton University Press, 2000).

18 The use of 'per capita consumption' as a metric is fraught with an interpretive issue as a socially meaningful definition. Since the price of sugar was initially high and its availability relatively scarce, despite growing and relatively widespread consumption, it is probable that consumption of sugar (particularly refined versus raw cane) in China as elsewhere at this time was probably more skewed toward distinct and fairly well-to-do

TABLE 1.1 *Sugar production and consumption in Qing China, c. 1750*

- Population (Estimates)
  - 170 to 225 million inhabitants
- Production (Location and Estimates):
  - Concentrated in the south and southeast, excludes Sichuan
  - Volume:
    - Guangdong: 672 million pounds/year
    - Taiwan: 104 million pounds/year
    - Fujian: 86 million pounds/year
- Imports (Estimates):
  - Vietnam (1730): 80 million pounds/year
- Exports (Estimates):
  - 1792: 11 million pounds/year
- Per capita consumption (Estimates):
  - 3.8 to 5.5 pounds/year

POMERANZ WITH OTHERS

Bin Wong,[19] in a slightly earlier work, and Pomeranz were primarily addressing the advanced nature of specific regions of Qing China's economy. There is great utility in their work, estimates and methods. I rely on and have carefully selected some of their evidence in this essay. While I also engage, primarily, some of Pomeranz's findings, it is important to remember that my essay addresses a fundamentally different issue than either Wong or Pomeranz.

Pomeranz's observations and arguments about sugar in Qing China are summarized in Table 1.1. He estimated that China's population was around 170 to 225 million inhabitants' c. 1750.[20] Using works of Mazumdar and

subset of society. Regardless of this caveat, the manifold problems related to use of population sizes in China with other parts of the world at this time and its imprecision as an indicator of individual consuming patterns, we shall employ it, since it establishes a rough order of magnitude in the volume of sugar produced, commercialized, and consumed by one with another population.

19 See R. Bin Wong, *China Transformed: Historical Change and the Limits of European Experience* (Ithaca and London: Cornell University Press, 1997).

20 Readers should remember that this is a summation of Pomeranz's findings as a point of departure for comparision and discussion. Specialists (outlined in personal correspondence from Elvin) dealing with China's population and its demographic make-up during the Ming-Qing period suggest that an estimate of the population of 'China' in 1750 from 170 to 225 million may be on the low side. Why? There is evidence that suggests that

Marks,[21] he confirmed that production of sugar was highly concentrated geographically. Excluding production figures for Sichuan, he estimated that around the same date total annual production of sugar in China was around 862 million pounds, with Guangdong producing by far the most 672 million, Fujian 86 million and Taiwan 104 million. Imports from Vietnam, the only suggested external supplier, were estimated from an earlier date (1730) at 80 million pounds per year. With the above, he estimated that per capita consumption of sugar was between 3.8 to 5.5 pounds per year in China around 1750, which is a rate that compares quite favorably with contemporaneous lower per capita rates of sugar consumption in parts of Europe.[22] It is true that per capita consumption of sugar in China c. 1750 would have been lower if we employed an alternative estimate for China's total population, for example, of around 250 to 275 million inhabitants. However, the per capita consumption rate of sugar in China would not have fallen under 3 pounds per year under any of these scenarios, which is the point that Pomeranz has made and we agree: estimated contemporaneous per capita consumption of sugar rates in China c. 1750 compared favorably with those rates in parts of Europe.

Some additional observations may be deduced and advanced about sugar in Qing China from Pomeranz's discussion and work of others and are summarized in Table 1.2. Using Mazumdar's estimate that cultivated sugar yields by producers was 2,400 pounds per acre and that six *mu* equaled one acre, the total number of acres or *mu*, respectively, that were required to produce

---

China's population had quite possibly already reached 200 million by about 1600. See Shui-Yuen Yim, "Famine Relief Statistics as a Guide to the Population of Sixteenth-Century China: A Case-Study of Honan Province," *Ch'ing-shih wen-t'i* 3:9 (1978), p. 18. There is no question or doubt that there was serious loss of population during the Ming-Qing transition (the middle of the 17th century). How large was the loss and how fast the recovery was are both problematic. Consequently (and for brevity's sake I am summarizing a great deal of specialized study here), the crux of the discussion hinges on the estimated size of population loss, the rate(s) of population recovery and growth, and, co-terminously, incremental population growth produced by changes in the geographical meaning of 'China' and its territorial expansion over the eighteenth century to reach one estimate of 430 million or another for China's total population by 1850. For the 430 million estimate, see Ping-ti Ho, *Studies on the Population of China, 1368–1953* (Cambridge, Mass.: Harvard University Press, 1959), p. 278. For further discussion, see, for example, Mark Elvin and Josephine Fox. "Marriages, Births, and Deaths in the Lower Yangzi Valley during the Later Eighteenth Century." in Clara Wing-chung Ho (ed.) *Windows on the Chinese World: Reflections by Five Historians* (Lanham: Lexington Books, 2009).

21 See Robert B. Marks, *Tigers, Rice, Silk, & Silt: Environment and Economy in Late Imperial South China* (New York: Cambridge University Press, 1998).

22 See Pomeranz, *Great Divergence*, pp. 120–122.

TABLE 1.2 *Sugar production and consumption in Qing China, c. 1750*

- Estimated Yield:
  - Around 2,400 pounds/acre
- Production Estimates:
  - Guangdong: 672 million pounds/year = 2.8 million acres
  - Taiwan: 104 million pounds/year = 43.3 thousand acres
  - Fujian: 86 million pounds/year = 35.8 thousand acres
  - Total in acres: 856 million pounds/year = 2,879,168
  - Total in *mu*: = 17.3 million
- Estimated Annual Total Exports:
  - 1792: 11 million pounds/year = 4,667 acres
  - 1834: 34 million pounds/year = 14,167 acres

SOUZA USING POMERANZ AND OTHERS

the total annual amount of sugar in China was around 2.9 million acres or 17.3 million *mu*.

Using figures for late in the eighteenth century (1792) and early nineteenth century (1832), Pomeranz mentions that Chinese exports of sugar to Japan, South Asia and elsewhere were rather small, only 11.2 million pounds in 1792 and only around 20% of those exports were destined for Japan. He also suggests that exports of Chinese sugar were growing and forty years later had more than trebled. The majority of these sugar exports, however, were not destined for Japan but South Asia. Based on my calculations from Pomeranz's and others information, the amount of land in use to produce sugar for export was extraordinarily small in comparison with total land in use producing sugar in general for consumption within China.

Total production of sugar in specific regions of south China and its role as a cash crop in the development of a commercialized economy was significant. Although quantities exported were small relative to quantities produced, sugar's role in development of China's maritime trade cannot be dismissed. Why? There are two primary reasons. The first is present today in international trade theory: trade can introduce demand for refinement or enhancement in technology and presentation of the quality or the range of quality(–ies) in the production of a commodity that produces benefits in its internal and external markets and satisfies the exporter, importer, and consumer at the end-market. The second, as we shall examine in greater detail below, is that availability of sugar as a coarse, gruff or ballast good was fundamental in making trade between China and Japan economically and logistically viable – to such an extent that there was a symbiotic relationship between Chinese sugar and Japanese copper.

Sugar production in general was significant in development of a commercialized economy in south China. Chinese sugar exports were employed and became heavily embroiled in China's maritime trade with Japan in the late sixteenth and into the nineteenth centuries, although we shall concentrate comments on the long eighteenth century. Nagazumi has edited a large number of Dutch records that document involvement of some 1,319 junks from China and Southeast Asia to Japan from 1641 to 1831 (over a span of 190 years, with 114 years reporting activity and 76 not). Figure 1.2 indicates the annual distribution of the numbers of junks sailing to Japan in these and from additional sources.[23] Over this period, when and where indicated, junks are reported as having sailed from sixteen Chinese ports: from Nanjing in Jiangsu province (1); from Ningbo, Danshan, Dinghai, Wenzhou, Zhapu, Zhoushan, and Rui'an in Zhejian province (7); Fuzhou, Shacheng, Quanzhou, Xiamen, Anhai, Zhangzhou in Fujian province (6); Taiwan (1); and Guangzhou in Guangdong province (1). Additional sailings of Chinese junks from four regions of Southeast Asia: Vietnam: Tonkin and Annam: the latter also being mentioned as Giao Chỉ, its

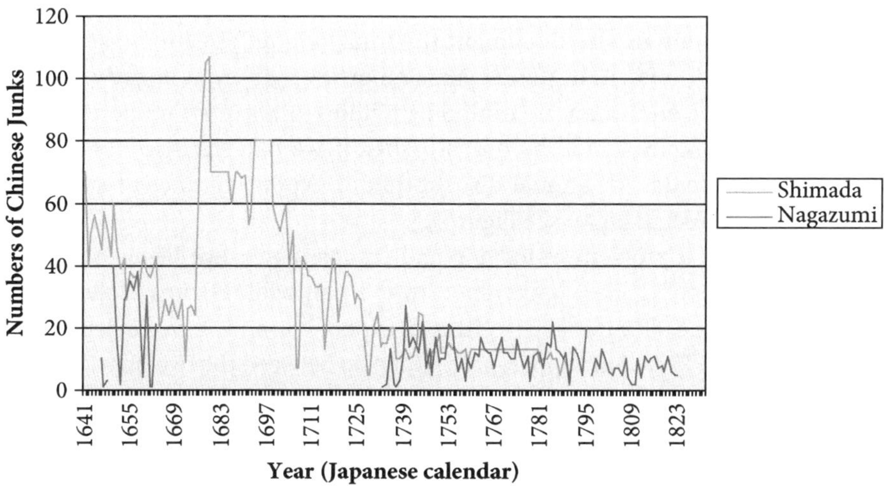

FIGURE 1.2 *Total annual number of reporting Chinese junks to Japan, 1641–1831 (Shimada is the complete unbroken line; Nagazumi is the partial or interrupted unbroken line)*

23 See Ryuto Shimada, *The Intra-Asian Trade in Japanese Copper by the Dutch East India Company During the Eighteenth Century* (Leiden; Boston: Brill, 2006), p. 197; the suggested discrepancies in the table are actually variations caused by use of the European calendar year in Nagazumi and use of the Japanese calendar year in sources employed by Shimada.

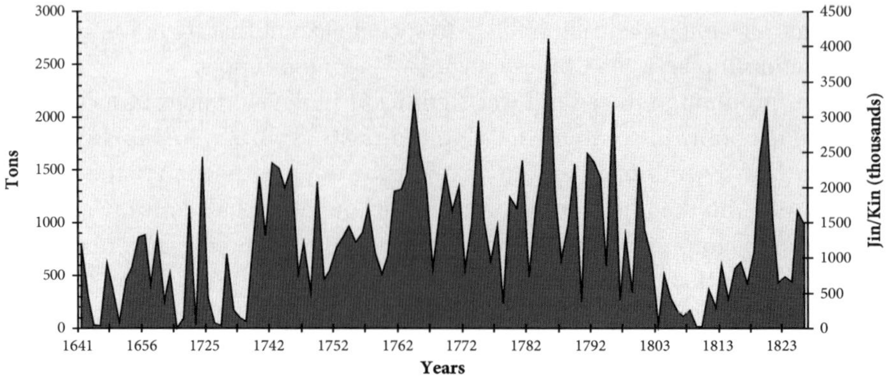

FIGURE 1.3 *Total annual Chinese sugar exports to Japan, 1641–1831*
NAGAZUMI/PARTIAL VOC RECORDS

synonym in Vietnamese, and Quang Nam, a name of one of its provinces and site of one of its primary port cities, Hoi An; Cambodia; Siam, including a separate mention of Patani; and Java: Batavia or Kelapa. In two instances, names of prominent junk owners: Iquan or Zheng Zhilong 鄭芝龍 and his son Koxinga 國姓爺, the popular appellation for Zheng Chenggong 鄭成, is mentioned and in five instances junks are named; in the rest, they are numbered.

Nagazumi's sources also document the total volume of Chinese sugar, primarily, exported to Japan in the 114 years reporting activity as slightly over 128 million *jin* or *kin*, equivalent to around 1.3 million *piculs* or 171 million pounds. Obviously, this figure would be much higher, if we had statistics for missing non-reporting years. For annual distribution of export volumes of sugar carried by these junks to Japan see Figure 1.3.

Now, there is a problem in judging and comparing by eye Figure 1.2, which gives the number of Chinese junks reporting to Japan, while Figure 1.3 follows with the annual volume of Chinese sugar that was exported to and arrived in Japan, over the same period. There is no apparent relationship between the two. To resolve this conundrum, we must answer several questions: (1) Did the mean total carrying capacity of a junk loaded with sugar vary over time; did sugar's mean percentage of total cargo vary; or was there a combination of factors at work? (2)

What is the likely explanation for the spikes/fluctualtions in annual volume of Chinese sugar exported to Japan? Despite lacunae, underlying factual records are sufficiently detailed to permit us to answer what was likely to have been going on here and why. It is also important to stress that certain trade items, such as sugar and other coarse, gruff, and dense commodities (including sugar, zinc and alum) were of fundamental importance to the safety of the operation of a ship, since they served as ballast which provided balance for the vessel's transit in the water. In addition to serving as ballast, they were paying ballast goods, that is: commodities that not only served a technical and logistical purpose but were also important in commerce, since their exchange and sale significantly contributed to the profitability of the trade between two countries.

Figure 1.2 establishes that from the middle of the seventeenth century (1641) to the third decade of the eighteenth century (c.1730) the number of junks arriving annually in trading Chinese sugar to Japan ranged very roughly from 20 to over 100. Over the next hundred years, from the third decade of the eighteenth century (c.1730) to the fourth decade of the nineteenth century (1841), the number of junks arriving annually and trading Chinese sugar to Japan rarely surpassed 20, and were usually fewer than that figure. However, over the same sub-periodization, it appears (see Figure 1.3) that from the middle of the seventeenth century (1641) to the third decade of the eighteenth century (c.1730) the volume of Chinese sugar sold annually in Japan ranged very roughly from neglible to around 1,700 tons. Over the next hundred years, from the third decade of the eighteenth century (c.1730) to the fourth decade of the nineteenth century (1841), the volume of Chinese sugar sold annually in Japan ranged from around 1,500 to 2,700 tons. Ancillary evidence provided by Shimada concerning the numbers of Chinese junks and volumes of Japanese copper shipped by them to China substantiate and corroborate the feasibility and logic of our estimates and comments made below on commercial behavior and practice.

There are less serial data to answer definitively whether there were significant variations in Chinese sugar's mean percentage of total cargo in this trade. Why? We would have to have serial data for the entire period for all trade items, volumes and prices generally involved. These cargo data would have to be classified and organized further by function i.e. whether and which commodities were potentially saleable 'ballast', of roughly the same density. In this case and for over this entire period, there were three commodities that fit this description and criteria: sugar, zinc and alum.[24] The scenario that is envisaged here is that there was competition in price, quantity availability and profitability over

24 For a thorough discussion with quantification of this issue, see George Bryan Souza, "Ballast Goods: Chinese Maritime Trade in Zinc and Sugar in the Seventeenth and Eighteenth Centuries," in Dietmar Rothermund and Roderick Ptak (eds.) *Emporia, Commodities and Entrepreneurs in Asian Maritime Trade, c.1400–1750* (Stuttgart: Steiner Verlag 1990) and George Bryan Souza, "Country Trade and Chinese Alum: Raw Material Supply in Asia's Textile Production in the Seventeenth and Eighteenth Centuries," *Revista de Cultura* 11 (2004).

time between each of these ballast goods per unit either (i) of weight (thinking in terms of ballast), or (ii) of ounce of silver spent (thinking in terms of commodities being traded), or some sort of optimal mix of the three that is partly at least determined by what will work navigationally in terms of ships loaded with them. Although clumsily sketched, this profit-driven variation in the mix of preferred ballast scenario provides the basis of an explanation for at least some of the sudden leaps and plunges around the annual mean amount of total Chinese sugar transported to Japan each year (which appears to have been around 700 tons).

Respecting our caveat concerning serial data availability and reliability, observations and comparisons that we made above obviously establish that the mean total carrying capacity of Chinese junks grew as the number of junks involved declined over the entire period.[25] As a rough rule of thumb, it is probable that the average mean total carrying capacity of Chinese junks involved in Sino-Japanese maritime trade from the middle of the seventeenth century (1641) to the third decade of the eighteenth century (c.1730) averaged from 30 to 50 tons per junk; and over the next hundred years, from the third decade of the eighteenth century (c.1730) to the fourth decade of the nineteenth century (1841), Chinese junk average mean total carrying capacity had quadrupled or trebled to around 120 to 150 tons per junk. Chinese sugar's mean percentage of total cargo varied, but it was the primary commodity in volume used for profitable or paying ballast trade purposes. While we have examined individually each of these factors, it is more logical and probable that a combination of these factors is more likely to explain the spikes/fluctualtions in annual volumes of Chinese sugar exported to Japan.

Since quality of sugar was dependent on refining and processing, there were distinctions in quality of sugar exported from China and sold in Japan. Diversity of qualities produced and commercialized oscillated, primarily, around the level of molasses that was or was not left during processing, making distinctions between the types of sugar based upon color: white, brown, and muscovado (dark or black) or relating to method of process or shape: candy and loaf or cake, which were mirrored in respective prices and, on occasion, subject to differentiation by levels or gradation within each respective type of sugar. Composition of types of sugars by volumes and percentages of total amount of sugar exported from China to Japan over this period is shown in

---

25 These rough estimates were made: (1) based on early seventeenth century observations and calculations by Dutch employees of the VOC in Japan on the size and carrying capacities of Chinese junks trading to that country; and (2) annual total imported and exported cargoes divided by the reported number of junks trading in that year.

Figure 1.4. Although there were differences in price reflecting value added for each type of sugar, they do not appear to register any measurable quantifiable significance. It does not look as if variations in type or quality of sugar, as in Figure 1.4, would have been likely to generate big enough jumps or fluctuations in overall sugar sales: in particular three-quarters of the sugar mix seems to have been 'white'.

If we take scant records available based upon Nagazumi and Mazumdar, as shown in Table 1.3, for the market price of sugar at Guangzhou, prices realized on sales of Chinese sugar at Nagasaki, the only *entrepôt* for trade from China with Japan, and prices realized on sales of sugar in Beijing, a major Chinese market, it is possible to establish, examine, and compare their differentials as evidence of transaction, risk and opportunity costs and profit expectations of commercialization of sugar in and between external and internal markets. With regard to external markets, in 1705, for example, respective market prices of white and candy sugars at Guangzhou were 2.5 and 4 taels and at Nagasaki 7 and near 11 taels per *picul* or 100 *jin*/*kin*. Clearly and obviously, differentials between cost price in China and sales price realized in Japan of 4.5 and 6.8 per *picul* or 100 *jin*/*kin* establish that commerce in Chinese sugar with Japan was profitable and that these differentials were acceptable for Chinese merchants involved in this trade. With regard to internal Chinese markets in 1792, for example, respective market prices of white and candy sugars at Guangzhou were 5 and 10 taels and at Beijing, the imperial household paid 10 to 17 taels per *picul* or 100 *jin*/*kin*, although the source that Mazumdar cited does not clarify whether prices paid were specifically for white and candy sugars.[26] Nevertheless,

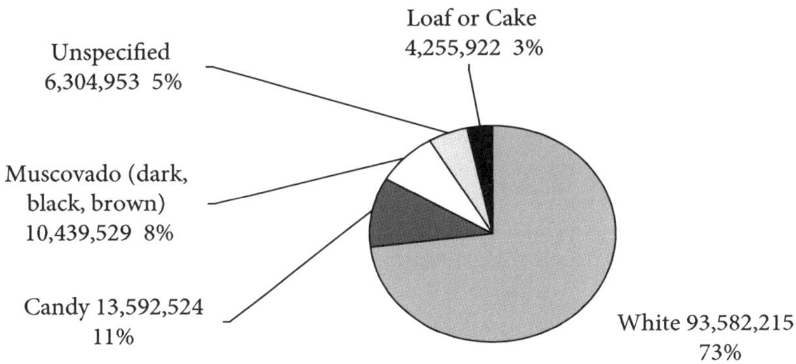

FIGURE 1.4 *Sugar to Japan, 1641–1831: Composition of total volume.* 128 MILLION JIN/KIN AND %

26 Mazumdar, *Sugar and Society in China*, pp. 54–55.

TABLE 1.3 *Sugar prices in China at Guangzhou and in Japan, 1620–1810*

Year	China	China	Japan	Japan	Japan	Japan
	White	Candy	White	Candy	Brown	Muscovado
1620	1.4	–	–	–	–	–
1637	2.6	–	–	–	–	–
1640	–	–	5.5	6.0	–	2.9
1644	–	–	6.8	8.0	–	5.0
1645	–	–	6.0	8.5	–	2.3
1646	–	–	3.5	5.5	–	2.0
1648	–	–	9.4	–	–	6.5
1654	–	–	8.0	9.0	–	6.0
1664	4.5	–	–	–	–	–
1684	1.6	–	–	–	–	–
1698	–	–	5.4	9.5	–	2.5
1699	–	–	5.6	8.2	5.3	3.8
1700	–	–	–	–	–	3.7
1701	–	–	5.2	8.0	5.2	2.7
1703	–	–	7.4	9.6	–	4.1
1704	–	–	7.6	8.7	–	5.7
1705	2.5	4.0	7.0	10.8	6.1	4.8
1706	–	–	6.2	11.1	–	4.3
1711	1.8	–	–	–	–	–
1723	3.0	6.0	–	–	–	–
1724	3.0	5.8	–	–	–	–
1732	2.4	5.0	–	–	–	–
1733	2.8	4.4	–	–	–	–
1751	3.0	5.0	–	–	–	–
1774	4.0	9.4	–	–	–	–
1792	5.0	10.0	–	–	–	–
1810	6.5	10.0	–	–	–	–

AVERAGE PRICES IN *TAELS* PER *PICUL* OR 100 *JIN/KIN*

suggested possible and probable differentials between cost price of white and candy sugars at Guangzhou with their probable sales prices realized at Beijing of 5 and 7 taels per *picul* or 100 *jin/kin* logically ratify and establish that commerce in sugar internally was profitable, and that these differentials were acceptable for Chinese merchants involved to cover transaction, risk and opportunity costs and met profit expectations for this trade.

Although profitable, but relatively small scale in comparison with the size of China's internal market, there was at least one additional major factor from the Chinese perspective that favored sugar's inclusion in maritime trade with Japan. China's primary interest in the trade was driven by state and private merchant interests in obtaining Japanese copper to incorporate the metal into Qing monetary policies for manufacture of coin. Simply put, the additional major factor was that of all of China's exportable commodities, sugar was particularly important because it was bulky and relatively low cost, but also a profitable commodity available in volume and in weight that functioned as ballast for outward junks journey to Japan. In view of limited use of alternative ballast goods (for example, zinc and alum),[27] without sugar availability in quantity, it is possible that junks involved in this trade would have encountered severe commercial and structural difficulties in locating and loading suitable alternative commodities in volume necessary to serve as ballast. Without sufficient ballast on one leg of the voyage, the number and size of junks involved and prospects of loading quantities of copper on board returning junks would, possibly, have been jeopardized. It is also possible that the quality and types of sugar demanded in Japan may have caused improvements in sugar processing techniques in south China that may have, it is speculated, been incorporated for the internal Chinese market or vice-versa. Implications of the importance of sugar and of commodity chain analysis in the history of China's economic development as outlined in this paragraph cannot be over-stated. From the Chinese perspective, the reason for Sino-Japanese trade over this period was to obtain copper. Sugar was incorporated into and made this trade economically and logistically viable. A symbiotic relationship between two objects – sugar and copper – was created and the contribution of sugar in facilitating Qing monetary policy was of major significance. Hinterlands of south China not only produced significant wealth in the form of sugar but that sugar fueled delivery of fundamentally important quantities of Japanese copper to provincial and central mints.

From the Japanese perspective, however, inclusion and acceptance of Chinese sugar in maritime trade with Japan had important repercussions within the Tokugawa economy. Initially, in the sixteenth and into the seventeenth century, apparently, there was little domestic sugarcane production,

27 For Chinese sugar, zinc, and alum as ballast goods and in maritime trade, see citations in note 24 and for additional discussion concerning zinc mining, smelting, refining, and commercialization, see Hailian Chen and George Bryan Souza, "Zinc in Ming and Early Qing China, ca. 1400 – ca. 1680s," in Ulrich Theobald, et al, (eds), *Sino-Japanese Trade, Commodity Chains, Regional Economies and the Environment: Monies, Markets and Finance in China and East Asia, April 2010 Conference Proceedings* (Leiden, Brill, forthcoming).

and demand for sugar was met from other sweetening alternatives available in Japan. Based upon internal demand for sugar that had been established and had grown very modestly as a result of maritime sugar imports from China, after the Satsuma-han established control over the Ryukyu islands, and that domain and the shogunate identified revenue potential that sugarcane produced in those islands, sugar cultivation on a large scale was initiated and production significantly expanded in the Ryukyu's via importation of Chinese refining techniques in the seventeenth and eighteenth centuries. Production of sugar in those islands was organized to provide revenues for the Satsuma-han and de-facto to compete and substitute for importation of sugar from China into the internal Japanese economy as much as possible. Sugar production in the Ryukyu Islands never eliminated, as we have seen, maritime trade in the commodity from China, but it did diminish the volume of Chinese sugar marketed in Japan. Furthermore, it is apparent that internal demand for sugar in the Tokugawa period had experienced some, apparently, minimal growth and by the early nineteenth century sugarcane was also cultivated and sugar produced in smaller amounts in southern Kyushu around Kagoshima, Shikoku, and western Honshu.

A summary of salient features about sugar in Tokugawa Japan is presented in Table 1.4. It is known that Tokugawa Japan experienced zero population growth from 1721 to 1846[28] and total population is estimated at around 27 to 30 million inhabitants around 1830. Innes[29] provides two quantitative estimates for sugar annually produced in the Ryukyu's and exported to mainland islands of Japan in the 1830s. They were (1) 5 to 6 million *jin*, or 6.5 to 7.9 million pounds; or (2) 6 to 7 million *jin* or 8 to 9 million pounds. For our purposes, the average of those two estimates is used to produce an estimate of 6 million *jin*, or 7.9 million pounds for the quantity of sugar annually produced in the Ryukyu's and exported to Japan in the 1830s. Despite present difficulties in finding reliable sources and estimates, an arbitrary figure of around 1 million *jin* or 1.3 million pounds is assigned as a hypothetical figure for sugar production from

28 The statistical near-standstill of Japan's population during the long 18th century is a fact. However, it was also an illusion of aggregation to some extent, since there was quite noticeable change in population during this period within different regions and domains, especially between north and south, which more-or-less offset each other to yield a seemingly static total. For a thorough look at and discussion of the details, see Irene Barnes Taeuber, *The Population of Japan* (Princeton: Princeton University Press, 1958).

29 See Robert LeRoy Innes, "The Door Ajar: Japan's Foreign Trade in the Seventeenth Century," Ph.D dissertation, University of Michigan, 1980, p. 515; and Mazumdar, *Sugar and Society in China*, pp. 174–175.

TABLE 1.4 *Sugar production and consumption in Tokugawa Japan, c. 1830*

- Population
  - Estimated at around 27 to 30 million inhabitants
  - Zero population growth 1721–1846
- Production:
  - Ryukyu islands
    - Innes' estimates (c. 1830s) around:
      - 5–6 million *jin*: 6.5 – 7.9 million pounds/year
      - 6–7 million *jin*: 8–9 million pounds/year
    - My estimate (c. 1830):
      - 6 million *jin*: 7.9 million pounds/year
  - Mainland Japan
    - No data presently available
    - Arbitrary estimate (c. 1830):
      - 1 million *jin*: 1.3 million pounds/year
- Chinese Imports (annual average over period):
  - 1750–1799:
    - 1.5 million *jin*: 2 million pounds/year
  - 1800–1831:
    - 650,000 *jin*: 870,000 pounds/year
- Chinese Imports (reported):
  - 1831:
    - 1.3 million *jin*: 1.7 million pounds/year
- Total estimated Japanese production and imports (c. 1830):
  - 8.3 million *jin*: 11 million pounds/year
- Per capita consumption (Estimates):
  - 0.36 to 0.4 pounds/year

SOUZA WITH OTHERS

the southern most parts of mainland islands of Japan in 1830. Nagazumi's Dutch sources suggest that an annual average of Chinese sugar imported into Japan was 1.5 million *jin* or 2 million pounds from 1750 to 1799. From 1800 to 1831, the annual average of Chinese sugar imported into Japan declined to 650,000 *jin*, or 870,000 pounds, although Chinese sugar imports rose to 1.3 million *jin* or 1.7 million pounds in 1831. In conclusion, it is estimated that total Japanese production plus imports of sugar c. 1830 was 8.3 million *jin* or 11 million pounds. Consequently, based upon the above data and assumptions, it is tentatively and conservatively estimated that per capita consumption of sugar in Tokugawa Japan around 1830 was between 0.36 to 0.4 pounds per year, which is a rate that does not compare favorably with earlier and contemporaneous higher per capita consumption of sugar rates in China and Europe.

Hinterlands, Commodities, Commercialization and Monies in Early Modern Asian History

Our examination of Chinese sugar-producing hinterlands, sugar's commodity chain and production, commercial, and currency circuits in Qing China and Tokugawa Japan over the long eighteenth century is completed in this final section. Furthermore, our model presents an example of salient interpretive benefits derived from using and interconnecting commodity chain analysis with expansion of hinterland cash-crop production, and commercial and currency circuits: it culminates with estimation of the annual value of sugar production and amount of monies that sugar producers were paid in south China around 1750. Subsequently, we ask and answer the following questions: Why are hinterlands, commodities, commercialization, and monies important in the history of production, commercial expansion and economic development in early modern Asia? And, finally, How useful is this model and methodology?

We can estimate annual value of sugar production and the amount of money or monies paid to producers in south China around 1750, by making a number of assumptions about the internal Chinese market price for white and candy sugar at Guangzhou from Table 1.6, its behavior in Fujian and Taiwan markets, and incorporating these data with Pomeranz and others' estimates for China's sugar production. Assumptions include: (1) market prices at Guangzhou (the only market for which we have information) was the same or generally the same as market prices in Fujian and Taiwan; (2) while acknowledging additional types of sugars at different prices, prices for white and candy sugar – the bulk of production – and a composite average price for white and candy sugar are sufficient for our purposes; (3) China's sugar producers are assumed to have been paid at market prices in Guangzhou, Fujian and Taiwan; and (4) an arbitrary percentage of 66–50% may be reduced from market price for sugar at Guangzhou to obtain the realized price to sugar farmers in the hinterlands, the other third or half covering merchant opportunity cost and profit expectations in commercializing the commodity. Neither transaction costs nor producer net profit is estimated.

Based on assumptions outlined above, plus Pomeranz' estimate of total production of sugar in China (Guangdong, Taiwan, and Fujian) at 862 million pounds or around 6.5 million *piculs*, a composite average market price of 4 taels per *picul* in 1751, and price reduced by one-third (2.67 taels per *picul*) or one half (2 taels per *picul*), suggest an annual price that producers realized. I estimate that gross annual income of sugar producers was around 17.4 to 13 million taels in China (Guangdong, Taiwan, and Fujian) in the mid-eighteenth century.

There is a direct spatial relationship between this estimate of gross income received annually by sugar producers in hinterlands or production circuits of Guangdong, Taiwan, and Fujian vis-à-vis the co-terminus currency circuit for sugar. Simply stated: the geographically delimited and finite areas in China where sugarcane was produced: Guangdong, Taiwan, and Fujian i.e. China's sugar production circuits, logically shared the same space with the currency circuits in its currency circuit counterpart. Thus, the estimated quantity of monies or media of exchange (17.4 to 13 million taels) was paid to sugar producers in mid-eighteenth century Oing China.

There are two further fundamental comments and preliminary observations on this issue.

The first point is more micro-economic. To the degree that there is sufficient evidence about potential sugar producer behavior both as producer and consumer, along with practical seasonal demands made upon that producer, it should be possible to model (under different scenarios) volumes and seasonality of the demand for money or monies, for individual producers by types and conditions or an entire collective or group. Elaboration of such a model is planned, but is not included in this article. Obviously, it is contemplated that such a model will be of utility in visualizing how, when, where, and why a volume of money or monies was used, demanded, and turned over in a reasonably defined and compact space over time. No exaggerated claim for exactitude of approximate magnitudes of money in this space is being advanced, but it is argued that ability to make such estimates has significant potential to improve discussions concerning visualization of commercial activities, their inter-connected and comparative relationships with economic development in Early Modern Asian History.

The second point is more macro-economic and has broader historiographical implications. To the degree that there is sufficient evidence from existing secondary literature and further monographic research oriented towards production circuits of other highly commercialized and specialized individual commodity chain(s) in addition to sugar in Qing China – such as, for example, salt, raw cotton, tea, rice, indigo, turmeric, safflower, saffron, tobacco, opium, timber, copper, zinc, lead, tin, coal, raw silk, linen, wool, cotton and silk textiles, metal-working and organized and grouped by economic sectors or categories of production such as, for example, agriculture, forestry, mining, and handicrafts – it should be possible to replicate the type of analysis performed in this article for sugar in China, for some or all commodity chains not only in Late Imperial China but for most of Asia. The majority of these examples are commodities that were grown, cut and harvested, mined, or produced in spatially delimited areas in hinterlands, which in part explains the historian's perennial interest in their conception and relationships to other spaces, state formation, and economic development. It is advocated that historians exhaustively examine individual commodity chains not by production within geographical boundaries that coincide with treatment coinciding with nation state development but rather by functional or economic productive categories across regions and globally and group them. I am, for example, referring to individual commodities from the agricultural sector that shifted from being produced for subsistence to surplus and vented for cash and those that were produced exclusively for cash. The same objective is true, for example, for all other primary categories of productive activity i.e. mining and handicrafts. I advocate that the results from such historical investigations will provide the background and framework for analysis comparing and examining groupings and development of commodities by commercial or economic sector within a locality, region, intra-region or other, interconnecting those internal and external market relationships, via maritime and overland trade, with general and spatially specific internal monetary flows and economic development in early modern Asian history.

This essay does not suggest that commodity chains and their analysis have been un-examined. For example, while developing ideas on the formation of a world system,[30] Wallerstein identified commodity chains that played a role in the rise of capitalism and an emerging global economy by linking peripheries with Europe.[31] Frank used the example of colonial heritage in organization and exploitation of primary commodities in Latin America to articulate his ideas concerning dependency theory[32] and for his argument that divergent

30 It is characterized as a set of mechanisms which redistributes resources from the *periphery* to the *core*. In his terminology, the *core* is the developed, industrialized part of the world, and the *periphery* is the "underdeveloped," typically raw materials-exporting, poor part of the world; the *market* being the means by which the *core* exploits the *periphery*.

31 See Terence K. Hopkins and Immanuel Wallerstein, "Commodity Chains in the World-Economy prior to 1800," *Review* (*Fernand Braudel Center*) 10:1 (1986) and Immanuel Maurice Wallerstein,. *The Modern World-System*, 4 vols. (New York: Academic Press, 1974–2011).

32 Defined as a body of social science theories predicated on the notion that resources flow from a 'periphery' of poor and underdeveloped states to a 'core' of wealthy states,

historical developmental paths were significant factors in why economic development in certain parts of the world lagged behind in comparison with others. Recent work by Topik and others has returned to the question of dependency in Latin America and developed sound empirically driven examinations of individual commodity chains that suggests that creoles and indigenous agents and their agencies in developing commodity production were not as dependent as earlier work has suggested, and that peripheral relations with colonial or neo-colonial centers or cores are of greater historical complexity and fluidity.[33] And Topik and Wells have intriguingly employed examination of commodity chains to their logical and broadest unit of analysis – an emerging world economy.[34]

This essay, rather, argues and advocates that historical research, examination and analysis of commodity chains in Asia and elsewhere has to be performed. Results of which have to be incorporated into the history of Asia's regional, intra-regional, and global or world economic development in order to remedy our lacunae in understanding as to when, how, and to what degree or levels of intensity certain diverse regions of the world were politically, economically, socially, and culturally inter-connected and inter-acted.

It advances a structure and a methodological tool that facillates further examination of complex relationships among groups of commodities within all mentioned circuits. We acknowledge examples of commodities with complex circumstances and exceptional relationships that may suggest that our model is potentially insufficient and, perhaps, further refinement of commodity chain analysis is required to incorporate, refine, and explicate distinctions. For example, an individual commodity – opium – as Bello's work and others have shown could be "legal" or "illegal" within specific segments of these circuits and could function contemporaneously as commodity and currency.[35]

---

enriching the latter at the expense of the former. It is a central contention of dependency theory that poor states are impoverished and rich ones enriched by the way poor states are integrated into the 'world system'.

33 See Steven C. Topik, Carlos Marichal, and Zephyr L. Frank, (eds.) *From Silver to Cocaine: Latin American Commodity Chains and the Building of the World Economy, 1500–2000* (Durham: Duke University Press, 2006).

34 See Steven C. Topik and Allen Wells, "Commodity Chains in a Global Economy," in Emily S. Rosenberg, (ed.) *A World Connecting, 1870–1945* (Cambridge, Mass.: Belknap Press of Harvard University Press, 2012). I wish to thank Professor Topik for sharing a final draft version of this essay with me.

35 See, for example, David Anthony Bello, *Opium and the Limits of Empire: Drug Prohibition in the Chinese Interior, 1729–1850* (Cambridge, Mass.: Harvard University Asia Center/ Harvard University Press, 2005).

By using commodity chain analysis and linking expansion of hinterland cash-crop production circuits with commercial and currency circuits, the possible volume and turnover of monies or media of exchange paid to producers by merchants involved in commercialization of a specific good at a specific time is possible. Beyond its utility in aggregating and quantifying, and regardless of potential distinctions in its use as mentioned above, we argue that our model is one of the most comprehensive and inclusive anaylitical tools available to establish a platform from which all objects may be examined and their stories told with the widest treatment and examination of their capacity to produce wealth, establish power, contribute to knowledge and suggest meaning to mankind.

Conclusions

The conceptual and theoretical importance of hinterlands, commodity chains, production, and commercial and currency circuits in early modern Asian history were discussed in this essay. Crucial issues and questions dealing with place(s), space(s), and time relationships were explored by (re-)examining the well-known and well-studied example of an Asian hinterland: the case of cash-crop sugar production in South China over the long eighteenth century. Sugar in Qing China and Tokugawa Japan was examined as an example of a good produced in a hinterland; a (generic) commodity, its commodity chain, production, and commercial and currency circuits were defined, explored, and modeled to answer key questions about their interconnected nature and economic and spatial relationships.

It is axiomatic, in my opinion, that historians who deal with any place in space and over time perennially face the issue of how to situate and define those relationships. Hinterland or hinterlands are one (but not necessarily the one and only) way of making such delimitations. All alternatives, frontiers or borderlands for example, have their rationale and were elliptically mentioned and some literature concerning them cited. But we restrict our examination to hinterland or hinterlands. Why? First, while we were not averse to engaging conceptually or theoretically with alternatives (and there was concern related to essay length), in our opinion these alternatives do not address to the same degree or the same depth issues of place, space, and time in relation to economic development that are central to this essay. Second, regardless of a plethora of studies, historians return time and again to this theme, since each place, space and time examined produces a unique story. But, within seeming uniqueness and exceptionality of historical evidence produced for each place, space and time, there are characteristics and a component to the story that are seemingly omnipresent, or as Liebermann has pointed out yield seemingly strange parallels.[36]

We chose to tease out and explore historical evidence for one commodity, sugar, and an analytical model of its commodity chain and circuits in examination of hinterlands in South China. At a heuristic level, by linking expansion of hinterland cash-crop production with commercial and currency circuits, for example, the volume and turnover of monies or media of exchange paid to producers by merchants involved in commercialization of one cash-crop can be estimated. At the abstract level, our model structures examination of complex relationships between an object or objects (primarily, but not obligatorily, inanimate) that have been commoditized and found in a place or places (hinterlands and central places in this instance), in space (physically and metaphysically) and their inter-actions with human agency and the environment. It provides a framework that is holistic as well as rigorous in dealing with historical evidence without being dogmatic or reducing it to mechanical or formulaic treatment.

This essay has shown that individual commodities, their chains, and production, commercial, and currency circuits at heuristic and abstract levels must be examined and integrated into analysis of networks of commodity chains and circuits that functioned in spaces including hinterlands in order to develop an essential methodological tool for understanding and visualizing the history of economic development and evolution and dynamism of commercial expansion in general and in particular in Asia. Expanding research and incorporating this methodology is fundamental toward developing new directions for study and comparison of economic development in early modern Asian history.

---

36 See Victor B. Lieberman, *Strange Parallels: Southeast Asia in Global Context, c. 800–1830*, 2 vols. (Cambridge; New York: Cambridge University Press, 2003–2009).

CHAPTER 2

Hydraulic Metaphor

A Model of Global and Local Connectivity[1]

Dennis O. Flynn and Marie A. Lee

Introduction

Trade histories normally focus on exports/imports between port cities, yet actual trade is (and always has been) far more complex than mere bilateral coast-to-coast exchange. While a particular hinterland may indeed produce a negligible proportion of a particular item, it is sometimes the case that *combined* hinterland output dominates. By the same token, relatively little of a commodity may end up in a single hinterland location, yet hinterland end-markets *combined* can dominate. Historical neglect of hinterlands is at least partly due to inadequacies inherent in conventional supply and demand concepts at the foundational building-blocks level of economic theory.

This essay offers intuitive, visual representations of hinterlands in local, regional, and global contexts via a Hydraulic Metaphor[2] that is based upon an unconventional supply–demand model that is more comprehensive than standard supply–demand; moreover, our visual Hydraulic Metaphor version is specifically designed for comprehension by non-economists. Our aim is to showcase Pedro Machado's archival-based case-study on eighteenth-century textile trade between western India and eastern Africa, work based upon primary-source research of large-scale international textile trade that depended fundamentally upon hinterland end-markets in Africa and hinterland production-centers in India.[3] Not only did residents of Indian hinterlands and African hinterlands not

1 An early version of this essay was published as a working paper in *Empires, Systems, and Maritime Networks: Reconstructing Supra-Regional Histories in pre-19th Century Asia*, Working Paper Series 05: New Perspectives of Global Economic History (December 2011), 1–32. Professor FUJITA Kayoko graciously convened a Grant-in-Aid Research Project (FY2009–2011, Category B, No. 90454983) workshop at Ritsumeikan Asia Pacific University in Beppu, Oita, Japan, on 29 May 2011, which was funded by the Grants-in-Aid for Scientific Research program of the Japan Society for Promotion of Science.

2 Water provides a useful market metaphor because liquids flow from location to location, are stored within locations, and their stocks are depleted via consumption and evaporation/decay; markets for transferable goods are easily visualized in similar stocks-flows terms.

3 Pedro Machado, "Clothes of a New Fashion: Indian Ocean Networks of Exchange and Cloth Zones of Contact in Africa and India in the Eighteenth and Nineteenth Centuries," In *How*

© KONINKLIJKE BRILL NV, LEIDEN, 2015 | DOI 10.1163/9789004283909_004

interact with each other directly, Banyan merchants who coordinated these distant overseas markets also interacted directly with residents of *neither* hinterland group. Our Hydraulic Metaphor exposes logic of market connections within local spaces and also among distant places, and does so in a way that can be visualized. An additional aim of this chapter is to use Machado's fascinating case study to illustrate how non-economists can themselves apply Hydraulic Metaphor logic to an endless list of case studies involving any place, space, or time period.

Conceptual Background

The most fundamental dichotomy in Economics since the late-19th century has involved bifurcation of economic theory into microeconomic concepts vis-à-vis distinct (and often incompatible) macroeconomic concepts. From Greek, 'micro' implies small and 'macro' signifies large. Conventional Laws of Supply and Demand are microeconomic concepts that pertain to *individual* (non-monetary) products. Macroeconomic supply–demand concepts, on the other hand, diverge fundamentally from microeconomic counterparts. For one thing, macroeconomic theory *aggregates* across distinct products, while microeconomic theorists consciously restrict analyses to *individual* products and *individual* behaviors. In short, microeconomic theory focuses on individual products and individual entities; macroeconomics, on the contrary, offers theoretical concepts based upon *aggregation* across dissimilar items. Moreover, it is arguable that *the* core of macroeconomics is comprised of monetary aggregates.

While theoretical monetary economics is intentionally left aside for purposes of this essay, brief mention should be made of the fact that each of the world's four main monetary substances from the 16th through 19th centuries – silver, gold, brass-copper,[4] and cowry shells – was produced in specific locations around the globe; each substance gravitated to distinct end-markets around

India Clothed the World the World of South Asian Textiles, 1500–1850, edited by Giorgio Riello and Tirthankar Roy, 53–84 (Leiden; Boston: Brill, 2009).

4 Although "copper cash" and "bronze coin" terminology pervades Asian monetary history scholarship, Souza and Chen and Souza argue convincingly that these coins were in fact fabricated of brass, see George Bryan Souza, "Ballast Goods: Chinese Maritime Trade in Zinc and Sugar in the Seventeenth and Eighteenth Centuries," In *Emporia, Commodities and Entrepreneurs in Asian Maritime Trade, C.1400–1750*, edited by Dietmar Rothermund and Roderick Ptak., (Stuttgart: Steiner Verlag 1990), 291–315; and Hailian Chen and George Bryan Souza, "Zinc in Ming and Early Qing China, ca. 1400–1680s." In *The Many Shapes of the Coin: International Trade, Monetary Metals, and Money in Religion in China and East Asia (Conference Proceedings of the 2010 "Monies, Markets and Finance in East Asia" Workshop)*, edited by Jin Cao and Ulrich Theobald. (Leiden: Brill, forthcoming).

the world; moreover, each substance traversed specific global trade routes (as well as being exchanged for each other over extensive time periods, such as a century). Actual monetary history at the global level, in other words, contradicts all conventional monetary theories, in the sense that modern theory insists upon consolidation of diverse monetary substances into a conceptual unit "money," while it is clear from global monetary history that each monetary substance requires independent analysis. In short, understanding centuries of global monetary history requires abandonment of "macro-aggregate" approaches that add together fundamentally dissimilar monetary objects such as silver, gold, brass, and cowries.[5] Indeed, aggregation of the world's main monetary substances into any catch-all "money" taxonomy guarantees confusion; thorough training in conventional macro-money theory, in other words, precludes perception of central themes in global monetary history. It was in fact the failure of conventional monetary aggregates to account for evidence from global history that prompted creation of the Unified Theory of Prices (UTP), including the Hydraulic Metaphor version offered in this essay. Only later did we discover that the UTP is "unified" in the sense that the model applies equally to monetary and non-monetary topics alike, thereby obviating need for (1) macroeconomic aggregation techniques, and hence need for (2) the fundamental microeconomics-macroeconomics dichotomy itself.[6]

The central concept of this essay has to do with "end-markets" (a concept that, to our knowledge, does not exist in conventional economics). Think about trade via port-city systems such as Long Beach/Los Angeles, Hong Kong, Istanbul, Buenos Aires, Rotterdam, or any other important *entrepôt*.

---

5 Note that objection to "aggregation" here refers to dangers inherent in adding together dissimilar substances in context of supply–demand theory; we ourselves participate, on the other hand, in quantitative aggregation across spaces of virtually-identical products (such as a particular textile).

6 See W.E. Mason, "The Neoclassical Dichotomizaton of Economic Theory," *Economic Inquiry* 12 (1974), 567–576. For a more complete statement of the argument of this paragraph, see Dennis O. Flynn and Arturo Giráldez, eds. *Metals and Monies in an Emerging Global Economy*, (Aldershot, Hampshire, Great Britain; Brookfield, Vt.: Variorum, 1997), xv–xl; Dennis O. Flynn, "Link-Unit-of-Account versus Ratio-Unit-of-Account Moneys: Seventeenth-Century Dutch Mint Policy," in *Empires, Systems, and Maritime Networks: Reconstructing Supra-Regional Histories in Pre-19th Century Asia,* Working Paper Series 05 (December 2011), 33–62 (Ritsumeikan Asia Pacific University in Beppu, Oita, Japan); and Dennis O. Flynn and Marie A Lee, "Link-Unit-of-Account versus Ratio-Unit-of-Account Moneys: Seventeenth-Century Dutch Mint Policy," in edited by Jane Kate Leonard and Ulrich Theobald, *Small Currencies Matter: Trade and Transactions in Early Modern East Asian Economies: Third International Workshop of the Research Group 'Monies, Markets, and Finance in China and East Asia, 1600–1900', 1–3 October 2008,* (Leiden: Brill, forthcoming).

The Unified Theory of Prices focuses on a straightforward question: What determines how much of a particular trade item remains in the port city itself, versus the portion of the trade item that comes to rest in any number of large and small market areas connected to that main port city? The UTP states that the magnitude of each "end-market" – that is, the amount of the trade item that comes to rest in a particular location – depends upon population of the end-market area, combined wealth of each end-market's populace, tastes and preferences for the item in question, and related considerations. Thus, one would not be surprised to discover that more high-end BMW imports find a home in Los Angeles than in, say, Death Valley, California. More well-to-do people live in LA than in Death Valley, so the number of new BMWs owned in LA is much higher than in Death Valley. Similarly, a less-populous city such as Las Vegas, Nevada is expected to contain fewer new BMWs (of a particular model) than Los Angeles, but certainly Las Vegas attracts more new BMWs than are attracted to end-markets in Death Valley. The main innovation of the Unified Theory of Prices is provision of mechanisms that describe these sorts of common-sense realities in theoretical terms. A central feature of the UTP is "Inventory Demand," a concept best explained in context of three interrelated sets of supply-and-demand concepts. We next outline UTP demand-and-supply concepts, devices applied (in this essay) to commodities traded in global, regional and local markets in a particular historical setting.

Keep in mind that our "inventory stocks" concept includes inventories of any tangible item owned by anyone, including producers, shippers, wholesalers, retailers, households, and government entities. All existing units of an item owned by an entity at a given point in time constitute that entity's "Inventory Stock." Inventories are not restricted to business inventories, for instance, since even relatively poor individuals own inventory stocks of mundane items such as bread, shirts, and pencils. The Unified Theory of Prices identifies mechanisms that determine why specific quantities of overall inventory stocks, not more and not less, are held by entities in particular places at a point in time, as well as identifying mechanisms that alter inventory holdings over time. The UTP recognizes three distinct notions of demand as well as three distinct notions of supply:

Supply Side	Demand Side
Production Supply (adds to stock) = PS	Purchase Demand (adds to stock) = PD
Inventory Supply (existing stock) = IS	Inventory Demand (desired stock) = ID
Sales Supply (depletes stock) = SS	Consumption Demand (depletes stock) = CD

Production Supply (PS) adds to existing stocks of a good over time, other things equal, simply because newly-created units augment the pre-existing stock of the item under consideration. Inventory Supply (IS), on the other hand, simply refers to the item's existing stock at a point in time. Sales Supply (SS) depletes existing inventory holdings (IS) over time, other things equal, because sale of units from inventory holdings necessarily implies decline in seller ownership over time; by definition, items sold are by no longer owned by the seller. In sum, Production Supply (PS) enhances Inventory Supply (IS) through new production, while Sales Supply (SS) depletes Inventory Supply (IS) through sales.

On the demand side, Purchase Demand (PD) adds to one's existing stock (IS) of a good over time, other things equal, since purchase implies ownership of more units of the item in question. Inventory Demand (ID) refers to quantity of the item a person/entity *is willing and able to own*, other things equal, given wealth and individual tastes/preferences. Consumption Demand (CD) depletes inventory holdings (IS), other things equal, since one literally cannot "eat one's cake and have it too." In sum, Purchase Demand (PD) augments Inventory Supply (IS) while Consumption Demand (CD) depletes Inventory Supply (IS).

There are three versions of the Unified Theory of Prices: (1) a mathematical version,[7] (2) a graphical version, and (3) an intuitive and visual Hydraulic Metaphor version that is easiest for non-economists to comprehend. We now turn to step-by-step construction of an intuitive "Hydraulic Metaphor" that visually demonstrates essential features of the Unified Theory of Prices. Once familiarity with terminology and basic visualization via the Hydraulic Metaphor is (hopefully) achieved, we shall then apply Hydraulic Metaphor methodology in order to highlight central features of Machado's case-study.

7 The only published exposition of mathematical foundations that underlie the UTP is a bare-bones treatment (Appendix A: Derivation of Stock Demand) in Kerry W. Doherty and Dennis O. Flynn, "A microeconomic quantity theory of money and the price revolution," in *Precious Metals, Coinage and the Changes of Monetary Structures in Latin America, Europe and Asia,* edited by E.G. van Cauwenberghe, (Leuven: Leuven University Press, 1989), 185–208 [republished in Dennis O. Flynn, *A Price Theory of Monies: Evolving lessons in monetary history,* (Wetteren: Moneta, 2009). A more complete (unpublished) mathematical version, "Consumer Demand in Comparative-Static and Dynamic Analysis," (July 1986) can be found on our website at: www.unifiedtheoyrofprices.org Both of these 1980s essays contain some poor terminological choices: for instance, even the title of the 1989 essay contains the phrase "Quantity Theory of Money," yet application of the Unified Theory of Prices actually yields a "Price Theory of Monies," not a Quantity Theory of Money. Unfortunate terminological choices notwithstanding, inventory demand functions were derived via utility analysis in these early essays, and inventory demand is foundational for Unified Theory of Prices models.

In the process, we will soon emphasize the extent to which long-distance trade in textiles from western India into eastern Africa depended upon key players within distant hinterlands.

Hydraulic Metaphor for an Isolated Market Area

We begin with the simplest view: an isolated market not yet permitted to trade with the outside world. Three UTP supply concepts – production supply, inventory supply, and sales supply – are visualized in hydraulic terms in Figure 2.1. Production Supply (PS) simply refers to fresh production at a site. The producer must maintain an inventory of its own good in order to have new product on hand to sell (SS_{PROD} = sales supply) into nearby Market A. Market A's Inventory Supply (IS_A) refers to the total amount of the product held by all parties within that location; in other words, the volume of liquid within Location A's container represents that location's inventory stock (IS_A).

Figure 2.1 also shows three UTP demand concepts in hydraulic terms – purchase demand, inventory demand, and consumption demand. The volume-capacity of the container represents Inventory Demand (ID_A): ID_A represents the quantity of the item people in Location A *are willing and able* to hold at a given price. Purchase demand (PD_A) for individual entities in Location A

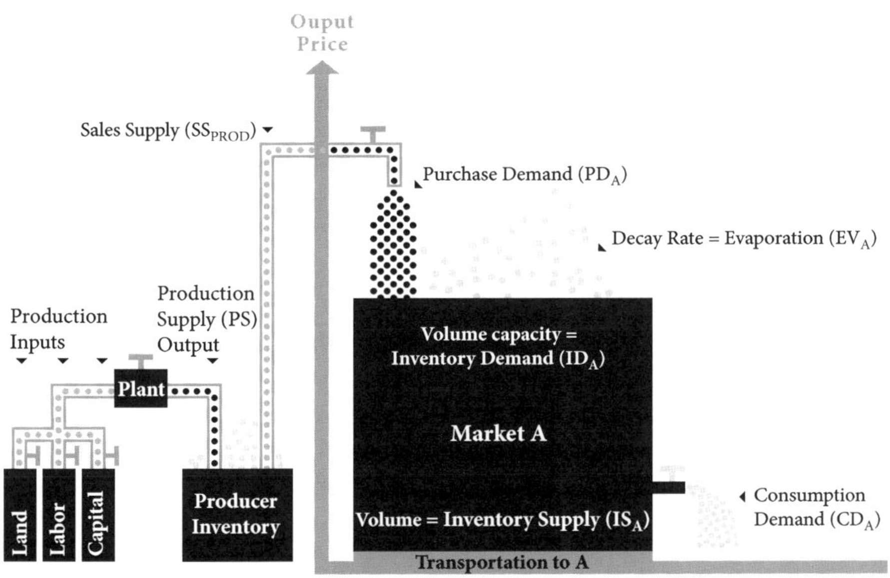

FIGURE 2.1 *Steady state for a reproducible and consumable good*

involves additions to inventory-stocks of the purchaser.[8] Consumption demand (CD_A) depletes inventory holdings in Location A. For visual simplicity, additions to the inventory of any location are depicted as "darkly-shaded-bubble inflows" of liquid, while subtractions from a location's inventory are depicted as "lightly-shaded-bubble outflows" of liquid. "Lightly-shaded-bubble outflows" shown rising from the liquid stock (IS) in Figure 2.1 are labeled "evaporation = decay" and represent subtractions from that location's inventory stock (e.g. wear and tear). For visual simplicity, all subtractions from inventories are represented as lightly-shaded-bubble outflows. Thus, consumption demand (CD_A) is represented as a lightly-shaded-bubble outflow because units consumed are units subtracted from inventory holdings.[9] According to this scheme, Producer sales (SS_{PROD}) are depicted as lightly-shaded-bubble outflows in the upper-portion of the flow of product from

8 The single stream between the Plant and Area A is labeled sales supply (SS_{PLT}) toward the top of its flow, and is labeled purchase demand (PD_A) toward the bottom of its flow. In other words, what appears as sales supply (from the Plant vantage point) appears as purchase demand (from the vantage of those in Area A). Unlike conventional microeconomics, entities are allowed to buy and sell items simultaneously.

9 Note that "consumption" demand for a good under the UTP is characterized by two simultaneous requirements: (1) the activity must generate utility (satisfaction) and (2) it must also deplete inventory. These assumptions are more restrictive than those of conventional microeconomics. Neoclassical economists sometimes describe ownership of a piece of art (e.g. a painting) in utility terms, for example, by assuming that the painting (an inventory item in our view) emits "painting services" (time-dimensioned flows) that are "consumed" (in a utility-generating sense). According to UTP assumptions, however, consumption does not occur in this instance because the painting remains intact after viewing; since the painting-inventory (one) has not been depleted, in other words, there can be no "consumption" of the painting according to our restrictive definition. Rather than conceptualize inventories, including paintings, in metaphysical terms that essentially convert inventory stocks into consumption flows, the UTP simply acknowledges that owning things (inventories) renders satisfaction. At issue is more than semantics. If the source of painting services consumed (on the demand side) is the painting (inventory), then what are the characteristics of the painting's production-supply-of-services function? Does the painting emit more painting services as the price of the painting rises? And on the demand side: would one experience as much pleasure viewing an expensive painting owned by Steve Wynn as would Mr. Wynn (standing proudly at one's side at his casino in Las Vegas or Macau); or might one instead feel pitifully inadequate standing beside a member of the wealthy elite? UTP answers are straightforward: The quantity inventory supply of an original painting is one irrespective of its price, and "pride-of-ownership" exists in reality (in addition, potential wealth appreciation is acknowledged and described when appraised-price rises). In short, the UTP posits two sources of utility (satisfaction): from consumption (as in conventional microeconomics) and also satisfaction from ownership.

Producer Inventory into Market A; note that lightly-shaded-bubble-outflow sales supply (SS_{PROD}) undergoes metamorphosis into darkly-shaded-bubble-inflow purchase demand (PD_A) when viewed from the perspective of buyers in Market A. In other words, Sales Supply from the Producer's point of view is identical to Purchase Demand from the point of view of buyers in Market A; ownership of newly-manufactured items is transferred from the producer to customers in Market A. We represent Producer Sales Supply as a lightly-shaded-bubble outflow because sales deplete Producer inventories, while purchase demand is shown as a darkly-shaded-bubble inflow because items purchased enlarge inventories held in Market A. Any ownership exchange can be viewed from the perspective of inventory-depleting sales supply, or alternatively from the perspective of inventory-enlarging purchase demand. This ($SS_{PROD} = PD_A$) exchange represents the rate at which inventories are transferred (relocated) from the producer to Market A residents.

So long as additions to Market A inventory (via purchase from the production site) equal subtractions from Market A inventory (due to decay plus consumption), the situation in Figure 2.1 depicts "steady state" (assuming that price yields normal profits). That is, the system regenerates itself over time, assuming undisturbed conditions. "Steady state" is the dynamic equivalent to "equilibrium" in comparative-static analysis.[10]

Figure 2.2 shows a system in initial *dis*equilibrium, in contrast to Figure 2.1, in the sense that existing market price and quantity do not self-regenerate over time. The vertical height of the container-base represents price of the item; the upward arrow beneath the container indicates price rising due to the fact that Inventory demand (ID_A = container capacity) is greater than Inventory Supply (IS_A = contents of the container). Unfilled storage capacity implies temporary inventory shortage in Market A, in other words, which explains why price is initially rising above the steady-state price depicted in Figure 2.1; people in Market A wish to hold more than they actually hold at this instant. As price rises, *Quantity* of Inventory Demand for the good declines (under standard assumption of negatively-sloped demand functions); this decline in quantity of inventory demand is shown visually through slight shrinkage of container volume capacity in Figure 2.2 relative to container volume capacity in Figure 2.1.[11]

---

10 To view and interact with a dynamic version of the Hydraulic Metaphor, contact www.unifiedtheoryofprices.org.

11 Reduction of inventory capacity of the container in response to a rise in price refers to the commonsense observation that customer's wish to own fewer units of an item when its price rises.

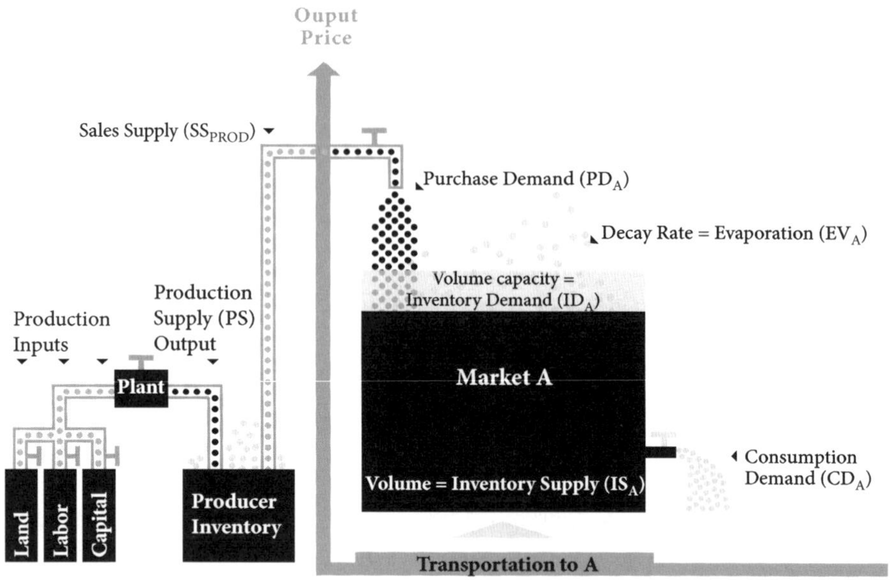

FIGURE 2.2 *Temporary Disequilibrium: Inventory Demand* (ID_A) *exceeds Inventory Supply* (IS_A)

As price rises, quantity of inventory demand (container volume capacity) continues to shrink until IS_A equals ID_A, as shown in Figure 2.3; again, container capacity shrinks simply because people desire to hold smaller inventories as the price of the good rises. As will be explained in a moment, Figure 2.3 depicts non-steady-state *dis*equilibrium even though inventory demand equals inventory supply.

The elevated price shown in Figure 2.3, of course, provides incentive for the Producer to ramp up production. Since high price would lead to a more vigorous production than before ($PS_{PROD}' > PS_{PROD}$) due to elevated price, larger transfers of new units into Market A overpower depletions due to Market A consumption (CD_A) plus Market A decay (=evaporation, EV_A). Since enlarged production is now adding units faster than subtractions due to consumption plus decay, inventory supply (IS_A) must grow. Assuming existence of wholesale storage facilities, yet-to-be-sold inventories in Market A appear as cross-hatched "excess inventories" (EI_A) atop Market A inventories in Figure 2.4. Market A residents can be induced to take possession of all newly-enhanced wholesale inventory stocks (cross-hatched in Figure 2.4), but price reduction within Market A is required to attract additional purchases. Market forces depress price automatically, in other words, whenever inventory stocks ($=IS_A + EI_A$) exceed inventory demand at the existing, elevated price. As enhanced production continues to enter Market A due to favorable price, ever-rising

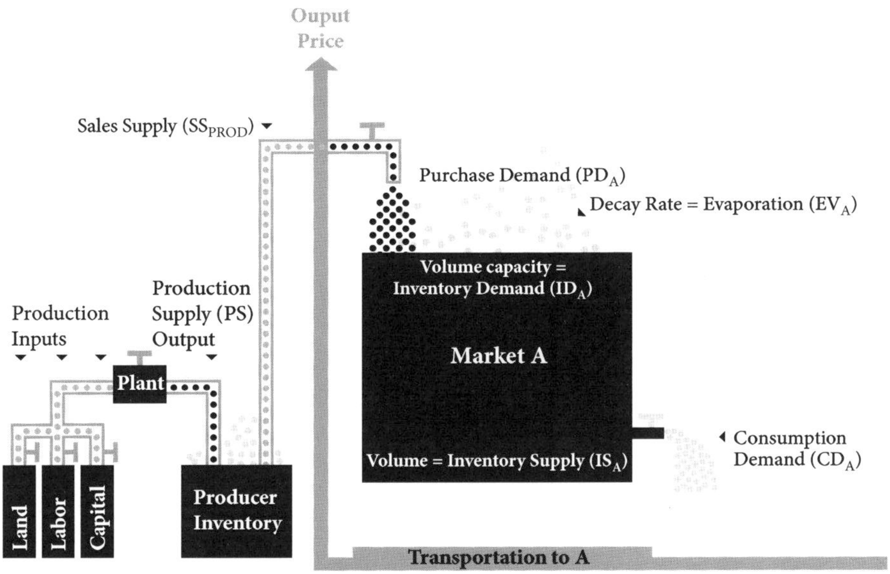

FIGURE 2.3 *Temporary Disequilibrium, although Inventory Demand* (ID_A) = *Inventory Supply* (IS_A)

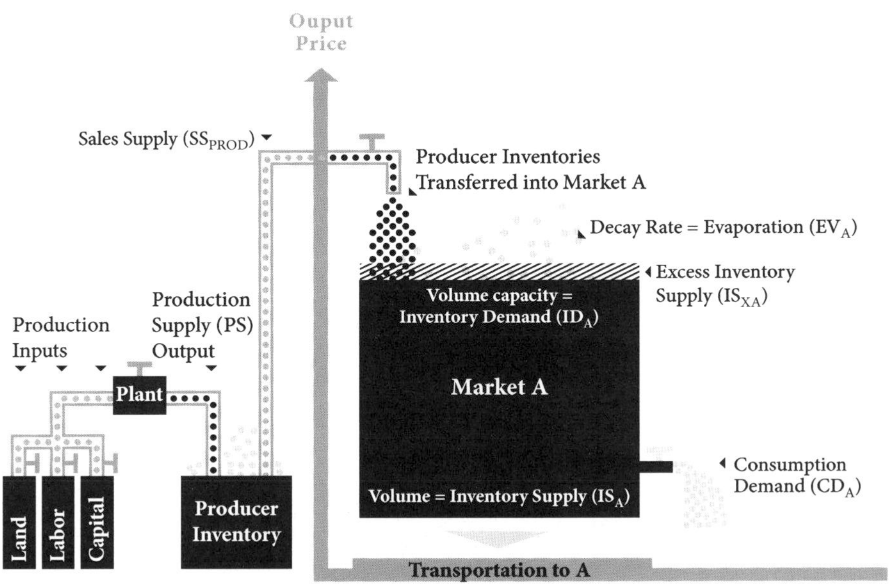

FIGURE 2.4 *Producer transfers product to Market A in anticipation of sale*

inventory supply puts downward pressure on price; falling price in Market A, in turn, causes *quantity* of inventory demand to rise (since people desire to hold a larger quantity of the good as its price falls).

The container base eventually subsides to floor level, as depicted in the snapshot view of the system once steady-state equilibrium has been reasserted at floor-level price shown in Figure 2.5. Price has declined to equilibrium level (floor) such that subsequent additions ($PS_{PROD} = PD_A$) to Market-A inventory once again precisely offset Market-A inventory subtractions due to consumption demand (CD_A) and evaporation (EV_A); the system self-replicates in Figure 2.5, other things equal, from one period to the next. Note that this "steady state" equilibration process has thus far been described without reference to trade beyond this isolated space.

Hydraulic Metaphor with Trade

Figure 2.6 depicts two interconnected market areas for a specific good. Note that supply and demand conditions in Market A and Market B reflect steady-state conditions, inasmuch as existing inventory holdings match desired inventory holdings at prices that generate normal profits within each market.

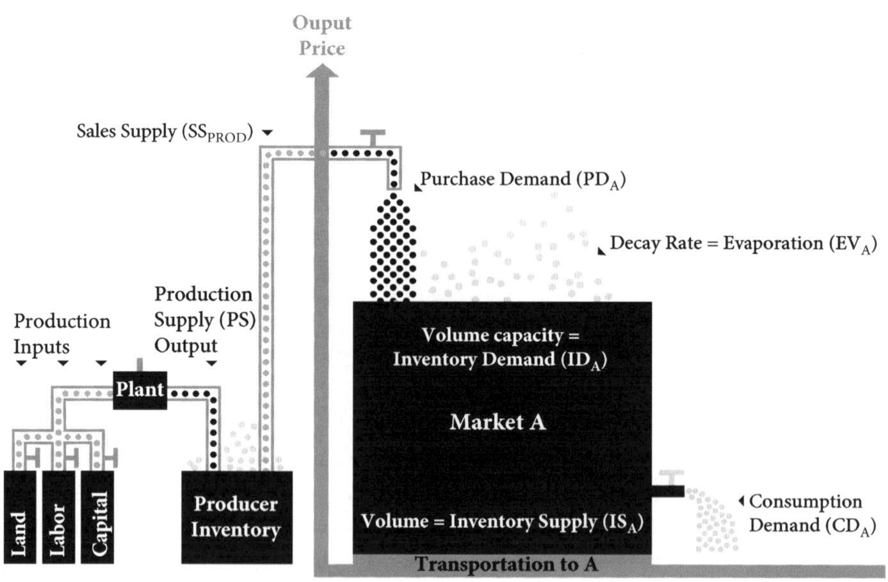

FIGURE 2.5 *Steady-state price and quantity reasserted*

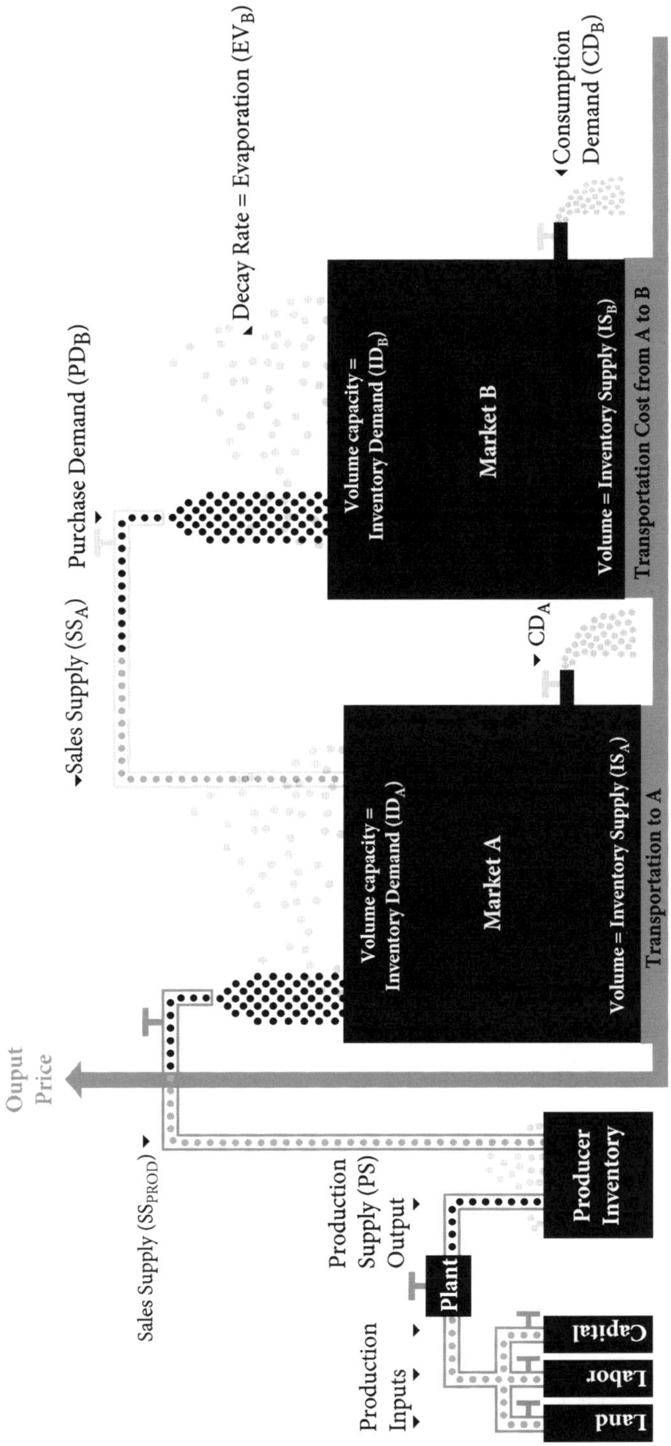

FIGURE 2.6 *Steady-state in each connected market*

Next, some market disturbance – for example, a natural disaster – reduces inventory holdings in Market B, which causes price to rise in Market B. Figure 2.7 depicts price elevation in Market B, but without sufficient time *yet* for price to have risen in Market B as fully as it soon will; thus, ID_B exceeds IS_B temporarily (i.e. the Market B container is not full).

Once *quantity* of Inventory Demand has had time to fully shrink in response to an even higher price in Market B shown in Figure 2.8, then $IS_B = ID_B$ equality will come to pass. Price in Market B now exceeds price in Market A by a considerable margin in Figure 2.8, as indicated by the fact that the base of Container B is higher than the base of Container A was in Figure 2.7. Arbitrage gains can now be realized through purchase of the good at a relatively low price in Market A, followed by relocation and resale of the good in Market B at a higher price.

Figure 2.9 depicts an intermediate stage of adjustment during the arbitrage phase of exchange between market areas. High price in Market B (relative to Market A) has induced transfer of some inventory holdings from Market A to Market B. Assuming that market prices have not yet had time to react fully to depletion of Market A inventories (as a result of transfers into Market B), IS_A temporarily sinks below ID_A (i.e. container A in Figure 2.9 is no longer full). This simply means that enhanced transfer of goods into Market B causes a temporary inventory shortage in Market A ($IS_A < ID_A$); this temporary inventory-shortage in Market A hence puts upward pressure on price in Market A (indicated by upward arrow under Market A). Simultaneously, sale/transfer of the good into Market B bolsters inventory supply in Market B ($IS_B > ID_B$), which puts downward pressure on price in Market B (indicated by a downward arrow under Market B). Under assumption that price has not yet had time to adjust as fully as it eventually will, excess inventory supply in Market B (IS_{XB}) is depicted as a cross-hatched container-area that hovers above container B in Figure 2.9; IS_{XB} (excess inventories), in turn, that puts downward pressure on price in Market B (indicated by a downward arrow under Market B in Figure 2.9).

Figure 2.10 projects the same forces as Figure 2.9, except that price has had more time to adjust upward in Figure 2.10-Market A (relative to Figure 2.9-Market A), reflected by increased elevation of the base of container A (caused by the temporary inventory shortage depicted in Figure 2.9). Note that Figure 2.10-Container A capacity is smaller than the capacity of Figure 2.9-Container A; reduction of Container A capacity reflects the fact that *quantity* of inventory demand is assumed to decline as price rises. By parallel reasoning, "excess inventory supply" ($IS_{XB} = IS_B - ID_B$) in Market B causes Market B price to decline, which is reflected by lowering of the base of Figure 2.10-Container B (vis-à-vis

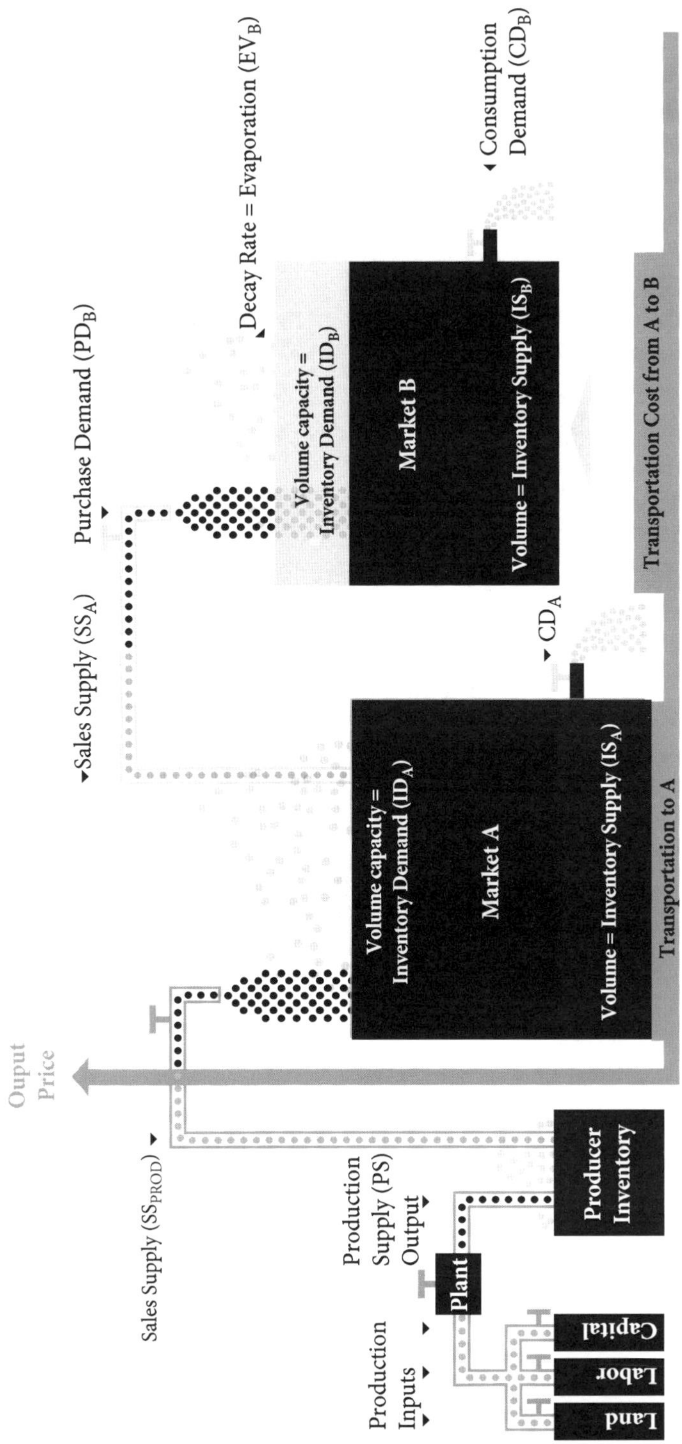

FIGURE 2.7 *Price divergence among market areas*

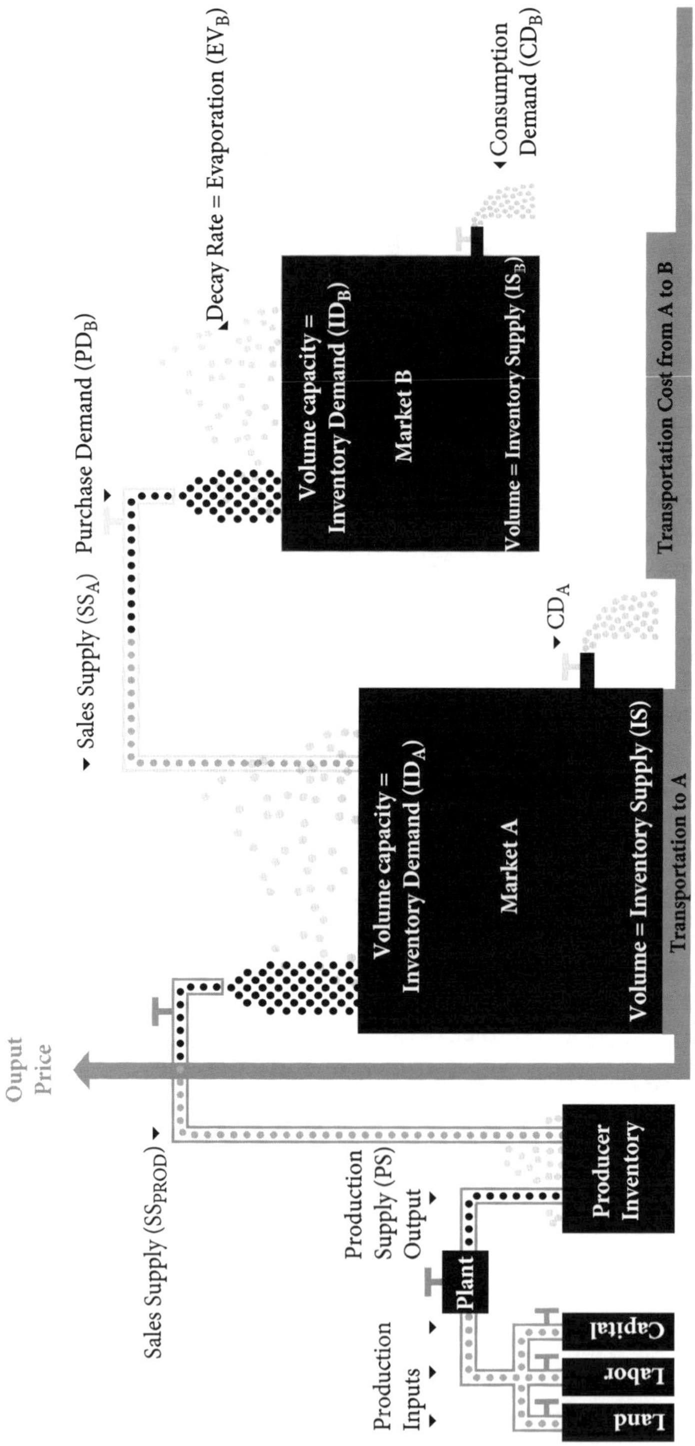

FIGURE 2.8 *Arbitrage between markets*

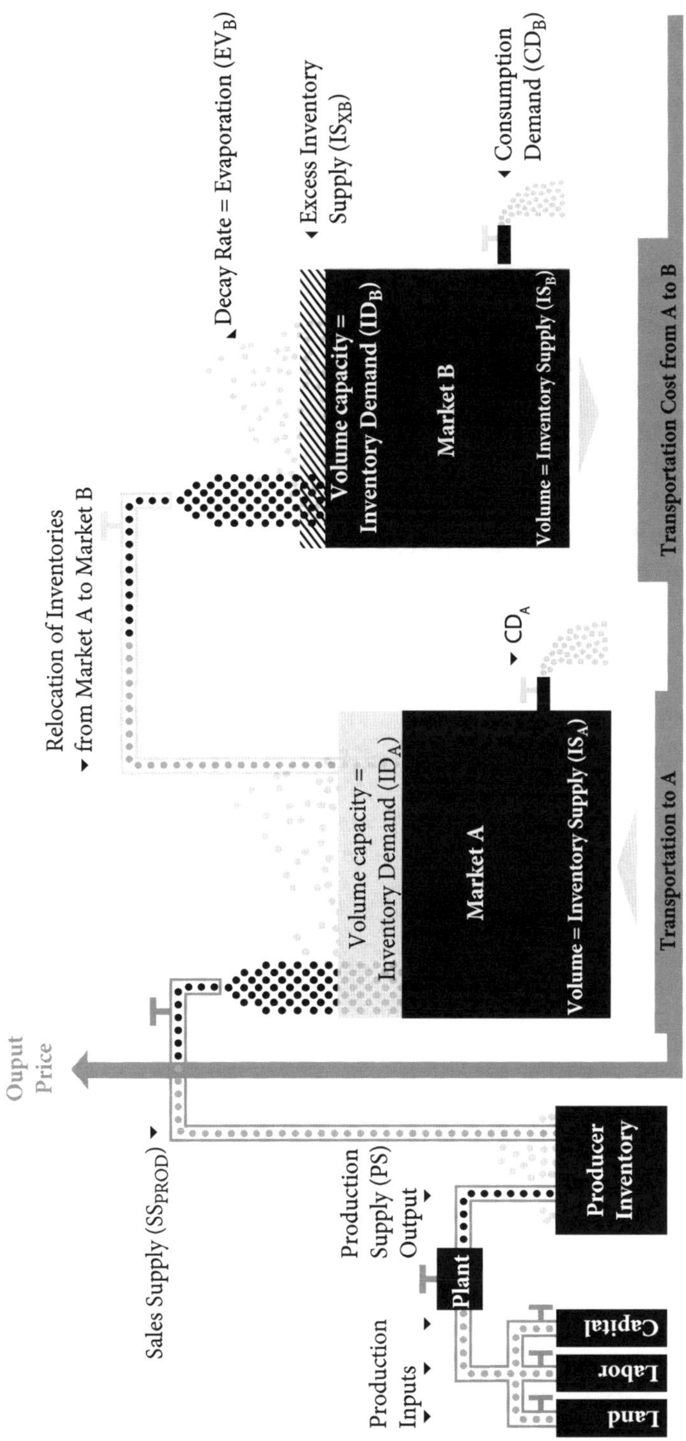

FIGURE 2.9 *Price pressures and inventory transfer during arbitrage trade*

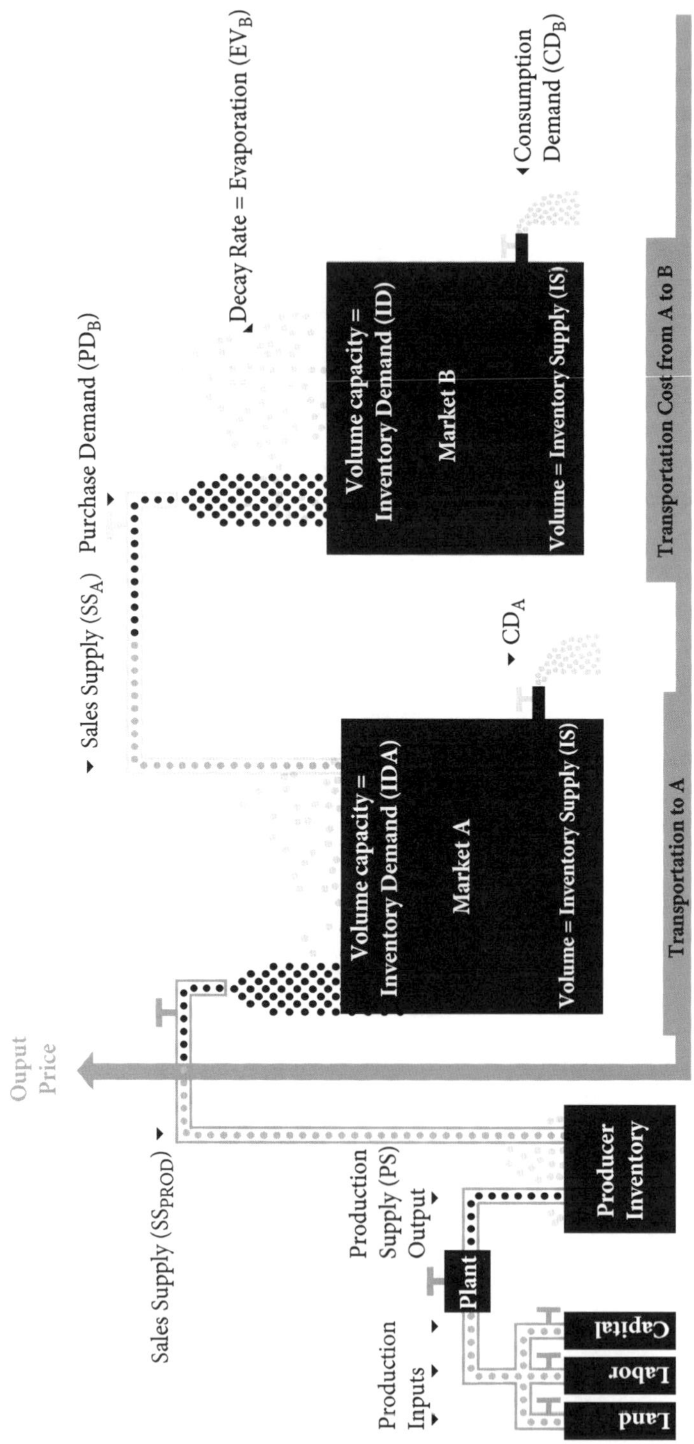

FIGURE 2.10 *Arbitrage transition on path to steady-state*

elevation of the base of Figure 2.9-Container B). Note again that Figure 2.10-Container B capacity is larger than Figure 2.9-Container B capacity, reflecting an assumed increase in *quantity* of inventory demand in Market B as price declines in Market B. In short, price in Figure 2.10-Market A rises while Figure 2.10-Market B price falls (relative to respective prices in Figure 2.9); in other words, arbitrage trade acts to reduce price differences among connected market areas. Thus, arbitrage trade automatically self-eliminates arbitrage possibilities (as arbitrage trade is occurring).

Figure 2.10 projects an attractive situation from the producer point of view. Prices in Market A and Market B both yield profits greater than original steady-state (normal) profits implicit in construction of Figures 2.1 and 2.5. High price and elevated profits induce increased *quantity* of production (PS_{PROD}) and increased sales supply (SS_{PROD}) into Market A and into Market B. At the same time, elevated prices in Market A and Market B simultaneously provoke reduced *quantities* consumed (CD_A) in Market A and Market B; decay declines in both markets as well (since decay is assumed a fixed percentage of inventory holdings).

To simplify matters, let's assume that the producer is able to sell its product into both Market A and Market B simultaneously (a situation *not* shown visually in this essay) in response to unusually-high price in both market areas. Ramped up production would eventually be transferred to both Market A and Market B; that is, larger-than-normal transfers of inventory quantities enter each end-market simultaneously.[12] Of course, higher inventory stocks in each end-market puts downward pressure on price, as before, in both market areas simultaneously. Prices in both end-markets ultimately decline until only normal profits prevail everywhere; price equilibration occurs in all markets (net of transportation costs) when only normal profits prevail everywhere. Such a steady-state situation is depicted in Figure 2.11, where both containers have come to rest once again on respective bases that reflect prices consistent with normal profits. A key conclusion is that Inventory Demand (i.e. container capacity) determines "end-market" quantities (i.e. Inventory Supply) that finally come to rest in each market area. Similar to living things in biological models, the Unified Theory of Prices describes forces that determine steady-state "populations" (i.e. inventories of animate and inanimate market objects) that come to rest in individual places, spaces, and times.

---

12 We could insist that enhanced production must pass through Market A prior to re-export to Market B, as before, but we seek to simplify the story here.

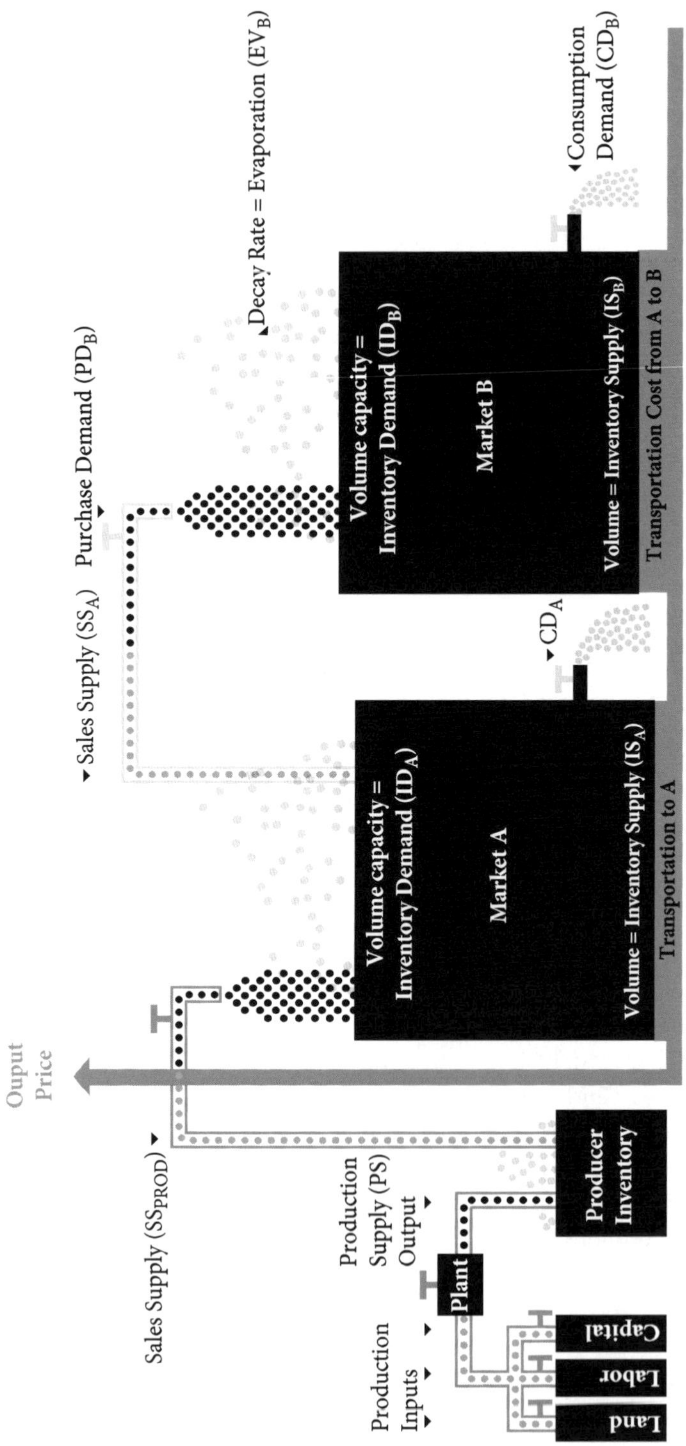

FIGURE 2.11 *Steady-state throughout connected market areas*

Gujarati Textiles into East Africa via a Hydraulic Metaphor Lens

Pedro Machado has recently argued convincingly that the conventional literature on East African trade distorts reality due to near-total emphasis on ivory, slaves and other African exports; Machado protests that exports represent only one side of the story. Trade involves exchange of export goods for import goods, hence a balanced picture can be achieved only through investigation of African *imports*, including textiles from India, in addition to conventional emphasis upon African exports. Textiles fulfilled many functions, including clothing, dining, wall hangings and so on, but also served as a type of money in East Africa: Cotton textiles were regarded as "currency that is accepted in ports" and a "primary measure of value for which ivory, slaves and other commodities were exchanged across the Indian Ocean in areas that effectively constituted cloth currency zones of contact."[13] Textiles in Africa served non-monetary functions as well, of course, and dire consequences confronted merchants caught off-guard by changing African tastes for textiles. Machado has uncovered a web of transoceanic linkages that connected textile producers in Gujarat (northwest India) with end-market customers in East, East-Central and Southeast Africa during the eighteenth and nineteenth centuries. This portion of our essay highlights aspects of trade history unveiled by Machado's research. Application of the Hydraulic Metaphor outlined above is helpful for keeping track of key determinants of complex, long-distance trade connections among producers, merchants, and customers from diverse cultures. Banyan merchants from India possessed special skills that enabled them to navigate distant connections, allowing them to dominate the Gujarati textiles trade into East Africa. Gujarati merchants had been involved in the African textile trade for centuries previously, but goods had been shipped aboard Portuguese vessels as a result of monopolistic Portuguese Crown policies early on. Portuguese policy shifted during the eighteenth century, however, to an increasingly free-trade regime based upon regulation and taxation in place of monopoly. As a result, "Vaniya [Banyan merchants] assumed complete control over the direct shipment of textiles to Africa, and thus were able to command a powerful presence in an openly competitive environment."[14]

13 Pedro Machado, "Clothes of a New Fashion: Indian Ocean Networks of Exchange and Cloth Zones of Contact in Africa and India in the Eighteenth and Nineteenth Centuries," In *How India Clothed the World the World of South Asian Textiles, 1500–1850*, edited by Giorgio Riello and Tirthankar Roy, 57.

14 Ibid., 61.

Gujarati weavers concentrated in/near major urban centers that offered plentiful labor, close proximity to raw cotton, and clean water required for dyeing. Jambusar developed into an urban center "where the bulk of western Indian textiles for the African markets were manufactured."[15] Astute Banyan merchants negotiated purchase of Gujarati textiles, not directly with weavers, but through brokers (via verbal contracts) who represented weavers. Lacking direct contact with Indian weavers, the Banyan network nonetheless managed to accurately transmit detailed information indirectly (via brokers in Gujarat) to Gujarati weavers regarding specific African tastes and preferences.

The Banyan merchant network gained detailed knowledge of shifting consumer preferences for each specific African market without having ventured into African hinterland end-markets either. Collaboration with African agents (some themselves slaves) provided Gujarati merchants an indispensable edge over rivals:

> The Vaniya unfailingly understood very early on that commercial success depended in large part on being attuned to the changing regional differences of textile demand in East-Central and South-East Africa. Because they did not venture into interior markets, critical information was provided to them…by the *patamares* and *vashambadzi*, with whom the Vaniya maintained contact on a regular basis.[16]

In short, Banyan merchants custom-ordered textiles based upon detailed information gleaned from African agents with first-hand knowledge of tastes and preferences specific to individual end-markets in African hinterlands. Detailed preferences gleaned from African specialists were transmitted to Gujarati brokers in India, who then negotiated contracts on behalf of weavers and assured that customized, quality textiles were produced. Thus, Banyan merchants refrained from visiting locations of hinterland production as well as hinterland end-markets. Raw cotton and other resources required by the Jambusar textile industry were produced in the Gujarati hinterland. Machado describes Banyan merchants as unparalleled "mediators of cross-cultural and cross-regional contact" with management skills (and thereby access to knowledge) that led to domination of this important transoceanic textile trade for generations.

Our Hydraulic Metaphor offers visual representation of key forces at work across distant "cross-cultural and cross-regional" markets uncovered by

15 Ibid., 57.
16 Ibid., 66–67.

Machado, forces easily overlooked by readers in the absence of such a model. Island *entrepôts* played important roles on both sides of this Indian Ocean trade, as was the case for many crucial trade linkages around the globe, since islands facilitated control and taxation of trade items in relative isolation from outside disturbances (including smuggling). By the end of the 18th century, some 400,000 textile pieces per year were routed from Jambusar through a nearby island, Diu, a "small and infertile island…[that had been]…a poor and unproductive area…" that nonetheless became a logistical linchpin due to its location "close to Gujarati production centers…[which] meant Diu was potentially well placed to take advantage of this vast hinterland for its textile supplies."[17] An additional 200,000 pieces annually reached Mozambique Island via Daman, a secondary Indian *entrepôt* to the south of Diu.[18] Textiles were temporarily sequestered in warehouses at Diu and Daman, awaiting transfer to East-Africa-bound ships.

Mozambique Island, off the coast of East African, furnished a similar *entrepôt* function for Banyan merchants on the receiving end, where Guajarati textiles were recorded, sorted, and temporarily stored in order to be properly funneled to specific East African market centers. Figure 2.12 offers a simplified picture of the Banyan merchant trade network, with emphasis upon inventory-theoretic considerations.[19] Recall that volume capacity for a particular container represents a location's inventory demand under the Hydraulic Metaphor; here, container capacity represents the quantity of a specific textile that locals wish to hold in inventory at prevailing prices (all else constant). Thus, the Jambusar container is intentionally represented as a large vessel, since Jambusar was a populous and vibrant commercial city during the time under consideration. Given that Jambusar contained a large and relatively wealthy population, it stands to reason that some of the textiles purchased in Jambusar must have been retained locally in order to satisfy inventory demand by Jambusar residents (including retail merchants). During periods of population growth and prosperity (not shown here), expansion of Jambusar's inventory demand would be represented by expansion of that city's container-volume capacity. If growth in volume capacity (i.e. increase in inventory demand) were to (temporarily) outpace growth of the actual volume residing inside of the

17 Ibid., 71–72.

18 Ibid., 62.

19 Note that all Hydraulic Metaphor figures presented from this point onward abstract from arbitrage (and other) complexities sketched earlier in this essay. We intentionally simplify in order to focus attention on the dominant role played by Inventory Demand in determining end-market resting places for products discussed herein.

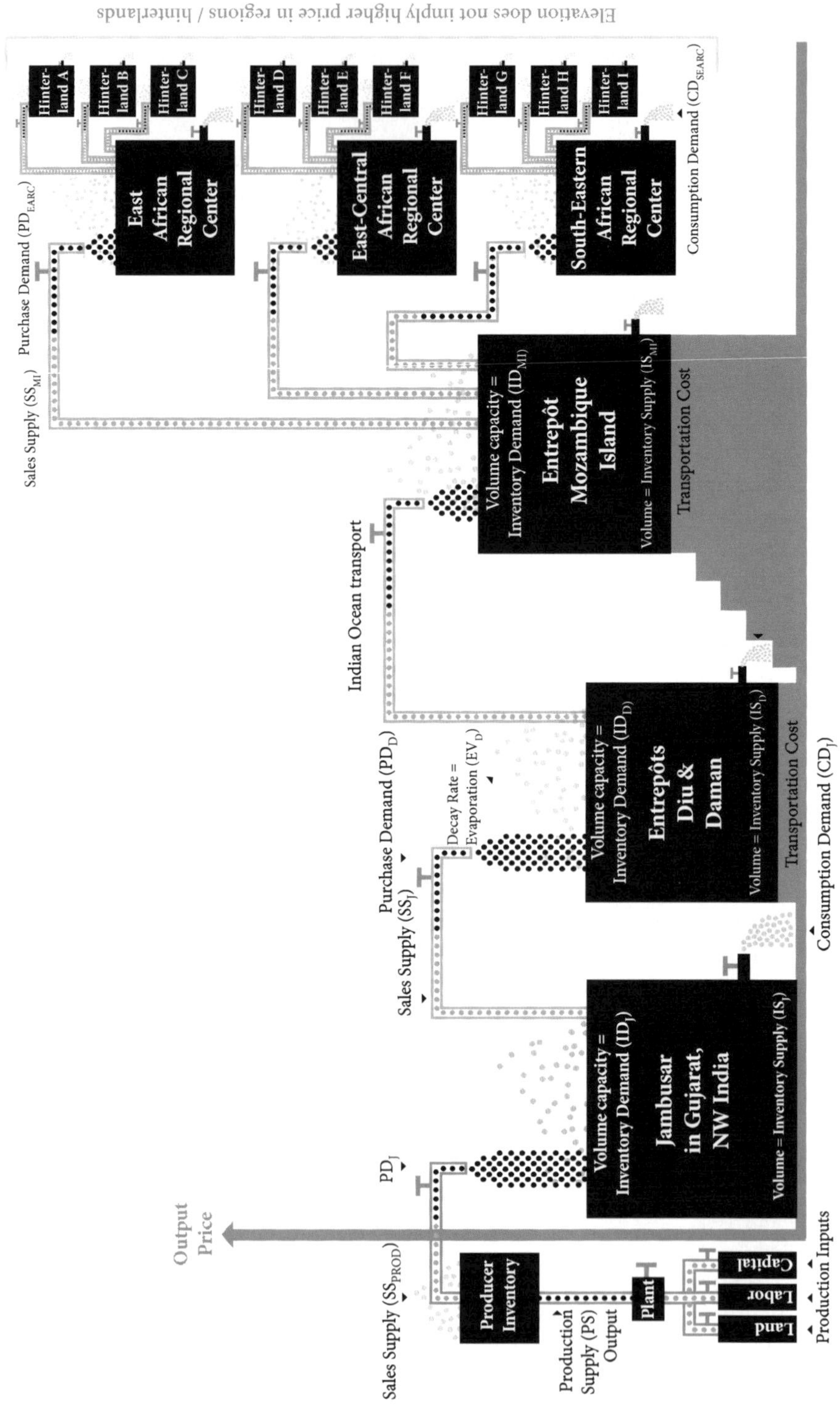

FIGURE 2.12 *Indian textiles into East Africa*

container (i.e. inventory supply), then the textile's price in Jambusar would rise for a time (again, not shown here), whereupon market mechanisms (described earlier in this essay) would induce an enhanced production rate; inventory supply would eventually expand to satisfy growth in inventory demand (i.e. the container would fill up) at prices that would eventually generate normal profits. This analysis is symmetrical in the sense that, were Jambusar's economy to contract during a down cycle (perhaps including loss of population), shrinking inventory demand would translate into shrinkage of container volume-capacity; volume of liquid held (inventory supply) would also shrink inevitably as a consequence of such a reduction in demand-side capacity. Inventory demand rules the roost, in other words, in the sense that inventory demand ultimately determines the amount of a good that remains within each place and space (i.e. inventory supply adjusts to satisfy inventory demand, and *not* the other way around). Simplistic as this image may appear, the Hydraulic Metaphor facilitates visualization of how and why goods reside at particular locations. Wherever concentrations of wealth and population exist, other things equal, individual components of wealth – including textiles – concentrate in the form of inventories held. Whenever an area suffers loss of wealth and/or population – due, say, to closure of a large manufacturing plant or an environmental/infrastructure disaster – individual forms of portable wealth (including textiles) tend to exit the depressed area (i.e. they are exported). If the good in question decays relatively quickly (e.g. bananas) and/or residents consume it at a rapid rate, then maintenance of an inventory stock requires a sufficiently high rate of import (purchase demand) to offset a three-pronged drain on existing inventory stocks – (1) decay, (2) consumption demand, and (3) sales supply (to outside regions). If the item is non-consumable and decay is imperceptive (e.g. diamonds), on the other hand, then inventory stock can be maintained by simply importing (purchase demand) at the same rate the item is exported (sales supply). Just about any scenario imaginable can be described via the Hydraulic Metaphor. Note that the metaphor represented in Figure 2.12 applies to inventory analyses of hinterlands as well as major cities/regions alike.

Entrepôt Diu (together with nearby Daman) is represented in Figure 2.12 as a place with substantial inventory demand and inventory supply (arbitrarily drawn in magnitude similar to inventories in Jambusar itself). Large inventory holdings at Diu could indeed be realistic, but only during certain time-intervals in a seasonal cycle. Warehouses on Diu must have bulged with inventories on the eve of loading of textiles onto Mozambique-bound ships.

The container labeled "Entrepôts Diu and Daman" in Figure 2.13 represents full warehouses just prior to loading of cargo aboard ships. Figure 2.13

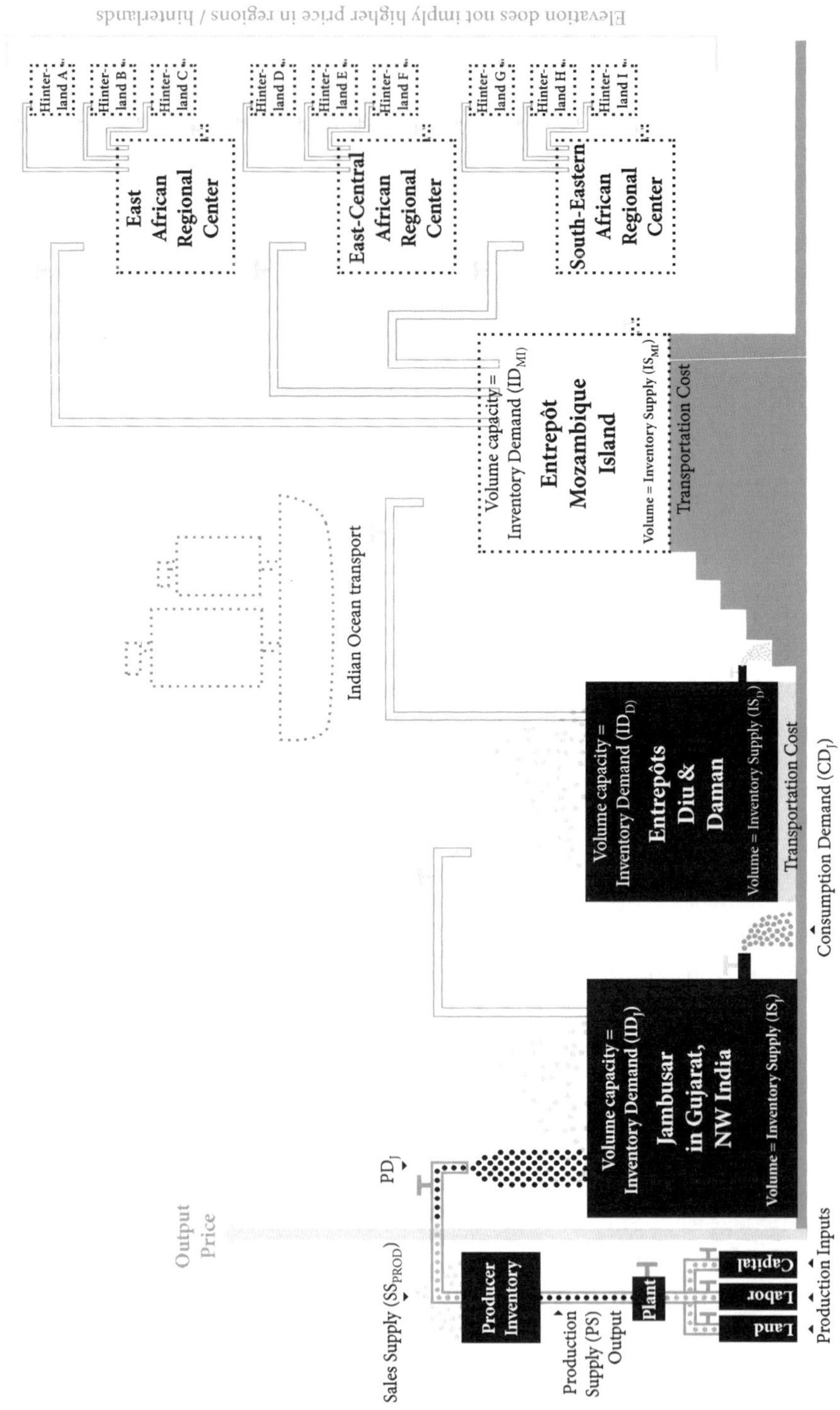

FIGURE 2.13 *Textiles in Diu & Daman warehouses*

also indicates that a portion of textile output remained in Jambusar itself, a populous and vibrant city in its own right. The quantity of a specific textile remaining in Jambusar was determined by the magnitude of that city's inventory demand for it. Jambusar's inventory demand, in turn, was determined by (a) the amount of wealth in that city, by (b) the extent to which residents chose to hold a fraction of their wealth in the form of the particular textile (i.e. tastes and preferences), and by (c) the rate of wear and tear of textiles already held (i.e. depleted stocks require replenishment).

Once ships were fully loaded, on the other hand, container volume capacity for Diu would shrivel, reflecting the fact that textiles had been loaded aboard ship (after having been warehoused at Diu/Daman). Figures 2.13, 2.14, 2.15 and 2.16 add time sequences that reflect inventory transfers that occur from one discrete time to another discrete time (an aspect intentionally ignored in Figure 2.12).

Figure 2.14 introduces an outbound ship loaded with textiles from Diu and destined for Mozambique Island. Diu's container in Figure 2.14 is shown empty – reflecting the fact that textiles were recently loaded aboard ship – and drawn with dashed container walls that show what the size of inventory demand had been *prior to loading of the ship* (a reminder that merchants no longer wish to hold inventories at Diu warehouses until the next export cycle). The Mozambique Island container is similarly shown both empty and with dashed container walls (to remind us that merchants *will wish to hold* textile inventories at this East African *entrepôt* at the time of scheduled ship arrival, although they currently wish to hold zero inventories on Mozambique Island). Since current-season textiles are en route at sea, they obviously could not be held simultaneously in any *entrepôt* warehouse.

Figure 2.15 depicts successful arrival of the textile ship and unloading of cargo into warehouses on Mozambique Island; the ship is now shown empty with dashed walls to indicate prior inventory demand aboard ship (while sailing across the Indian Ocean previously). In other words, dashed ship walls denote the magnitude of inventory demand that had existed aboard ship *prior to* its arrival at Mozambique Island. Cargo must have been sorted during the off-loading process in order to direct specialized textiles into appropriate sections of warehouses (for temporary storage), since specific textiles were earmarked for predetermined end-markets (that depended upon projected tastes in each local market). The reader is asked to keep in mind that diverse textiles had been earmarked for specific African markets (since it is difficult for us to exhibit such distinctions via black-and-white images shown here).

Figure 2.16 depicts arrival of new textiles both at regional centers along the African coast, as well as arrival at end markets in African hinterlands.

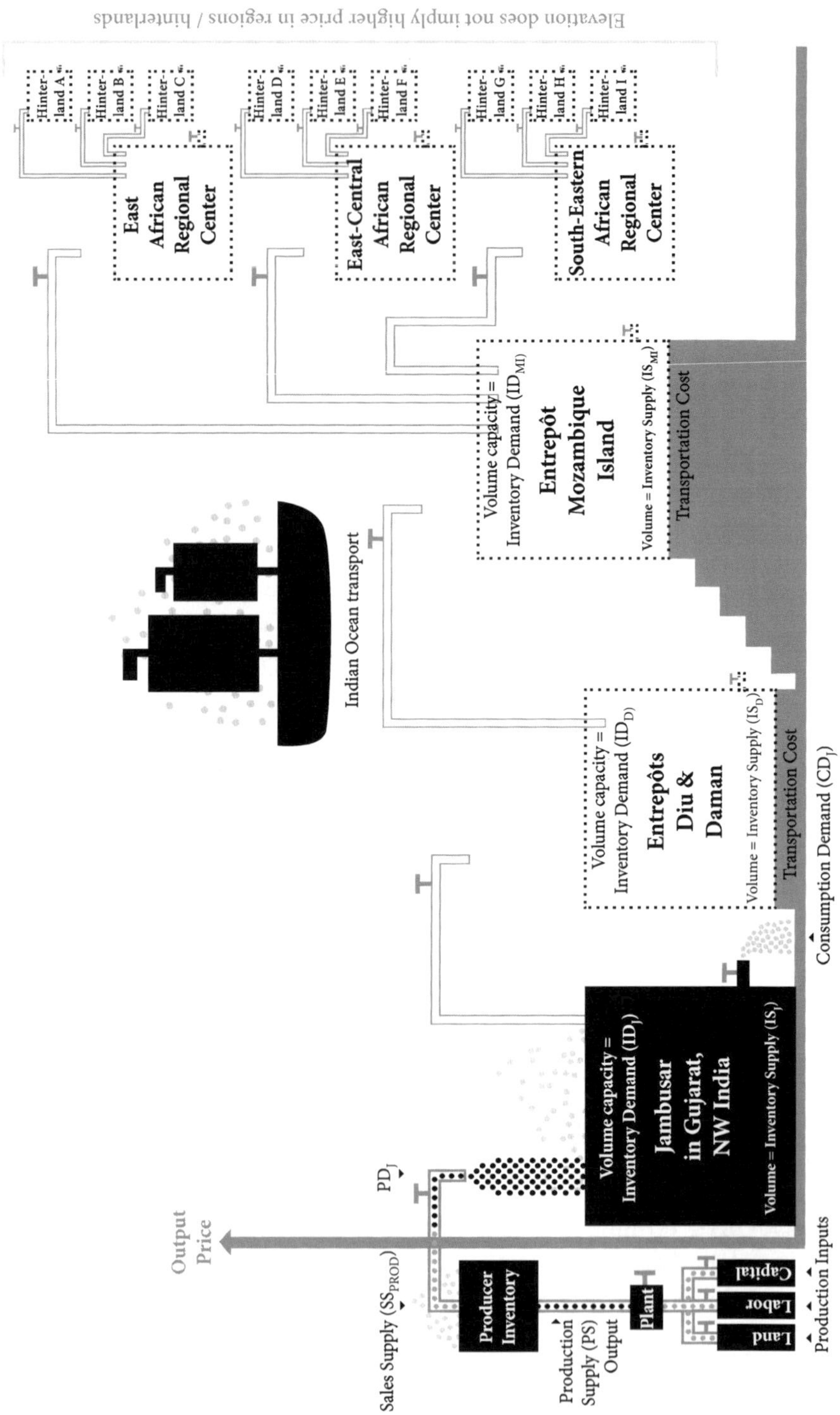

FIGURE 2.14 *Textiles at Sea*

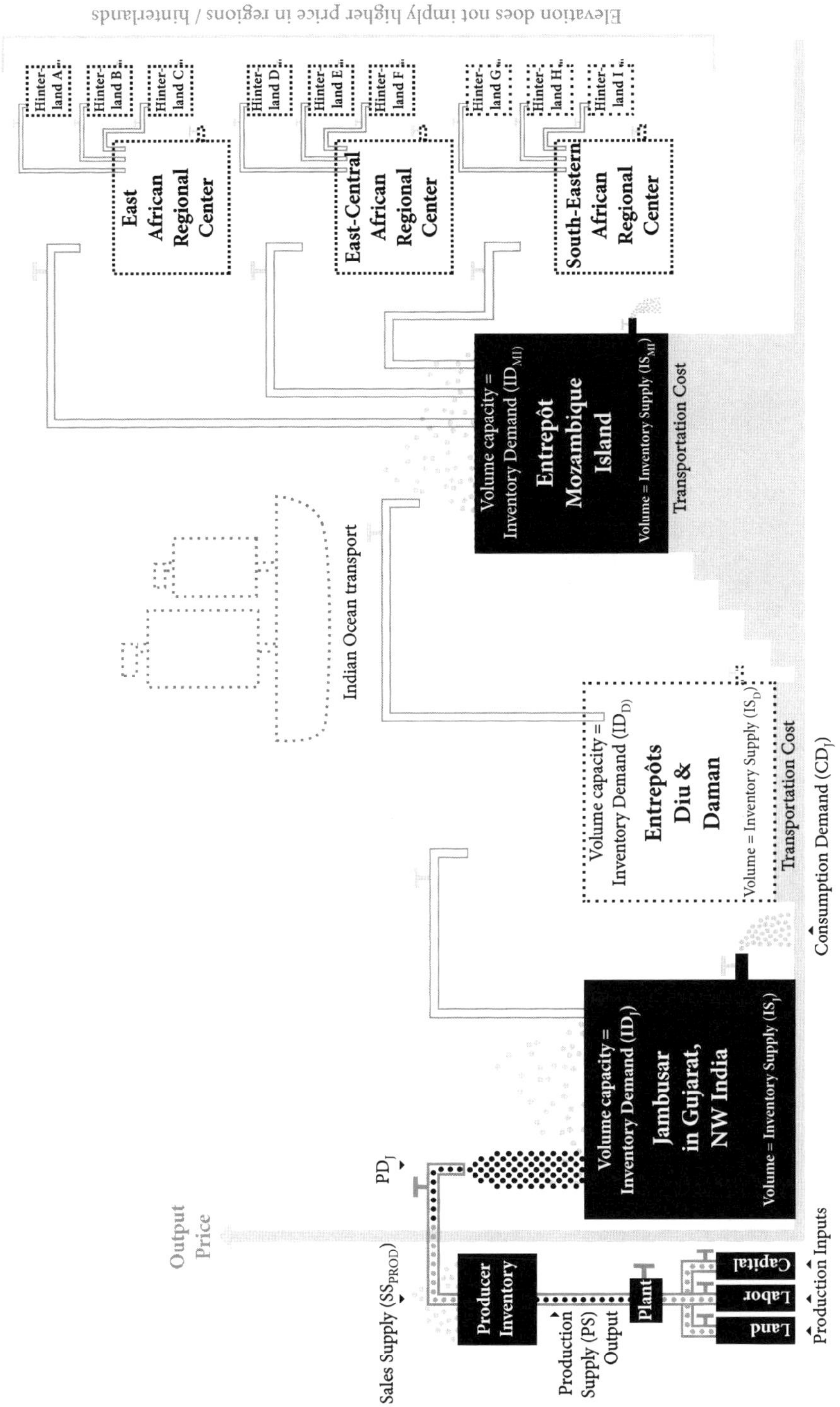

FIGURE 2.15 *Textile warehouses on Mozambique Island*

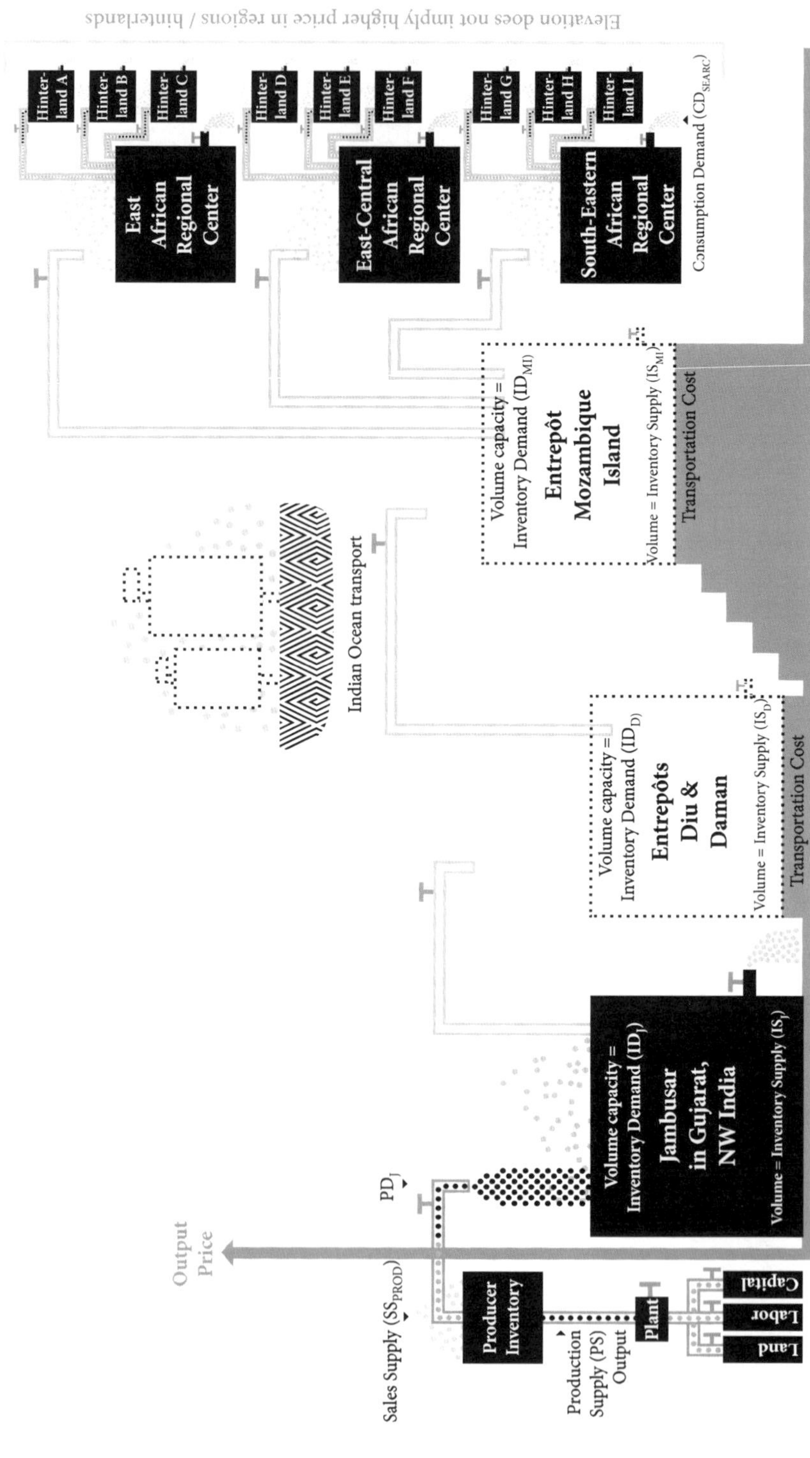

FIGURE 2.16 *Textile end-markets within Africa*

Warehouses on Mozambique Island are shown empty, with dashed walls, representing the fact that current-season textiles have already been re-exported to final destinations.

An important aspect of interregional trade is intentionally ignored in this essay: namely, cargo simultaneously exported from East Africa (e.g. ivory, gold, and slaves) in exchange for specialized textile imports from Gujarat. In the interest of brevity, the very African exports that Pedro Machado complains were previously overemphasized in the mainstream literature are intentionally underemphasized here. Even so, Africa-to-Gujarat exports receive at least abstract acknowledgment via depiction of a return ship full of (unspecified) cargo in Figure 2.16. The Hydraulic Metaphor could just as easily be applied to trade in the widely-acknowledged African export goods, assuming that accurate and detailed scholarly information exists. Ivory, gold and slaves were goods produced in African hinterlands, after all, and they were relocated to specific domestic and overseas market areas based upon extent of Inventory Demand (volume capacities) at each locality; moreover, decay rates (which in the case of slaves, means sickness and death) affected each market. Hydraulic Metaphor methodology is applicable to all goods, including crucial factor-of-production inputs that are often concentrated in hinterlands, scattered across urban and rural landscapes at regional and global levels.

Conclusion

This essay offers a theoretical model applicable to any topic in trade history, including impacts *from* hinterland areas as well as impacts *upon* hinterlands. Pedro Machado's research on eighteenth-century Indian textile exports into East Africa is featured because of his explicit consideration of central roles played by seemingly-remote hinterland areas. Banyan merchants coordinated distant overseas markets, yet these entrepreneurs had direct contact with neither hinterland producers in India nor hinterland end-market buyers in African hinterlands. Rather, African *agents* provided detailed information to Banyan merchants regarding local tastes in specific East African locations; Banyan merchants conveyed detailed orders to Gujarati *brokers*, in turn, whose job was to coordinate labor and materials – including those from hinterlands of west India – required for timely production of custom-ordered textiles based upon hinterland and urban center tastes in specific East African locations. Distant agents and brokers were unknown to each other, as of course was the case for customers in respective hinterlands separated by thousands of miles. Yet, hinterland players were the *sin qua non* for a large-scale transoceanic trade system that was flexible, durable, and coordinated by remarkably multicultural merchant entrepreneurs.

The Hydraulic Metaphor proposed in this essay attempts to clarify forces at work along entire supply chains that connected distant market areas, including hinterlands. The Hydraulic Metaphor identifies three distinct supply concepts: production supply (which increases inventories), sales supply (which decreases inventories), and accumulated inventories (inventory supplies themselves). Three distinct demand concepts are also introduced: purchase demand (which raises inventories), consumption demand (which reduces inventories), and inventory demand (desired inventory holdings). The model offers a hydraulic metaphor because liquids are easy to visualize in terms of stocks and flows: inflows fill (dark bubbles) the "container pool," outflows drain (light bubbles) the container pool, and pool capacity determines how much liquid accumulates within the pool itself.[20]

Indian textiles trade illustrates centrality of the model's focus on "inventory demand," which determines the amount of a particular textile that remains in each specific location. In terminology of the model, volume of Inventory Supply (amount of liquid) that settles in a given place is strictly determined by Inventory Demand (container capacity). Substantial textile inventories remained in large and vibrant cities such as Jambusar, for instance, because that city was heavily populated with relatively wealthy people whose comparatively capacious chests, closets, and buildings beckoned to be filled. On the other hand, relatively small textile inventories were destined for each particular hinterland village area – due to lesser concentrations of population and wealth – yet *combined* hinterland inventory demand could indeed be (and was) substantial. Similarly, production supply within a particular hinterland locality could be relatively small, yet *combined* hinterland production could in some cases dominate. Roles played by hinterlands through history must be

20 The Hydraulic Metaphor's use of liquid "pools" must not be confused with "systems of linked pools" proposed by Kishimoto in 2009, whose pools refer strictly to time-dimensioned flow concepts. Centerpiece of our Hydraulic Metaphor is mathematical (not shown in this essay) derivation of Inventory Demand (the size of each pool), which determines the amount of product that remains and accumulates in any given location. Kishimoto's linked-pools provide a useful metaphor, however, especially when combined with the inventory stocks metaphor proposed herein; our metaphor explains determinants of sizes of respective "pools" or "containers." The two metaphors should be seen as complements, rather than substitutes. See Mio Kishimoto, "New Studies on Statecraft in Mid-and Late-Qing China: Qing Intellectuals and Their Debates on Economic Policies," *International Journal of Asian Studies*, 6, 1 (2009), 87–102.

examined on a case-by-case basis. Presupposition of hinterland insignificance in context of global economic history and global history generally, in other words, is a significant oversight that this volume aspires to illuminate and to begin to correct.

George Souza's opening chapter features commodity chain analysis, which helps disentangle complex interdependencies among commodity markets that are often ignored. First, Souza explains similarities between south China's sugar exports destined for important domestic end-markets vis-à-vis international sugar exports (destined for end-market Japan, for instance). Second, he emphasizes sugar's key role as ballast for stabilizing sailing vessels, stability required in order to export non-sugar commodities from China. Third, Souza calls attention to often-ignored linkages between south China sugar exports (to both domestic end-markets and international end-markets) compared with attention devoted to goods imported into sugar production centers located in south China. For example, sugar exported to Japan was essentially swapped for Japanese copper imports; Japanese copper was in turn the principle ingredient in mintage of Chinese copper (more accurately, brass) coins. In short, Souza's commodity chain analysis focuses attention on connections, continuities and interdependence among markets, in sharp contrast to conventional conceptualization of each market in isolation.

Although this essay focuses almost exclusively on west Indian textile exports into East Africa, our Hydraulic Metaphor (a version of the Unified Theory of Prices) is consistent with Souza's model of commodity chain analysis. For instance, he advocates analysis of specific monetary imports (say, the Carolus dollar into highly-specific Chinese end-markets) in the context of a theory that applies equally to non-monetary commodities. Although "such a model is planned, but not elaborated in this article," Souza states that estimation of monetary magnitudes for specific places "has significant potential to improve discussions concerning visualization of commercial activities, their inter-connected and comparative relationships with economic development in Early Modern Asian History." Not only do we agree with Souza's plea for visualization of interrelationships among monetary and non-monetary trade items, our recently-published article provides precisely this type of monetary-and-non-monetary visualization in connection to East Asian history during an earlier time period.[21] In a nutshell, we think of monetary items – say, a specific coin such as a Carolus dollar – in inventory-demand terms. For instance, to

21 Dennis O. Flynn and Marie A. Lee, "East Asian Trade before/after 1590s Occupation of Korea: Modeling Imports and Exports in Global Context," *Asian Review of World Histories* 1:1 (January 2013), 117–149.

the extent to which a particular area (whether urban or hinterland) expresses demand to hold a particular type of tangible money, quantities of that money are imported in amounts precisely sufficient to fill "monetary container capacity" (i.e. desired inventory stocks) for that place.[22] Wear and tear of coins requires importation in order to maintain inventory stock, but this statement applies equally to non-monetary stocks. Growth in population and wealth enlarges container capacity for a specific coin, but this statement once again holds true for any non-monetary product. The bottom line is that markets for many items are deeply interrelated, as suggested by commodity chain analysis. With respect to hinterlands, to the extent that an export boom – whether export of a monetary metal or some other item – enhances wealth within a hinterland, then inventory demand for numerous items in the hinterland would be expected to expand. Localized inventory stocks grow with the addition of net imports, of course, and this process continues until inventory demand is satiated. Applicability of the model to monetary and non-monetary items alike is indeed the reason for featuring the word "unified" in the Unified Theory of Prices.[23]

Research by Nadri on hinterland-port relationships within Gujarat complements research by Machado in the sense that both address local, regional, and global dynamics that involve hinterlands. Mughal conquest of Gujarat in 1573, for instance, yielded political stability, peace and security that propelled Surat to prominence among Indian Ocean ports. Gujarat's surging exports depended upon production of primary goods within India. By the same token, expanding raw materials production (such as indigo and raw cotton) caused population and wealth to surge within Indian hinterlands; in consequence, Indian

22 Assuming absence of insurmountable obstacles to trade, of course.

23 Conceptualization of a unit-of-account money in terms of which to express values of media-of-exchange monies has presented by far the most difficult technical challenge in integration of monies (such as actual coins discussed by Souza) into a general Unified Theory of Prices. For an early version that claims to solve the main technical hurdle, see Dennis O. Flynn, "Link-Unit-of-Account versus Ratio-Unit-of-Account Moneys: Seventeenth-Century Dutch Mint Policy," in *Empires, Systems, and Maritime Networks: Reconstructing Supra-Regional Histories in Pre-19th Century Asia,* Working Paper Series 05 (December 2011), 33–62 (Ritsumeikan Asia Pacific University in Beppu, Oita, Japan). For a more polished version, see Dennis O. Flynn and Marie A Lee, "Link-Unit-of-Account versus Ratio-Unit-of-Account Moneys: Seventeenth-Century Dutch Mint Policy," in edited by Jane Kate Leonard and Ulrich Theobald, *Small Currencies Matter: Trade and Transactions in Early Modern East Asian Economies: Third International Workshop of the Research Group 'Monies, Markets, and Finance in China and East Asia, 1600–1900', 1–3 October 2008,* (Leiden: Brill, forthcoming).

hinterlands themselves became attractive end-markets for finished products funneled through port cities such as Surat. In addition, Surat became a major end-market in its own right, although less prominent later on when it devolved into a feeder port for the expanding port of Bombay. In sum, both primary goods production and finished goods production are sources of wealth. The hydraulic metaphor provides visual depiction of mechanisms that determine how and where components of wealth come to rest. Concentrations of affluent human populations determine places and spaces where end-market goods concentrate.

Ota's case study of late-18th/early-19th-century Banten provides a fascinating glimpse at historical dynamics within one borderlands region of Southeast Asia. Pepper production requires significant access to water, which helps explain profit-seeking-VOC-initiated pepper production along rivers and streams in hinterlands of Banten. Export of pepper into Chinese markets turned out to be unprofitable, yet the failed project did yield eagerness for cash within the local economy. The profit motive caused locals to switch from pepper to production of rice (although never self-sufficient), coffee, and especially export of sugar. Thousands of cultivators migrated into the interior, initially to produce sugar but also to secure firewood required for operation of sugar mills. Sugar mills shifted westward within the hinterland in search of new sources of firewood over time. Chinese entrepreneurs gained control of sugar production, while Chinese laborers dominated the sugar labor force. Importation of various finished products was required to satisfy demand by workers, of course, including opium that was imported and monopolized by sugar mill owners for sale to their own workers. Dynamic Chinese communities that were uncontrolled by any outside power emerged within a hinterland setting that was fundamentally linked to the widespread and expanding India-Sino-Southeast Asian trade system. As Ota's case study makes clear, this seemingly-remote hinterland region was firmly linked to global markets, both as provider of raw materials and as end-market for imported finished products (as well as products from the hinterland's hinterlands). In this case, human population migrated into areas abundant in timber as well as rivers and streams; in turn, these human populations attracted populations of imported goods as well as goods produced domestically. "Inventory" terminology of the Hydraulic Metaphor refers to ownership of goods, which are "populations" of domestically-produced as well as imported inventories. Ordinary household goods populate our living spaces today. The Hydraulic Metaphor is an economic model reminiscent of biological models designed to describe and explain steady-state populations of plants and animals. Indeed, humans and things they own are components – and increasingly determinants – of an ecosystem today that continues to evolve from sixteenth-century roots that are global. Hinterlands have played indispensable roles throughout five centuries of global history. The Hydraulic Metaphor and commodity chain analysis provide powerful tools that enhance conceptualization of physical and technological connections across place, space, and time.

CHAPTER 3

The Dynamics of Port-Hinterland Relationships in Eighteenth-Century Gujarat

Ghulam A. Nadri

Introduction

This paper examines the relationship between ports and their hinterlands in eighteenth-century Gujarat and explores changes in their respective economic roles and functions. Scholars have variously defined hinterlands and ports and have identified several types of them on the basis of their location and economic roles.[1] My definition of hinterland as a region that is economically closely linked with a port or a port city draws from the literature and largely follows *Encyclopaedia Britannica* that defines it as "hinterland, also called '*umland*', tributary region, either rural or urban or both, that is closely linked economically with a nearby town or city" and also classifies it into 'export' and 'import' hinterlands.[2]

Most ports and port-cities in early modern India performed two major economic functions. First, they served as maritime terminals where commodities from the inland territories were brought, exchanged, and transported to overseas destinations, and second, as terminals from where goods imported from overseas were distributed in the interior. The interior that constituted a port's hinterland, likewise, played an important economic role in two major ways. As an export hinterland, it supplied goods to the port(s) mainly for overseas markets that comprised its 'export foreland' and as an import hinterland, it consumed the merchandise brought from numerous overseas destinations that constituted its 'import foreland'.[3] The hinterlands, thus, cannot be understood

1 Atiya Habeeb Kidwai, "Conceptual and Methodological Issues: Ports, Port Cities and Port-Hinterlands," in Indu Banga, ed., *Ports and Their Hinterlands in India, 1700–1950* (New Delhi: Manohar, 1992), 17–22.

2 *Encyclopaedia Britannica Online* http://www.britannica.com/EBchecked/topic/266517/hinterland.

3 The overseas markets to which commodities were exported or from where goods were imported into the hinterlands for consumption, comprised the forelands of the port such markets were connected with. In the former case the overseas markets constituted the export foreland and in the latter import foreland. Ibid.

© KONINKLIJKE BRILL NV, LEIDEN, 2015 | DOI 10.1163/9789004283909_005

without reference to ports and forelands with which they were intimately connected.

While ports (and port cities) were more or less defined physical spaces, their hinterlands were not. Hinterlands form a conceptual category identifiable only in relation to the ports they served. The way hinterlands related with a port was complex and contingent on the nature of commercial contacts they maintained with other ports. A port's hinterland, therefore, might also simultaneously serve another port (or more ports) or might not continue any more economic services to the port it had served before. It is, therefore, interesting to see how the geographical limits of a port's hinterland shrank or expanded over a period of time, and to explore how political and economic conditions in the interior re-defined its relationships with the port. It is also important to note that, in conceptualizing the hinterland, our reference points are people and commodities that moved and circulated along the port-hinterland axis. Physical spaces contiguous to a port or port-city are relevant to this conceptualisation only if they constituted a geographical area within which intensive or extensive exchanges and consumption occurred.

No matter how one defines a port or its hinterland, it seems there always existed between the two a complex relationship of interdependence and complementarities. The rise or fall of their commercial fortunes depended on variables such as volume and value of maritime trade, production and consumption of commodities, and the size and strength of the merchant class. The growth or decline of each of these variables depended largely on long-term political stability in the region and the peace and security that the state and its rulers were able to provide to their subjects. Conflict and instability, which often accompanied a regime change, adversely affected the economy and dislocated trade and production, resulting in a significant reconfiguration of the demographic and spatial attributes of ports and their hinterlands. These dynamics were most visible in eighteenth-century Gujarat, when its political economy underwent a major transformation.[4] Internal political changes in Gujarat and shifts

4 The economic implications of these changes in Gujarat have been studied by many scholars. See for example Ghulam A. Nadri, *Eighteenth-Century Gujarat: The Dynamics of Its Political Economy, 1750–1800* (Leiden: Brill, 2009); Lakshmi Subramanian, *Indigenous Capital and Imperial Expansion: Bombay, Surat and the West Coast* (New Delhi: OUP, 1996); Ashin Das Gupta, *Indian Merchants and the Decline of Surat, 1700–1750* (Wiesbaden: Franz Steiner, 1979); idem, *The Trading World of Indian Ocean Merchants: Collected Essays of Ashin Das Gupta*, comp., Uma Das Gupta (New Delhi: OUP, 2001). This was not unique to Gujarat, the political economies of other parts of India and the Islamic world too experienced this transition in the eighteenth century. For studies on Bengal and Coromandel, see Sushil Chaudhury, *From*

in the commodity composition of Indian Ocean maritime trade during this period substantially affected the port-hinterland relationship. But before we track the changes that occurred in the fortunes of Gujarat's major ports and their hinterlands, let us first outline the significance of this region in Indian Ocean maritime trade prior to the eighteenth century (See Map 3.1).

Gujarat in Indian Ocean Trade

Gujarat, on the north-western coast of India, has played an important role in the subcontinent's maritime trade since the pre-historic times. A number of major and minor ports served as trade terminals, where merchandise from the widespread production centres were collected, exchanged, and exported to numerous oceanic destinations.[5] The pre-eminence of Gujarat in Indian Ocean trade since the early centuries of the last millennium is well documented. Its ports and commodities are mentioned in the Cairo Geniza records of the Jewish merchants, whose trading networks connected the Red Sea ports with the western coast of India, including Gujarat in the twelfth and thirteenth centuries.[6] The conquest of Gujarat by Sultan Alauddin Khalji of the Delhi Sultanate in 1298 evidently added to the importance of this region in Indian Ocean trade as it accelerated commercial exchange between coastal north-western India and Delhi, the Sultanate's capital and the upper Ganga and Yamuna deltas.[7] Gujarat's prominence grew further during the period of the

Prosperity to Decline: Eighteenth Century Bengal (New Delhi: Manohar, 1995); Prasannan Parthasarathi, *The Transition to a Colonial Economy: Weavers, Merchants and Kings in South India, 1720–1800* (Cambridge: CUP, 2001). For other studies on the eighteenth-century developments in India and other parts of Asia, see the contributions in Seema Alavi, ed., *The Eighteenth Century in India: Debates in Indian History and Society* (New Delhi: OUP, 2002); P.J. Marshall, ed., *The Eighteenth Century in Indian History: Evolution or Revolution?* (New Delhi: OUP, 2003); and Leonard Blussé and Femme Gaastra, eds., *On the Eighteenth Century as a Category of Asian History: Van Leur in Retrospect* (Aldershot: Ashgate, 1998).

5 Shireen Moosvi, "The Gujarat Ports and their Hinterland: The Economic Relationship," in Banga, *Ports and Their Hinterlands*, 121–122.

6 Shelomo D. Goitein and Mordechai Akiva Friedman, *India Traders of the Middle Ages: Documents from the Cairo Geniza ('India Book')* (Leiden: Brill, 2008); Roxani E. Margariti, *Aden and the Indian Ocean Trade: 150 Years in the Life of a Medieval Arab Port* (Chapel Hill: The University of North Carolina Press, 2007).

7 The market regulations of the Sultan stipulated large-scale imports of merchandise into the capital city from distant places. Gujarat, already well connected with West Asian ports, must have been a major source of precious metals such as gold and silver, and horses. Tapan

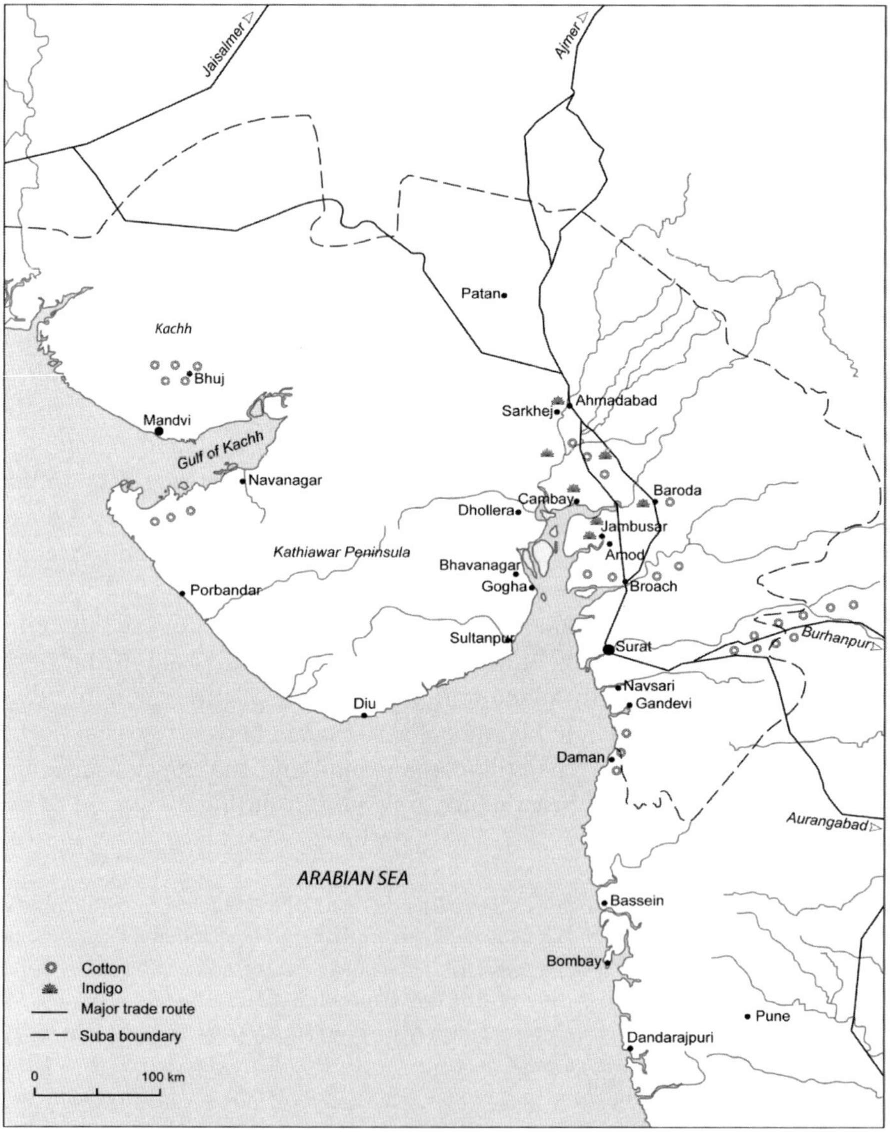

MAP 3.1 *Gujarat*

Raychaudhuri and Irfan Habib, eds., *The Cambridge Economic History of India, vol. 1 (c. 1200–c. 1750)* (Cambridge: CUP, 1982), 82–84, 125–159.

Gujarat Sultanate (1348–1573), when Cambay emerged as the chief maritime terminal and a popular destination for Asian merchants and their ships. Contemporary travelers and chroniclers have left testimonies to Cambay's pivotal role in Indian Ocean trade.[8] Tomé Pires wrote, 'Cambay stretches out two arms, with her right arm she reaches out towards Aden and with the other towards Malacca, as the most important places to sail to'.[9]

In the early modern period, maritime trade played an important role in the lives of the people of Gujarat and, in many ways, was instrumental in shaping their fortunes. This was largely because the region marketed a variety of textiles, indigo, sugar, and other commodities, which were in high demand in Asia and Europe. These commodities came from numerous inland production centres of Gujarat and neighbouring provinces. Tomé Pires says, 'a great deal of Cambay merchandise comes from Rajput, Mandu and Delhi, and [Cambay] distributes their goods for them, because the other provinces, that is Delhi, Mandu, Indo [Sind], and others, are inland, while Cambay has a sea-coast'.[10] Gujarat itself produced a large part of the merchandise exported from Cambay. The central and southern parts of the region were particularly endowed with natural advantages, such as black and sandy soil and a suitable climate for the production of high-value cash crops like cotton and indigo.

Imports of indigo, cotton textiles, sugar, and other products from northern India and the Deccan into Cambay may have been limited due to the political boundaries and customs barriers. This was even more so in the early sixteenth century, when northern and western India were gripped by a prolonged struggle for political power between the Mughals and the Afghans and the Mughals and the Rajputs.[11] This was also the time when the maritime space of Gujarat and western India, until then free for all merchants and seafarers, turned into an arena in which prolonged contests for sovereignty and control were played out between the Portuguese and coastal western Indian rulers. This must have adversely affected the fortunes of Cambay and its hinterlands. By the 1560s, however, Mughal Emperor Akbar (1556–1605) had firmly established the

8 Michael Pearson, *The Indian Ocean* (New York: Routledge, 2003), p. 94; Rubi Maloni, 'Europeans in Seventeenth Century Gujarat: Presence and Response', *Social Scientist*, 36/3–4 (2008), 67–70.

9 Tomé Pires quoted in André Wink, *Al-Hind: The Making of the Indo-Islamic World*, vol. 3 (Leiden: Brill, 2004), p. 196.

10 Ibid., 37.

11 J.F. Richards, *The New Cambridge History of India 1.5, The Mughal Empire* (Cambridge: CUP, 1993).

Mughal rule in northern India, ushering in a new phase of political stability, internal peace and prosperity.

The Mughal conquest of Gujarat in 1573 eliminated the barrier that had long separated coastal western India from the productive interior in the north and the east. The Mughal imperial frontier extended to the Arabian Sea and the long spell of political stability in the Empire contributed immensely to Gujarat's prominence in Indian Ocean trade.[12] This was accompanied by a major structural change in Gujarat's commerce. Surat, a port located in the south, on the banks of the river Tapti and formerly of no particular significance, rose to prominence at the expense of Cambay. By the early seventeenth century, it had become the Empire's chief port and earned the appellations of *bandar-i mubarak* (the blessed port) and the 'gateway to Mecca', due to the role it came to play in the *hajj* traffic between Gujarat (and North India) and Mecca.[13] Surat's hinterland extended up to the Mughal provinces of Delhi, Agra, and Awadh in northern India and Malwa and subsequently the Deccan in central and southern India. The political unity forged by the Mughal Empire in northern India and the ensuing elimination of customs barriers smoothed and accelerated the flow of merchants and merchandise between Suart and its widespread hinterlands. Large quantities of Bayana (in Bharatpur district, Rajasthan) indigo, sugar, and a variety of textiles from the imperial heartland (the provinces of Agra, Delhi and Awadh) came to Gujarat for exportation to various Indian Ocean and transoceanic destinations.[14] Similarly, commodities like pepper, fine spices, precious and non-precious metals began to be imported into Surat by Asian and European merchants and the English East India Company (EIC) and the *Verenigde Oost-Indische Compagnie* (VOC, or the Dutch East India Company) for distribution and consumption in the hinterlands. During this period, the economy of the Mughal Empire was integrated into the global economy sustained by the intra-Asian and Euro-Asian maritime trading networks of the Indian Ocean-China Sea complex. Surat played a key role in

---

12 An added factor in the commercial prominence of Surat and Gujarat was the establishment of two stable political states in West Asia; namely the Safavid Empire in Iran and the Ottoman Empire in the Middle East. Gupta, *Indian Merchants and the Decline of Surat.*

13 Michael Pearson has examined this aspect in detail in his book *Pilgrimage to Mecca: the Indian Experience, 1500–1800* (Princeton: Markus Wiener, 1996).

14 The European Companies procured a large quantity of indigo and textiles from their factories in Agra or obtained these through their brokers in Surat. Om Prakash, *European Commercial Enterprise in Pre-Colonial India* (Cambridge: CUP, 1998); H.W. van Santen, "De Verenigde Oost-Indische Compagnie in Gujarat en Hindustan, 1620–1660" (PhD Dissertation, Leiden University, 1982).

this integration by commercially linking Gujarat and Mughal north India with many parts of Asia and Europe.

These developments implied that some restructuring in agricultural and commercial production of Gujarat and its surroundings would also take place. The agronomy of Gujarat had been highly commercialised since the sixteenth century and, in accordance with the domestic and external demand, a variety of cash crops occupied a large proportion of cultivable land. In the early seventeenth century, indigo and cotton were two major cash crops grown in various parts of Gujarat. Indigo was grown and manufactured in Sarkhej (near Ahamadabad), Jambusar (near Baroda), Dholka, and Cambay.[15] The best indigo that was exported in large quantities to Europe, however, came from Bayana and villages around it.[16] Cotton was produced on a large scale in central and southern Gujarat mainly between Ahmadabad and Surat. Broach and the villages in its vicinity were particularly known for high-quality cotton and textiles, a position they retained in the next century as well. Cotton was also produced in some villages in the principalities of Nawanagar and Kachh.

In the second half of the century, however, the European demand for Indian indigo waned rather quickly because of its large-scale supplies from Europe's trans-Atlantic colonies at relatively low costs. Around the same time, there began a surge in the demand for Indian textiles in Europe on account of a fashion change.[17] Such developments arising out of the changes taking place in Surat's forelands may have necessitated some adjustments in commodity production in the interior and also may have reconfigured the relationship between Surat and its hinterlands. Due to the limitations of primary sources, it is difficult to measure the impact these developments must have had on indigo growers and producers in the Bayana and Sarkhej regions or on the prices and production of food grains and other articles of common local consumption.

15 Ghulam A. Nadri, "Indigo Industry and Trade in Gujarat in the Seventeenth Century" (M. Phil. Dissertation, Aligarh Muslim University, 1996); Moosvi, "Gujarat Ports and their Hinterland," p. 125.

16 Francisco Pelsaert, *De Geschriften van Francisco Pelsaert over Mughal Indië, 1627: Kroniek en Remonstrantie*, eds., D.H.A. Kolff and H.W. van Santen, ('s-Gravenhage: Martinus Nijhoff, 1979), 259–263.

17 K.N. Chaudhuri, *The Trading World of Asia and the English East India Company, 1660–1760* (New Delhi: Cambridge University Press, 1978), 277–283; Prakash, *European Commercial Enterprise in Pre-Colonial India*, 337, 349. The share of textiles in the total sale value of VOC imports in Amsterdam rose from 15 per cent to about 25 per cent around 1670 and to 45 per cent by 1700. Femme S. Gaastra, "The Textile Trade of the VOC: the Dutch Response to the English Challenge," *South Asia: the Journal of South Asian Studies*, XIX (Special Issue 1996), 87.

Under such conditions, peasants may have turned to cultivating cotton, which was increasingly in demand in the burgeoning textile industry in Gujarat and Bengal.[18] As long as the hinterlands remained accessible from Surat and market forces governed the production and exchange relations between the two, peasants, manufacturers, and merchants had no difficulty in adjusting to new situations. This would, however, change in the early eighteenth century when political instability and economic dislocation gripped over Gujarat.

Gujarat in the Eighteenth Century: The Internal Dynamics

Until the early years of the eighteenth century, the Mughals were successful in maintaining the power equilibrium in Gujarat by articulating state policies and exercising sovereignty in a way that would accommodate local political aspirations instead of completely eliminating them.[19] After Emperor Aurangzeb's death in 1707, however, the Mughal imperial centre was no longer able to exercise effective political control in Gujarat. The first half of the eighteenth century witnessed a tussle for political power and control of the region's revenue resources first among some Mughal nobles, then between the Mughals and the Marathas, and finally between the English, and the Mughals and Marathas. By the 1750s, the Marathas had taken over a large part of central and southern Gujarat including Ahmadabad and the English had sneaked in the corridors of power. In 1759, the EIC took over the Mughal Castle of Surat and came to share political sovereignty and fiscal resources in Gujarat with the Mughals.[20]

The contest for power and the ensuing political changes in Gujarat affected the port-hinterland relationship in three major ways. Firstly, they disrupted the long-established production and exchange patterns. As cities and production

18 Until the mid-eighteenth century, cotton was not cultivated in Bengal and its textile industry depended heavily on the imports of raw cotton from Gujarat. British Library, Bombay Commercial Proceedings, 49, Consultations at Bombay, 9 June 1789, pp. 154–156.

19 For details, see Farhat Hasan, *State and Locality in Mughal India: Power Relations in Western India, c. 1572–1730* (Cambridge: CUP, 2004).

20 On the latter aspect, there is a good literature. Lakshmi Subramanian, "Banias and the British: the Role of Indigenous Credit in the Process of Imperial Expansion in Western India in the Second Half of the Eighteenth Century," *Modern Asian Studies*, 21/3 (1987), 473–510; Michelguglielmo Torri, "Mughal Nobles, Indian Merchants and the Beginning of British Conquest in Western India: The Case of Surat, 1756–1759," *Modern Asian Studies*, 32/2 (1998), 257–315; Nadri, *Eighteenth-Century Gujarat*, 15–19.

centres in the interior became unsafe, manufacturers and merchants had to relocate or reorient themselves to a new craft or a different profession. Secondly, Surat lost access, at least temporarily, to its distant hinterlands. Trade between Surat and Agra, for instance, was disrupted to an extent that the European Companies were compelled to close down their trading establishments in the interior. The Dutch closed down their factory in Agra in 1713 on account of difficulties in the purchase, sale, and transportation of merchandise.[21] Thirdly, as large number of merchants and manufacturers relocated in Surat and Cambay, the social relations of production there were severely affected. Although a large concentration of producers certainly helped these port cities to meet the growing European and Asian demand for textiles and other commodities, it also gave rise to widespread social tensions.

Textile production in Gujarat was concentrated in urban areas. Cities like Ahmadabad, Cambay, Broach, Baroda, Bhuj, Navanagar, and Surat, and many other small towns, were places where merchants and artisans lived and had their workshops. In the unsettled political conditions of the early eighteenth century, many of these cities and their dwellers suffered heavily. Mercantile property in Ahmadabad, a major commercial mart of Gujarat, was exposed to insecurity and extortion at the hands of the local Mughal officials.[22] Merchants and producers responded to this situation in different ways. Merchants either succumbed to the pressure and acquiesced to official importunity or, sometimes, resisted it by pleading and petitioning to higher imperial authorities and by temporarily withdrawing from businesses and even from the city.[23] Under uncongenial circumstances, producers, especially weavers, usually migrated to other cities where the prospects of peace and good working conditions were better. In the early eighteenth century, the weavers of Ahmadabad moved to Cambay, Surat, and even Bombay to escape the misfortunes that befell that city

21 Nadri, *Eighteenth-Century Gujarat*, 86–87.

22 The eyewitness accounts of the insecurity of merchants' property and extortion given by I'timad Ali Khan (*Mirat-ul Haqaiq*, MS dirary, Bodleian Library, Oxford) and Ali Mohammad Khan (*Mirat-i Ahmadi*, 2 vols., Baroda: Oriental Institute, 1928) provide detailed description of merchants' plight and their resistance; Ghulam A. Nadri, "The Trading World of Indian Ocean Merchants in Pre-Colonial Gujarat, 1600–1750," in Om Prakash, ed., *The Trading World of the Indian Ocean, 1500–1800* (New Delhi: Pearson, 2012), 236–241.

23 Douglas Haynes, "From Avoidance to Confrontation? A Contestatory History of Merchant-State Relations in Surat, 1600–1924," in Douglas Haynes and Gyan Prakash, ed., *Contesting Power: Resistance and Everyday Social Relations in South Asia* (New Delhi: OUP, 1991), 239–289.

whereas some merchants and artisans moved to the east and settled down in Banaras.[24] When Cambay became inhospitable on account of disputes between the local governor and the Marathas, weavers, artisans, and craftsmen migrated to Surat and Bombay. This is evident from the British attempts in the 1790s to induce them to return to Cambay.[25] Unstable conditions rendered it impossible for the European Companies to carry on trade at these places. The VOC discontinued the Ahmadabad factory in 1742 and withdrew itself from Cambay in 1744 because with diminished production and consumption, these places were no longer profitable for the Company.[26] In 1750, the only factory subordinate to Surat that the VOC maintained in Gujarat was in Broach, and this remained fairly important for the Company's cotton and textile purchases in the subsequent decades. These developments indicate that the hinterland, with which Surat could economically closely link, shrank substantially in the early eighteenth century. It lost its access to a large part of northern India as the flow of merchandise between Surat and places like Agra, Delhi, and Awadh was disrupted. Commodities from these provinces began to flow eastward to Bengal through the Ganges and its tributary river waterways.[27] It was because of the relative political stability that the Maratha regime sought to ensure in Gujarat and beyond, and local merchants' perseverance that Surat regained access to its distant hinterlands in the second half of the century.[28]

24 In 1789, the English Resident at Puna, Charles Warre Mallet, wrote, 'I am informed that several families of Guzerat silk manufacturers, *soucarrs* and others, distressed by oppression of the farmers of this state who rule that province, have fled and settled at Benaras, where they practice their former occupations'. Bombay Commercial Proceedings, 49, Consultations at Bombay, 9 June 1789, p. 156. Aniruddha Ray, "Cambay and its Hinterland: Early Eighteenth Century," in Banga, *Ports and Their Hinterlands in India*, p. 141.

25 British Library, Bombay Commercial Proceedings, 55, Consultations at Bombay, 27 March 1795, pp. 200–203; ibid., Consultations at Bombay, 23 June 1795, pp. 459–465; British Library, Factory Records: Surat (Hereafter FRS), 73, Proceedings, Surat, 14 March 1795, pp. 181–121; FRS 77, Proceedings, Surat, 18 Jan. 1798, pp. 41–45; K.N. Chaudhuri, "Some Reflections on the Town and Country in Mughal India," *Modern Asian Studies*, 12/1 (1978), 77–96.

26 National Archive, The Hague, Hoge Regering te Batavia [HRB], 837, Consideratie wegens de vrije vaart en handel [Consideration on permitted trade], Jan Schreuder, Surat, 1746, item 268; HRB, 843, Beschrijving van Souratta [An account of Surat], D. van Rheeden, Surat, 1758, p. 27.

27 C.A. Bayly, "Inland Port Cities in North India: Calcutta and the Gangetic Plains, 1780–1900," in Dilip K. Basu, ed., *The Rise and Growth of the Colonial Port Cities in Asia* (California: UPA, 1985), 15, 29.

28 For details on the mid-century recovery in the commercial fortunes of Gujarat, see Nadri, *Eighteenth-Century Gujarat*, Chapter 5.

While Surat lost access to some parts of its hinterlands in the early eighteenth century, it attracted a large number of weavers and manufacturers from the areas affected by political instability. Consequently, its textile-manufacturing sector expanded rapidly and the output grew substantially. In the late eighteenth century, it boasted its textile industry with more than 15,700 looms, which provided employment for thousands of weaving families.[29] It became the largest supplier of textiles to the European Companies and Asian traders in western India. This had some implications for the rest of Gujarat as well. Some regions that had formerly produced textiles and complemented Surat's total exports now supplied raw material to the metropolis. Broach, for example, was renowned for its textile production, but in the late eighteenth century it was no longer seen by European and Asian traders as a major textile supplier.[30] Instead, Broach came to be recognized as the producer and supplier of high-quality cotton in the subcontinent. More than three-fourths of the total cotton produced in the district of Broach went to Surat and a large part of that was exported to Bengal, China, and Europe.[31] Moreover, some new areas emerged as major suppliers of this raw material. For example, Bhavanagar, on the west of the Gulf of Cambay, emerged as a major producer of cotton, reportedly producing 14,000 *candies* (the weight of a *candy* varied between 784 and 880 pounds avoirdupois) in 1789, of which 12,500 candies (about 90 per cent) were exported.[32] In 1800, Bombay received from Gujarat about 60,000 *candies* for export purposes.[33] Gujarat had never before exported such a large quantity of raw cotton. Such modifications in the commodity composition represent a change in Surat's export hinterlands.

A noticeable change occurred in the constitution of Surat's import hinterland as a consequence of the changing composition of imports into Surat and overall maritime trade. This is illustrated by the trajectory of imports and

---

29 FRS, 73, Proceedings, Surat, 24 Dec. 1795, pp. 794–797; Bombay Commercial Proceedings, 57, Consultations at Bombay, 2 Jan. 1796, pp. 18–22; Lakshmi Subramanian, "Capital and Crowd in a Declining Asian Port City: The Anglo-Bania Order and the Surat Riots of 1795," *Modern Asian Studies*, 19/2 (1985), 221.

30 Even though the VOC maintained a factory at Broach, its contribution to the total volume of textiles purchased by the Company in Gujarat was by no means significant.

31 Broach, together with Jambusar and Amod, produced about 24,000 *candies* of cotton out of which 18,500 candies were exported. Bombay Commercial Proceedings, 49, Consultations at Bombay, 11 Sept. 1789 (John Griffith's report on cotton, Surat, 22 Aug. 1789), pp. 247–250.

32 Ibid.

33 British Library, Home Miscellaneous [hereafter Home Misc.], 476, D. Scotts to Jonathan Duncan, 23 May 1801, pp. 141–145.

consumption of sugar in Gujarat. In the seventeenth century, the European Companies and private traders and Asian merchants procured sugar from northern India or bought it in Surat and exported to West Asia and Europe. This was no longer so in the eighteenth century. The Companies and merchants began to import large quantities of sugar from East and Southeast Asia, Mauritius, and Brazil. The VOC alone on an average imported about 0.7 million Dutch pounds of castor sugar into Surat every year during 1701–1745 and the average annual imports rose to about 1.9 million pounds during 1745–1792.[34] Sugar imports from other sources were also enormous and, sometimes, exceeded those of the VOC.[35] Large imports of Chinese and Javanese sugar, if on one hand, adversely affected the sugar industry in Bengal and interrupted its production in Gujarat and northern India, they also, on the other, played an important role in reconstituting Surat's import hinterland. It helped Surat to establish commercial contacts with some new areas that began to receive supplies of imported sugar from the port. For example, Tibet, not known before for any commercial links with Surat, became a major consumer of sugar in the second half of the eighteenth century. The Deccan too, emerged as a major market to which much sugar was annually carried from Surat by local merchants.

While these developments were taking place in the hinterlands, Surat itself underwent a change in its economic role. It emerged as a major producer of textiles in the second half of the eighteenth century as a number of weavers and craftsmen immigrated to the city. Such a concentration of weavers belonging to various castes and ethnic groups was bound to have some social implications. As the demand for textiles grew in Surat many new groups of people took to weaving. According to a report prepared in 1795 by the EIC officials in Surat, weavers of various caste and religious denominations, such as Momin, Tahi, Bohra, Bungar, Bandara, Khatri, Kunbi (both Muslim and Hindu), and Parsi, were engaged in textile production for the market.[36] Some of these castes

---

34 These averages are taken from the Company's annual imports and sales of sugar in Surat (*ware rendement*) in the eighteenth century. Nadri, *Eighteenth-Century Gujarat*, 216–217 (Appendix 8).

35 The average annual imports of sugar into Surat by the English and other European and Asian merchants for the years 1768–70, 1772, and 1776 amounted to about 4.8 million Dutch pounds. VOC 3238, Shipping list, 1768, pp. 9–15; VOC 3268, Shipping list, 1769, pp. 37–42; VOC 3297, Shipping list, 1770, ff. 16^r–19^v; VOC 3354, Shipping list, 1772, ff.84^r–86^v; VOC 3462, Shipping list, 1776, ff.17^r–19^v.

36 FRS 73, Proceedings, Surat, 11 Sept. 1795, pp. 453–454, ibid., Proceedings, Surat, 24 Dec. 1795, pp. 792–800; Bombay Commercial Proceedings, 57, Consultations at Bombay, 2 Jan. 1796, pp. 18–22; Subramanian, "Capital and Crowd in a Declining Asian Port City."

presumably entered into this industry to take advantage of the growing demand for textiles. Some, at least, began to produce the variety of cloth other groups had specialised in. Those who had, since generations, produced particular types of cloth were naturally keen on protecting their professional interests and, therefore, considered the newcomers a threat to their business. In 1742, some weavers of Surat refused to work for the English Company in protest against the Muslim immigrant weavers.[37] The Khatri weavers, similarly, resisted the Kunbis who, in the second half of the eighteenth century, produced the sort of textiles the former had specialised in.[38] The Khatris persisted in their demand and, in 1800, finally succeeded in persuading the English chief at Surat and the local government to withdraw the license that the Kunbi weavers had earlier obtained from the Mughal governor of Surat.[39]

While the increasing demand created employment opportunities for new social groups in professions and crafts, that had been conventionally associated with certain castes, it rendered social relationships much complicated and estranged. The so-called Surat 'riots' of 1788 involving Muslims and Parsis and of 1795 involving Muslim weavers and Hindu moneylenders were basically manifestations of professional rivalry and fiercely competing commercial interests of the groups involved.[40]

Gujarat in the Eighteenth Century: the External Dynamics

The fall of the Safavid Empire in 1722 impacted the port-hinterland relationship in Gujarat and the region's overall commercial fortunes. Persia was a major export/import foreland of Surat and Cambay and the political crisis there caused a substantial reduction in the volume and value of Gujarat's trade

37 K.N. Chaudhuri, "The Structure of Indian Textile Industry in the Seventeenth and Eighteenth Centuries," *Indian Economic and Social History Review*, 11/2–3 (1974), 172.

38 FRS 79, Proceedings, Surat, 18 March 1800, p. 182; ibid., Proceedings, Surat, 20 March 1800, p. 164.

39 FRS 79, Proceedings, Surat, 18 March 1800, p. 164. In 1742, some Kunbi weavers obtained from Surat's governor, Safdar Khan, the permission to manufacture *saris*, the long cloth that Khatris traditionally produced. Bombay Commercial Proceedings, 56, Consultations at Bombay, 27 Oct. 1795, pp. 807–809.

40 FRS 66, Proceedings, Surat, 1 Dec. 1788, pp. 331–333; Subramanian, "Capital and Crowd in a Declining Asian Port City"; idem, "The Eighteenth Century Social Order in Surat: A Reply and an Excursus on the Riots of 1788 and 1795," *Modern Asian Studies*, 25/2 (1985), 321–365.

with that region.[41] However, with the consolidation of the Omani Empire under the al-Busaidis in the second half of the eighteenth century, the maritime trade of Surat with the Persian Gulf somewhat revived.[42]

Another factor adversely affecting the port-hinterland relationship in Gujarat was the change in the commodity composition of intra-Asian and Euro-Asian trade. Bengal began to produce cotton on a large scale and its textile industry was no longer dependent on cotton supplies from Gujarat.[43] According to an estimate made in 1789, more than eighty-five per cent of cotton used in textile production in Bengal was produced locally.[44] As a result, the lucrative exchange of Gujarat cotton for Bengal silk declined. The diminishing import of Bengal silk possibly motivated a number of Gujarati silk-textile manufacturers to migrate to Banaras and Bengal. This loss of market for Gujarat cotton, however, was made up by a huge demand for this raw material in China and Europe.

The demand for Gujarat cotton for exportation to China was substantial in the late eighteenth and early nineteenth centuries. The EIC exported large quantities of cotton to that market every year.[45] More of this article was

41 Ashin Das Gupta has attributed the decline of Surat to the disintegration of the Safavid Empire among other factors. Gupta, *Indian Merchants and the Decline of Surat*. The crisis also severely damaged the trading interests of the European Companies in the Arabian Seas. Willem Floor, "The Decline of the Dutch East India Company in Bandar Abbas (1747–1759)," *Moyen Orient & Océan Indien*, 6 (1989), pp. 45–67; Ben Slot, "At the Backdoor of the Levant: Anglo-Dutch Competition in the Persian Gulf, 1623–1766," in Hamilton Alastair (ed.), *Friends and Rivals in the East: Studies in Anglo-Dutch Relations in the Levant from the Seventeenth to the Early Nineteenth Century* (Leiden: Brill, 2000), pp. 117–133. The VOC's total annual value of goods sold in Persia declined by seventy-eight percent after 1722. Ghulam A. Nadri, "The Dutch Intra-Asian Trade in Sugar in the Eighteenth Century," *International Journal of Maritime History*, 20, 1 (2008), pp. 63–96.

42 This is evident from references to Surat ships sailing to the Persian Gulf ports in the second half of the eighteenth century. Nadri, *Eighteenth-Century Gujarat*, 54–66.

43 The English Resident at Pune, Charles Ware Mallet, noted that 'the demand for Guzarat cotton in Bengal has greatly decreased this of late years, owing to the increased cultivation of it at home'. Bombay Commercial Proceedings, 49, Consultations at Bombay, 9 June 1789, p. 154.

44 Thus, by the late 1780s, Bengal needed only about 20,000 bales of cotton from outside to meet its total requirement of 147,000 bales in the textiles industry. Home Misc., 434, George Smith to Governor General Charles Cornwallis, Calcutta, 26 Oct. 1789, p. 334.

45 In 1769, it exported about 30,000 bales (a bale was half of a candy or 345 Dutch pounds) from Gujarat mainly to China. FRS 49, Proceedings, Surat, 5 Nov. 1769, pp. 95–96. In 1789, the Company's exports of cotton from Gujarat to China amounted to 30,000 bales. Bombay Commercial Proceedings, 47, Consultations at Bombay, 11 May 1789, pp. 65–68.

exported by private European merchants, who invested in this trade primarily for remitting money to Europe.[46] In 1787, for example, they exported more than 63,000 bales of Gujarat cotton to China.[47] During this period, the export of raw cotton from India to Britain too became significant. For the British, it even became a matter of national importance since Britain was losing money on buying cotton from non-British colonial markets.[48] It was, therefore, considered more profitable to purchase it in Gujarat using bills of exchange issued in Bengal in favour of Surat and Bombay. In 1789, it was reported that British textile manufacturers aimed to buy 20,000 bales (6,000,000 lbs.) of good quality cotton from Gujarat every year.[49] European demand for Gujarat cotton remained significant in the subsequent period and grew further in the early nineteenth century.[50] This surge in the demand induced peasants to grow cotton. Consequently, cotton production in Gujarat increased substantially in the last decades of the century. Dr. Hove's account of his journey through numerous villages in Broach in the 1780s testifies to the extensive cultivation of cotton in the district.[51]

The fierce competition among cotton buyers implied a greater degree of commercialisation of agriculture and penetration of merchant capital in the rural economy by means of loans and advances to peasants against future deliveries. This brought cotton producing villages into a direct economic relationship with the global cotton market as the fortunes of a large number of peasants, merchants, and brokers came to depend on the external demand for the raw material. They took advantage of the competition among buyers and

46 They lent money on respondentia at low rates and offered freight services to prospective cotton exporters to China. The principal capital with interest was paid to their agents in China, which was then invested in purchasing tea for Europe. In this way, a large amount of wealth was remitted to Europe.

47 Pamela Nightingale, *Trade and Empire in Western India, 1784–1806* (Cambridge: CUP, 1970), 23. The export of cotton to China by private British traders increased so much that the London authorities expressed their concern and complained that the Company was unable to take full advantage of the boom in cotton exports. Bombay Commercial Proceedings, 49, Consultations at Bombay, 26 Oct. 1789, pp. 289–290; ibid, Consultations at Bombay, 20 Nov. 1789, pp. 321–322.

48 About two-thirds of the total cotton consumption in Britain that exceeded 22 million lbs avoirdupois was purchased from the non-British (foreign) merchants/places. Home Misc., 434, pp. 321–336.

49 Ibid., 321–325.

50 In 1819, there were about 50,000 bales of Surat cotton unsold in the Company's warehouse in England. Home Misc., 374, Extract Letter to Bombay, 22 Dec. 1819, p. 513.

51 Home Misc., 374, Extracts from Dr. Hove's Journal, 1787.

benefited from an expanding demand for cotton. This is evident from the rise in cotton prices in the eighteenth century and from the frequent complaints the EIC officials in Gujarat made against Asian and European merchants frantically buying cotton and raising its price.[52] They also, sometimes, exposed their cotton to dew or water to make it weight more. They did it to avoid delivering it to the EIC from whom they had received advances and to sell it, instead, to others at higher prices than what the Company paid.[53] It transpires from references to such manipulative practices that the competitive market in Gujarat added to the complexities of relationship among peasants, brokers, merchants, and the EIC and private English traders.

Coastal Gujarat in the Eighteenth Century: The Structural Dynamics

So far, we identified the changes in Surat's relationship with its hinterlands and in their respective economic roles caused by several internal and external circumstances in the eighteenth century. But, how did Surat relate with other major and minor ports on the coast of Gujarat and western India and how the role, position, and fortunes of one port changed in relation to the other are questions that need to be addressed. The changes occurring in the fortunes of some ports contributed to Surat's rising fortunes and the dynamism of its relationship with the hinterlands. By the late eighteenth century, the nature of port-hinterland relationship in Gujarat became more complex than before. Hinterlands came to be shared, at times contested, by several ports leading to Surat's loss of primacy in the maritime trade of the western Indian Ocean.

Despite being the most prominent Gujarat port, Surat was still one among many ports along the coast in the Gulfs of Cambay and Kachh. For a long time and even into the eighteenth century, the ports and port cities of Broach, Bhavanagar, Ghoga, Cambay, Navanagar, Mandvi, and many other minor ones served as feeder ports to Surat. Together, they formed a 'port system' or 'port

52 In 1790, a contractor of the EIC, Rawal Malikchand Motichand, attributed his inability to procure the stipulated quantity of cotton for the Company to its excessively high price due to the shortage of cotton and stiff competition for it among buyers. Bombay Commercial Proceedings, 50, Consultations at Bombay, 4 May 1790, pp. 105–107; ibid., Consultations at Bombay, 27 Dec. 1790, pp. 305–306; Home Misc., 374, Extract Letter to Bombay, 22 Dec. 1819, pp. 525–526.

53 Bombay Commercial Proceedings, 50, Consultations at Bombay, 4 May 1790, p. 107; Home Misc., 374, Extract Letter to Bombay, 22 Feb. 1811, pp. 250–251.

complex' of Gujarat in which Surat was the most prominent and served as a port city, a trade emporium, an *entrepôt*, as well as a 'gate-way' city.[54] Goods and merchandise intended for distant overseas markets were collected in and transmitted from the feeder ports to Surat and then on to their respective destinations. A similar 'port complex' existed in the Gulf of Kachh, with Mandvi as the chief port on the north-western coast of the Gulf. A series of minor ports along the coast, including Anjar, Tuna, Mondera, Lakhpat Bandar, Oranga Bandar on the northern rim, and Bedi Bandar, Jhakar, and Navanagar on the southern shore served as feeder ports to Mandvi. There existed between these two port complexes, as among the ports within each complex, a relationship of complementarities and competitiveness. Mandvi was connected with Surat and as a feeder port, it contributed to the latter's commercial fortunes by exchanging cotton, textiles, and some minerals for spices, sugar, copper, ivory and other commodities.

A regular flow of merchandise between the two ports was maintained by mostly local merchants. For some years in the 1750s, the VOC had a subordinate factory in Mandvi primarily to obtain cotton and textiles and to dispose of sugar, copper, and other imports.[55] Simultaneously, Mandvi competed with Surat both in accessing north Indian hinterlands and harnessing commercial benefits of the forelands in West Asia. Ships laden with textiles and other commodities sailed directly from Mandvi to various ports in the Red Sea, the Persian Gulf, and on the Malabar Coast.[56] Similar 'port complex' operated on the Kathiawar Coast, with Diu as its leading port. This too, stood in complementary and competitive relationships with Surat and Mandvi-led complexes. The Bania merchants of Diu procured textiles in Jambusar, which was also Surat's hinterland, and supplied to the markets of east-central and south-east Africa in the late eighteenth and nineteenth centuries.[57] Diu competed with

54 For the definition and characteristics of a 'port complex' and of various types of ports, see Kidwai, "Conceptual and Methodological Issues."

55 Ghulam A. Nadri, "Exploring the Gulf of Kachh: Regional Economy and Trade in the Eighteenth Century," *Journal of the Economic and Social History of the Orient*, 51/3 (2008), 474–479.

56 In 1753, the captain of a VOC ship reported that 25 ships from Mandvi arrived in Mokha and complained that the merchants sold their textiles and other goods and obtained gold ducats at higher rates than what the VOC allowed its servants to buy. VOC 2842, Resoluties, Surat, 26 Sept. 1753, pp. 341–345. Ashin Das Gupta, *Malabar in Asian Trade, 1740–1800* (Cambridge: CUP, 1967), 25, 91–92, 146; Nadri, "Exploring the Gulf of Kachh," 473–474.

57 Pedro Machado, "Cloths of a New Fashion: Indian Ocean Networks of Exchange and Cloth Zones of Contact in Africa and India in the Eighteenth and Nineteenth Centuries," in

Surat in sharing the hinterlands and with Mandvi in sharing the forelands because the latter also maintained close commercial links with the East African Coast. Similar relationships of cooperation and competition existed between ports within a complex. Port cities like Surat, Cambay, and Bhavanagar complemented each other through supplies of commodities and competed in accessing the hinterlands and forelands.

An important development in the port system on the Gujarat coast was the restructuring of the port complex, in which the English port of Bombay came to play a dominant role. Since the acquisition of Bombay in the early 1660s, the Company had been trying to develop it as its main trading port in western India. Throughout the eighteenth century, Bombay competed with Surat in accessing the hinterlands in northern and north-western India and the forelands in West and Southeast Asia. Surat, however, retained its pre-eminent position and ships continued to sail from there to the Red Sea, the Persian Gulf, and to other major destinations in East and Southeast Asia.[58] By the end of the century, however, Bombay had taken over the role of the most important port city in the western Indian Ocean. The EIC's takeover of Surat in 1800 and of Gujarat in 1818 further strengthened Bombay's position as western India's foremost port city. In the new port complex of Gujarat in the early nineteenth century, however, Bombay and Surat stood in a complex relationship of competition and complementarities. Surat was reduced to the position of a feeder port to Bombay, yet many ships continued to sail from there to the Red Sea ports and other major Indian Ocean destinations.[59]

Conclusions

The fortunes of Gujarat's ports and their hinterlands changed perceptibly during the eighteenth century. Surat increasingly lost commercial connections with Delhi, Agra, and Awadh, which as export hinterlands had formerly

---

Giorgio Riello and Tirthankar Roy, eds., *How India Clothed the World: The World of South Asian Textiles, 1500–1850* (Leiden: Brill, 2009), 53–84.

58 Nadri, *Eighteenth-Century Gujarat*, 54–66; idem, "Sailing in Hazardous Waters: Maritime Merchants of Gujarat in the Second half of the Eighteenth Century," in Prakash, ed., *The Trading World of the Indian Ocean*, 255–284.

59 Surat's trade with West Asia was still rather substantial in the early nineteenth century. According to a report, the average annual value of imports during 1802–03 and 1805–06 from the Red Sea alone to Surat and Bombay amounted to £331,175 (about 3.31 million Rupees). Home Misc. 494, Regarding Mr. Jacobs' proposal for a trade with Abyssinia and the eastern parts of Africa, East India House, London, 24 Dec. 1807, p. 521.

contributed to Gujarat's total exports of indigo and textiles. However, the ports of Gujarat continued to cater to large European and Asian demand by supplying textiles and cotton produced mainly within Gujarat. The structure of import hinterland too changed, as new imports found new territories to which they were distributed from Surat. The Deccan and Tibet were commercially closely connected with Gujarat, as they came to serve as Surat's import hinterlands. Such reconfigurations of the hinterlands led to greater concentration, and possibly intensification, of production in Gujarat which together with the rising demand for textiles and cotton and changes of regimes impacted the market and production relations. However, unlike Bengal and other places where under similar circumstances peasants and artisans were subjected to oppressive and exploitative production relations, those of Gujarat maintained their relative autonomy in the market place.[60]

Changes in the economic role of the hinterlands affected the structure of Gujarat's port complexes and the relationships among the constituent ports. While the ports complemented each other by exchanging commodities, they also competed for access to economic resources. The competition was intense in the eighteenth century when the hinterlands and forelands that were earlier economically closely connected with the ports of Gujarat shrank on account of several internal and external developments. Commodity production, nevertheless, intensified in the hinterlands still accessible to Surat, which together with large imports of sugar and other commodities helped it regain access to much of north and north-western Indian hinterlands and the West Asian forelands in the second half of the eighteenth century. In the reconstituted port complex of Gujarat in the early nineteenth century, however, Bombay overshadowed Surat in so far as direct access to major oceanic forelands was concerned. To access the hinterland, the colonial port city still heavily depended on Surat.

60 There is a rich literature on textiles industry in late eighteenth-century Bengal and the Coromandel Coast that underscores coercive market forces and oppression of weavers, artisans, and merchants. Hameeda Hossain, *The Company Weavers of Bengal, the East India Company and the Organization of Textile Production in Bengal, 1750–1813* (Delhi: OUP, 1988); Chaudhury, *From Prosperity to Decline*; S. Arasaratnam, "Weavers, Merchants and the Company: The Handloom Industry in South-eastern India, 1750–1790," *Indian Economic and Social History Review*, 17/3 (1980), 257–281; Parthasarathi, *The Transition to a Colonial Economy*; Om Prakash, "From Negotiation to Coercion: Textile Manufacturing in India in the Eighteenth Century," *Modern Asian Studies*, 41/6 (2007), 1331–1368.

CHAPTER 4

Ports, Hinterlands and Merchant Networks

*Armenians in Bengal in the Eighteenth Century**

Bhaswati Bhattacharya

Ports have very poetically been called 'brides of the sea'.[1] In terms of geography and urban history, a port denotes a location where people and goods can enter or leave a country, and hinterland refers to the area lying immediately behind the port, or the surrounding countryside. Ports are, however, not necessarily sea ports and, as Christopher Bayly has demonstrated, inland river ports function in very much the same way as coastal ports as part of a complex trading institution.[2] Economic activity at a sea port in pre-modern India, as in other parts of the world, was very much dependent on ships coming from ports far and near. These ships carried gold and silver, and took back sundry goods ranging from the luxurious and exotic to the trivial, and if they stayed away for some reason, life at the port was uncertain. This aspect of a port's relationship with the sea inspired the historian Ashin Das Gupta to maintain that, in order to understand the developments at a certain port, one has to look across the sea

* The original sources used in this paper are, unless otherwise mentioned, the last wills and accounts of estates of Armenian merchants produced before the Mayor's Court in Calcutta for the grant of probate. These are to be found at the High Court in Calcutta (Kolkata). The documents were usually folded and tied up with a cord before they were filed. Many of the documents are so brittle that it is impossible to open them without ruining them. Such documents could not be consulted.

Many of the wills were first written in Armenian and then translated into English by an Armenian. Transcribing Armenian names must have posed a serious difficulty to the translators. The old writing often used two to three consonants without any vowel in between. 'Mnskn' in the document was transcribed as Manasakan, Minasakan, or even as Manatsakan. Moreover, in the cosmopolitan milieu in India the pronunciation/spelling of the names was simplified. Hyrapiet became Arapiet, Harutyun became Aratoon (also spelt as Arratoon or Arrathoon), Astvatsattur became Tsattur, Tsatoor and Sattoor, and Khachik became Catchik or Khatchik. In referring to the sources I have left the original spelling while in the document I have used one accepted form throughout the text.

1 F. Broeze (ed.) *Brides of the sea: Port Cities of Asia from the 16th–20th Centuries* (New South Wales: University Press, 1989); Broeze borrowed the epithet from Mohammad Said Farsi, architect, and Mayor of the Yemeni port of Jedda, p. 1.

2 C.A. Bayly, "Inland port cities in North India: Calcutta and the Gangetic plains, 1780–1900," in D.K. Basu (ed.), *Rise and growth of the colonial port cities in Asia* (Berkeley: University Press of America, 1985).

© KONINKLIJKE BRILL NV, LEIDEN, 2015 | DOI 10.1163/9789004283909_006

at places with maritime contacts with that port. Das Gupta's work on Surat, however, attested to the fact that, if a port was a bride of the sea, then the sea was only one of Surat's many bridegrooms, for if the sea flirted with Surat by making advances through the romantic and splendid sailing ships, all the mortals that flocked to Surat were dependent on its immediate hinterland, which supplied provisions. Moreover, it was the caravans of bullock carts that provided Surat with commodities from the hinterland, which not only comprised weavers' villages and production centers throughout Gujarat but stretched as far as Agra and Patna. These commodities could be exchanged at Surat for the money brought by the ships, thus bringing Surat its glory. The credit networks of Surat's merchant bankers connected the port with banking and trading activity all over the country and, via the channels of overland and overseas commerce, with countries bordering on the Indian Ocean. Surat was therefore one of the outlets for capital, goods and traffic from the hinterland, and all these activities faced disjuncture once the port was severed from its hinterland as a result of political turmoil in the hinterland in the late seventeenth and eighteenth century.[3]

Armenians are known as one of the Asian communities specializing in overland commerce. Armenia was strategically located on the overland caravan routes connecting Asia with Europe. Members of this ethnic community formed a dominant group within that commerce, which took Armenians to countries situated along the various silk routes stretching through Central Asia, Persia, Russia and Turkey. They scattered to numerous parts of Asia through overland and maritime trade and were already familiar with the subcontinent's commerce by the time the East India companies arrived in the Indian Ocean. Focusing on the activity of Armenian merchants in Bengal in the eighteenth century, this paper will demonstrate how spatially separated members of a merchant community like that of the Armenians, operating in different capacities at different locations, formed part of the processes linking ports with their hinterland and beyond.

Even after we come across Armenians engaged in maritime trade in Portuguese sources, they continued to participate in the overland trade to India for a long time. This was largely possible because, since the close of the

3 Ashin Das Gupta, *Indian merchants and the decline of Surat, ca. 1750* (Wiesbaden: Frans Steiner, 1979). Later research, however, has shown that unlike what Das Gupta maintained, Surat retained much of its trade in the late eighteenth century. L. Subramanian, *Indigenous Capital and Imperial Expansion: Bombay, Surat and the West Coast* (Oxford: Oxford University Press, 1999); G.A. Nadri, *Eighteenth-century Gujarat: The Dynamics of its Political Economy, 1750–1800* (Leiden: Brill, 2009).

sixteenth century, the land-based empires of the Safavids, Uzbeks and Mughals had provided a broadly similar commercial and linguistic environment over the extensive land mass stretching from West to South Asia, with Persian as the most widely used language for administrative and cultural purposes.[4] The extensive stretch along the major thoroughfare that had linked Central Asia with Agra since the end of the sixteenth century experienced a relative degree of urbanization.[5] The caravan route used by merchants engaged in trans-imperial commerce brought Armenian, Persian and Turkish merchants to India. Kandahar, an important post on the northwest frontier of the Mughal Empire, was a nodal point on this caravan route.[6] A long chain of markets of various categories catering to local and long-distance trade connected Lahore and Multan in the west and Agra, Patna, Murshidabad and Dacca in Bengal in the east through overland and riverine routes, and was supplied with agricultural and proto-industrial products from the regions it covered.[7]

The Mughal Emperor Akbar was knowledgeable of the Armenians and was personally acquainted with a number of those in his court. He apparently invited an Armenian named Jacob, and his son, to settle at Agra. The idea was that Jacob would persuade his fellow countrymen from the Punjab and other areas to follow the imperial court to Agra.[8] Akbar's contacts with the Jesuit priests at Goa were mediated by an Armenian called Dominic or Domingo Pires. This name is not typically Armenian, but it was common practice among

---

4 S.F. Dale, *Indian Merchants and Eurasian Trade, 1600–1750* (Delhi: Foundation Books, First Indian edition, 1994), 7–13.

5 Jean Deloche, *Transport and Communications in India prior to Steam Locomotion*, 2 vols., trans. James Walker (Delhi: Oxford University Press, 1993–94), vol. 1, p. 34.

6 Niels Steensgaard, "The Route through Quandahar: The Significance of the Overland Trade from India to the West in the Seventeenth Century," in Sushil Chaudhury and Michel Morineau (eds.), *Merchants, Companies and Trade: Europe and Asia in the Early Modern Era* (Cambridge: Cambridge University Press, 1999); For the overland route linking India with Central and West Asia, see Jos J.L. Gommans, *The Rise of the Indo-Afghan empire, c. 1710–1780* (Leiden: Brill, 1995); for the Sindhi diaspora, see C. Markovitz, *The Global World of Indian Merchants* (Cambridge: Cambridge University Press, 2000) and Scott C. Levi, *The Indian Diaspora in Central Asia and its Trade, 1550–1900* (Leiden: Brill, 2002); for Armenians taking this route, see J. Russell, "Two Armenian Graffities from Ziârat, Pakistan," *Revue Etude Armeninnes*, 16 (1988–89), pp. 471–475.

7 B.R. Grover, "An Integrated Pattern of Commercial Life in the Rural Society of North India during the Seventeenth and Eighteenth Centuries" in S. Subrahmanyam (ed.), *Money and Market in India, 1100–1700* (Delhi: Oxford University Press, 1994), pp. 219–255.

8 Mesrovb Seth, *Armenians in India: From the Earliest Times to the Present Day – a work of Original Research* (Delhi: Oxford Book House etc., reprint, 1983[1937]), pp. 1–2.

Armenians in the diaspora – as we shall see later – to adapt their name to new situations and even to convert, as part of their business strategy.[9] While they already spoke Persian in addition to Armenian, contact with the Portuguese in the Indian Ocean ensured that many Armenians picked up at least some knowledge of that language as well.[10] The Armenians' familiarity with the markets and trade in Asia was a further quality that the Europeans – especially the English and the French – felt they could make use of. It was generally assumed that, as they were Christians, they were closer to European culture.[11] Consequently, time and again throughout the sixteenth to the mid-eighteenth century, we find Armenians mediating between the Mughals and the Europeans.

A landmark in the history of the Armenians in the early seventeenth century boosted the Armenian drive towards the East during the ensuing period. As a part of his war strategy against the Ottomans, the Safavid Emperor Shah Abbas evacuated the rich Armenian city of Julfa, forcing the inhabitants to move and settle in different parts of Persia. The wealthy merchants of the city were brought to settle in the outskirts of Isfahan, baptized by the émigrés as New Julfa. Shah Abbas was aware of the Armenian merchants' fame in the silk trade in the Ottoman Empire and the Mediterranean ports, and it has been argued that the Shah was using the Armenians as a political tool against the feudal forces in Iran, in order to establish his monopoly over the silk trade.[12] Other scholars have cited the symbiotic relationship between the Shah and the Armenians.[13] The proximity of India – Iran's main trading partner – prompted an increasing number of Armenian merchants from Iran (Safavid Persia), especially New Julfa, to frequent India. This was a time when relative peace and prosperity in India induced many Persians to flee there, in the hope of better

9 For conversion among Armenians in India see B. Bhattacharya, "Armenian European relationship in India, 1500–1800: No Armenian Foundation for European Empire?" *The Journal of the Economic and Social History of the Orient,* 48, 2 (2005), pp. 277–322.

10 See the memoires of Francois Martin where he recalled that on board the ship bound for Fort Dauphin in Madagascar, *khoja* Margar, who had just been recruited to sort out the problems of the French Company in Asia won everyone's heart by praying in Italian and 'Frank'. Francois Martin, *Mémoires: Travels to Africa, Persia and India, 1664–1670,* ed. and trans. Aniruddha Ray, (Calcutta: Subarnarekha, 1990), (henceforth *Mémoires*), p. 281.

11 For different aspects of the Armenian relationship with Europeans, see Bhattacharya, "Armenian European relationship."

12 Ina Baghdiantz-McCabe, *The Shah's Silk for Europe's Silver: The Eurasian Trade of the Julfa Armenians in Safavid Iran and India, 1530–1750* (Atlanta: Scholars Press, 1999), p. 33.

13 Edmund Herzig, "The Armenian Merchants of New Julfa, Isfahan: a Study in Pre-Modern Asian Trade" (D. Phil. Thesis, Oxford, 1991); Rudi Matthee, *The Politics of Trade in Safavid Iran: Silk for Silver, 1600–1730* (Cambridge: Cambridge University Press, 1999).

opportunities.[14] On the other hand, religious intolerance toward Armenians and the intra-community disputes resulting from the conversion of Armenians to Catholicism and Islam in late Safavid Persia, coupled with political dislocation following the Afghan invasion of the 1720s, and, finally, the tyrannical rule under Nadir Shah after 1745, ensured a steady flow of Armenians into India.[15] Ports under Europeans, especially the English, made special efforts to attract Armenians to their settlements.

On their arrival in the Indian subcontinent, the European companies were granted a number of economic privileges. Generally, the companies sent ambassadors to the Mughal Emperor, requesting a permit (*farman, parwana*) to trade at certain ports, which they received in return for a fixed annual fee payable to the imperial treasury. They also reinforced certain settlements, which developed as Portuguese, Danish, Dutch, English, and French enclaves in the Indian Ocean. We have no knowledge of Armenians applying jointly for such privileges, or sending a mission to the Mughals. This was perhaps because members of this stateless diaspora operated individually, either on their own behalf or for their principal, who was often the patriarch of a family firm that was also based in India by the eighteenth century. The merchants generally traveled with other Asian merchants, and lodged at caravanserais or places rented together with fellow travellers.[16]

Gradually, as more members of the community started settling down, certain quarters of towns became associated with this ethnic group, such as

---

14 Sanjay Subrahmanyam, "Iranians Abroad: Intra-Asian Elite Migration and Early Modern State Formation," *Journal of Asian Studies*, 51, 2 (1992); also Ina Baghdiantz McCabe, "Global trading ambitions in diaspora: the Armenians and their Eurasian silk trade, 1530–1750," in Ina Baghdiantz McCabe, Gelina Harlaftis, and Ioanna Pepelasis Minoglou, (eds.), *Diaspora Entrepreneurial Networks: Four Centuries of History* (Oxford and New York, NY: Berg, 2005), pp. 27–48; Muzaffar Alam and Sanjay Subrahmanyam, *Indo-Persian Travels in the Age of Discoveries, 1400–1800*, (Cambridge: Cambridge University Press, 2007), pp. 176, 241.

15 V. Ghougassian, *The Armenian Diocese of New Julfa in the Seventeenth Century* (Atlanta, GA: Scholars Press, 1998); Herzig, Edmund, "The Armenian Merchants of New Julfa, Isfahan: A Study in Pre-Modern Asian Trade" (D. Phil. Thesis, Oxford, 1991), pp. 90–95.

16 When the Abbé Carré was in Bijapur, the caravanserais of that place were full of foreign merchants. Ill as the priest was, he sent for an Armenian or Persian merchant who could help him find his way. The messenger found several Armenians, but they were travelling with a lot of merchandise, and as they lodged with other foreign merchants at a caravanserai the end of the town, they did not dare leave their goods behind and accompany the messenger to meet the abbé. *The Travels of Abbé Carré in India and the Near East, 1672 to 1674*, ed. Charles Fowcett, trans. Lady Fawcett, 3 vols. (London: the Hakluyt Society, 1947–8), vol. 1, p. 270.

Armenian Street in Calcutta and Madras, and the Armanitola in Dacca. Armenian merchants (like their Indian counterparts) did not enjoy the exemption from payment of tolls, either at Hugli, Calcutta or Chandernagore. Though they sought protection under European flags, they were supposed to pay the customs duties in full, unless they had negotiated the matter with the harbor master beforehand.[17] Sometimes they tried to evade payment by smuggling goods in and out, often at the cost of trouble with the authorities ("*de thol voor de grootste gedeelte smokkelende daar zij hier ook grote liefhebbers van zijn, en nu en dan eens voor bloeden moeten*").[18] The question of toll payment generated manifold disputes between Armenian merchants and Mughal officials. To avoid trouble with the indigenous government, a Dutch chief at Chinsura noted that it would be wise to leave the Armenians alone and not bring *all* Armenians under Dutch protection.[19]

If haggling over tolls with Mughal officials sometimes ended in a skirmish, and even if some Dutchmen were cynical about the way Armenian merchants operated, Armenians often enjoyed a distinct position in comparison with other Asian merchants. This distinction though, was different from those enjoyed by Europeans, and the appreciation of their diligence was not untainted. The distinction was based on the understanding that they could be very useful and particularly so in some contexts, especially on the part of their local European benefactors who were jealous of the knowledge and wide range of contacts of the Armenians they had to depend on.

Bengal, as the granary of India in the early modern period, was abundant in food grains, sugar, salt, and betel nut. Before Calcutta started to grow at the beginning of the eighteenth century, at the time the Bengal subah of the Mughal Empire was also beginning to function as a semi-autonomous state, the major ports of the region were Hugli (in Bengal) and Balasore (in present day Orissa). While land routes connected the small production centers with the medium-sized and big towns, an extensive system of navigable rivers, especially the Ganges and its tributaries, provided excellent facilities for inland shipping. Although rice and numerous varieties of cotton textiles were

17 Nationaal Archief (henceforth N.A.) VOC 2849, Memorandum of director Louis Taillefert, for Adriaan Bisdom, 27 October 1755, f. 167v.

18 Ibid.; also *Calendar of Persian Correspondence: Being Letters, referring mainly to Affairs in Bengal, which passed between some of the Company's Servants and Indian Rulers and Notables*, vol. 1, 1759–1767 (Calcutta: Government of India Press, 1911), document no. 720.

19 N.A., Memorandum of director Louis Taillefert; similar comments were made by the next director Van der Velde in his memorandum, HRB 244, 4 April, 1757, f. 17v. Tharkan Agamal and a few others worked for the Dutch Company.

produced in lower Bengal, the hinterland catering for Bengal's ports stretched as far as Bihar, Awadh and Benares. The transfer of the provincial capital from Biharsharif to Patna and the construction of an overland road connecting Patna with Sonargaon (east of Dacca) in Southeast Bengal had been realized by Sher Shah in the sixteenth century. The consolidation of Mughal rule over Bengal in the early seventeenth century seems to have boosted commercial traffic between Bihar and Bengal. Patna's geographical location on the Ganges, forming the main link between northern India and Bengal, had led to its emergence as an entrepot in the seventeenth century, with a plentiful supply of cotton and silk textiles, rice and other grains, sugar, opium, and oilseeds from its hinterland.[20] Lying between the two off-shoots of the Ganges flowing southwards to Calcutta, Murshidabad was also conveniently located for river traffic. The region's major products were silk, brass and bell-metal ware. The major industry consisted of silk winding and weaving silk cloth. In addition to Murshidabad, the capital of Bengal since the early eighteenth century, there was a conglomeration of commercial towns, including Jangipur, Azimganj, Jiaganj and Khagra-Berhampur, and there was a brisk trade at Murshidabad in rice, pulses, gram, oilseeds, raw silk, woven silk, salt, cotton goods, sugar, tobacco, jute, gunny bag, ivory ornaments, spices and precious stones. The raw silk purchased by the Europeans came almost exclusively from the area around Kasimbazar.[21] Further southeast, connected to the Ganges-Padma river system, Dacca's excellent location allowed the city to develop into an entrepot of river-borne trade connecting the eastern and western parts of Bengal, and Bengal with the heartland of India.[22] The fertile hinterland provided a rich variety of rice, textiles and other goods. The world market that had penetrated the interior of India via ports such as Surat and Hugli was still highly active in cities such as Patna, Murshidabad and Dacca. The merger of the provinces of Bihar and Bengal in 1733 integrated the two economies. Textiles, saltpeter, sugar, opium and indigo, for instance, were taken downstream to Chandernagore, Hugli and Calcutta, for export overseas. Agricultural

---

20 Kumkum Chatterjee, *Merchants, Politics and Society in Early Modern India: Bihar, 1733–1820* (Leiden: Brill, 1996), pp. 13–17.

21 Om Prakash, *The Dutch East India Company and the Economy of Bengal, 1630–1720* (Princeton: Princeton University Press, 1985), p. 55; for a reconstruction of the urban society at Murshidabad in the late eighteenth century, see Gautam Bhadra, "Social Groups and Relations in the Town of Murshidabad, 1765–1793," *Indian Historical Review*, 2, 2 (1976), pp. 312–338.

22 Richard Eaton, *The Rise of Islam and the Bengal Frontier, 1204–1760,* (Berkeley: University of California Press, 1993), Chapter 2.

products and manufactures from small towns and villages in the hinterland were sent upstream to entrepots such as Patna, but were also distributed through networks of other medium-sized and small market towns.

In the seventeenth century, Armenians in Bengal were settled two kilometers south of Hugli, at Chinsura, the headquarters of the Dutch in Bengal, where they lived in houses they rented in the Company's territory.[23] When the Dutch were attempting to secure a foothold for their commerce in Bengal in the 1630s, it was an Armenian who accompanied them to the nawab of Dacca.[24] Joseph and Hovannes, the two sons of *Khoja* Margar, who had assisted the French in obtaining the permit to trade at Masulipatnam, were successful traders, based at Chinsura, and they financed the building of the Armenian Church there in 1695–97. This connection with the French had taken Armenians to Chandernagore as well. In the interior, they had had a settlement at Saidabad (near Berhampur), in the silk growing region of Murshidabad, since 1665. Their other settlement was in Dacca. They invested mostly in ready money, and some minerals, which they themselves exchanged for cloth in the weavers' villages. The Armenian settlement in Calcutta seems to have started at around the turn of the seventeenth century, when the English settlement began to grow.[25] The Church of Holy Nazareth on Armenian Street in Calcutta was built in 1724. Up to at least the mid-eighteenth century, the Armenians conducted a considerable volume of trade in the Red Sea, Persia and Southeast and East Asia and were investing seven to eight thousand guilders annually in textiles in Dacca alone.[26]

Customarily, individual or family firms of Armenian merchants entered into a *commenda* or commission agency contract with an agent, by advancing him a sum of money.[27] The agent was expected to invest the capital in buying/

---

23 NA, HRB 244, Memorandum, Van der Velde 4 April, 1757, f. 17v.

24 NA, Account of the costs incurred when six of us, together with an Armenian and a few pions, were taken in chains to Assalimchaen the nawab of Decca, early September 1636. VOC 1122 Coromandel ff. 651–652. The role of the Armenian here is not clear. It is possible he was consulted by the Dutch who were planning to send an embassy to Islam Khan. The costs included those for dress material and making charge of 4 *kaba*s for the Armenian Martin.

25 For the role of the Armenians in the establishment of the English rule in India, see Bhattacharya, "Armenian European relationship in India."

26 NA, Resolution at Hugli, 23 January 1744, VOC 8795, f. 846.

27 For discussions on this institution, see Edmund Herzig, "The Family Firm in the Commercial Organisation of the Julfa Armenians," in J. Calmard (ed.), *Études Safavides*, (Paris: Institut Français de recherche en Iran, 1993), pp. 287–303 and Sebouh Aslanian, "The Circulation of Men and Credit: The Role of the *Commenda* and the Family Firm in

selling commodities for the firm in return for a commission, depending on his age and experience, and the nature of the contract. Often, the agent deposited his own capital as part of the total investment, or received an additional amount to invest on his own account. Profit from an enterprise was divided according to the share in the investment. The agents crisscrossed from one production center to another in the hinterland. The initial capital invested could be doubled or tripled within a couple of decades and the arrangement left enough room for the agent to accumulate a fortune for himself, provided he worked hard.[28]

As Armenians in Bengal (like in other parts of India) traded in partnership with family members based in Persia and in other parts of India, there was a constant circulation of capital, goods, and information, carried by merchants traveling to and fro. Nazar Jacob, the founder of the Armenian Church in Calcutta, shuttled between Calcutta and Madras and worked as an agent for Avetik, Sarhad and Tarkhan in Bengal.[29] A merchant based in Calcutta could instruct his partners in Basra to lend capital to his agent there against a bond issued on him. The agent would borrow the money against a security, buy goods, and ship or take them to Calcutta. Avak di Aratoon of Calcutta worked as an agent for both Mirza Petrus of Calcutta and Petrus' partner, Aga Minas di Elias, in Basra. In addition to this business, Avak started a separate venture together with Thomas Boddam, in which they deposited two thousand and six thousand rupees respectively. Avak appears to have been operating between Calcutta and Basra on behalf of merchants at both ends.[30] Similarly, there was Margar di Sattoor of Basra, nephew and agent of Khachik di Khojamal, who worked as a link between Khachik in Calcutta and his partners in Isfahan.[31]

Julfan Society," *Journal of the Economic and Social History of the Orient* (henceforth *JESHO*), 50, 2–3 (2007), pp. 124–171. My paper (see the note below) illustrates how the system worked in India.

28 B. Bhattacharya, "The 'Book of Will' of Petrus Woskan (1680–1751): Some Insights into the Global Commercial Network of the Armenians in the Indian Ocean," *JESHO*, 51, 1 (2008), pp. 67–98.

29 Ibid.

30 Calcutta High Court (henceforth CHC), Original Site (henceforth OS) Old Will (henceforth OW) 342 the will of Avak di Aratoon, December 2, 1758. Document 10 appended to the thesis of Edmund Herzig is an instruction issued by Mirza di Petrus to Aga Minas di Elias in Basra to advance capital to Avak to be invested in goods in Basra for shipment to Calcutta. Herzig, "The Armenian Merchants," pp. 328–330.

31 *Khoja* Khachik di Khojamal was active in Bengal trade from 1740. For Khachik and his agent Margar di Sattoor, see Bhattacharya, "The 'Book of Will' of Petrus Woskan"; for Margar di Sattoor borrowing money from Basra merchants on a bill issued on Khachik in

While merchants such as Avak and Margar maintained the link between Calcutta and the outer world, the careers of *khoja* Wajid, *khoja* Gregory and *khoja* Petrus Aratoon in the trade and politics of Bengal in the mid-eighteenth century illustrate how Armenian portfolio capitalists combined their success in overseas commerce with trade and politics in the hinterland.[32] As we know, the Conspiracy of Plassey demonstrated how the vested interests of the court officials, indigenous merchants, bankers and foreign trading companies combined to create a rupture that changed the course of India's history. A number of Armenian merchant diplomats played a crucial role in the negotiations between the Bengal nawabs and the English during the eventful years preceding the climax. The person known as the 'merchant prince' of Bengal in the 1740s and 1750s was the Armenian *khoja* Wajid. In all probability, it was the father of *khoja* Wajid, referred to as Mhamet Faziel in Dutch company papers, who had embraced Islam. The English, keen to have Armenians on their side in exploring opportunities in Asia, kept referring to Wajid by his original nationality, as Armenian, whereas the Dutch, who had the tendency to be politically correct, referred to him as a 'Moor', a term loosely applied to Muslims.[33] He was settled in Hugli and conducted transactions with the French through their lodge at Chandernagore and the Dutch through their lodge at Chinsura. Wajid owned at least five ships and conducted extensive overseas trade with Mocha and Basra. Wajid was also known to have owned a fleet of 2,000 boats, for transporting goods such as saltpeter down the Ganges.[34] He had close contacts with the Jagat Seths' banking house and other Patna merchants, and participated in the inland trade to Patna and Surat. He had large stakes in Bengal's salt trade and the opium and saltpeter trade of Bihar, where his interests in the

---

Bengal, see Edmund Herzig, Appendix, document 7, pp. 315–318; there was also *khoja* Mkartich who traveled between Calcutta, Madras and Basra, Tamil Nadu Archives (henceforth TNA), Copies of Wills, Probates, vol. 9 the will of Petrus Woskan.

32 Sushil Chaudhury has written extensively on *khoja* Wajid. See his "Merchants, companies and rulers: Bengal in the Eighteenth Century," *Journal of the Economic and Social History of the Orient*, 31, 1 (1988), pp. 93–94, and "International Trade in Bengal Silk and the Comparative Role of Asians and Europeans, circa. 1700–1757," *Modern Asian Studies*, 29, 2 (1995), pp. 373–386.

33 Sushil Chaudhuri maintains that there is no evidence to show that Wajid converted to Islam and that he perhaps adopted the name for strategic purposes. My position is based on the consistent reference to Wajid in Dutch records as a "moor." If his father had adopted Islam, there is no reason why Europeans in eighteenth-century Bengal would record such an incident. On the other hand, it was not uncommon for Armenians to convert to another faith. It is also possible that *khoja* Mhamet Faziel married an Armenian woman.

34 Chatterjee, *Merchants, Politics and Society*, p. 50.

production areas were looked after by his brother *khoja* Ashraf.[35] Through his contacts in the nawab Alivardi's darbar, he was able to secure the salt firm in 1752 and the saltpeter firm in 1753. For a few years, before the Battle of Plassey brought the English East India Company political control over Bengal, Wajid enjoyed the monopoly on saltpeter and salt. On behalf of the nawab Siraj-ud-Daula, he maintained diplomatic negotiations with the European companies and represented the French in the nawab's darbar.[36] For a long time, Wajid endeavored to counterbalance the power of the English in the nawab's court with that of the French, but the growing political and military power of the English, manifested in their activity in Coromandel, followed by the recapture of Calcutta and the plunder of Hugli, seem to have persuaded Wajid not to alienate them, but to join in the conspiracy against the nawab. Soon after the victory at Plassey, suspected of conspiring with the Dutch and the French, Wajid was captured and he consumed poison in prison.

Khoja Petrus Aratoon was another prominent Armenian merchant in eighteenth-century Bengal. Born into a New Julfa family, it is not known when Aratoon and Hosanna's three sons had left for India. *Khoja* Gregory Aratoon, initially a cloth merchant in Hugli, rose to become commander-in-chief in the army of the nawab Mir Qasim (1760–64), who called him Gurgin Khan.[37] *Khoja* Barseek Aratoon had settled in Saidabad and traded in salt, owning warehouses in the interior at Rangpur and Dinajpur.[38] *Khoja* Petrus was close to the Mughal court at Murshibad, but lived in Calcutta from 1748.[39] He was married to Dastagool, daughter of Aga Minas of a branch of the Minassian family of New Julfa which had settled in Bengal. Petrus came into the limelight for the first time in the wake of the dispute between Siraj ud Daula, the nawab of Bengal, and the Fort William Council in Calcutta. In 1756, when the nawab briefly captured Fort William forcing Governor Drake and other members of the Council

35 Ibid. p. 72.

36 S.C. Hill (ed.), *Bengal in 1756–57: A Selection of Public and Private Papers dealing with the Affairs of the British in Bengal during the Reign of Siraj-uddaula,* 3 vols. (London: J. Murray, 1905), vol. 1, pp. 3–5; vol. 3, Appendix III, translation of the first part of a memoir by Monsieur Jean Law, chief of the French factory at Kasimbazar, p. 187.

37 For a recent reconstruction of the remarkable career of this Armenian portfolio capitalist see B. Bhattacharya, "Between Fact and Fiction: Khoja Gregory alias Gurgin Khan, the 'Evil Genius' of Mir Qasim," in J.J.L. Gommans and Om Prakash (eds.) *Circumambulations in South Asian History: Essays in Honour of Prof. D.H.A. Kolff* (Leiden: Brill, 2003), pp. 133–158.

38 Willem Bolts, *Considerations on Indian Affairs* [(London: s. n., 1772)], pp. 185–186.

39 R.C. Temple, "Side-lights on Omichund: An Echo of the Intrigues before Plassey," *Indian Antiquary*, [2nd series, 47], (1918), pp. 265–74.

to leave Calcutta for Fulta, it was Petrus who supplied the English with provisions, and this service in a time of need earned him the trust of Colonel Clive, who was to depend heavily on Petrus' embassy in his diplomacy with the nawab. Mesrovb Seth carefully chronicled the service Petrus offered the English during the Conspiracy of Plassey.[40] The fact that he bore the entire expenses for restoring the old and ruined Armenian Church at Saidabad as late as 1758 testifies to the importance attached to the place by members of the community. Petrus also financed the repair and embellishment of the Armenian Church in Calcutta, where two additional altars were built in 1763: one in memory of his brother Gregory, assassinated that same year, and the other to immortalize his own memory.[41] He was close to Warren Hastings, the governor and, later, governor general of Bengal (1771–85). While all this suggests he was an influential merchant with close contacts in politics, the account of his estates discussed here for the first time gives us some idea of the actual wealth of Petrus, who died on 29 August 1778.

The inventory of Petrus' estate as it was presented to the court by his son Aratoon Petrus in 1789 showed a total of Rs 393,130.[42] The goods left by Petrus in his house featured a variety of textiles of numerous origins. These included piece goods, from a variety of locations (table 4.1).[43]

It is possible that the piece goods from Europe were purchased in Calcutta from European Company or private merchants, but it is also possible that Petrus had received them as gifts from his European friends and partners. Armenians, rich and poor, could send a consignment of goods with merchants

40 Seth, *Armenians in India,* pp. 325–359.

41 Ibid.

42 CHC, OS, OW 1373 contains the will of one Sarhad Arratoon. Sarhad stated in his will (written in 1767) that he was indebted to Petrus Arratoon for 32,529 Arcot Rupees and he hoped Petrus would relinquish his claim. Indeed, this amount does not appear in the account of Petrus discussed here.
There were different denominations of rupee in use in eighteenth century India. The accounts produced before the High Court discussed in this paper were, unless otherwise indicated, in 'current rupee', sometimes with the Arcot rupee equivalent. I have taken the figures in 'current rupee' which was equivalent to approximately 2s 3d before 1770 and 2s thereafter. See P.J. Marshall, *East Indian Fortunes: The British in Bengal in the Eighteenth Century* (Oxford: Clarendon Press, 1976), p. [vii], and table iv on p. 223 for the currencies in Bengal and the rates of conversion.

43 The following account of Petrus' assets, etc. has been collected from CHC, OS, OW 2623: Inventory and account sales of the whole effects and goods, etc. belonging to Petruse Arratoon deceased which were bought by the legal heirs of the said deceased as per their real value, dated 16th February 1789, signed by Arratoon Petruse.

TABLE 4.1 *Piece goods in the estate of Petrus Aratoon*

Quantity (in pieces)	Source	Cost price in current rupees
13	Kasimbazar and Murshidabad	112
16	Dacca	328
21	(silk piece goods) China	325
28	Balasore and Santipore	342
54	Brocade with gold and silver thread work from Benares	1,701
65	Chintz and white textiles from Madras	900
18	Masulipatnam	100
16	Surat and Multan	245
7	Europe	110
96	Shawls of different colors and qualities	3,220
(321)		(7,383)

traveling to a specific destination, be it Basra, Bombay, Canton or Manila. The consignee would send goods in return, for sale at the original port. The Chinese silk piece goods could have been brought by Armenians sailing to China and those from Masulipatnam and Madras brought by ships engaged in coastal trade. The Benares, Multan and Surat varieties could be purchased from Armenians or other up-country merchants, via agents at Murshidabad and Saidabad.

The rest of the varieties must have been procured by members of Petrus' network from the production centers at Balasore (in Orissa), Dacca, Murshidabad and Santipore. Armenian settlements at Chinsura, Saidabad, Dacca and elsewhere ensured that there were enough male members in the community to be drawn into the network, and religion and commerce went hand in hand.[44] From these bases, members of the community spread to other urban and rural centers, acting as contacts for others engaged in the broader economy of the Indian Ocean trade. Ablahad, the son of Isaac, who was trading at Dacca, died there in 1757. While his estate was worth approximately 9,822 Arcot

44 Cf. CHC, OS, OW 796 the will of Arratoon Jacob, 12th May, 1766: "…I have given to Padre Carrapeat 150 rupees to invest in goods at Saidabad on my account which must be delivered to my executor Coja Zachariah." Arratoon valued his estate at approximately Rs. 1,000; also CHC, OS, OW 1855 the will of Agazar Sattoor who had invested 5,500 Arcot rupees in Dacca textiles.

rupees, he seems to have been engaged in trade, buying and selling Japanese copper, small quantities of cloth, silver spoons, cups and saucers, muskets and pistols. His estate included one silver snuff box, one brass bassoon, one copper pot and three copper plates. The credit side of his estate showed that on board the *Prince George* he had received one bag of gold and silver coins from Basra, which he sold for 5,513.14 Arcot rupees. One Nayal Dalal of Dacca owed him a thousand rupees on a bond.[45] The tragic story of Aratoon Thaddeus Kalantar helps illustrate how Armenians were familiar with the production centers of the interior of Bengal. Aratoon, the son of Thaddeus and nephew of Gregory, both merchants in Madras, was in the service of a merchant in Calcutta and accompanied his master to Dinajpur (North Bengal). Before he left for Dinajpur, he engaged someone for purchasing opium. This opium, together with the cloth and four bags of rice that Aratoon left with Mr. John Ben (at Dinajpur), was to be delivered by Mr. Ben to Saidabad. At Dinajpur, Aratoon also met Carapet Jacob, who received two hundred rupees from him. He left five pieces of chintz with Margar Carapet for sale at Dacca and two pieces of *charkona duria* with Carapet Sattoor (at Saidabad). The young man fell unexpectedly ill, perhaps at Dinajpur, and breathed his last either there or in Saidabad.[46] Similarly, Johannes Phanoos, living in Surul, traded in sugar and textiles while working for Khachik Minas of the Minassian family originally of New Julfa but settled at (the Danish settlement of) Serampore.[47]

The other goods sold from Petrus' estate were 414 pieces of silver and gold plates worth Rs 9,240; 37 agate handles with gold work for Moorish daggers worth Rs 1,850; mirrors and other glassware worth Rs 800; carriages and horses worth Rs 1,300 and jewelry, including costly rings, tiaras and necklaces, to the value of Rs 33,000. The sale of the estate, including these goods, yielded Rs 163,358.

---

45 CHC, OS, OW 200 the [nuncupative] will of Ablahad. The will was put on paper by the executor *khoja* Israel who attested that the will was according to the last wishes of Ablahad; cf. ibid., OW 1541 the will of Aviet Gregory, who was operating in Bengal since 1724.

46 TNA, Mayor's Court records, Copies of wills, probates…vol. 24, Will of Arratoon Thaddeus Calandar, ff. 74–75. Arratoon appointed Carapet Sattoor his attorney and requested him to collect his dues and send all his belongings to his uncle at Madars.

47 CHC, OS, O.W. 5557: the will of Johannes Phanoos. Surul is a village in south Birbhum in West Bengal. The area grew rice, oilseeds, mulberry and sugarcane while the principal manufactures were lac, silk and tassar. cf. CHC, OS, OW 4522 the will of Arratoon Johannes. Arratoon was based at Saidabad but invested at Sheerpur [Sripur near Dacca] through his agent Chattoor Thoman. Gautam Bhadra has also discussed this will in "Social Groups."

The accounts still open at Petrus' death included business transactions with Stephanus Aga of Basra. Stephanus had sent pearls, which were sold per weight and in strings, in Calcutta and at Saidabad for Rs 30,499.

The Armenians' contribution to developing the skyline of colonial Calcutta in the late nineteenth and twentieth century is well documented. As pioneers of the real estate business in the city not only did they build three churches, but they can also claim credit for building some of the finest buildings in the heart of the city, such as the Galstaun Mansions (Queen's Mansions at the corner of Park Street and Russel Street), Harrington Mansions, and the Galstaun Park (later purchased by the nizam of Hyderabad, who renamed it Saba Mansion, A.J.C. Bose Road), the Stephen Court (adjoining Galstaun Mansions) and the Grand Hotel. Johannes Galstaun, who donated Rs 25,000 for the construction of the Victoria Memorial Building, developed and beautified central and south Calcutta, where he had 350 houses built.[48] Many members of the community were living in these quarters in the colonial period, which also bears witness to the fact that many Armenians were involved in the hospitality sector, catering for the growing tourism industry. Real estate baron Aratoon Stephen built the Grand Hotel in Calcutta and the Hotel Mount Everest in Darjeeling. The hotels Astor, Astoria, Carlton, Fairlawn, Kenilworth, Lytton and New Kenilworth were also owned by Armenians.[49]

Armenians engaging in real estate business was not new in colonial times, though. Already in the eighteenth century, we find big and small merchants from the community building and purchasing houses. This was one way of investing the profit from commerce, and the house and/or rooms could be rented out to itinerant merchants, newcomers, and Armenian families residing there.[50]

48 Jaya Chaliha and Bunny Gupta, "The Armenians in Calcutta," in S. Chaudhuri ed. *Calcutta: the Living City; Vol. 1. The Past* (Calcutta: OUP, 1990), pp. 54–55; Susmita Bhattacharya, "The Armenians of Calcutta," in Himadri Banerjee et al. (eds.) *Calcutta Mosaic: Essay and Interviews on the Minority Communities of Calcutta* (New Delhi: Anthem Press, 2009).

49 Of these only the Fairlawn and the New Kenilworth are still run by Armenians. The octogenarian Violet Smith, owner of the Fairlawn is still around, though the formalities are now looked after by her daughter living in England. The New Kenilworth was run for a long time by Mrs. Joyce Purdy (Sarkies), who towards the end of her life was unable to run the place, due partly to extremely poor eyesight. After she passed away, her son David Purdy, who was living in England, went back and thoroughly renovated the place.

50 See CHC, OS, OW 1559, 13 December, 1768, the will of Jacob Johannes. The estate of Jacob was worth Rs. 4427 out of which the house he owned cost Rs. 3715; OW 4522, the will of Aratoon Johannes who had a house in Saidabad; OW 5108, the estate of Masy Baba John (Martiros) whose houses were rented to the members of the community; Khachik Arakiel discussed below also had several houses in Calcutta, Dacca and Saidabad; cf. *khoja* Petrus

Petrus Aratoon's investment in real estate, not only at various locations in Calcutta, but also in Bhatpara, Chinsura, Serampore, Saidabad and Dacca, is important in this context. The papers mentioned above include a list of the following immovable property as belonging to Petrus, together with the sale price:

TABLE 4.2 *Immovable property left by Petrus Aratoon*

2 'upper roomed'[51] houses facing the Armenian Church	Rs 19,000
1 'upper roomed' house at Moorhgee Huttah[52]	Rs 5,000
1 'upper roomed' house on the Armenian Street	Rs (illegible)
1 large dwelling house of the deceased (Petrus Aratoon)[53]	Rs 20,000
1 'lower roomed' house adjacent to the Greek Church	Rs 2,000
1 'lower roomed' house at Moorghee Huttah	Rs 2,000
1 large garden house adjacent to the deceased's garden house (Calcutta)	Rs 12,000
1 lower roomed house adjacent to the said garden house	Rs 1,000
1 garden house in Serampore	Rs 11,000
1 lower roomed house in Chinsura	Rs 2,000
1 large house in Dacca	Rs 4,000
(Estates) and gardens	
1 large plot of land consisting of a large tank, Calcutta	Rs 6,500
1 large plot of land adjacent to Kasim Ali's house, Calcutta	Rs 2,000
1 small plot of land adjacent to Manekji's house	Rs 2,000
1 large plot of land housing the stables (Calcutta)	Rs 5,000
1 garden at Syaldah, near Calcutta	Rs 600

Woskan, an Armenian merchant of Madras in the eighteenth century owned more than forty houses in that port city, Bhattacharya, "The 'Book of Will' of Petrus Woskan."

51 Refers to a construction with two floors, the ground floor and the first floor; 'lower roomed house' stands for a building with a single storey.

52 Literally 'chicken market', the Barabazar area in Calcutta. With the conglomeration of the indigenous Bengali elite in the northern part and the Europeans in the southern part of the growing urban space of Calcutta, areas like *Murgihata* were the intermediate zones where Armenians, Eurasians, Greek, Portuguese and other communities lived. Such space has been defined as the 'Gray Town' – in between the 'Black Town' and 'White Town' often demarcating the living quarters of different ethnic groups in a colonial city. See Pradip Sinha, *Calcutta in Urban History* (Calcutta: Firma KLM, 1978), pp. 7–8.

53 Unfortunately the location of this house is not mentioned. But the location of all his other houses on this list is mentioned and we know that Petrus was a resident of Calcutta from 1748.

TABLE 4.2 *Immovable property left by Petrus Aratoon* (cont.)

1 large plot of land at 'Gheeriza bazar'[54] Saidabad	Rs 1,000
1 plot of land at Bhatpara[55]	Rs 500
1 *taluk* or revenue land called Sutle (illegible)[56] within the limits of Beelkool[57]	Rs 10,000
Total value of Petrus' real estate	Rs 105,600[58]

In other words, more than a quarter of the total value of Petrus' estate was in real estate. Rs 150,215 was paid to the estate by Muhammad Reza Khan, on account of the principal sum of Rs 101,765 he had borrowed from *khoja* Gregory and transferred to Petrus' account after Gregory's death.[59] We have to remember that by the time Petrus died some time had passed since Plassey, and the accounts of Petrus' estate should be judged in the context of the post-Plassey developments in Bengal and elsewhere in India. Following the political victory in 1757, the employees of the English East India Company entered into reckless competition to enrich themselves through private trade and attempted to clip the wings of any Armenians or indigenous merchants with vested interests in these fields standing in the way of ambitious English traders.[60]

54 Denoting the market place adjoining/near the '*girja*'; the word used for church in Bengal (from the Portuguese igreja).

55 Sailing down the Hugli, Bhatpara lies on the left or the eastern bank of the river while Chinsura and Chandernagore lie on the other side.

56 *Taluk* was a fiscal arrangement under the Mughals granting the right to collect rent of an estate in perpetuity. There could be several *talukdars* in a *zamindari*.

57 Not identified.

58 This was part of the Rs. 163,358 mentioned above.

59 Muhammad Reza Khan who migrated from Persia during the rule of nawab Alivardi Khan of Bengal (1740–56) was closely associated with the events leading to the end of the Mughal rule and the beginning of the Company rule in Bengal. After the British secured the right to revenue collection in Bengal in 1765, Reza Khan was appointed *naib diwan*, the official in charge of executing the disposal of the revenue on behalf of the Company. He was the virtual ruler of Bengal during 1765–1770. See Abdul Majed Khan, *The Transition in Bengal, 1756–1775: A Study of Saiyid Muhammad Reza Khan* (Cambridge: Cambridge University Press, 1969).

60 Two conflicting parties of the English in contemporary Bengal provided two accounts of the incidents during this period; see H. Vansittart, *A Narrative of the Transactions in Bengal 1760–1764*, eds. A.C. Banerjee and B.K. Ghosh (Kolkata: K.P. Bagchi, 1976) and Willem Bolts, *Considerations on Indian Affairs* (London: [s. n.], 1772). Also Marshall, *East Indian Fortunes*, p. 268; also Willem Kuiters, *The British in Bengal 1756–1773: A Society in*

The revenue-payee land mentioned in the list is perhaps the bestowal of the *zamindari* by Mir Qasim, which was frowned upon by the members of the Fort William Council, who complained that Petrus was a man of business, moving from camp to camp, and asked the nawab to return the *zamindari* to its previous owner.[61] The nawab, however, replied that the previous owner was not paying his dues and he had promised a *zamindari* to Petrus and could not possibly revoke his order.[62] Even before the victory at Plassey, the members of the Fort William Council in Calcutta were suspicious of the intentions of Petrus, who had acted as the 'nawab's spy'. The charge came up again later, when his brother Gregory became the commander-in-chief to the nawab Mir Qasim and a number of members of the Fort William Council wanted Petrus to leave the settlement. Henry Vansittart, the president, pointed out that that would be an arbitrary step considering his service; but Petrus was forbidden to act as the *vakil* to the nawab in future.[63] An order issued in 1765 forbade the Armenians and their agents to reside at the manufacturing centers, as this interrupted the Company's trade.[64] A private trading society set up that year broke open Barseek's salt warehouses at Rangpur and Dinajpur and carried away salt worth Rs 60,432 at prices current.[65] By an edict issued in 1768, Armenian and Portuguese merchants and their descendents were forbidden to take part in any trade beyond the borders of Bengal, Bihar and Orissa.[66] As indicated above, however, investing in real estate and lending at interest were two other modes of business preferred by Armenians settled in India.[67]

A large part of the estate consisted of bonds for money lent to different persons. This credit network included Armenians, Hindus, Europeans and Muslims. There were two bonds issued by Mir Suleiman Khan in favor of Petrus for Rs 12,000. One bill of exchange was issued by Gopal Das on account of his debt to Petrus' estate. Raja Ramlochan had a claim of Rs 22,000 on Petrus' estate. Another Rs 19,104 was paid from the estate to Mrs. Merkatoon Sarhad. Rs 30,734 was paid to the estate of Solomon David, an Armenian from Bagdad,

---

Transition Seen Through the Biography of a Rebel: William Bolts (1739–1808) (Paris: Les Indes Savantes, 2002).

61 *Calendar of Persian Correspondence,* vol. 1, nos. 721 and 971. *Zamindar* is a land-owner.

62 James Long, *Selections from unpublished Records of the Government: For the years 1748 to 1767 inclusive relating mainly to the social condition of Bengal,* ed. Mahadev Saha. (Calcutta: Firma KLM, 1973), document no. 517 (from Nawab Kasim Ali Khan, December 1760).

63 Ibid., document no. 647 (Proceedings, 24 March 1763).

64 Ibid., document no. 827 (to Francis Sykes, 1765).

65 Bolts, *Considerations on Indian Affairs,* pp. 185–186.

66 Ibid., p. 199.

67 See TNA, the will of Petrus Woskan who had 42 houses in Madras in the 1940s.

through Pogos Mirza, the estate administrator.[68] Extremely interesting is the list of 'dubious debts' accompanying these papers. While the largest amount was due from an Armenian (Rs 15,134.4.6; from Aga Aratoon Aga Satoor), the debtors came from various social strata and across religious boundaries, and the total amounted to Rs 92,264.5.6.[69] The debtors included Rani Bhavani, *de jure* zamindar of Rajshahi (Bangladesh), 'the Sircars of Dacca', the *zamindar* of Tamluk and about fifty others names.[70] The list of Petrus' irrecoverable debts from the landowners of Bengal dating from 1789 testifies to the hardship imposed on them after the English received the right to collect the revenues in Bengal in 1765.

If Petrus' estates detail how an Armenian merchant of considerable importance based at a sea port functioned, the wills of lesser merchants operating inland show how the entire network was maintained. A good case in point is Mahdesy Aratoon, son of the priest Gasper, based at Dacca, who passed away in 1773. Before talking about Mahdesy, however, we would like to take a brief look at the Arakiel family as, in his will, Mahdesy mentions *khoja* Khachik Arakiel, an eminent and powerful merchant in Calcutta in the late eighteenth century, known for his benevolence. Khachik's father came from Gentloom, and his mother was a member of the Kalantar family (of New Julfa).[71] Khachik and his brothers Jacob John, Sattoor and Gregory, and sisters Gulistan and Dishkun, seem to have settled in different places in Bengal. While Khachik was

---

68 Cf. *khoja* Khachik having a demand on an Armenian merchant from Agulis, CHC, OS, OW 224.

69 CHC, OS, OW 2623 "An account of doubtful debts due from the following persons, to the estate of Petrus Arratoon deceased, dated 16th February, 1789". Also see *Calendar*, vol. II, document no. 1124 the Company's letter to Muhammad Reza Khan September 12, 1768 desiring his assistance in collecting *khoja* Petrus' money due from the *zamindars*. Document no. 1188 dated November 12, 1768 in the same volume Reza Khan replied that he had issued pressing orders to the *zamindars* and *amils* (collectors) in the dependencies of Murshidabad and particularly the son of the deceased Mir Haji, an inhabitant of Azimabad to settle their accounts with Petrus. Rani Bhavani was indebted for Rs. 2,536 on a bond issued in 1760.

70 Cf. CHC, OS, OW 224 *khoja* Khachik had a demand on Hudychand Sharraf; OW 4522 the will of Arratoon Johannes who had a demand on Roopchand Pramanic at Sheerpore.

71 According to Mesrovb Seth, Arrakiel (son of Khachik), father of the Khachik in this paper, died in Dacca which implies that he had moved with his entire family sometime in the early eighteenth century. Seth however mentions on p. 453 (footnote) that Arrakiel died at Dacca in 1742 while the list of graves inside the Roman Catholic Church in Dacca he presented on p. 571 shows one Arakiel dying in 1722. Moreover, Seth says that Arakiel was a native of Julfa.

based mainly in Calcutta, Jacob John was based at Saidapet, from where, in addition to carrying on his own trade, he also looked after Khachik's interests in Patna. Though the brothers traded individually, their business interests were thus intertwined. Khachik operated as an attorney for Michael Martiros of Basra, while Jacob John had a trading account in pearls, together with the said Michael Martiros.[72] Khachik made lavish endowments to the Church of Holy Nazareth in Calcutta. He paid for the construction of the compound wall of the church, embellished the interior of the building, built a parsonage inside the church and had the clock adorning the belfry ordered from London. When the news of King George III's recovery reached Calcutta, Khachik celebrated the incident by relinquishing the debts of 138 debtors confined to the prison of the Calcutta Court of Requests.[73] On his death, he left property of Rs 800,000 in cash, goods, houses, East India Company bonds, silver plates and gold jewelry, etc.[74]

Mahdesy himself seems to have been illiterate, as the will bearing his name stated "I…, knowing no writing at all, have put my seal to this my last will and testament." He appointed *khoja* Johannes, son of the priest Daniel as executor of his will. Mahdesy's total assets amounted to a modest Rs 3,123. It is not clear whether Mahdesy worked as an agent for Khachik. Usually, if a lesser Armenian merchant worked as an agent for a senior powerful merchant, the latter advanced capital against a bond issued by the agent. If the agent invested his own capital in a venture, the agent's will categorically stated the name of his principal(s), the amount received by him on different accounts and the share of the various partners in a particular enterprise. Above all, as the agent was trading on behalf of the principal, he expressed his gratitude to his benefactor, even when there was no account running. Mahdesy did not refer to any such bond or transaction with Khachik at all, save for his debt of Rs 57. It is remarkable – and in my view a source of strength for the Armenian network, for it is generally understood that in a hierarchical system the lesser agents toiled for the capitalists who exploited them – that a merchant of Arakiel's stature was dealing on behalf of a small merchant such as Mahdesy. It is better to have a look at the relevant part of this will:

72 The payments made by Jacob John to Michael and to Khachik acting as attorney of Michael CHC, OS, OW 1858, The estate of Jacob John Arrakiel in account with Coja Gregory Arrakiel administrator. Unfortunately, we do not have the account of the estates of Khachik Arakiel.

73 Seth, *Armenians in India*, pp. 448–457.

74 CHC, OS, OW, Will of Catchick Arakiel, 21 May 1790; Jacob John's fortunes were worth Arcot Rupees 26,632.5.3 OW 1858.

> I have a demand on Coja Sarkees Menassagan[75] upon (bond) which remains now in the hands of…Coja Catchick Arrakeel. I have one thousand rupees in the hands of the said Coja Catchik which I have delivered him with orders to invest the same in Radnagore goods…[76] I have sent to Bombay through the means of the said Catchik Arrakeel 1 bale containing 200 pieces of Dacca *dureas*.[77] I have 800 rupees at Dacca invested in goods, part of which is ready and part unready, or not whitened (unbleached). I have a further demand on Johannes Baboom, a barber, upon a bond; I have left an account by Coja Johannes (son of) Padre Daniel. In the year 1770 I have delivered goods to him, and he sent them to Madras. I have further delivered him at different times goods and other commodities, and have likewise had from him goods, money and other commodities, the account of which is in his possession….He is to take possession of the sundries, chest, one coconut hookah or hubble bubble,[78] silver mounted; a pair of silver spoons and other things all belonging to me.[79]

The credit side of the will noted that Khachik Arakiel had 200 pieces of Radhanagar *soosie*s sold at auction on behalf of Mahdesy for Rs 1,363. After deducting the auction master's charge, Rs 1,293 was credited to Mahdesy's account.[80]

---

75 This Sarkies was perhaps the same 'Sarkes Munasekar' who had arrived in Bengal in 1755 when he traveled up to Malda. After he had made several sea voyages he returned to Bengal in 1771 when he became the agent at Malda for supplying cloth worth Rs. 30 to 40,000 annually to Armenians; N.K. Sinha, *The Economic History of Bengal: From Plassey to the Permanent Settlement*, 3 vols. (Calcutta: Firma KLM, 1956–70). vol. 1, pp. 235–236. Among the papers in Calcutta High Court, there is a will of Sarkies Minasakan of Erevan (Armenia) filed on 24th April 1798. The incomplete account of estate shows that he had transactions with a merchant called Bulchand and had sent a small parcel of textiles to Batavia OW 5184. For another Sarkies working as agent in Malda in the 1740s see Bhattacharya, "The "Book of Will" of Petrus Woskan."

76 Radhanagar in Midnapur district in Southwest Bengal was a thriving centre for the production of textiles, especially the mixed silk-and-cotton variety called *soosie*s or *souse*s.

77 Striped or checked cloth of a silk and cotton mix.

78 Water-pipe.

79 Calcutta High Court, O.W. no. 2079 dated Dacca, 12th November, 1773.

80 *Khoja* Petrus Woskan, the prominent Madras merchant in the first half of the eighteenth century also carried out similar transactions on behalf of his agents, see Bhattacharya, "The 'Book of Will' of Petrus Woskan."

Conclusion

Historically, attracting trade has been a major function of ports, and a driving force guiding the relationship between a port and its hinterland. By focusing on Bengal in the mid and late eighteenth century, this paper aims to shed light on a particular merchant network – that of the Armenians – spread over geographical locations spanning the ports and hinterlands of several countries, tackling the complex task of organizing the logistics of their commerce.

As for the Armenian merchants of New Julfa, it has been argued that their network in the seventeenth century was a closed coalition of merchants, based on trust. Merchants of New Julfa, who followed the Apostolic Church and shared the same cultural traits and historical experience, built up a coalition exclusively for themselves. It was restricted to those who had been evacuated from Julfa and settled in New Julfa, who spoke the Julfa dialect of Eastern Armenian, were adherents of the same Apostolic faith, and, moreover, followed the written and unwritten rules determining membership of this elite circle.[81]

The organization of commerce by Armenian merchants in Bengal demonstrates how the foothold they had gained in the region in the course of the seventeenth century, in places such as Chinsura, Saidabad and Dacca, made them part of the process connecting the region to the economy of North and Northwestern India and beyond.[82] The capital – both financial and human – and the information that went into building that network was extended to and welcomed by the growing European settlements in the seventeenth and early eighteenth century. By the mid-eighteenth century, Armenian agents could be found in many production centers in interior Bengal, working for Armenian and European masters.

The wills of Armenians operating in Bengal since at least the 1730s show that mutual dependence on the part of the network members was crucial for its functioning. Although they operated individually, brothers, sons, sons-in-law, nephews and other close and extended family members were often employed as the firm's agents or partners.[83] When a merchant had no family to rely on, he

81 See e.g. Sebouh Aslanian, "Social Capital, 'Trust' and the Role of Networks in Julfan Trade: Informal and Semi-Informal Institutions at Work," *Journal of Global History*, 1 (2006), pp. 383–402.

82 Cf. Levon Khachikian, "The Ledger of the Merchant Hovannes Joughayetsi," *Journal of the Asiatic Society of Bengal*, 4th series, 8 (1966), pp. 153–186.

83 Khachik Arakiel categorically mentioned Mkartich and Johannes, the two grandsons of his uncle in his will. After his death, both of them were to continue to work as agents; the

depended on members of the community at large. Armenians who had settled in various places across Mughal Bengal and beyond belonged to an informal network, which included members of the community from Agulis, Bagdad, Gentloom and New Julfa, for instance.[84] Being obliged to operate subtly, manipulating their way between the Europeans looking for more privileges and power and the indigenous rulers bent on checking European power, their network had to be elastic. Living in a foreign country next to Hindus and Muslims and trading shoulder to shoulder with them, they could not possibly have avoided entering into business relationships with members of other ethnic groups. The long-standing credit relationship forged by merchants such as Ablahad, Khachik Khojamal and Petrus with individuals across religious boundaries shows that they had gone there to stay. A cut and dried formula, such as a coalition of New Julfa merchants based on a shared church, language, culture and history, is therefore too restrictive to understand the organization of members of the Armenian diaspora in Bengal (and other parts of India).

Secondly, although merchants in Bengal worked in close co-operation with their counterparts in Basra and New Julfa, there is no reference to any central organization in New Julfa controlling the activity of these merchants. All contracts mentioned in the wills were between individuals representing individual (family) firms, and the choice of witnesses was not fixed.

Thirdly, the network stretching from Dacca, Dinajpur, and Saidabad to Calcutta, Madras, Bombay, and Basra was extremely flexible, giving lesser merchants a distinct autonomy, allowing them to act independently as soon as they were able. A small merchant in this network in the interior of Bengal could dispatch goods as far away as Basra or Batavia, or even further, to be sold on his own account, using the network of an established *khoja* and others in the chain. The role of a big merchant in the link was equally flexible: in addition to balancing his position among the cosmopolitan elite, he ensured not only that the small merchant's modest consignment reached its destination but also that the profit from the investment reached the smaller merchant or his family. This shows how the network was not one in which the hardworking commenda agents toiled for the capitalist *khojas*, who were sleeping partners, but one that was as dependent on the efficiency and knowledge of the agents as on the integrity and sense of responsibility of the bigger merchants in the network.

---

former was to live at Saidabad with his family, together with Khachik's brother Gregory; the latter was expected to go and live at Dacca; CHC, OS, OW 4172.

84 See my "Armenian European Relationship" for the earlier period.

Fourthly, restrained though their movement was in the post-Plassey period, the careers of Petrus Woskan and Khacik Arakiel demonstrate how a number of Armenian merchants acquired fortunes comparable to some of the opulent families in contemporary Bengal.[85] As a consequence of the uncertainties caused by the tyrannical regime of Nadir Shah in Persia, streams of Armenians continued to flow into India up to the late eighteenth century; a trend that would persist in the colonial period. After the initial setback during the transitional period in the eighteenth century, Armenians in India were to feel safe under the umbrella of a much larger Christian nation for some time to come, and would be busy adapting to the changing circumstances once more.

---

85 Cf. Gokul Chandra Ghosal, the Calcutta merchant who died in 1779 left a fortune of Rs. 600,687-11-8 behind. The estate of Ramdulal De, the Calcutta merchant trading to the USA in the early nineteenth century amounted to Rs. 678,750. Sinha, *Calcutta in Urban History*, Appendix III, "Estates of some opulent families of Calcutta," pp. 144–147 and 154–155 respectively.

CHAPTER 5

Linking Hinterlands with Colonial Port Towns

Madras and Pondicherry in Early Modern India

Tsukasa Mizushima

Ports and Hinterlands in Early Modern India

This paper discusses and clarifies the features of economic development and the significance of the role of European colonial port towns in early modern India. By juxtaposing Madras and Pondicherry with indigenous societies in the port-hinterland axis, it focuses upon structural changes caused in indigenous societies by the development of maritime trade, rather than upon commodities or trading patterns, as most studies have attempted.

Historical and ecological differences among Asian regions produced varied reactions to the rapid developments in maritime trade in the long eighteenth century. Southeast Asia, for instance, already had a number of long-established ports, which functioned not only as trading hubs but also as political centers. Due to low population density and the limited capacity of local markets in their hinterlands, these ports often exported local commodities to distant markets, including India, China and Europe.

Hirosue, in his study on Southeast Asian ports,[1] argues that port rulers tried to segregate hinterlands from Europeans by fabricating legends in order to mystify the hinterlands. This strategy seemed essential for them to protect their monopoly in commodity transactions with hinterlands and to keep out outsiders. Once the power of port rulers was usurped by Europeans, however, the whole structural relationship came to be placed under the Europeans' control, and the hinterlands also became fully integrated with the ports.

China, on the other hand, took a different path. Pomeranz, in his study of Huang-Yung, in northern China, argues that some localities were closely integrated and became centers of commercial and political activities, while others became disconnected from mainstream development and designated as hinterlands.[2]

1 Masashi Hirosue, *Tonan Ajia no Kousi Sekai* [*Port Cities in Southeast Asia*] (Tokyo: Iwanami Shoten, 2004).

2 K. Pomeranz, *The Making of a Hinterland: State, Society, and Economy in Inland North China, 1853–1937* (Berkeley, Los Angeles, Oxford: University of California Press, 1993).

© KONINKLIJKE BRILL NV, LEIDEN, 2015 | DOI 10.1163/9789004283909_007

In this case, the state's role and power were significant enough to transform the relationship between ports and hinterlands.

Coastal areas in India had totally different features. India had a long history of maritime trade, as far back as the Roman period. The ancient South Indian kingdoms, such as Pallava and Chola, had ports and conducted extensive maritime activities extending over Sri Lanka, the Malay Peninsula and beyond. Most of the indigenous rulers of India's early modern states, on the other hand, seemed to rely more on revenues from agrarian activities than on maritime trade. As the European ports emerging in early modern India, such as Madras and Pondicherry, were mostly located at previously vacant coastal sites, far from the political and economic centers in the interior, they could more or less maintain autonomy from political interference by the Indian powers until the mid-eighteenth century.

To activate trade and facilitate regular shipping, the European commercial powers promised such privileges as tax exemption and subsidies, in order to increase the population of their ports. It was actually essential for their survival to attract as many merchants as possible both from pre-existing ports and interior towns. The fortification of ports and the claiming of extraterritorial rights for the Europeans as well as locals residing in port towns also provided a shelter that few Indian rulers could promise in that period.

During the seventeenth and eighteenth centuries, the colonial ports attracted large Indian populations and grew rapidly to become leading commercial centers. Calcutta (Kolkata), Bombay (Mumbai) and Madras (Chennai) were among them. On the other hand, pre-existing Indian towns in the interior gradually lost their politico-economic importance and became hinterlands, stratified under the colonial port towns. The major issues discussed below are the causes and processes of transformation that South Indian society experienced in the early modern period and the specific role played by colonial ports in this transformation.

Two Economic Systems in Early Modern India

The dominant production system in early modern South India (and in other parts of India) was a subsistence economy, organized for reproducing local societies. A unique system of reproducing local societies had emerged and developed over several centuries (probably since the late Chola period). An extremely elaborate division of labor was commonly observed during the period, linked to allocating specific proportional shares in the whole produce to certain roles necessary for reproducing local societies. Colonial administrators posted in South India in the early colonial period referred to it as the *mirasi* system.[3]

It is important to note that not only those engaged in agriculture but also non-agriculturists were incorporated into the system. In the late eighteenth century, a surprisingly high percentage of the population in South Indian society was non-agricultural. As illustrated in Table 5.1, as many as 45 percent of households were basically engaged in non-agricultural activities in the 1770s.[4] Many people in the mirasi system had non-agricultural occupations. Barbers, washermen, carpenters, smiths, priests and astrologers, for instance, provided other members of the local societies with essential services. For their services, they were allocated certain proportional shares in kind in the whole local produce, without involving any cash transaction. In other words, the mirasi system was not a commodity exchange system, but a service exchange system within local societies, even though there was an extreme division of labor.

TABLE 5.1 *Occupational structure in the Jagir in the 1770s*

Peasantry and cattle-keeping		
Vellalas	7,411	11.9%
Pallys	9,693	15.5%
Pariars	11,052	17.7%
Reddys	1417	2.3%
Kammawars	1,005	1.6%
Cow-keepers	2,573	4.1%
Shanars	812	1.3%
sub-total	33,963	54.3%
Crafts & industry		
Weavers	4,011	6.4%
Cotton-Refiners	85	0.1%
Carpenters	536	0.9%

3 For details, see T. Mizushima, "The Mirasi System as Social Grammar: State, Local Society, and Raiyat in Eighteenth-Nineteenth Century South India," in M. Kimura and A. Tanabe (eds.), *The State in India: Past and Present*, (Delhi: Oxford University Press, 2006), pp. 140–201.

4 A related topic is discussed by Kumar in her paper titled "The Forgotten Sector: Services in Madras Presidency in the First Half of the Nineteenth Century," in Dharma Kumar, *Colonialism, Property and the State*, (Delhi: Oxford University Press, 1998), pp. 55–89. Kumar concludes that the "services sector in South India at the beginning of the nineteenth century was large, almost certainly considerably larger in terms of employment than the industries sector." (*Ibid*, p. 87).

Ironsmiths	394	0.6%
Artificers	45	0.1%
Braziers	36	0.1%
Gold & Silver smiths	209	0.3%
Vegetable oil manufacturers	637	1.0%
Pot-makers	389	0.6%
Wood-cutters	596	1.0%
Salt manufacturers	39	0.1%
Fishermen	590	0.9%
Shoemakers	78	0.1%
Stone-cutters	89	0.1%
Others (approx.)	500	0.8%
Sub-total	8,234	13.2%
Merchants, traders and bankers		
Chettys	2,051	3.3%
Other Traders	1,839	2.9%
Shroffs	422	0.7%
Sub-total	4,312	6.9%
Essential Services		
Barbers	664	1.1%
Washermen	862	1.4%
Medicine-men	159	0.3%
Sub-total	1685	2.7%
Scholarship, higher learning, ritual performances, and culture		
Brahmins	6,646	10.6%
Pandarams	1054	1.7%
Devadasis	622	1.0%
Valluvans	137	0.2%
Wochuns	173	0.3%
Musicians	27	0.0%
kootadi	25	0.0%
Sub-total	8,684	13.9%
Administration		
Kanakkupillai (Registry/ Record-Keeping/Accountancy)	1660	2.7%
Panisevans	314	0.5%
Sub-total	1974	3.2%

TABLE 5.1 *Occupational structure in the Jagir in the 1770s* (cont.)

Militia	2,186	3.5%
Moormen	671	1.1%
Fakirs	62	0.1%
Sub-total	733	1.2%
Other Households	758	1.2%
Total Households	62,529	100.0%

SOURCE: PREPARED FROM J.K. BAJAJ AND M.D. SRINIVAS, "INDIAN ECONOMY AND POLITY IN THE EIGHTEENTH CENTURY: THE CHENGALPATTU SURVEY, 1767–74," IN *INDIAN ECONOMY AND POLITY* (MADRAS: CENTRE FOR POLICY STUDY, 1995), PP. 72–3.

Distinctive during this period was the co-existence of highly developed commodity production, including the cotton textile industry, and the service exchange or mirasi system. Indian cotton textile production, as we know, was extensively involved in overseas trade in the Indian Ocean region and beyond for centuries prior to and throughout our period. The next issue to investigate is the relationship between the mirasi system and the textile industry.

An examination of the lists of share recipients in the mirasi system shows that neither weavers nor merchants were found among them. This is interesting, as it indicates that those in the weaving industry and in commerce were not within the system. Weavers producing textiles might have been incorporated into the mirasi system prior to the eighteenth century, by producing textiles for local villagers, similar to the way that carpenters in the mirasi system prepared agricultural equipments for farmers. By our period, however, weavers and merchants had clearly been excluded – or had excluded themselves – from participating. In the case of weavers, their spatial distribution is one piece of evidence that supports this claim. Table 5.2, which was prepared from the village records of the Jagir at the beginning of the nineteenth century, indicates that there were a number of 'weaving villages', where dozens of weavers lived. Other villages, in contrast, registered a few or no weavers. Weavers working in small numbers in villages probably produced textiles for local markets, whereas weavers concentrated in weaving villages must have worked for remote markets, including those overseas. In any event, this evidence documents the fact that, by the eighteenth century, weavers in weaving villages were no longer participating members of the mirasi system.[5] Since merchant activities crossed

5 Unlike weavers, dyers, painters, and other specialists in the textile industry, spinners were still incorporated in the local reproduction system. The reason could be that most of

TABLE 5.2 *The number of weavers in a village in the Jagir*

Number of looms in a village	Number of villages
0	2,135
1–4	51
5–9	40
10–19	25
20–49	22
50–99	11
103	1
145	1
183	1
193	1
248	1
Total	2,289

SOURCE: PREPARED BY MIZUSHIMA FROM *ZAMINDARI STATEMENT* (STATEMENT RELATING TO THE PERMANENT SETTLEMENT OF JAGIR FORWARDED AS ENCLOSURES TO MR. GREENWAY'S LETTER, 29TH MARCH, 1801), VOLS. 20–22.

localities, which sometimes extended to remote markets, we can easily understand why they were, similarly, outside the system.

Early modern India therefore observed the two economic systems, functioning in parallel. Our next task is to examine the relationship between the two.

---

the spinners were the wives of agriculturists and practised spinning as a sideline. There were some Pariah professional spinners who produced the highest quality yarn. These Pariahs, however, were still categorized as 'Untouchables' and had yet to be categorized as distinctive occupational community. For details, see T. Mizushima, "Features of Economic Development in Early Modern India," in *Multiple Paths of Economic Development in Global History: Proceedings of the Symposium in Commemoration of the Executive Committee Meeting of the IEHA, November 8–9, 2008* (Kyoto and Osaka: Centre for Southeast Asian Studies, Kyoto University and the Graduate School of Letters, Osaka University, 2009), pp. 95–104. As to the importance of female spinners in Indian economy, see, Ian C. Wendt, "Four Centuries of Decline? Understanding the Changing Structure of the South Indian Textile Industry," in Giorgio Riello and Tirthankar Roy (eds.), *How India Clothed the World: The World of South Asian Textiles, 1500–1850* (Leiden and Boston: Brill, 2009), pp. 193–215, and Prasannan Parthasarathi, "Historical Issues of Deindustrialization in Nineteenth-Century South India," *Ibid.*, pp. 415–435.

Port Town and the Development of a Market Economy

India's textile production was destined not only for overseas but also for domestic markets. According to Om Prakash, in eighteenth-century Bengal, one tenth of the one million textile industry workers were engaged in producing textiles for overseas markets, meaning that nine tenths were employed for domestic markets.[6] Brennig argues similarly with regard to the Godavari delta, the most important weaving center for calicoes. He says that the area could probably produce at least twice the amount of cloth exported by the Dutch and English Companies in 1682.[7] Although we have no exact figures, it would not be wrong to assume that at least some weavers worked for domestic markets. We should bear in mind that local societies during this period were reproduced by the service exchange system, without involving any commercial transactions. If the dominant economic system during the period was based upon a service exchange system without involving market transactions, however, then where were the domestic consumers? Another phenomenon relevant to this issue was the mushrooming of bazaars in various parts of India, indicating a wide spread of cash transactions in daily lives. In that case, where was the niche in the subsistence economy into which commercial transactions could penetrate?

One possible answer is the demand from royal courts, armies, and temples. Records from the late eighteenth century show that their combined share in the whole produce was considerable, amounting to between two fifths and a half. Their consumption, however, could not be large or consistent enough to allow the growth of considerable populations engaged in the textile industry, if we consider the small percentage of the population that these sections represent.

Though it is not the objective here to investigate the birth of commodity transactions in the locality, one possible answer lies in a symbiotic relationship between textile production and a part of subsistence production in various localities. Incidentally, the prevalence of the subsistence production system did not necessarily signify a classless society. Even though services were exchanged without involving money transactions among local members, share proportions allocated to respective service providers varied greatly. As will be discussed later, village landlords, referred to as *mirasidar* in South India, for

6 Om Prakash, *The New Cambridge History of India; Vol. 2. Part 5. European Commercial Enterprise in Pre-Colonial India* (Cambridge: Cambridge University Press, 1998), p. 317.

7 Joseph J. Brennig, "Textile Producers and Production in Late Seventeenth Century Coromandel," *Indian Economic and Social History Review*, 23 (1986), p. 345.

instance, secured a far larger share than other share recipients in the mirasi system. It was quite possible for them to throw surplus produce into the grain market and present themselves as important consumers of not only textiles but also other commodities. The aforementioned mushrooming of bazaars also indicates the development of a market economy, involving many sections of the population able to secure some surplus in the mirasi system.

Opportunities for broader sectors of people to participate in market transactions were found in the development of the rural-urban grain trade, a process closely related to the growth of colonial port towns during the period. The next section investigates this process.

Development of Colonial Port Towns and Grain Trade

One of the salient economic features over our period was the influx of a large amount of bullion into South India's colonial ports. As we know, bullion was by far the most important commodity for procuring large quantities of Indian textiles. Two types of change were generated by the influx. Firstly, the politico-economic importance of port towns increased. Deepening political unrest, exemplified by the Carnatic Wars, for instance, provided good opportunities for European powers – which possessed not only superior military equipment but also relatively greater financial strength, supported by bullion transferred from outside – to gain more political control in the region. As a shortage of war expenditure, which often occurred due to the difficulty of collecting revenue in unsettled political situations, made it extremely difficult for Indian rulers to maintain an army for long,[8] the timely arrival of a European fleet with bullion could change the tide of war. The relative safety of port towns from invading armies also attracted the families of leading local rulers. In this climate, colonial towns under the British or the French gradually emerged as core politico-economic centers. By the end of the eighteenth century, Madras had gradually become the most important center in South India.

Secondly, the urban population in the port towns increased. Almost all colonial ports were newly born in the seventeenth and eighteenth centuries, and grew rapidly into major urban centers under the conditions mentioned above. An important point here is that they started providing a large consumer market. Colonial port towns such as Madras and Pondicherry, whose population sometimes numbered a few hundred thousand, necessitated constant grain

8 Since *sipahi* and other soldiers on the battlefields were all hired soldiers, any delay of payment often made them abandon war fronts and go over to the enemy side.

imports from either the hinterlands or other coastal areas, such as Andhra and Bengal. An important contemporary source of the period, *The Private Diary of Ananda Ranga Pillai*, contains several dozen references to grain imports into Pondicherry. As the regular supply of paddy and other grain was essential for the prosperity of colonial towns, Ananda Ranga Pillai, a courtier to the French Governor Dupleix, was instructed to supply information. The references are listed in Table 5.3.

It seems grain was actively transacted during our period. In early colonial records, the most detailed descriptions of grain trade were usually recorded in the military correspondences of the English East India Company. As it was essential to secure grain dealers for any military operation, information on these dealers was eagerly collected and reported. These included the correspondences on the *Banjaries*, or grain transporter-cum-dealer groups, recorded during the war with Tipu Sultan in the late eighteenth century.[9] The records say that Lieutenant Colonel Read was "directed to take immediate measures for entering into engagements with these useful people [Banjaries]," and Read sent "a very clear and satisfactory report," that he "hoped to collect in about three months from the date of our engagements upward of fifty six thousand Benjarries [sic.] or dealers in grain on their own account, and that the number of carriers of grain who might be collected in that time would be also very considerable…"[10]

The large number of grain dealers mentioned in this record implies active grain transactions in the period. Banjaries, according to a contemporary record, were "the people…whose sole occupation is the dealing in grain upon their own account, and who find constant employ in supplying districts with that article, where it is scarce, from other where it abounds, large towns, and armies."[11] Notwithstanding the survival of the service exchange system in localities, large amounts of grain were extracted from within the mirasi system and passed into market transactions through the hands of these dealers and others.

Growth of colonial port towns offered stable markets for grain trade. As I have attempted to calculate on other occasions, the amount of grain trade

9 Most of the related correspondences on Banjary are compiled in "Measures adopted for securing the Assistance of the Benjarries" (1313, *Board's Collections*, Oriental and India Office Collections, British Library, F/4/59).

10 "Extract of Military Letter from Fort St. George, 2/1/1799" (1313, *Board's Collections*, Oriental and India Office Collections, British Library, F/4/59): Paragraphs 47–48.

11 "Extract of Fort St. George Military and Political Consultations, 4/12/1798" (1313, *Board's Collections*, Oriental and India Office Collections, British Library, F/4/59).

TABLE 5.3 *Grain transactions recorded in the diary of Ananda Ranga Pillai*

Date	Goods	Volume/Value	Produced at or coming from	Brought to/by	Buyer	Remarks
10.11.1747	Grain	500–600 Bullock-load	South of Ariyankuppam			Waiting over the river.
do.	Paddy	400 Garce	Gingee & Valudavur forts		Company	Going to buy if the price comes down.
28.11.1747	Paddy	300–400 Bullock-load		Market		Daily brought to the market.
2.12.1747	Paddy	400 Garce		Market	Company	Ordered to buy.
27. 1.1748	Wheat	50–60 Palla	Arcot and Lalapettai	A. Ayyan	Company	Ordered to buy.
2. 2.1748	Maize			Market		
14. 2.1748	Wheat	2000 Bags	Merchant of Madras		Company	
do.	Wheat	2857 Rupees	Cuddapah	M. Lucas	Company	Written not to buy any more.
16. 2.1748	Paddy	40 Bullock-load			Priest	The buyer paid no dues.
do.	Paddy	300 Bullock-load		Market		
do.	Paddy	40–50 Garce	Out-villages		Company	Brought to the Company till today.
20. 2.1748	Paddy	500 Bullock-load		Market		
21. 2.1748	Paddy	725 Bullock-load		Market		
do.	Rice	57 Bullock-load		Market		
23. 2.1748	Paddy	454 Bullock-load		Market		
do.	Rice	53 Bullock-load		do.		
do.	Cumbu	73 Bullock-load		do.		
24. 2.1748	Paddy	610 Bullock-load		Market		

TABLE 5.3 *Grain transactions recorded in the diary of Ananda Ranga Pillai* (cont.)

Date	Goods	Volume/Value	Produced at or coming from	Brought to/by	Buyer	Remarks
26. 2.1748	Paddy	36 Garce	Out-villages		Company	Brought to the Company till today.
5. 3.1748	Paddy	785 Bullock-load		Market		
do.	Sugar	12 Bullock-load		do.		
do.	Sugar	12 Packages		do.		
6. 3.1748	Paddy	6–7 Garce		Market		Sold yesterday and today.
do.	Paddy	100 Garce	Out-villages			Stocked by the Company till today.
do.		20–25 Garce	Alisapakkam	Market		
do.		30–34 Garce	Northward	Market		
do.		27–30 Garce				Already stocked by the Company.
do.		190–200 Garce				
10. 3.1748	Paddy	700–900 Bullock-load		Market		
16. 3.1748	Paddy	940 Bullock-load		Market		
22. 3.1748	Paddy			M. Mudali	Company	To be given to the Company as pledge.
do.	Paddy	100 Garce	Out-villages (?)		Company	Brought to the Company till today.
do.	Paddy	500–600 Garce	Utramallur, Salavakkam			Ordered to buy for the Company.
23. 3.1748	Paddy	1257 Bullock-load		Market		
13. 8.1748	Paddy	0				No arrival.
16. 8.1748	Paddy	20 Bullock-load		Market		New arrival.
18. 8.1748	Paddy	10 Bullock-load		Market		
do.	Rice	11 Bullock-load		Market		

do.	Rice	4 Bullock-load	Arcot	Coja Sultan		Permissions sought to bring in rice.
7. 9.1748	Paddy	6 Garce	Country	A.R. Pillai	Company	
6.10.1748	Paddy	8 Garce 415 vallam	Out-villages		Company	
22.10.1748	Paddy		Villupuram			Ordered to buy as there was no stock.
do.	Paddy	300–400 Garce				Ordered to procure from somewhere.
18.11.1748	Paddy	400 Bullock-load		Market		Brought in till noon.
19.11.1748	Paddy	468 Bullock-load		Market		Brought in yesterday.
do.	Rice	24 Bullock-load		do.		do.
do.	Horse-gram	23 Bullock-load		do.		do.
do.	Cumbu	8 Bullock-load		do.		do.
do.	Castor	17 Bullock-load		do.		do.
do.	Ragi	5 Bullock-load		do.		do.
do.	Ghee	23 Duppers		do.		do.
do.	Nut	2 Bales		do.		do.
do.	Paddy	200 Bullock-load		Market		Brought in from dawn to 11 a.m.

SOURCE: *THE PRIVATE DIARY OF ANANDA RANGA PILLAI*, TRANSLATED AND EDITED BY J.F. PRICE AND K. RANGACHARI, 12 VOLS. (MADRAS: GOVERNMENT PRESS, 1904–1928; REPRINT, NEW DELHI: ASIAN EDUCATIONAL SERVICES, 1985).

Notes:
Out-village – suburban villages near Pondicherry
Market – Pondicherry market

between Madras or Pondicherry and their respective hinterlands in the eighteenth century was considerable.[12] The population of Madras in the mid-eighteenth century may be estimated around 150,000 and that of Pondicherry 50,000,[13] while the value of the grain trade probably amounted to between two and three million rupees for Madras and one million rupees for Pondicherry.[14]

The participation of European commercial powers in the textile trade, the influx of bullion, the population growth in port towns, and the growth of grain trade between port towns and hinterlands all enhanced the integrity of the regional economy. That integrity embodied the structural relationship between ports and hinterlands. While the interior became hinterlands to supply grain and migrants to port towns, leading colonial port towns became politico-economic centers, enforcing hegemonic control over hinterlands.

Incidentally, the deepening integrity transformed the mirasi system that had functioned as the fundamental economic system for centuries.

Finally, we will examine the transformation process in the hinterlands.

Transformation of the Hinterland

The development of textile trade from the seventeenth century onwards gradually transformed the social structure of hinterlands in several ways. Firstly, there was urbanization. Not only port towns but also hinterlands experienced a certain degree of urbanization, although not to the extent of Madras and other port towns. Merchants and weavers did migrate to port towns, but the majority remained in the interior or moved to local textile centers in the proximity of cotton producing areas. However, these centers in the interior were

12 T. Mizushima, "Globaler Handel und binnenwirtschaftliche Entwicklung. Südindische Hafenstädte in der vorkolonialen Zeit," *Hamburger Wirtschafts-Chronik*, Neue Folge, Band 7 (2007/2008), pp. 117–50.

13 There are a good number of estimates of the urban population in the colonial port towns. As to Madras and Pondicherry, see, for instances, Susan M. Neild, "Colonial Urbanism: The Development of Madras City in the Eighteenth and Nineteenth Centuries," *Modern Asian Studies*, 13, 2 (1979), p. 227; N.S. Ramaswami, *The Founding of Madras* (New Delhi: Orient Longman, 1977), pp. 55, 57; H.D. Love, *Vestiges of Old Madras, 1640–1800* (London: Govt. of India, 1913), vol. 1, p. 547; Om Prakash, *The New Cambridge History of India; Vol. 2. Part 5*, p. 148; J.F. Richards, "European City-States on the Coromandel Coast," in P.M. Joshi and M.A. Nayeem (eds.), *Studies in the Foreign Relations of India* (Hyderabad: State Archives, Government of Andhra Pradesh, 1975), p. 514; Catherine Manning, *Fortunes a Faire: The French in Asian Trade, 1719–48* (Aldershot, UK: Variorum, 1996), p. 51.

14 Mizushima, "Globaler…," op. cit.

connected and integrated with port towns through commodity chains of bullion, textiles, and grain. Until the end of the eighteenth century, these chains were maintained by Indian merchants, who often moved to colonial ports. Ananda Ranga Pillai, for instance, was based in Pondicherry, but had branches in Arcot, Lalapettai, Tanjavur, Porto Novo and other towns in the interior, dealing in cotton threads, cotton cloth, opium, areca nut, and English broad cloth, for example.[15]

Through caste and community networks, leading merchants transacted commodities between the interior and colonial port towns. As we mentioned, some of them had jointly invested in overseas trade with servants of the European East India Companies.[16]

Relationships between local towns, on the other hand, became disjointed or reorganized in response to geo-spatial changes centralized on colonial port towns. Each locality was assigned a number of specific roles, according to European commercial interests, and was organized in pyramidal order, with colonial port towns at the top.

The transformation in the interior did not end within the economic sphere. An emerging new social order – the top of which was now occupied not by traditionally high castes, but by Europeans or Indian upstarts in port towns – also transformed the pre-existent social order. Indian merchants, for instance, used to have autonomy and settled disputes among the Indian residents by a meeting of influential Indians.[17] Later, when the Indian communities became more dependent upon Europeans for finance and markets, disputes were often brought before European Governors or other high officials in port towns for settlement.[18]

Disruption of the social norm and order, as well as anxiety about one's social position in the new colonial towns, was often reflected in so-called right-hand/left-hand conflicts during the period.[19] An interesting phenomenon related to

---

15 See, for instances, the entries in the following dates. 15/5/1740, 29/12/1740, 11/10/1746, 3/5/1747, 16/6/1746, and 3/7/1748. *The Private Diary of Ananda Ranga Pillai*, trans. and eds. J.F. Price and K. Rangachari, 12 vols. (Madras: Government Press, 1904–1928; reprint, New Delhi: Asian Educational Services, 1985).

16 *Ibid.*, 6/8/1746, 24/10/1746, 1/11/1746, 9/7/1748, 4/10/1748, 18/3/1750, 19/6/1750, 30/6/1752.

17 They were called *mahajan* or *mahanattar* in Pondicherry.

18 T. Mizushima, "Nattars in Pondicherry in Mid-Eighteenth Century," in *Proceedings of the International Conference-Seminar of Tamil Studies*, vol. 2 (Madras: Kalakshetra Publications Press, 1981), pp. 14.37–14.48.

19 As to the right-hand and left-hand conflicts, see, for instances, A. Appadurai, "Right and Left Hand Castes in South India," *Indian Economic and Social History Review*, 11, 2 & 3

this was the frequent occurrence of similar types of right-hand/left-hand conflict, even in the interior. The deepening integrity with port towns certainly had a similar high impact on people's lives in the interior.

Another related change in hinterlands was their closer linkage with the trend of cash wages and commodity prices of port towns. The cash economy and new employment relations responding to requirements from overseas markets became a norm, which slowly penetrated into the subsistence economy in the hinterland. Cultivators in the interior began responding to fluctuations in demand and prices in port towns, changing their crops accordingly. In the course of this development, people became more involved in commodity transactions

Of the many recipients of shares in the mirasi system, the *mirasidar* class secured a much higher proportion. Mirasidars were those thought to be descendants of the first settlers or conquerors of the area. There were mirasidars in almost every village in the Tamil country in the late eighteenth century. Jagir counted a total of 9,499 mirasidars in around 2,200 villages.[20] They generally belonged to either Brahmin or Mudaliar communities. There were also, however, many mirasidars belonging to other communities. They had undisputed claims on all the resources in the localities, ranging from pastoral right to forest entry. The proportion they received of the entire produce in the locality is not clear from contemporary village records, but it was most probably around one tenth.[21] They were the core class, which maintained the socio-economic order in the mirasi system in the locality.

(1974), pp. 216–259; B.E.F. Beck, *Peasant Society in Konku : A Study of Right and Left Sub-Castes in South India* (Vancouver: University of British Columbia Press, 1972).

20 "Abstract State of the Number of Meerassee Shares and of Meerassee Holders in the Several Districts of the Jagheer in Fusly 1207 shewing also the Quantity of Meerassee unclaimed & occupied by Pyacarries" (2,115–2,116, *Board's Collections*, Oriental and India Office Collections, British Library, F/4/112).

21 Revenue records during the period paid attention to the divisional proportion only between the state and localities. As mirasidars secured their share privately from the rest of the cultivators in the locality and their share was of a private nature, it is difficult to find evidence of them. One tenth was usually the share collected by the *zamindars*, *nattars* (leading representatives of the locality), and other lords. See, for instances, T. Mizushima, "From Mirasidar to Pattadar: South India in the Late Nineteenth Century," *Indian Economic and Social History Review*, 39, 2 & 3 (2002), pp. 259–284; id., *Nattar and the Socio-Economic Change in South India in the 18th-19th Centuries*, Study of Languages and Cultures of Asia and Africa, Monograph Series No.19 (Tokyo: Institute for the Study of Language and Cultures in Asia and Africa, Tokyo University of Foreign Studies, 1986), p. 71.

The mirasidar class also played an important role in rural-urban commodity transactions. They, as mentioned above, threw their surplus produce into the grain market, which was often connected with colonial port towns. They must also have been the core class constituting the consumer market for Indian textiles in the hinterland. Textiles purchased by mirasidars were distributed among other subordinate classes in the locality as gifts at festivals and other occasions.[22]

Significant for the mirasi system during this period is that some mirasidars started breaking away from the system. Their deepening involvement in the market economy even made them abandon the centuries-old reproduction system based upon the service exchange relationship among local members. Mirasidars now sought a shift from the share distribution system to a more individual control over resources. For a more efficient functioning of their control over local resources, the socio-economic entity of the local society needed to be divided into individual villages under their respective control.

Against this backdrop, a number of sale and mortgage transactions of mirasidar shares took place in the eighteenth century. Compiled from the *Barnard Report*, Table 5.4 shows the cases in the Ponneri area in the Jagir, and demonstrates that transactions took place across caste communities and localities. We can find considerable numbers of similar transactions in other areas over our period, symbolizing the collapse not only of the mirasi system but also of local societies, which were increasingly involved in developing commodity transactions. Hinterlands evidently underwent an overall transformation in the early modern period.

Conclusion: Colonial Social Structure

This paper has attempted to assess the impact of the development of colonial port towns upon the indigenous structure of the interior, and examined the interior's placement in the position of hinterland. This process was in parallel with the colonization of Indian society in the decades to come.

Among the many features of transformation experienced, it was probably the deprivation of social 'security' that affected people's lives most. In the Indian agrarian economy, where there was a recurrent excessive shortage of

22 It is known that new cloth was distributed by landlords as a gift to their agricultural laborers at the time of *Pongal* or the festival of the new harvest. The Tamilnadu state government has continued the custom of distributing new cloth at Pongal up to today.

TABLE 5.4 *Transactions of Mirasidar Share in Ponneri recorded in the Barnard report*

Barnard report (Page No.)	Village name	Location (Map code)	Description of transaction
Ponneri-014	Coommungalum	Ponneri-115B	Ancient landholders Palli, from whom Chettis purchased the landholdership. And from the Chettis Tuliva Vellaler purchased. Thus changeable shares 5 Fixed
Ponneri-018	Kistnaporum	Ponneri-115A	Ancient landholders are Palli, from whom the Chettis purchased the landholdership. And from whom bought Tuliva Vellaler who are landholders now.
Ponneri-040	Woppalum	Ponneri-152C	1. Kanamaula Vencaten's share purchased by Andeappean residing at Coodvary [?], 1. Rahaviah have one [unreadable] residing at Chennacavanum [Ponneri-157A], 2. Sooriya Sola & c. residing at Coommungalum [Ponneri-115B]
Ponneri-122	Tottacaud	Ponneri-052A	Kondaikatti Vellala of Nuthvoil [Ponneri-051A] who mortgaged their village to Nunda Gopauler.
Ponneri-128	Poolidarvacum	Ponneri-045B	Kondaikatti Vellalars 3, Cowkeepers bought Share 1
Ponneri-154	Naithvoil	Unidentified	Kondaikatti Vellaler, Nunda Gopauler who bought landholdership
Ponneri-160	Ennoor	Ponneri-044A	Landholder resides at Poolidavacum [Ponneri-045B] & Auttypade [Ponneri-043A]. Kondaikatti Vellaler landholder & cowkeeper who purchased landholdership: Kondaikatti Vellaler – 6, Kondaikatti Vellaler purchased from above landholders – 5, Cowkeeper purchased from above landholders – 1
Ponneri-252	Cunacumbacum	Ponneri-145A	Gentoo Bramin, Vishnu Bramins, share 30. Rakeapa Mudali purchased the landholdership, share 2.
Ponneri-254	Tirooparoo	Ponneri-143K	Gentoo Bramins of Cunasumpacum [Ponneri-145A]. Arsoor [Ponneri-183A] Vencatachel Modaly purchased part of land & has taken for mortgage the other part of land from Gentoo Brahmin landholders of Tirooparoo [Ponneri-143K].

Ponneri-264	Codypullum	Ponneri-016A	Kavarais who purchased landholdership
Ponneri-266	Mahafoose Cawn Petta	Ponneri-035A	Nabob Mahafoose Cawn purchased landholdership from Condighetty Vellaler landholder
Ponneri-268	Chinnamullavoil	Ponneri-037A	Kavarai landholders of Codepullom [Ponneri-016A], Kavarai Cooppe Chetti who purchased landholdership
Ponneri-270	Parymullavoil	Ponneri-037C	Gentoo Bramin landholders of unknown place, another Gentoo Bramin residing at Garacanbacum [?] & Ragooputy Pandit Stul Mojumdar residing at Ponary [Ponneri-115C], Vengamrajah Niyogee residing at Aroomunda [Ponneri-017A] (who purchased landholdership)
Ponneri-302	Soorapade	Ponneri-029A	Kondaikatti Vellaler landholders, from whom purchased the landholdership by Luchumajee Pundit of Ponary [Ponneri-115C]

SOURCE: *JAGHIRE – BARNARD'S SURVEY ACCOUNTS OF PONNARY* (VOL. 68).

Notes:

1. [?] – Location not identified
2. The spellings of the personal and caste names in the description of transactions are original.
3. Map Code is prepared from the 1971 Census village code. Village names are identified with the hamlet names recorded in the topographical map prepared in the 1960s and 1970s. Where there are more than two hamlets in a Census village, an alphabetical suffix is added to each hamlet at random.
4. landholder – mirasidar, landholdership – mirasidar share

resources, the share distribution of local produce under the mirasi system functioned as a kind of social security, especially in times of famine. In the mirasi system, the interests of the residents as well as the state were negotiated by adjusting proportional shares among recipients. A similar situation could be observed in the textile industry. Textile workers usually had intermediaries, such as head weavers, brokers, and merchants, who mediated for them with the market. As the colonial economy developed, however, these 'safety valves', or whatever exploitative features could be observed among them, disappeared. The Raiyatwari system, for instance, entirely broke up not only local societies but also villages into an assemblage of individual land lots held by respective raiyats or landholders. The close relationship between local members, maintained through the service exchange system, was also destroyed at the time of Raiyatwari settlement, when the notion of 'shares in the whole produce' disappeared with the abolishment of shares. The colonial government also tried to establish control over textile producers by sending their own agents directly in the late eighteenth century.[23]

Face-to-face contacts between the British colonial power and Indian producers through the colonial land system created extremely unbalanced relations between rulers and ruled. The establishment of the leading colonial port town as the colonial capital, having political, economic, and social hegemony over hinterlands, progressed in parallel, seriously aggravating the unbalanced relations. As in many other Asian countries, the historical development of relations between colonial port towns and hinterlands was the development of colonial history itself.[24]

---

23 S. Arasaratnam, "Weavers, Merchants and Company: The Handloom Industry in Southeastern India 1750–1790," in S. Subrahmanyam (ed.), *Merchants, Markets and the State in Early Modern India* (Delhi: Oxford University Press, 1990), pp. 204–212; Prasannan Parthasarathi, *The Transition to a Colonial Economy: Weavers, Merchants and Kings in South India, 1720–1800*, (Cambridge: Cambridge University Press, 2001), pp. 5–6.

24 A similar view is discussed by Robert J. Ross and Gerard J. Telkamp, "Introduction," in Robert J. Ross and Gerard J. Telkamp (eds.), *Colonial Cities* (Dordrecht: Martinus Nijhoff Publishers, 1985), pp. 1–6.

CHAPTER 6

Maritime Asian Trade and Colonization of Penang, c. 1786–1830

Tomotaka Kawamura

Introduction

Southeast Asia and especially the Indonesian archipelago had long been an important transit zone for trade, culture and religion.[1] The region was a frontier zone, where spices and exotic products had been procured by Muslim, Hindu, Malay and Chinese merchants long before direct European contacts. Since the sixteenth century, Europeans had also paid much attention to trading and the cultural world of Southeast Asia, founding the chartered companies in attempts to monopolize the East India trade. In the late eighteenth century, Britain came to dominate maritime Southeast Asia more than any other European imperial power. In 1786, acting as an agent for the English East India Company (hereafter, EIC), Francis Light occupied the small island of Penang (named Prince of Wales Island) on the western edge of the Archipelago. Georgetown became the most prosperous port city on the island. Occupation of Penang by the EIC could be seen as a harbinger of Britain's growing empire in the Indonesian Archipelago and along the China coast.

This essay examines the socio-economic conditions of early Penang. It analyzes the characteristics of maritime trade, population, internal improvements, and agricultural cultivation between 1786 and 1820. The study goal is to assess the extent to which the economic development of Penang's hinterland was correlated with the expansion of its maritime trade during this period. Studies of the European presence in Southeast Asia are used to consider the early history of Penang. Generally speaking, it has long been argued that British expansion in Southeast Asia was shaped by (a) world-wide expansion of British commercial/industrial capitalism, (b) prosperity in British India, (c) opportunities presented by China and (d) international, particularly Anglo-French, competition in the nineteenth century.[2] Christopher Bayly's original viewpoint,

---

1 C.A. Bayly, *Imperial Meridian: The British Empire and the World, 1780–1830* (Harlow: Longman, 1989), p. 63.

2 D.R. SarDesai, *British Trade and Expansion in Southeast Asia, 1830–1914* (New Delhi: Allied, 1977); A.J. Stockwell, "British Expansion and Rule in South-East Asia," in Wm. Roger Louis

© KONINKLIJKE BRILL NV, LEIDEN, 2015 | DOI 10.1163/9789004283909_008

on the other hand, stresses turbulence in Muslim Asia, as well as the growth of the intercontinental spice trade, which attracted European (especially British) aggressive intervention in Southeast Asian economics and politics during the eighteenth century.[3] From this global viewpoint, it could be argued that Penang was acquired principally as a trading center and naval base for the protection of Britain's China trade. In the mid-1790s, French invasion of the Low Countries gave substance to the threat that the French might seize Dutch possessions in Southeast Asia. The British occupied the Dutch Moluccas and the port of Malacca in 1795. In 1800, Britain purchased Province Wellesley, a tract of land on the Peninsula opposite Penang, from Kedah. Malacca returned to Dutch possession in 1818, but was again administrated by Britain in 1824. Penang, Malacca and Singapore were integrated in 1826 and became known collectively by the name Straits Settlements. They were administrated under the control of the Bengal Governor in Calcutta.

Studies of Southeast Asia's maritime history are also required for a balanced view. Anthony Reid stresses an era between 1740 and 1840 as the so-called 'Chinese century', for example, with expanding Chinese junk trade and migration, notwithstanding firm establishment of European dominance in the region.[4] This period marked a major increase in the tempo of commerce throughout Southeast Asia, largely influenced (especially on the mainland) by economic growth in China. From the late eighteenth century onwards, Southeast Asia saw an increase in Chinese shipping in Southeast Asian waters; a growing influx of Chinese migrants; an increase in Chinese settlements, trading networks and Chinese trade; vigorous Chinese involvement in agriculture, mining and revenue farms, and an increase in the Chinese population in many port towns and their hinterlands. At the same time, the long coastline of southern Indochina and Siam was a major element in this moment of dynamic Southeast Asian economic growth and state building. Studies of the 'Chinese century' are closely related to the so-called 'intra-Asian trade' thesis by Kaoru

(editor-in-chief), *The Oxford History of the British Empire,* Vol. III: Andrew Porter (ed.), *The Nineteenth Century*, (Oxford: Oxford University Press, 1999), pp. 372–375.

3 Bayly, *Imperial Meridian*, p. 64.

4 Anthony Reid, "Chinese Trade and Southeast Asian Economic Expansion in the Later Eighteenth and Nineteenth Centuries: An Overview," in Nola Cooke and Li Tana (eds.), *Water Frontier: Commerce and the Chinese in the Lower Mekong, 1750–1880* (Lanham: Rowman & Littlefield Publishers, 2004), pp. 21–34; Leonard Blusse and F.S. Gaastra (eds.), *On the Eighteenth Century as a Category of Asian History: Van Leur in Retrospect* (Aldershot and Brookfield: Ashgate, 1998); Anthony Reid and Radin Fernando, "Shipping on Melaka and Singapore as an Index of Growth, 1760–1840," *South Asia*, 19 (1996), pp. 80–82.

Sugihara, Takeshi Hamashita and other Japanese scholars.[5] Sugihara promotes the interesting argument that intra-regional trade in early nineteenth-century Asia, less directly affected by the Western impact, should be granted far deeper consideration.[6] He also points out that Penang acted as a center for long-distance and regional trade in the Bay of Bengal until the 1820s.

In such a context, this essay provides a new explanation for developments in early Penang. Drawing upon recent research and a number of archival sources, I address three key issues. Firstly: How can the trade and society of early Penang be characterized? Secondly: How important was Penang's role in maritime Asia during the long eighteenth century? And, thirdly: To what extent can the growth of Asian maritime trade be related to Penang's colonization? This essay attempts to assess Penang's importance for Britain's growing empire in Southeast Asia and along the China coast, as well as for the development of Asian maritime trade.

Penang's Maritime Trade

According to the Cain and Hopkins thesis, the EIC was originally seen as an impressive overseas manifestation of an alliance between land and finance (so-called 'gentlemanly capitalism') during the eighteenth and early nineteenth centuries. The EIC became a vehicle for London-based merchants and financiers, however, rather than provincial British manufactures and industrialists. It has been suggested that the EIC's principle and purpose was to promote British imperial expansion in India, Southeast Asia and the Far East.[7] Consequently, one reason the EIC acquired Penang was to develop British trade and finance in Asia, with linkage to the city's interests, especially via the

---

5 Kaoru Sugihara, *Ajiakan Boueki no Keisei to Kozo* [The Formation and Structure of Intra-Asian Trade] (Kyoto: Mineruva Shobo, 1996); Takeshi Hamashita, *Hon Kon: Ajia no Nettowaku-Toshi* [Hong Kong: A Network-City of Asia] (Tokyo: Chikuma Shobo, 1996).

6 Kaoru Sugihara, "19 Seiki Zenhan no Ajia Koekiken: Tokeitekikousatu [Intra-Asian Trade in the First Half of the Nineteenth Century: A Statistic Inquire]," in Naoto Kagotani and Kohei Wakimura (eds.), *Teikoku to Ajia Nettowaku, Choki no 19 Seiki* [Empire and Asian Network: The Long Nineteenth Century], (Kyoto: Sekai Shisosha, 2009), pp. 250–281.

7 P.J. Cain and A.G. Hopkins, *British Imperialism, 1688–2000* (Harlow: Pearson Education, 2nd edn. 2002), pp. 278–284. See also the excellent works: Anthony Webster, *Gentlemen Capitalists: British Imperialism in South East Asia 1770–1890* (London: Tauris Academic Studies, 1998), especially chapters 2 and 3; Anthony Webster, *The Twilight of the East India Company: The Evolution of Anglo-Asian Commerce and Politics 1790–1860* (Woodbridge: Boydell Press, 2009).

city's rapidly-expanding China trade and intra-Asian country trade between the late eighteenth and early nineteenth centuries. The need for a naval station in the Straits of Malacca as protection against other European powers during wartime became paramount to Britain's imperial presence in maritime Asia. A more central issue, however, was that the EIC expected Penang (and later Singapore) to become a great trading centre for collecting produce from the Malay Peninsula and eastern archipelago for shipment to China. The Straits Settlements (Penang, Malacca and Singapore) certainly witnessed a remarkable growth in trade throughout the nineteenth century.

The Straits Settlements were influenced by transit trade motives, and were essentially centers of exchange. Their prosperity resulted from (1) their location on the great trade route through the Straits of Malacca, and (2) their system of free trade. The remarkable growth of Singapore's trade, in particular, depended upon free trade at the southern entrance to the Straits Settlement. Penang's free trade system was introduced between 1786 and 1802 and temporarily abandoned between 1803 and 1826, but then reintroduced in 1827. Exact statistical data for Penang's trade is difficult to find before 1850, but some contemporary reports[8] provide useful information. Figure 6.1 is based on Braddell's *Statistics*, for example, and roughly illustrates a long-term transition of trade in Penang between 1789 and 1840, in Singapore from 1824, and in Malacca between 1825 and 1834. Penang's trade was valued at 23,261 pounds sterling in 1789, 481,438 pounds sterling in 1806 and 1,106,924 pounds sterling in 1811. Figure 6.1 clearly shows that Penang's trade grew extremely rapidly between 1789 and 1811. Penang's steady increase in general trade ended between 1810 and 1816 (although 1816 showed improvement). Decline was prominent in 1817, but there was steady improvement in the period from 1818 to 1822. Penang's trade can, to some extent, be compared with Singapore's trade from 1824 in Figure 6.1 (except for the years 1827–28 and 1830). The value of Singapore's trade already exceeded that of Penang's by 1824, and Singapore's lead widened at an increasing rate, with occasional declines. As Cowan suggested, however, Singapore's development did not result in a decline in Penang's trade. By the late 1820s, there was a division of trade areas between Singapore and Penang.[9]

---

8 T. Braddell, *Statistics of the Population, Commerce, Agriculture, Revenue and Government Establishments of the British Settlements in the Straits of Malacca* (Pinang: Gazette Printing Office, 1861); T.J. Newbold, with an introduction by C.M. Turnbull, *Political and Statistical Account of the British Settlements in the Straits of Malacca (1839)* (Oxford: Oxford University Press, 1971).

9 C.D. Cowan, "Early Penang and the rise of Singapore, 1805–1832," *Journal of the Malayan Branch of the Royal Asiatic Society*, 23, 2 (1950), pp. 11–12.

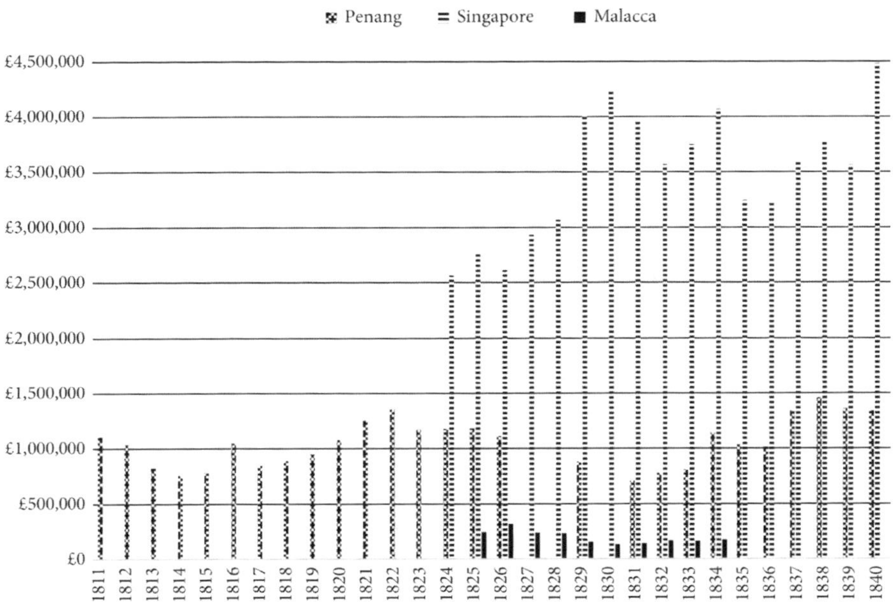

FIGURE 6.1 *Value of trade of Penang, Malacca and Singapore, 1789–1840*
SOURCE: T. BRADDELL, *STATISTICS OF THE POPULATION, COMMERCE, AGRICULTURE, REVENUE AND GOVERNMENT ESTABLISHMENTS OF THE BRITISH SETTLEMENTS IN THE STRAITS OF MALACCA* (PINANG: GAZETTE PRINTING OFFICE, 1861).

The Straits Settlements Factory Records (SSFR) offer detailed information on ships calling at Penang at the end of the eighteenth century. Figures 6.2, 6.3 and 6.4 are based on the SSFR. One finding is that, between 1786 and 1802, there was a steady increase in the total number of ships coming to Penang (Figure 6.2), the great majority of which were British. Note, however, that the number (other European/American and Asian ships) also increased at the beginning of the eighteenth century. The number of other European ships (mostly Portuguese and Dutch) did not grow so rapidly in that period. It was rather Asian ships, such as Malay, Indian, Moorish and Arab vessels, that steadily increased in number. Broadly speaking, British ships connected Penang to Bengal, Pedir, Malacca, China, Bombay, Junk Ceylon, Madras, Aceh, Selangor, Rangoon, Kedah, Macao and other Straits ports. Other European/American vessels were connected to Macao, Malacca, Bengal, Madras, Pegu, Pedir and other Straits ports. Small Asian ships connected local maritime networks with Kedah, Nagore, Malacca, Bengal and other Indian and Straits ports.

Alternatively, Penang's trade between 1788 and 1792 could be classified by regional categories, such as shipping to/from ports in the Indian subcontinent,

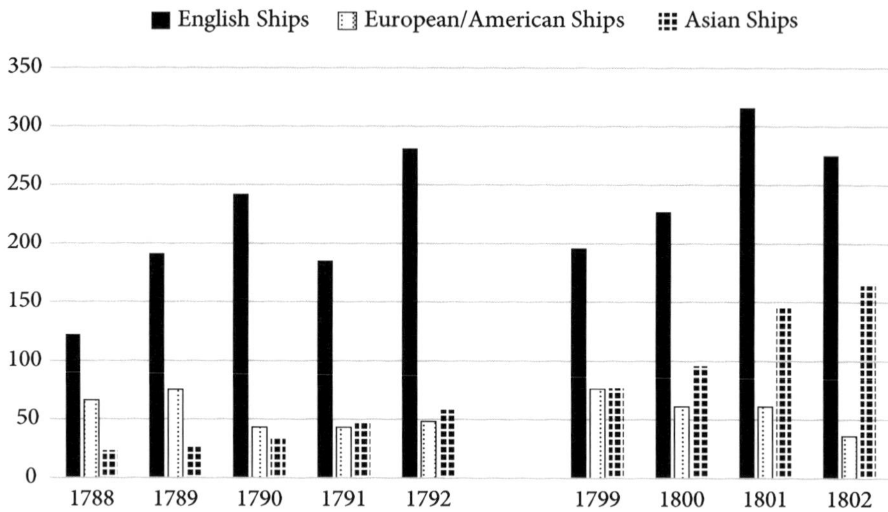

FIGURE 6.2 *Numbers of Ships incoming to Penang, 1786–1802*
SOURCES: SSFR, G/34/2-6; GEORGE LEITH, *A SHORT ACCOUNT OF THE SETTLEMENT, PRODUCE AND COMMERCE OF PRINCE OF WALES ISLAND IN THE STRAITS OF MALACCA* (LONDON: J. BOOTH, 1805), PP. 89–90.

the East coast of the Bay of Bengal, the Straits of Malacca, East Asia and other ports. Figure 6.3 illustrates the geographical dimension of Penang's trade. Prominent among Penang's trading partners were various Asian ports and regions, especially ports in the Indian subcontinent, the East coast of the Bay of Bengal and the Straits of Malacca.[10] Trading linkages with East Asia were important, but not relatively strong. Interestingly, Penang did not trade directly with England. Thus, Penang's trading world covered a vast maritime region surrounding the northern entrance of the Straits of Malacca, and also served to interconnect the Bay of Bengal with the South China Sea by means of the Straits.

Characteristics of Penang's trade in the 1780s–1790s are seen even in the late 1820s. The geography of Penang's trade in 1828/29 is reflected in Figure 6.4. It could be argued that Indian ports were Penang's most prominent trading partners, followed by Southeast Asian ports and regions. China was a significant trading partner for Penang exports, while there was far less trade with England. Close relations between Penang and Aceh emerged in this period. Indian cloth was re-exported by Penang to surrounding ports in the Straits of Malacca, and

10 See also S. Arasaratnam, *Maritime Commerce and English Power: Southeast India 1750–1800* (New Delhi: Sterling Publishers Private Ltd., 1996), p. 263.

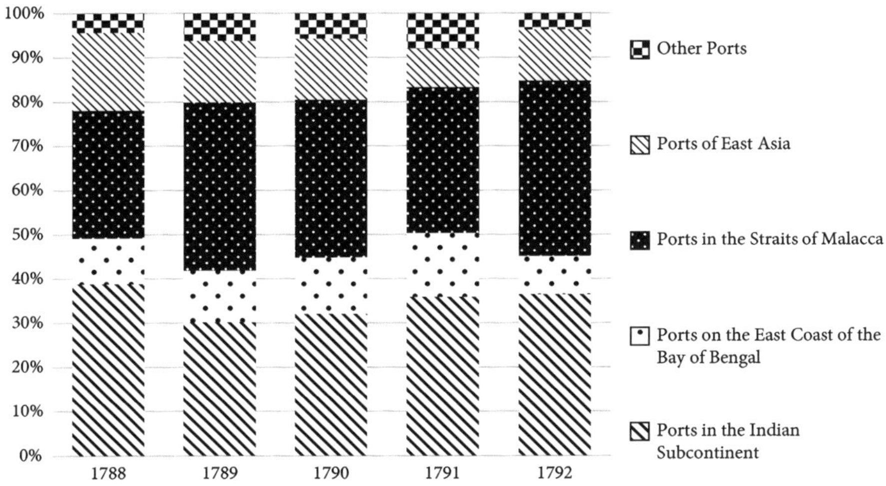

FIGURE 6.3 *Geographical pattern of Penang's trade, 1788–92*
SOURCE: SSFR, G/34/2-6

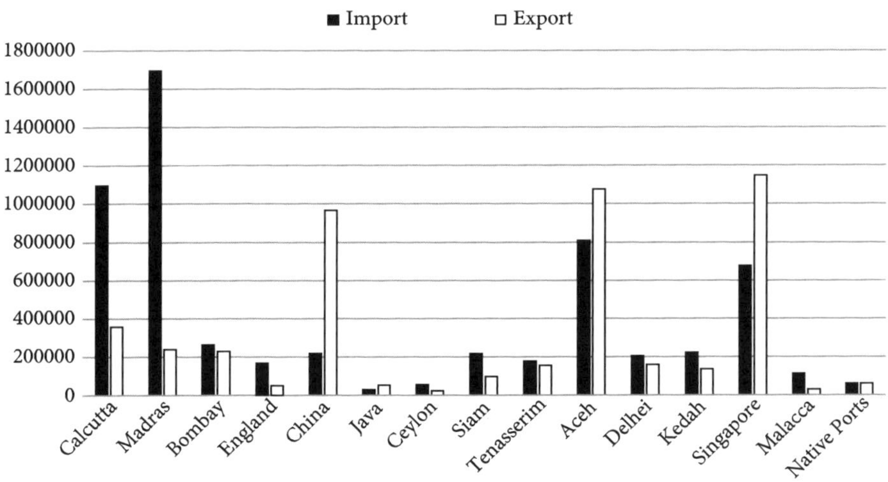

FIGURE 6.4 *Trade of Penang, 1828/29* (*Sicca Rupee*)
SOURCE: SSFR, G/34/162

large quantities of Indian piece goods and opium went to Aceh. The bulk of pepper and betel nuts was imported to Penang from Aceh and the neighboring west coast of Sumatra, brought entirely by native traders in their own boats. As Nordin Hussin points out, Aceh was very important to Penang's maritime prosperity.[11] That is, intra-Asian regional trade developed under the impact of British imperial power. In addition to Aceh, Singapore (founded in 1819) contributed significantly to the growth of Penang's regional trade in the Straits of Malacca. Penang's exports to Singapore mainly comprised India piece goods, which were counterbalanced by imports of British piece goods, sticklacs, sundries and other articles. These commodities were also re-exported from Penang to close neighbors, including Aceh.

The composition of Penang's commodity trade between 1809 and 1818 is shown in Figure 6.5. Indian articles (mainly cloth), opium and Malay tin comprised the major imports to and exports from Penang. Opium and Indian cloth entered Penang via British country traders and Indian long-distance merchants. Re-exported items were vital to merchants in Penang, as they had to find useful commodities to exchange for Chinese tea via British trade with Canton. Tin, mostly from the Malay Peninsula, was brought by Malay or Bugis traders. Table 6.1 shows that, even in the late 1820s, India piece goods, especially Indian cloth, opium and pepper, remained Penang's principal imports and exports. As exports consisted mostly of re-exports, Penang served as an important collection and distribution center for the north-western part of the Archipelago. Penang's trade commodities remained unchanged during the early nineteenth century, as Penang collected and distributed various commodities from Britain, India, the Malay Peninsula, the Archipelago and China. Indian goods, such as India piece goods and opium, were the chief commodities traded by British country traders and Indian merchants.

Population Increase

The Crawfurd's *Journal* of 1828 indicated that "when the English took possession of Penang in 1786, it was wholly uncultivated, and had no other inhabitants than a few occasional Malayan fishermen."[12] There were only 158 Malay settlers living on the island in 1786,[13] but from that year onwards, the almost uninhabited island swiftly began to attract a steady stream of settlers seeking their fortunes under EIC rule. Table 6.2 shows the total population of Penang between 1788 and 1833. This was 1,283 in 1789, 10,310 in 1801 and 13,885 in 1810.

11 Nordin Hussin, *Trade and Society in the Straits of Malacca: Dutch Melaka and English Penang, 1780–1830* (Singapore: NUS Press, 2007), pp. 92–93.

12 John Crawfurd, *Journal of an Embassy to the Courts of Siam and Cochin China* (London: Henry Colburn, 1st edn., 1828; reprint, London: Oxford University Press, 1967), p. 19.

13 Hussin, *Trade and Society*, p. 184.

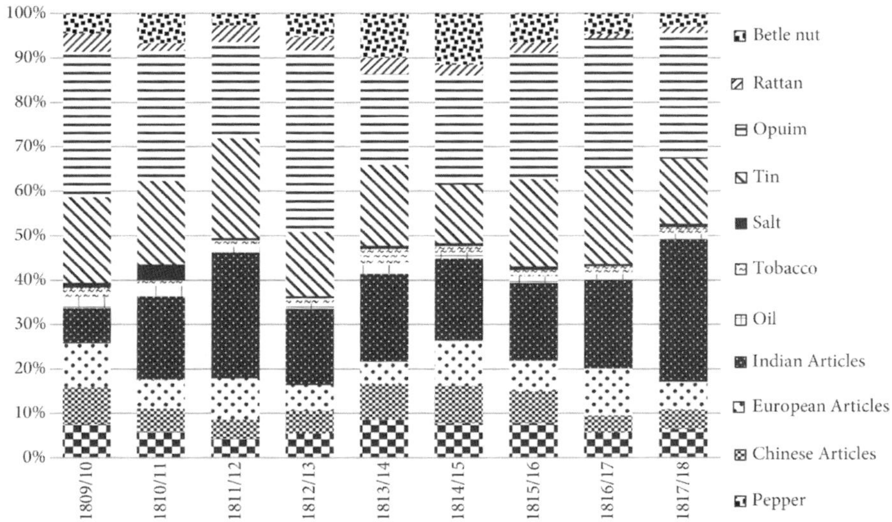

FIGURE 6.5 *Composition of commodities in Penang's trade, 1809/10–1817/18*
SOURCE: C.D. COWAN, "EARLY PENANG AND THE RISE OF SINGAPORE, 1805–1832," *JOURNAL OF THE MALAYAN BRANCH OF THE ROYAL ASIATIC SOCIETY*, 23, 2 (1950), P. 86.

TABLE 6.1 *Main commodities of Penang's trade (1828/29)*

Imported articles	%	Exported articles	%
India piece goods	34%	India piece goods	16%
Opium	14%	Opium	15%
Pepper & Spices	8%	Pepper & Spices	12%
Rice	7%	Betel nut	9%
Betel nut	5%	Tin	8%
British articles	4%	British piece goods	5%
Tobacco	3%	Bird nests	4%
Oil	2%	China sundries	3%
Tin	2%	Sticklac	3%
India sundries	2%	Beech de Mer	2%
Others	19%	Others	23%

SOURCE: SSFR, G/34/162

TABLE 6.2 *Total population (Penang)*

Year	Number
1788	1,283
1801	10,310
1805	14,000
1810	13,885
1822	51,207
1826	55,116
1828	60,551
1833	86,275

SOURCE: T.J. NEWBOLD, WITH AN INTRODUCTION BY C.M. TURNBULL, *POLITICAL AND STATISTICAL ACCOUNT OF THE BRITISH SETTLEMENTS IN THE STRAITS OF MALACCA (1839)* (OXFORD: OXFORD UNIVERSITY PRESS, 1971), PP. 54–55.

Since the population of Province Wellesley was included in census numbers from 1822, the total population of Penang surpassed 50,000 and subsequently reached 86,275 in 1833. Table 6.2 clearly shows that Penang experienced a rapid population increase between the late eighteenth century and the early nineteenth century.

Penang attracted immigrants from various places and regions in Asia, as shown in the EIC census on the composition of inhabitants. Categories of ethnic groups used in every census were roughly created on the basis of European knowledge, values and ideas, but to some extent those data reflect the nature of migrant societies in other colonial port towns in Asia. The 1788 population (Table 6.3) consisted of Europeans, Portuguese-Eurasians (descendants of Portuguese who had intermarried with Asians), Jawi-Pekans (a mixed race group of Muslim Indians and native Malays, Malays, and Chinese), with Jawi-Pekans/Malays and Chinese as the largest social groups.[14] The European population (mostly British) was always the smallest, and was an enclosed minority of the wealthiest elite. Malays arrived from throughout the Malay Peninsula, the island and Sumatra via Kedah to settle in Penang, including the Javanese, Bugis and Sumatrans. They lived mostly as paddy cultivators, wood cutters or workers clearing the jungle for spice cultivation in the island interior.[15]

14 Hussin, *Trade and Society*, pp. 185–186.

15 Hussin, *Trade and Society*, p. 307.

TABLE 6.3 *Census of Penang*

Census of 1788			Census of 1822		
Ethnic Groups	**Number**	**%**	**Ethnic Groups**	**Number**	**%**
Europeans*	19	1.48	Europeans*	400	2.9
Portuguese-Eurasians	197	15.35	Malays	3,367	24.43
Jawi-Pekans/Malays	530	41.3	Chinese	3,313	24.04
Chinese	537	41.85	Chulias	4,996	36.25
			Native Christians	763	5.53
			Achinese	60	0.43
			Bataks	294	2.13
			Bengalis	411	2.98
			Arabs	145	1.05
			Armenians	16	0.11
			Persians	11	0.07
			Cafferes (or Kafirs)*	4	0.02
Total	1,283	100	Total	13,781	100

* Not including Company servants

SOURCE: NORDIN HUSSIN, *TRADE AND SOCIETY IN THE STRAITS OF MALACCA: DUTCH MELAKA AND ENGLISH PENANG, 1780–1830* (SINGAPORE: NUS PRESS, 2007), PP. 185, 190.

In the 1788 census, the Chinese were identified as one of the largest groups of Penang society. Francis Light, founder of Penang, encouraged the immigration of the Chinese. Early arrivals were mostly merchants, traders and laborers from mainland China and Malacca, but the majority came from Kedah. They not only conducted long-distance trade but also practiced various occupations in towns and hinterland areas, including revenue farming, retail trade, handicrafts, agricultural planting and plantation laboring. Bazaar shops were principally kept by the Chinese. According to an 1822 report, of the Chinese from the two provinces of Canton and Fujian, three fourths of the former and roughly five sixths of the latter were unmarried young men.[16]

Ethnic Indian traders and merchants were among the earliest arrivals in Penang, the majority of whom had long been inhabitants of Kedah and Perlis. Other Indians soon joined them from such places as Prai, Selangor, Aceh, Borneo and India. Indian commercial immigrants, called 'Chooliar (Chulia)',

16 Crawfurd, *Journal of an Embassy*, p. 19.

came from a number of ports on the Coromandel Coast in South India, including Nagore, Negapatam, Porto Novo and Pondicherry.[17] The majority of Chulia were merchants, shopkeepers or coolies. A minority of Indian immigrants came from North India, mainly Bengalis, Parsis and Gujaratis, and were predominantly in the field of commerce, but the vast majority came from southern India. Nearly all Indian laborers and most petty traders came from South India. The number of Chulias rapidly increased and by 1822 they represented the largest ethnic group in Penang. The Malay group comprised 36.6% of the population, including Jawi-Pekans and Arabs, 24.4%, and Chinese, 24%.

Improvements to Georgetown

Georgetown was occupied in 1786 and named by Francis Light. It was expected to become a key port city on the island. Light decided to clear jungle at the point of arrival and constructed central thoroughfares converging on Fort Cornwallis, namely Light Street, Beach Street, Chulia Street and Pitt Street. Light had a small staff of around thirty, but a rapid increase in settlers required improvements and further geographical expansion of Georgetown.[18] Most inhabitants concentrated in the central town, and various groups were segregated according to ethnic living quarters. Europeans resided mainly in the northern part of Penang, especially near Fort Cornwallis. The majority of Chinese and Indians lived in the central business district, and most Malays lived in the southern part of the central business district.

The increasing flow of mixed immigrants into Georgetown caused administrative problems in the early days. Light realized the need to allot land to the settlers and the importance of providing policy to preserve the peace. After occupation of the island, Light's first public work was to sink a well at the head of Light Street, but no other amenities were provided for early settlers. Despite such a poor urban environment, by 1788 some two hundred houses had been built. Shop houses were built from palm roofs (*attap*), which created serious problems.[19] Georgetown inhabitants experienced three major fires in 1789, 1812 and 1814, for example, due to a lack of fire regulations, firefighting facilities and

17 Kernial Singh Sandhu, *Indians in Malaya: Some Aspects of their Immigration and Settlement (1786–1957)* (Cambridge: Cambridge University Press, 1969), p. 118.

18 F.G. Stevens, "A Contribution to the Early History of Prince of Wales' Island," *Journal of the Malayan Branch of the Royal Asiatic Society*, 7 (1929), pp. 389–390.

19 City Council of Georgetown, *Penang Past and Present 1786–1963: A Historical Account of the City of Georgetown since 1786* (Malaysia: Ganesh Printing Works, 1966), p. 1.

firemen.[20] Complaints were made about the expense and difficulty of procuring water for ships and, often, the bad quality of the water. Local governors, officers and residents realized the importance of access to safe, clean water for daily consumption and for ships. Moreover, most inhabitants were crowded into an ill-drained, swampy area round the harbor. The town had a very poor drainage system at the time, which contributed to the spread of tropical diseases, such as malaria and cholera, in unhealthy living conditions. Many people died of fever, and Light himself was a malaria victim.[21]

It was extremely difficult to construct streets, roads and drains in the 'quagmire'.[22] The serious problem of water supply, especially for naval and merchant vessels, was brought to the fore during George Leith's administration (1800–04). Leith embarked upon a reconstruction of the water transport system, and proposed that a stream should be brought to the town via pipes from a large reservoir near the harbor.[23] His plan was successful, and water was supplied to residents and ships by means of pipes from this reservoir. Robert Farquhar, Governor of Penang (1804–05), was more concerned about improvements to other public works and the infrastructure of Penang.[24] He proposed administrative schemes for island defenses, naval docks and a marine yard, and he was keen to improve the island's economic infrastructure and its habitants' living conditions. Farquhar devised a new water and canal system, taking fresh water from the interior. As the population and local agriculture increased, main roads, in particular, were required to further expand from Georgetown into the island's interior.[25] It was believed that roads could link the town with the most fertile and cultivated areas of pepper, spices and other agricultural production. Farquhar stressed that the rapid upgrading of the economies of the town and the island necessitated investment in communications.

Demand for labor in Penang, however, continued to exceed supply. In 1787, the high price of labor in Penang prompted Francis Light to request Bengal to send one hundred coolies. This workforce shortage was partially offset by the employment of slaves, but this did not last. In addition, it was a difficult task

---

20 Hussin, *Trade and Society*, pp. 149–154.

21 City Council of Georgetown, *Penang Past and Present*, p. 4.

22 City Council of Georgetown, *Penang Past and Present*, p. 1.

23 George Leith, *A Short Account of the Settlement, Produce and Commerce of Prince of Wales Island in the Straits of Malacca* (London: J. Booth, 1805), pp. 42–44.

24 Anthony Webster, "British Expansion in South-East Asia and the Role of Robert Farquhar, Lieutenant-Governor of Penang, 1804–5," *Journal of Imperial and Commonwealth History*, 23, 1 (1995), pp. 1–25.

25 Stevens, "A Contribution," p. 399; City Council of Georgetown, *Penang Past and Present*, p. 6.

for the government to raise revenues in Penang, which was a free port. One of the few options was to sell revenue farms for industries such as opium, liquors and gambling. Government revenue farms were monopolized by the Chinese, and originated from stiff competition and conflict among the Chinese. To tackle serious labor and financial problems, Penang's government began the practice of employing Indian convicts as low-cost laborers for social services and the construction of urban infrastructure. From George Leith's administration onwards, road building and drainage were supervised by the Committee of Assessors. In 1801, the Committee proposed the construction of a network of roads within the commercial town in an area bounded by Light Street, Beach Street, Chulia Street and Pitt Street. Leith asked Bengal's government to supply 130 Indian convicts. Farquhar also promoted the employment of convict labor to reduce financial costs for all major public works, including the construction and maintenance of streets, roads and the island's drainage system.[26]

Indian governments encouraged the transportation of convicts from South Asia to Southeast Asia, due to a shortage of jail facilities and to help maintain social order in British India. In 1788, Governor-General Charles Cornwallis recommended transporting convicts to Penang. From the 1790s onwards, Indian convicts were sent periodically to Penang from the Indian subcontinent.[27] The Indian convicts employed numbered 130 in 1800, increasing to 772 by 1805.[28] They were of great service as cheap forced labor, mainly for road construction and other public services. As mentioned above, keeping the town of Penang healthy remained a major concern in the early nineteenth century. A jungle and swamp tract of land south of the town was exceedingly unhealthy. In reality, Indian convict workers saved the government's budget and contributed to improving living conditions in Georgetown.

Penal destinations in the late eighteenth and first two decades of the nineteenth century included Benkulen, the Andaman, the island of Ambon, Java, Arakan, Tenasserim, Mauritius, Botany Bay, West Indies and Aden, but these were not developed into penal colonies for convicts from India. The Straits Settlements aggregated the largest number of Indian convicts in this period.[29] With the high mortality rate, roughly 200 new convicts per year were required,

26 Webster, "British Expansion in South-East Asia," p. 8.

27 Anand A. Yang, "Indian Convict Workers in Southeast Asia in the Late Eighteenth and Early Nineteenth Centuries," *Journal of World History*, 14, 2 (2003), pp. 191–192.

28 City Council of Georgetown, *Penang Past and Present*, pp. 4–5.

29 Stephen Nicholas and Peter R. Shergold, "Transportation as Global Migration," in Stephan Nicholas (ed.), *Convict Workers: Reinterpreting Australia's Past* (Cambridge: Cambridge University Press, 1988), p.30; Clare Anderson, *Convicts in the Indian Ocean: Transportation from South Asia to Mauritius, 1815–53* (London: Macmillan Press Ltd., 2000).

and some 15,000 moved into the Straits Settlements between 1790 and 1860. Female convicts were also transported to the Straits, but in comparatively small numbers, not exceeding 200 in any one year.[30] As indicated in Table 6.4, the total number of Indian convicts in Penang in 1824 reached 1,469, 998 of whom were sent from Bengal, 272 from Madras, 192 from Bombay and 7 from Ceylon. Singapore and Burma emerged as the principal penal destinations by the 1830s, but Penang remained an important settlement for Indian convicts.

Convicts were mainly assigned to 'public works' in Penang, such as the construction and maintenance of communication infrastructure. A high proportion of Indian convicts worked on Penang's roads and streets, clearing swamp and forestlands, constructing drainage ditches, and connecting pipes for fresh water to waterfalls and rivers in the hinterland. As Leith reported, bricks used for bridges and other public works were entirely made by convicts, under the supervision of European brick makers.[31] Convicts also carried out various duties in the government offices and the military base in Penang. By 1818, convicts were employed in a town hall, a warehouse, the customs house and the engineers' department, for example, and by the paymaster and storekeeper, the town major and his garrison, the hospital, junior civil servants and the military. Others also worked as servants for government officials and private individuals. Indian convict workers in Singapore worked under similar

TABLE 6.4 *Number of Indian convicts in the straits settlements, 1810–1873*

	Penang			Malacca			Singapore			Total
	Male	**Female**	**Total**	**Male**	**Female**	**Total**	**Male**	**Female**	**Total**	
1810			1,300							1,300
1824			1,469							1,469
1855			1,358			648			1,839	3,845
1860	1,163	93	1,255	532		532	2,151	124	2,275	4,063
1865	728	72	801	743	2	745	1,681	112	1,793	3,339

SOURCE: KERNIAL SINGH SANDHU, *INDIANS IN MALAYA: SOME ASPECTS OF THEIR IMMIGRATION AND SETTLEMENT (1786–1957)* (CAMBRIDGE: CAMBRIDGE UNIVERSITY PRESS, 1969), P. 135.

30 Sandhu, *Indians in Malaya*, pp. 133–136.

31 Leith, *A Short Account*, pp. 27–28.

circumstances from its foundation in 1819.[32] Evidently, hard work by criminals was essential to the colonization of Penang and Singapore during the first half of the nineteenth century.

Spice Cultivation in the Hinterland

Successive Penang governors during the period believed that Penang's importance should be judged, not by the size of local revenues, but by the additional wealth and revenues its trade generated for other Presidencies of India.[33] On the basis of this imperial policy, officials sought to stimulate various economic activities that would help the new colony to develop for the benefit of the Malay Peninsula and the eastern Archipelago. Agricultural development into the hinterland of Georgetown was therefore viewed as essential to Penang's economic performance. At that time, pepper, nutmeg and cloves remained major agricultural export items from Southeast Asia to Europe and China. By 1800, the Bengal administration also came to see Penang as an alternative to the Dutch Moluccas as a source of spice production. The development of export crops became a popular means for covering administrative costs in Penang.

During earlier periods, Penang's agriculture focused almost exclusively on the cultivation of pepper. Pepper planting began soon after Penang's foundation and it was the first export-oriented agriculture product developed on an island in the Straits of Malacca. Local pepper production was expected to attract spice trade to the new settlement, with revenues contributing to financing local administration. Pepper cultivation methods were imported to Penang from Sumatra, where pepper was a major export crop throughout the eighteenth century. Vines were introduced from Aceh in 1790. Southern and western valleys of the island were drier and therefore well suited to pepper and spice plantations. During the early 1790's, the EIC established 130 acres of experimental pepper gardens along slopes skirting the base of a hill near Amie's Mill, and also in the southern hinterland at Sungei Kluang and Ayre Itam. Many European residents also planted pepper vines on newly-acquired estates. By 1798, a total of 533,230 vines had been planted on an area measuring between seven and nine hundred acres. Between 1798 and 1801, a further three quarters of a million vines were planted, bringing the total planted area to between 1,700 and 2,200 acres.[34]

32 Yang, "Indian Convict Workers in Southeast Asia," pp. 200–203.

33 Cowan, "Early Penang and the Rise of Singapore," p. 8.

34 Stevens, "A Contribution," pp. 395–396.

A small number of clove plants was imported into Penang from Mauritius, under French rule in the early 1790s, but the planting was unsuccessful. Five thousand nutmeg and fifteen thousand clove plants were imported from Amboina in 1800, prompting experiments in cultivating cloves and nutmeg in Penang. The first nutmeg tree to bear fruit did so in 1802. In the same year, substantial quantities of plants (71,266 nutmeg and 55,264 clove plants) were introduced into Penang from the Moluccas, commencing large-scale production.[35] Besides clove and nutmeg trees, the Company garden contained cinnamon, coffee and many other plants. In 1804, the Bengal government instructed Farquhar to establish a special Board of Plantation to monitor and encourage agricultural production in Penang.[36]

The EIC Court of Directors in London, however, was always ambivalent toward spice planting in Penang. The costs were high and the returns slow and uncertain. In addition, poor management led to the death of plants. Bengal ordered cessation of production and the sale of the plantations in 1805. Farquhar reluctantly executed the order, but strove to ensure that cultivation would be continued privately in the future. In fact, government spice gardens at Ayer Itam were sold off cheaply in lots to European residents, most of whom started to grow pepper and other spice plants around their houses. One David Brown entered into speculation on a large scale.[37] Brown's valuable estate, Glugore, was situated about five miles out of Georgetown. Government officers were also encouraged to enter into spice cultivation. Chinese residents engaged in spice speculation in later years, and also occupied and planted comparatively small holdings in many parts of the island.

Penang's pepper cultivation was an interesting joint effect of superintending activity by Europeans and the industrious labor of the Chinese.[38] Malays specialized in cutting down large trees, but the remaining operations necessary for preparing ground cultivation were performed by Chinese laborers employed on a contract system.[39] Crawfurd reported that "all incurring this charges, with the loss of interest of capital for four years, until the gardens

35 James C. Jackson, *Planters and Speculators: Chinese and European Agriculture Enterprise in Malaya, 1786–1921* (Kuala Lumpur: University of Malaya Press, 1968), p. 101.

36 Webster, "British Expansion in South-East Asia," pp. 8–9.

37 Braddell, *Statistics*, p. 12.

38 Crawfurd, *Journal of an Embassy*, p. 18.

39 William Hunter, "Remarks on the Species of Pepper, which are found on Prince of Wales' Island," *Asiatick Research, or, Transactions of the Society*, 9 (1807), p. 385; J. Basten, *The Changing Balance of the Early Southeast Asian Pepper Trade* (Kuala Lumpur: Department of History, University of Malaya, 1960), p. 54.

begin to bear, they were let to Chinese cultivators on lease, the farmer paying one-third of the net produce as rent, and restoring the pepper gardens in good order."[40] Large plantations were thus generally developed with European capital and with Chinese contractors employing Chinese labor.[41]

Pepper and other spice cultivation in Penang met with bad fortune, however, but not for local reasons. The Decrees of Berlin (1806) and Milan (1807) had the effect of shutting the Company off from Continental European markets, and stocks of pepper, spices and coffee piled up in London warehouses.[42] Penang's pepper planters, unable to dispose of crops at a price that covered costs, were faced with ruin. Penang then witnessed a series of mercantilist experiments for expanding the export of staples in the 1810s. Coffee, cotton and hemp exports were attempted in response to instructions from London, which themselves fluctuated with changing European politics.[43] None of these experiments brought any great success, however. After the fall of Napoleon (1815), British trade with continental European countries resumed, and the growing demand for pepper in this period revived pepper cultivation in Penang.[44] Between 1816 and 1818, over 300,000 vines were planted, chiefly in the hinterland districts of Telok Tikus, Sungei Tiram, Paya Terubong, Sungei Nibong and Ayre Itam. In all, almost one and three quarter million pepper vines, occupying between two and three thousand acres, had been planted in Penang by 1818.[45]

Nevertheless, pepper trade growth was disappointing, as pepper prices had been falling on the London markets. Cut off from European markets, some Penang planters abandoned pepper cultivation between the late 1810s and mid-1820s. The decline of pepper plantations also led to a decrease in Penang's Chinese population during this period. According to censuses, there were 5,088 Chinese people in 1810, but only 3,128 in 1818.[46] Despite the decline of the London market, Penang's pepper trade survived, as reflected in trade figures for 1814 to 1822 in Table 6.5. Table 6.5 shows that the major part of Penang's imported pepper frequently came from the neighboring coast of Sumatra, especially Aceh and the West coast of Sumatra. In the 1810s, however, Penang's pepper (and also betel nut) imports suffered severely due to an unsettled state

40 Crawfurd, *Journal of an Embassy*, p. 18.
41 Jackson, *Planters and Speculators*, p. 99.
42 Cowan, "Early Penang and the Rise of Singapore," pp. 5, 39, 43.
43 Cowan, "Early Penang and the Rise of Singapore," pp. 33, 41, 43, 53.
44 Cowan, "Early Penang and the Rise of Singapore," p. 65.
45 Jackson, *Planters and Speculators*, p. 98.
46 Hussin, *Trade and Society*, pp. 187, 189.

TABLE 6.5 *Pepper trade of Penang*

	Imports			Exports				
	East Coast of Sumatra	Aceh, West Coast of Sumatra	Total	Britain	Europe & America	China	Bengal, Indian Ports & Mauritius	Total
	Piculs	Piculs	Sp.Drs.	Piculs	Piculs	Piculs	Piculs	Sp.Drs.
1814/15	2,846	18,798	118,163	4,500	3,178		18,103	180,472
1815/16	2,404	19,723	151,284	4,788	9,004	27,532	8,428	497,020
1816/17	1,748	9,534	88,800		16,280	7,901	13,725	547,272
1817/18	1,816	11,564	106,869		8,031	21,760	2,114	382,860
1818/19	5,514	2,957	79,640	2,186	6,579	13,026	3,413	277,244
1819/20	8,205	13,433	180,825	5,220	4,001	18,605	1,718	324,984
1820/21	15,667	15,988	290,486		4,080	40,892	14,604	714,910
1821/22	21,790	14,670	278,539	10,500	2,950	18,470	13,800	457,200
1822/23	30,277	8,373	303,290	8,086	4,625	30,674	12,304	584,691

SOURCE: C.D. COWAN, "EARLY PENANG AND THE RISE OF SINGAPORE, 1805–1832," *JOURNAL OF THE MALAYAN BRANCH OF THE ROYAL ASIATIC SOCIETY*, 23, 2 (1950), P. 140.

of affairs in Aceh. However, Aceh's trade difficulties stimulated pepper import from ports on the East coast of Sumatra in the early 1820s. As mentioned previously, Penang's pepper exports always fluctuated according to the demand for pepper in foreign markets. It is evident from Table 6.5 that China was constantly the principal market for pepper shipped from Penang during this period.[47] Besides China, Penang also directed large amounts of pepper re-exports to Bengal, Coromandel and Malabar Coasts, Burma, and Mauritius. In the early 1820s, quantities increased rapidly, compared with markets in Great Britain and other European countries.

Despite adverse circumstances in world markets during the 1810s, a small group of European planters shifted mainly to cultivating nutmeg and cloves,

47 Cowan, "Early Penang and the Rise of Singapore," pp. 139–141; Basten, *The Changing Balance*, pp. 58–59.

chiefly concentrated in the Sungei Glugor district, where David Brown's plantation was located, as indicated by John Crawfurd's 1822 report:

> The estate of Glugar is of a poor soil, and unfit for the growth of pepper. Mr. Brown has planted it with nutmeg and clove-tree, which are in full nearing, and have a very thriving appearance, the effect of skilful culture and of great care, despite of the sterility of the soil.[48]

During this period David Brown stood alone in Penang as a spice planter on an extensive scale.

Conclusion

This article examines maritime trade, immigrant society, and the colonial economy of early Penang in the late eighteenth and early nineteenth centuries. After its foundation as a British free port, Penang attracted many long-distance, regional and short-distance merchants, traders active in Asia, laborers and others. A rapid increase in Penang's population drastically transformed thriving Georgetown into a multi-ethnic/heterogeneous port town, inhabited primarily by immigrants. The overwhelming majority of inhabitants were not Europeans but Asian ethnic groups, such as Malays, Indians, and Chinese. The prosperity of Penang's maritime trade, and particularly the development of early Penang's spice economy, also provided great impetus for many Chinese pioneers to move into the hinterland by opening it up to growing markets in Western Europe and China. The local government encouraged the immigration of Chinese plantation laborers from the Malay Peninsula and China, suggesting that the 'Chinese century' was obviously an important factor for the cultivation and colonization of Penang.

Indian people, especially merchants from the Coromandel Coast, Bengal and the Malay Peninsula, however, were most prominent in early Penang. They specialized mainly in imports from the Indian subcontinent, and closer links between the eastern coast of India and the Straits of Malacca were the most important factor for the prosperity of Penang's maritime trade. Early Penang governors attempted to transform the island into a plantation colony by growing spices, and exporting them and raw materials to markets in Western Europe and China. The economic development of the island interior required the construction of infrastructure, such as roads, drainage, canals and other amenities

48 Crawfurd, *Journal of an Embassy*, p. 12.

needed to link Georgetown with the hinterland. The local government had suffered from labor shortages for public works since Penang's foundation. The solution involved the transportation of Indian convict workers from the Indian subcontinent. Thus, the 'Indian century' in the Straits of Malacca deserves far more consideration than they have been granted until now.

CHAPTER 7

Toward a Transborder, Market-Oriented Society

*Changing Hinterlands of Banten, c. 1760–1800**

Atsushi Ota

Introduction

The Sultanate of Banten (1520s–1813) has been viewed as a typical port polity. Scholars have focused mainly on its external trade, cosmopolitan cultures in the port city and trade impacts on state formation, while almost entirely neglecting hinterlands.[1] Because of the excessive focus on the port and trade, they have also generally neglected the period after 1684, when the Dutch East India Company (VOC) made the sultanate its vassal state and its external trade began to decline, apart from pepper exports under VOC monopoly.[2] These tendencies in previous studies give an impression that the hinterlands of Banten were detached from outside economies, especially after 1684.

This paper discusses the hinterlands of Banten in the late eighteenth century, aiming to argue that they experienced considerable socio-economic transformation because of their close connection to the outside world. I focus on two factors, which I argue brought about the transformation. The first factor

* This chapter reconsiders some issues discussed in my previous work that propel new perspectives based upon new data. Atsushi Ota, *Changes of Regime and Social Dynamics in West Java: Society, State, and the Outer World of Banten, 1750–1830* (Leiden and Boston: Brill, 2006). I am grateful to Siung-Ming Liao for creating the maps for me.

1 M.A.P. Meilink-Roelofsz, *Asian Trade and European Influence in the Indonesian Archipelago between 1500 and about 1630* (The Hague: Martinus Nijhoff, 1962), pp. 239–258; Freek Colombijn, "Foreign Influence on the State of Banten, 1596–1682," *Indonesian Circle*, 50 (1987), pp. 19–50; J. Kathirithamby-Wells, "Banten: A West Indonesian Port and Polity during the Sixteenth and Seventeenth Centuries," in J. Kathirithamby-Wells and John Villiers (eds.), *The Southeast Asian Port and Polity: Rise and Demise* (Singapore: Singapore University Press, 1990), pp. 107–125; Claude Guillot, *The Sultanate of Banten* (Jakarta: Gramedia, 1990); Claude Guillot, "Libre entreprise contre économie dirigée: guerres civiles à Banten, 1580–1609," *Archipel*, 43 (1992), pp. 57–72; Anthony Reid, *Southeast Asia in the Age of Commerce 1450–1680; Vol. 2. Expansion and Crisis* (New Haven and London: Yale University Press, 1993).

2 Works discussing the post-1684 period of Banten are Johan Talens, *Een feodale samenleving in koloniaal vaarwater: Staatvorming, koloniale expansie en economische onderontwikkeling in Banten, West-Java 1600–1750* (Hilversum: Verloren, 1999); Dinar Boontharm, "The Sultanate of Banten AD 1750–1808: A Social and Cultural History" (Ph.D. Dissertation, University of Hull, 2003); and Ota, *Changes of Regime*.

© KONINKLIJKE BRILL NV, LEIDEN, 2015 | DOI 10.1163/9789004283909_009

was the VOC policy to promote pepper cultivation in the hinterlands of Banten from 1763 to 1790. Though this policy was not very successful in terms of production increase, it significantly affected local society because it provided cash income to local elites and cultivators. Local elites first augmented their influence through pepper cultivation, but later they and ordinary cultivators began to look for other means to gain income, abandoning pepper production. The second factor involved the sugar industry, which had gradually migrated from the *ommelanden* (environs) of Batavia under VOC jurisdiction to the Sadane River area (borderland between the *ommelanden* and the Banten Sultanate) at the eastern edge of the Banten hinterlands. The industry attracted Chinese and Sundanese migrant workers, who developed 'clandestine' trade with outside traders.

Production of pepper and sugar was closely linked to the world economy. Along with tin, pepper was a principle Southeast Asian export item that the VOC strongly promoted for the Chinese market. China increasingly attracted European attention because of the lucrative tea trade. Provision of popular Southeast Asian products for the China market helped the Dutch, who did not have many trade items to offer the Chinese, to buy tea without using large quantities of silver.[3] Sugar was an important export commodity from Java to the Netherlands and to various places in Asia, including Gujarat.[4] In order to increase production, the VOC first took the initiative to promote pepper and sugar cultivation in the hinterlands of Banten. However, I will show that production of these crops soon went beyond state control, as it encouraged migration and transborder trade.

After describing the setting of the region in question, I discuss the economy and ruling system of hinterland society of the Banten region in the pre-1760 period. The Banten region (or Banten) refers to the tip of Java Island west of the Sadane River (Map 7.1).[5] Hinterland areas (or hinterlands) of Banten are taken here as areas apart from the northern coastal plain (or the lowland area). I then explain how the VOC started its policy to promote pepper production, and what sorts of impact it had on hinterland society. In a subsequent section, I discuss

3 Els M. Jacobs, *Merchant in Asia: The Trade of the Dutch East India Company during the Eighteenth Century* (Leiden: CNWS, 2006), p. 185.

4 Ota, *Changes of Regime*, p. 134; Ghulam A. Nadri, *Eighteenth-Century Gujarat: The Dynamics of Its Political Economy, 1750–1860* (Leiden and Boston: Brill, 2009), pp. 111–116.

5 The Banten region in this paper is therefore larger than the Banten Province in the colonial period, of which the western border lay on the Ci Durian. The capital of the sultanate, also called Banten, is referred to as Kota Banten in this paper, in order to distinguish it from the Banten region.

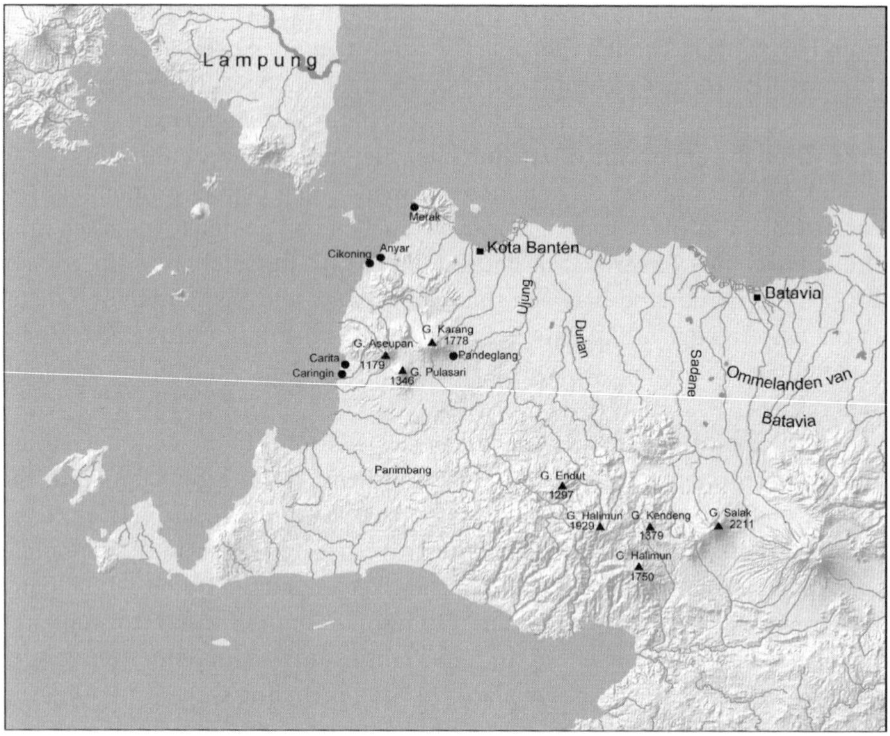

MAP 7.1 *The Banten region*

how the sugar industry (and other related economic activities) triggered the development of the Sadane River area into a borderland society, namely a society located between multiple states, yet characterized by weak central control, multiple ethnicities, and transborder communications.[6] Examining behaviors of local people, I aim to argue that the hinterlands of Banten transformed into a market-oriented society, increasingly connected to the outer world.

The Setting

Banten is not ecologically favored for agriculture. Apart from some small coastal plains in the north and southwest, large parts of the Banten region are covered with mountains and hills ranging from the Karang Mountains in the northwest

6 For good recent discussions on borderlands, see the research project "Borderlands: Ethnicity, identity, and Violence in the Shatter-Zone of Empires since 1848," Watson Institute for International Studies, Brown University, 2003–2007.

to the Kendang Mountains in the south (Map 7.1). According to Michael Charles Williams, the soil of Banten was markedly deficient in phosphates, magnesium, iron and lime. Concentration of organic matter is scanty, and the soil is quite porous as a result. Production of rice and commercial crops in Banten was the worst in all of Java throughout the Cultural System period (1830–1870).[7]

In terms of ecology, Banten can be divided into four zones: the north coastal plain, the slopes of the Karang Mountains, the slopes of the Kendang Mountains and the far south. On the north plain, wet rice cultivation developed since the sixteenth century,[8] but this area did not produce any secondary crop other than rice, and it had a high incidence of crop failure. The slopes of the Karang Mountains are the most fertile, probably due to their numerous streams and cool climate, which promoted the production of rice and some secondary crops in dry fields. As a result, relatively large settlements developed on the Karang slopes and basins in the late eighteenth century. Slopes of the Kendang Mountains were only sparsely populated, on the other hand, and rice cultivation in swidden and dry-field cultivation dominated. The far south was least developed, and is still thinly populated today.[9]

The Sundanese widely inhabited West Java. They were the original population in the Banten region and still comprised a majority in the central and southern areas. On the other hand, Javanese, originally from Central and East Java, migrated to the northern part of Banten, probably in the greatest numbers around the establishment of the Islamic kingdom of Banten in the early sixteenth century.[10] Javanese speakers resided on the northern coastal plain, while the population of the hinterlands was dominated by Sundanese speakers in the early twentieth century.[11] Eighteenth-century Dutch sources also confirm this distribution of the two language groups.[12]

7 Michael Williams, *Communism, Religion, and Revolt in Banten* (Athens, Ohio: Ohio University Center for International Studies, 1990), pp. 1–9.

8 According to a legend collected in the late nineteenth century, Javanese migrants brought rice cultivation when the Islamic kingdom was established in Banten in the 1520s. *Eindresumé van het bij Gouvernementsbesluit dd. 10 Juni 1867 No. 2 bevolen onderzoek naar de rechten van den inlander op den grond op Java en Madoera*, ed. Willem Bernardus Bergsma (Batavia: Ernst, 1876–1896), II, Bijlage A, p. 2.

9 Williams, *Communism, Religion, and Revolt*, pp. 1–2.

10 It was in 1642 that the ruler of the kingdom started to use the title sultan, and thus the term "sultanate" became appropriate.

11 S.J. Esser, "Talen," in Koninklijk Nederlands Aardrijkskundige Genootschap (ed.), *Atlas van Tropisch Nederland* (Batavia: Reproductiebedrijf van den Topografische dienst in Nederlands Indië, 1938).

12 Eighteenth-century Dutch sources distinguished the Bantenese (*Bantammers*) or Javanese (*Javanen*) living in the northern coastal plain and the Mountain Javanese

The Islamic kingdom of Banten was established in the 1520s. The Islamic teacher Faletehan (later also known as Sunan Gunung Jati), originally from North Sumatra, took control of the coastal port town of Banten, supported by Demak, the most powerful Islamic state in Java at that time. He made the town the capital (Kota Banten after this event) of his new kingdom. Subsequent rulers conquered the Hindu-Buddhist kingdom of Pajajaran in the inland area, and controlled the entire Banten region. The Lampung region in the southernmost part of Sumatra was also gradually incorporated into the Banten kingdom during the sixteenth and seventeenth centuries.[13]

Kota Banten soon developed into one of the most important intermediate ports in Southeast Asia by the end of the sixteenth century. While foreign traders exchanged various kinds of commodities with each other, virtually the sole export product from Banten was pepper, mostly produced at the foot of Mt. Karang.[14]

Early rulers also promoted irrigated rice cultivation around the capital. By the late seventeenth century, wet rice fields, a part of which must have been irrigated, were developed on a large scale on the north coastal plain.[15] Notably, this wet rice cultivation area is almost equivalent to the Javanese-speaking area. A legend circulating in the late nineteenth century connected the launch of wet rice cultivation with Javanese migration in the early sixteenth century.[16] In the Sundanese-speaking hinterlands, wet rice cultivation did not develop until the late eighteenth century. A late nineteenth-century study showed that about 400 rice-producing villages (*desa's*) on the northern coastal plain had been under the direct control of the sultan.[17] Probably since early times the ruler placed wet rice fields near the capital under direct control in order to increase production and thereby secure the food supply for the urban population.

In contrast, hinterland areas were not placed under the strong control of the ruler. Apart from some fighting against the Pajajaran Kingdom, early rulers of

---

(*Bergjavanen*) residing in the mountain areas. Nationaal Archief, Vereenigde Oost-Indische Compagnie, (hereafter VOC) 2843: 75–76, Commander J. van Suchtelen et al. in Banten to Governor-General and the East Indies Council in Batavia (hereafter Batavia), 15 October 1754.

13 Ota, *Changes of Regime*, pp. 15–16.

14 Willem Lodewycksz., *De eerste schipvaart naar Oost-Indië onder Cornelis de Houtman,1595–1597*, ed. G.P. Rouffaer and J.W. IJzerman (The Hague: Martinus Nijhoff, 1915 [1598]), I, pp. 128–129; Ota, *Changes of Regime*, pp. 17–18, 29.

15 Talens, *Een feodale samenleving*, p. 43; Ota, *Changes of Regime*, pp. 29, 178.

16 *Eindresumé*, II, Bijlage A, p. 2.

17 *Eindresumé*, II, p. 5; ibid., II, Bijlage A, p. 4.

Banten and their Javanese soldiers do not seem to have seriously fought against the local Sundanese population. In all likelihood, early rulers requested only that local people accept state authority, with little or no obligation to them. Early rulers emphasized their Islamic and Javanese roots and high culture in order to justify their rule.[18] The financial base of the state centered on trade ports and food-supplying areas on the north coastal plain, rather than the hinterlands. Pepper production in the Banten hinterlands declined in the course of the seventeenth century, as production in Lampung increased, but the sultan did not seriously attempt to improve production in Banten until the 1760s.[19]

Subsequent sultanate rulers competed fiercely and conflicted with the VOC, which established Asian headquarters in Batavia in 1619, through incessant wars and trade embargos. Finally however, internal conflict in 1682 resulted in an invitation for VOC military intervention, and the sultanate fell under VOC authority and became its vassal state in 1684. Although the VOC established monopoly on important trade items, it did not intervene in local politics until the 1760s.[20]

Pre-1760 Society

The difference between lowland and hinterland societies was obvious to eighteenth-century observers in Banten. According to the VOC Director

18 Atsushi Ota, "Orthodoxy and Reconciliation: Islamic Strategies in the Kingdom of Banten, c. 1520–1813," in Atsushi Ota, Masaaki Okamoto, and Ahmad Suaedy (eds.), *Islam in Contention: Rethinking Islam and State in Indonesia* (Kyoto: CSEAS; Taipei: CAPAS; Jakarta: Wahid Institute, 2010).

19 In Lampung, the Banten sultan repeatedly promulgated orders inscribed on copper plate (*piagem*, of which the existing old one was from 1662) to promote pepper cultivation. In Banten, however, no source indicates the promulgation of such orders. J.J. Meinsma, "Eene proklamatie van een Sultan van Bantam," *Bijdragen tot de Taal-, Land- en Volkenkunde van Nederlandsch-Indië, tijdschrift van het Koninklijk Instituut voor de Taal-, Land- en Volkenkunde van Nederlandsch-Indië* (hereafter *BKI*), third series, 8 (1873), pp. 152–157; H.N. van der Tuuk, "Naar aanleiding van eene proclamatie van den Sultan van Bantam," *Tijdschrift voor Indische Taal-, Land- en Volkenkunde* (published by the Bataviaasch Genootschap van Kunsten en Wetenschappen; hereafter *TBG*), 23 (1876), pp. 134–139; H.N. van der Tuuk, "Lampongsche pijagem's," *TBG*, 29 (1884), pp. 191–207; H.C. Humme, "Javaansche Inscriptie," *BKI*, fourth series, 8 (1884), pp. 1–17; J.L.A. Brandes, "Nog eenige Javaansche piagem's uit het mohammedaansche tijdvak, afkomstig van Mataram, Banten en Palembang," *TBG*, 32 (1889), pp. 557–601; *TBG*, 34 (1891), pp. 605–623; *TBG*, 35 (1892), pp. 110–126; *TBG*, 37 (1894), pp. 119–126; *TBG*, 42 (1900), pp. 131–134, 491–507; Theodore G.Th. Pigeaud, "Afkondigingen van Bantamsche Soeltans voor Lampoeng," *Djawa*, 9 (1929), pp. 123–159.

20 Ota, *Changes of Regime*, pp. 17–18.

General (later Governor General) in Batavia, Jacob Mossel, who visited Banten in 1747, Kota Banten was the only sizable town of about 10,000 residents in the sultanate. He stated that villages (*dorpen*) existed only along the coast, while in the extremely thinly populated hinterlands there were only hamlets (*gehugten*).[21]

Hinterlands were only loosely integrated into the state. The sultan, the highest authority of the state, had the right to appoint and dismiss court officials from among influential elite members called *ponggawa*. The *ponggawa* had rights over land and people in certain areas; partly in the lowland area but mostly in the hinterlands. The sultan sometimes granted land and people to the *ponggawa* as a reward, and took them away as punishment, although *ponggawa* hereditary rights were taken into consideration. A part of the *ponggawa* resided in the capital, appointed as court officials, and they and members of the royal family constituted the court elite. Other *ponggawa* remained on their land and formed the local elite. Local *ponggawa* provided workers in the palace called *mantri dalem* and only occasionally laborers for (re)construction work in and around the capital, but apart from this they did not bring any tribute to the sultan.[22]

The sultan obtained almost all his income from the lowland area. Mossel reported in 1747 (Table 7.1) that the sultan gained 60,000 Spanish Reals, about seventy percent of his income, from the export of pepper, which was mostly produced in Lampung at that time. Under a contract concluded with the VOC in 1684, the sultan secured the monopoly right to sell pepper produced in the sultanate to the Company at the fixed price of fifteen Spanish Reals per bahar. The sultan bought pepper from *ponggawa* or pepper traders at eight Spanish Reals per bahar; the difference between these prices became the sultan's income. The rest of the sultan's income was also mostly related to trade and commerce, such as the *shahbandary* (tax collected at ports), and market tax in port towns. Apart from the items mentioned by Mossel, the sultan collected a poll tax, in the form of half the income of cultivators under his direct control.[23] Even if we take this tax into consideration, it still seems safe to assume that the sultan did not depend financially upon tax income from hinterlands.

21 *De Opkomst van het Nederlandsche gezag in Oost-Indië Verzameling van onuitgegeven stukken uit het Oud-Koloniaal Archief*, ed. J.K.J. de Jonge, X, pp. 118–119, Director General Jacob Mossel in Banten to Batavia, 21 February 1747.

22 Ota, *Changes of Regime*, pp. 40–42, 48–50.

23 Arsip Nasional Republik Indonesia, Arsip Daerah Banten (hereafter ADB) 16: 18–19, Memorie van Overgave, Willem Hendrik van Ossenberch to Hugo Pieter Faure, 28 July 1761.

TABLE 7.1 *Income of the Sultan, 1747*

Pepper	**60,000**
The lease of seven sugar factories	3,000
Shahbandary, poll tax from Chinese, tax from markets etc.	8,000
Opium, arak, and topbanen	4,800
Shahbandary in Tanara, Cobong Panjang, Lontar, and Pontang	700
Salt and gold etc.	500
Diamonds	10,000
Total (Spanish Reals)	87,000

SOURCE: *OPKOMST* X: 122, DIRECTOR-GENERAL J. MOSSEL IN BANTEN TO BATAVIA, 21 FEB. 1747.

Most *ponggawa* had power bases in the hinterlands. Two population censuses, compiled at the Banten court by order of the sultan around 1700, are important sources for understanding the local ruling system. The censuses, covering people residing in the Banten region, organized the entire population into hundreds of units, each belonging to one patron (mostly to *ponggawa* but partly to the sultan).[24] Each unit consisted of the chief (*janten*), taxable men (called *kirnan, pakardi* and so on), young unmarried men (*prajaka*), old and disabled men (*jubag*) and others such as religious experts (*santri*). These types of people would have formed a 'communities' unit, in basic cooperative units of local society. The term *kirnan* means taxable men, although women were included in this category when husbands were not able to work for some reason. Probably other types of people were also grouped on the basis of tax categories. Such taxes must have been the financial base of the *ponggawa*, although amounts and details of taxes are not clear in eighteenth-century sources. As the sultan hardly intervened in patron-client relationships, the hinterlands seem to have enjoyed autonomy to a certain degree.

Summaries at the end of the two censuses show total numbers of people, respectively 31,848 and 36,302. These are numbers mentioned in the above-mentioned format, thus basically excluding women and children. Actual populations may have been three or four times these numbers.

24 The censuses thus do not include the people in the overseas territories of the sultanate in south Sumatra and west Kalimantan. Leiden University Library, Oriental Department (hereafter LOr) 2052, census of the population, Banten, 1696/97; LOr 2055, census of the population, Banten, c. 1700. For more detailed discussion on the censuses and local communities in Banten, see Ota, *Changes of Regime*, pp. 42–48.

In the lowland, rice was a popular crop among ordinary cultivators,[25] although they also grew indigo, arrack and sugar.[26] Rice production was not usually enough for domestic consumption, and imports from Cirebon and Batavia made up for the shortfall.[27]

Kota Banten imported daily consumption items such as cotton yarn, textiles, tobacco and 'bowls and plates' (probably Chinese porcelain or earthenware) from Batavia. Export items from Banten, such as coconuts, fruits, (dried) fish, and kapok – all produced in the lowland area – were directed to Batavia.[28]

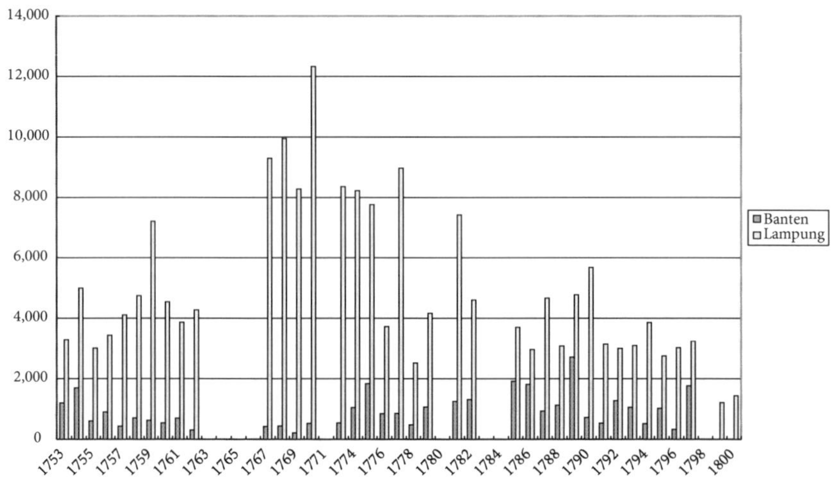

FIGURE 7.1 *Pepper delivery from the Banten hinterlands and Lampung.*[29]
Notes: No data for years not included in this figure. The figures in 1779 and 1880 indicate the total amount delivered from the Banten hinterlands and Lampung.
SOURCES: VOC 3094, 3214, 3248, 3277, 3306, 3417, 3444, 3469, 3498, 3527, 3555, 3626, 3652, 3736, 3762, 3814, 3909, 3965, CZOHB 118, 119, ADB 34.

25 For example, it was observed in the region just south of Kota Banten in 1763 that cultivators had switched from pepper to rice cultivation, because the latter was easier and more favourable for the life of the cultivators. VOC 3093: 16, Commander Hugo Pieter Faure in Banten to Batavia, 1 July 1763.

26 *Opkomst*, X, pp. 117–120, Director General Jacob Mossel in Banten to Batavia, 21 February 1747. However, the fact that Banten also imported arrack and indigo means that their production was lower than the domestic demand. VOC 3214: no pagination, list of ships coming from Batavia to Banten and their cargo, Banten, 1 January 1768.

27 Gerrit J. Knaap, *Shallow Waters, Rising Tide: Shipping and Trade in Java around 1775* (Leiden: KITLV Press, 1996), p. 95; ADB 16: 18, Memorie van Overgave, Willem Hendrik van Ossenberch to Hugo Pieter Faure, 28 July 1761.

28 VOC 3214: no pagination, list of ships coming from Batavia to Banten and those leaving Banten for Batavia, as well as their cargo, Banten, 1 January 1767.

29 The reason behind the sudden increase from the Banten hinterlands 1797 is not clear. However, the declining trend of the total delivery in 1799 and 1800 indicates that the

This trade connection shows that the economy of the lowland area of Banten was dependent to a considerable degree on Batavia, rather than on its own hinterlands.

In the hinterlands, rice was cultivated in dry fields in many places,[30] although the southwest coastal plain was not appropriate for rice cultivation.[31] People also cultivated coconuts, bananas and root vegetables for sustenance, in order to make up for insufficient rice.[32] The only cash crops grown in the hinterlands were pepper and nutmeg in the mid-eighteenth century. Pepper was produced in the Panimbang area,[33] but production decreased after 1753, a period for which the data are available (Figure 7.1). Nutmeg was cultivated from the 1730s on order of members of the royal family, but cultivation died out by the mid-1760s.[34] The hinterlands were neither economically important for the state center nor for those from outside because of the ecologically-determined small population and low production until the mid-1760s.

Local *ponggawa* hardly challenged the authority of the sultan, except for a few notable uprisings. The sultan's army usually suppressed revolts swiftly. Other elites' military power was no match for that of the sultan, even though he did not have a strong regular army and his soldiers consisted largely of Balinese, Bugis and other mercenaries. The sultan had a far larger income than the local *ponggawa*, while the financial base of the local elite must have been severely limited because of unfavorable ecological conditions. The Dutch always supported the sultan after 1684, even when he was unpopular in court circles, in order to avoid political turbulence that might lead to heavy military expense.[35]

The relationship between the hinterlands and the state center in Banten seems to have been more symbolic than based on economic and political interdependence. For a *ponggawa* in the hinterlands, receipt of a title or regalia from the sultan must have enhanced the *ponggawa*'s authority over local

increase in 1797 was a temporary phenomenon, and the delivery from the Banten hinterlands was declining after 1789.

30 Pandeglang and Cimanuk on the slope of Mt. Karang were well-known rice-producing places. VOC 3248: no pagination, pepper cultivation report, J. Benjamin Koehl to Commander J. Reijnouts in Banten, 8–9 July 1768.

31 VOC 3093: 16–17, Commander Hugo Pieter Faure in Banten to Batavia, 1 July 1763.

32 ADB 30: no pagination, pepper cultivation report, P. van Rhijn and F. van Chambon, Banten, 11 November 1790.

33 *Opkomst*, X, p. 120, Director General Jacob Mossel in Banten to Batavia, 21 February 1747.

34 *Opkomst*, X, pp. 120–121, Director-General J. Mossel in Banten to Batavia, 21 February 1747; VOC 3185: 61, pepper cultivation report, J.B. Koehl to J. Reijnouts in Banten, no date, 1766.

35 Talens, *Een feodale samenleving*; Ota, *Changes of Regime*, pp. 78–79.

society rivals. For the state center, the subjugation of hinterlands, entailing subjugation of a number of the *ponggawa*, must have enhanced the ruler's authority and thereby impressed potential rivals within and outside.

The symbolic importance of the hinterlands-center relationship was reaffirmed and strengthened at various ceremonies and customs, where the sultan's orders were solemnized, and local *ponggawa* emphasized that they represented the sultan's authority.[36] These ceremonies and customs indicate that the state center was a source of authority for the *ponggawa* in the hinterlands. The compilation of population censuses seems to have aimed to reconfirm patron-client networks between the sultan and the local *ponggawa*.

Promotion of Pepper Cultivation

Although some VOC officials were interested in pepper in the hinterlands of Banten from the 1740s,[37] it was not until 1763 that the VOC started to promote cultivation there. The commander of the VOC Banten factory, Hugo Pieter Faure, decided to order all men older than fifteen to plant 500 pepper vines each.[38] Growing demand in China and relatively high prices in Europe,[39] along with slow recovery in production in Lampung after a large-scale rebellion in 1750–52, would have spurred the VOC officials on to find an alternative production region. The sultan had conducted a survey on pepper cultivation in the hinterland since 1761 (probably at Faure's urging). The survey found that local *ponggawa* were enthusiastic about promoting pepper cultivation on their

36 In the capital, the sultan's orders were conveyed to the *ponggawa* at the heightened open-air platform called *paseban* in the middle of the open space (*alun-alun*), which any people could see, in front of the palace. The order was announced to the sound of drum (*gom-gom*) to solemnize the ceremony. The *ponggawa* passed the sultan's orders to his followers in a similar way in his land in the hinterlands. He announced the orders to the drum sound (*gom-gom*) in a small hut raised a few feet off the ground on pillars, in the middle of an open space in the village. When the sultan appointed a member of the *ponggawa* as his local representative, he conferred upon him the Javanese title of a court official and regalia such as clothes, a lance, a *kris* (decorated dagger), and a big parasol. Ota, *Changes of Regime*, pp. 56, 78–79.

37 For example, Jacob Mossel emphasized in his report of 1747 that the hinterlands were suitable for pepper cultivation. *Opkomst*, X, p. 120, Director General Jacob Mossel in Banten to Batavia, 21 February 1747.

38 This order followed traditional orders given by the sultan in previous times. VOC 3093: 15–16, Commander Hugo Pieter Faure in Banten to Batavia, 1 July 1763.

39 Jacobs, *Merchant in Asia*, p. 185.

land. Seeing this result, Faure decided to order local *ponggawa* to urge their people to cultivate more pepper vines.[40] Faure also decided that one or two VOC officials and an important court official should conduct an annual investigation tour to oversee proper cultivation in pepper gardens in the entire Banten region.[41]

Investigation of pepper cultivation started in 1763, and was conducted every year until 1790. The investigators visited about 300 kampongs (traditional villages)[42] annually, and created investigation reports noting the name of the kampong, its patron, the kampong chief, number of cultivators and numbers of newly planted pepper vines, young vines, and harvestable vines. Not all the investigation reports have survived, and the oldest surviving report is from 1765.

According to the investigation reports, pepper cultivation was conducted in kampongs dispersed throughout the hinterlands, apart from the far south area and not on the north coastal plain. It is difficult to geographically locate the kampongs listed in the investigation reports, as place names have been changed to a considerable degree. However, having examined the earliest modern map of the Banten region, created by the Topografische Richting (The Hague) on a scale of 1 to 100,000 in 1897, on the basis of a land survey in 1883–84, I have ascertained the locations of 128 kampongs (Map 7.2).[43]

Pepper gardens were established on slopes of hills and mountains, on land higher than that suitable for rice fields.[44] As pepper needed frequent watering, pepper-producing kampongs were located along rivers and streams.[45] This would also have made transporting harvest easier to a certain degree.[46]

---

40 VOC 3093: 15, Commander Hugo Pieter Faure in Banten to Batavia, 1 July 1763; ibid.: 27–28, 15 August 1763.

41 VOC 3093: 26–27, Commander Hugo Pieter Faure in Banten to Batavia, 15 August 1763.

42 Although the Dutch used several terms to refer to a village, I use this local term for villages in the hinterlands.

43 This map is earlier than the well-known series of 1-to-50,000 maps of Java and Madura, created in the 1920s by the Topografische Dienst (the successor of the Topografische Richting). For finding the location of each kampong, I carefully examined the descriptive information of the kampong locations included in the pepper investigation reports. I have also secondarily referred to the 1-to-50,000 maps.

44 Pepper inspection reports often mention that some places were too low for pepper cultivation and were more suitable for rice.

45 ADB 27: 36–37, pepper cultivation report, J.v.d. Boogaart and F. Chambon, Banten, 3 August 1789; ADB 30: 243r–244r, pepper cultivation report, J. v.d. Boogaart and F. Chambon, Banten, 20 November 1789; ibid.: no pagination, 11 November 1790.

46 Officials sent by the *ponggawa* carried pepper collected in his kampongs to Kota Banten by boat and cart, but mostly on foot. ADB 27: 26–27, pepper cultivation report, J. v.d. Boogaart and F. Chambon, Banten, 31 July 1789.

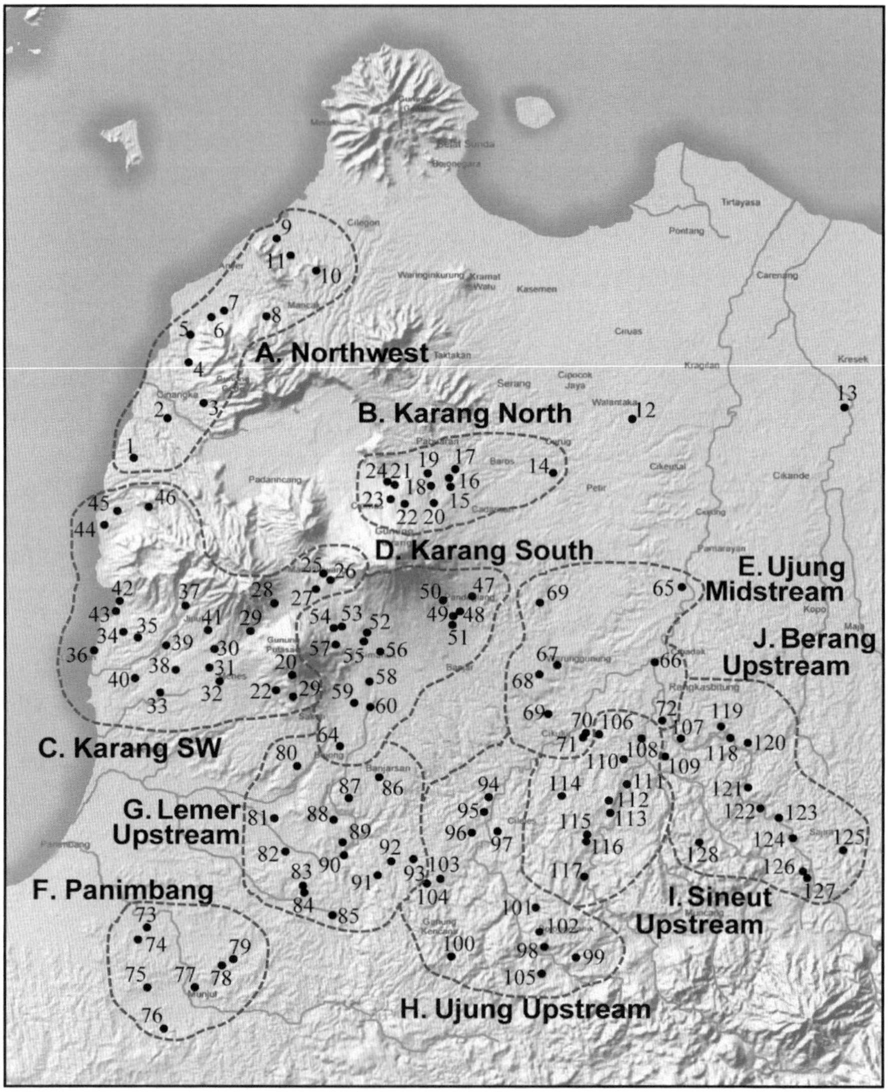

MAP 7.2 *Pepper-producing kampongs*

Cultivators seem to have opened new lands for pepper gardens, or to have switched part of existing fields to pepper gardens. They do not seem to have spent much time preparing pepper gardens, and switching from rice fields to pepper gardens and vice versa was common. People also cultivated rice (and probably other staple crops such as root vegetables) near their pepper gardens.[47] There is no evidence that authorities imported rice or other foodstuffs for pepper cultivators. These things mean that the introduction of pepper cultivation did not drastically change cultivators' lifestyles. Pepper cultivation in eighteenth-century Banten was not conducted in plantation style with intensive input of labor, but became part of the existing agricultural life of local people.

Impact of Pepper Cultivation on the Hinterland Society

Dutch policy to promote pepper cultivation achieved considerable results up to the late 1780s. Pepper production in Banten, which had dropped to almost zero in 1768, began to increase the next year, and increased continually until 1788, when it reached almost 2,000 bahar (Figure 7.1). Dutch and Bantenese investigators promoted pepper cultivation strongly, and often forcibly, especially in the early stage. Investigators arrested kampong chiefs and cultivators who neglected cultivation, and took them to Kota Banten for labor as punishment.[48] Many new kampongs were opened, especially in 1766, which was probably related to the opening of new pepper gardens.[49]

Pepper cultivation inspection reports indicate numbers of able-bodied men and names of their patrons in each pepper-producing kampong. Based on these data, it is possible to trace which kampongs and how many laborers each *ponggawa* controlled. The 128 pepper-producing kampongs for which the location was ascertained were mostly located along the streams of main rivers. Based on these rivers and streams, it is possible to group all the kampongs into ten areas (Map 7.2).

Figure 7.2 shows how the influential *ponggawa* expanded their power in local society during the period of pepper cultivation promotion policy. Pie graphs indicate ratios of kampongs and able-bodied men placed under the five most influential *ponggawa*, in terms of the number of kampongs under their influence, in each area. The general trend is that the number of kampongs and able-bodied men both increased slightly, and powerful *ponggawa* placed

47 For example, VOC 3093: 16, Commander Hugo Pieter Faure in Banten to Batavia, 1 July 1763; VOC 3277: 6–7, Hans Wiebens aan Commander Johannes Reijnouts, 4 July 1769.

48 VOC 3185: 61, pepper cultivation report, J.B. Koehl to J. Reijnouts in Banten, no date, 1766; VOC 3214: no pagination, J. Reijnouts to Batavia, 31 August 1767; VOC 3248: no pagination, J. Benjamin Koehl to Commander J. Reijnouts in Banten, 15 August 1768.

49 VOC 3185, pepper cultivation report, J.B. Koehl to J. Reijnouts in Banten, no date, 1766.

increasing numbers of kampongs and able-bodied men under their influence, before a setback in 1789–90. The increase in the numbers of kampongs and able-bodied men occurred due to the increasing concentration on growing pepper (the report recorded only pepper-producing kampongs and men), and did not mean an actual increase in kampongs and population. In each area, one or two *ponggawa* notably expanded influence, which means that a few powerful *ponggawa* came to dominate in many areas.

Pepper production in Banten increased almost in proportion to this expansion of powerful *ponggawa* influence (Figure 7.1). One can assume that the increase of pepper production and expansion of powerful *ponggawa* influence were correlated for the following reasons. Powerful *ponggawa* concentrated people in particular locations to promote pepper cultivation. For example, Raden Deman Boraksa in the Panimbang area forcibly relocated people from surrounding kampongs to Mampeng Kolot for pepper cultivation.[50] In important pepper-producing areas, in fact, the powerful *ponggawa* tended to control large numbers of kampongs and men. For example, in Panimbang, which was the major pepper-producing area in the pre-1765 period without other important industries (this land was not suitable for rice), a large number of people had already concentrated under one influential *ponggawa* in 1765, and one or two influential *ponggawa* were always dominant there (Figure 7.2). In areas where other industries such as trade and cash-crop cultivation had also developed, such as the Northwest and Karang Southwest areas,[51] on the other hand, the expansion of influential *ponggawa* power was not obvious. Unfortunately, the exact quantity of pepper production in each area is not clear from the sources.

Influential *ponggawa* forcibly took people from weak *ponggawa*.[52] *Ponggawa* were incessantly in conflict with each other for many reasons, and some indeed had military power (soldiers and weapons),[53] with which they could attack or overwhelm rivals. Banten censuses and Dutch sources both

50 ADB 27: 73–74, pepper cultivation report, J. v.d. Boogaart and F. Chambon, Banten, 23 August 1789.

51 *Opkomst*, X: 124, Director General Jacob Mossel in Banten to Batavia, 21 Feburary 1747; British Library, Mackenzie Collections Private (hereafter MCP) 4: 184–185, report by J. de Rovere van Breugel, 5 May 1788. The reason for the relatively small number of able-bodied men in 1765 in this area is that those placed under one influential *ponggawa* were not counted in this year for unknown reasons.

52 For example, ADB 25: 3–7, Commander Willem Hendrik van Ossenberch in Banten to Batavia, 12 July 1768.

53 VOC 3248: no pagination, pepper cultivation report, J. Benjamin Koehl to Commander J. Reijnouts in Banten, 9 July 1768; ADB 30: 123, pepper cultivation report, J. v.d. Boogaart and F. Chambon, Banten, 22 October 1792.

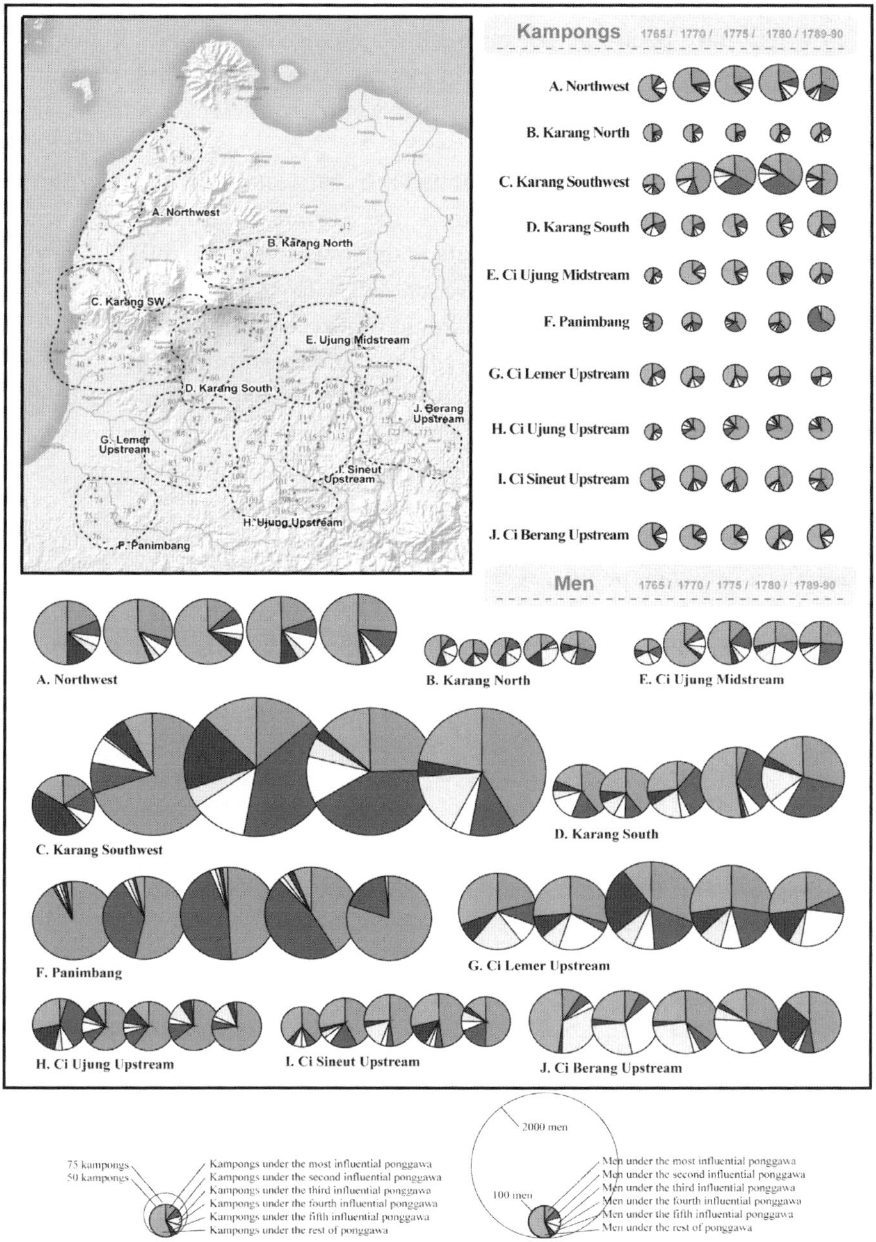

FIGURE 7.2 *Shifting influence of ponggawa over kampongs and people, 1765–1790*
SOURCES: PEPPER CULTIVATION REPORTS, 1765–1790. FOR INVENTORY INFORMATION OF THE SOURCES, SEE THE MAIN TEXT.

frequently mention that ordinary cultivators changed patrons. Forcible relocation would have been one reason behind a change of patrons, although the most frequently mentioned reason in pepper inspection reports was cultivators' spontaneous choice to flee from a heavy burden and seek a more generous patron.

New Javanese migrants, called Wetangers by the Dutch, also came to participate in pepper cultivation.[54] Wetangers first migrated to Kota Banten, where they were placed under the direct jurisdiction of the VOC, organized under the Chief of the Wetangers (*Hoofd der Wetangers*).[55] They engaged in various jobs in the capital for the VOC, such as guards at Company posts and patrol work off the coast.[56] However, because of meager pay and sometimes lack of payment by the VOC, they left the capital and migrated further to the hinterlands after the 1750s.[57] Groups of ten to twenty-five Wetangers lived in numerous kampongs under the protection of *ponggawa*. From the 1760s, they were engaged in pepper cultivation and became an important source of labor.[58]

The introduction of pepper cultivation would have made it easier for *ponggawa* to control their people, because cultivators now came to work for a much longer time on the same plots. In the hinterlands of Banten, where swidden or dry-field forms of cultivation were dominant, cultivators usually abandoned lands after three to four years' cultivation, and moved to open new fields in another place.[59] On the other hand, pepper vines needed five to seven years to bear fruit, and kept bearing until their twelfth to sixteenth year.[60] *Ponggawa* of

54 The Dutch distinguished the Wetangers from the long-settled Javanese-speaking population in the north coastal plain of Banten. The term Wetanger derived from the Javanese *Wetan*, meaning east.

55 ADB 24: 34–36, report by Commissioner P.A. van der Parra in Banten to Batavia, 9 October 1753; ADB 16: 49, Memorie van Overgave, Willem Hendrik van Ossenberch to Hugo Pieter Faure, 28 July 1761.

56 Hoog Regerings Batavia, Nationaal Archief, The Hague (hereafter HRB) 1005: 44, report by J. de Rovere van Breugel, Banten, no date, 1783.

57 VOC 2864: 148–149, Commander W.H. van Ossenberch to Batavia, 3 December 1755; HRB 1005: 66, report by J. de Rovere van Breugel, Banten, no date, 1783.

58 VOC 3185: 61, pepper cultivation report, J.B. Koehl to J. Reijnouts in Banten, no date, 1766; VOC 3214: no pagination, J. Reijnouts to Batavia, 31 August 1767; VOC 3248: no pagination, pepper cultivation report, J. Benjamin Koehl to Commander J. Reijnouts in Banten, 21 September 1768.

59 ADB 177: C-3, Statistiek van Residentie Bantam, 31 March 1821, *Resumé*, 162; *Eindresumé*, II, 12.

60 William Marsden, *A History of Sumatra* (Kuala Lumpur etc.: Oxford University Press, 1975 [1811]), pp. 134–139.

pepper cultivators thus did not have to worry about the frequent migration and disappearance of their people.

The number of able-bodied men shows large geographical differences. Apart from the above-mentioned Panimbang, Northwest and Karang Southwest areas, large numbers of men were recorded in the Karang South and Lemer Upstream areas. As these areas on the southern slopes of the Karang Mountains and their outskirts were relatively densely populated and fertile, influential *ponggawa* would have had more possibility to increase power through production of pepper and other crops. On the other hand, the population was small in upstream areas of Ujung, Sineut and Berang (Figure 7.2) on the slopes of the Kendang Mountains, which did not have important industry. Interestingly, it was especially in these areas that a few influential *ponggawa* became increasingly dominant toward 1790. Due to the absence of other important industries, the impact of pepper cultivation seems to have been stronger in these scarcely populated areas.

Some locally influential *ponggawa* gained high-ranking positions in the court because of their cooperation on pepper cultivation. Pangeran Suradilaga, whose power base was in the Karang Southwest area around 1770, was probably Shahbandar (harbor master) Kyai Aria Suradilaga. In 1763 he was appointed by the sultan to conduct an inspection tour, accompanying a VOC official.[61] The following year, he was appointed as the official in charge of the promotion of pepper cultivation. In 1766 he was promoted to Prime Minister (*rijksbestierder*) at the sultan's request and with the VOC's approval.[62] After the death of Kyai Aria Suradilaga, Ki Aria Trunajaya from the Panimbang area was appointed Prime Minister in 1773, later changing his name to Pangeran Dipanagara.[63] According to a Dutch report of 1779, the official in charge of the promotion of pepper cultivation was the third highest-ranking position in the sultan's court, after only the prime minister and Shahbandar.[64] In 1784 Raden Aria Wignyadiraja from the Karang Southwest area, who had been the official in charge of the promotion of pepper cultivation, took over the position of Prime Minister from Pangeran Dipanagara.[65] The fact that three

61 VOC 3093: 42, Commander Hugo Pieter Faure in Banten to Batavia, 28 Sepember 1763.

62 ADB 17: 13, Memorie van Overgave, Thomas Schippers to Johannes Reynouts, Banten, 31 May 1764; *Opkomst*, XI: 377, Memorie van Overgave, Johannes Reynouts to Willem Carpenter van Westerbeek, 20 January 1779.

63 VOC 3388: 12, Commander Johannes Reijnouts to Batavia, 30 April1773.

64 *Opkomst*, XI: 377–378, Memorie van Overgave, Johannes Reynouts to Willem Carpenter van Westerbeek, 20 January 1779.

65 ADB 18: 17, Memorie van Overgave, W.C. Engert to J. Reynouts, Banten, no date, 1781; VOC 3655: 793v, Generale Missiven, 31 December 1784.

successive prime ministers had their power bases in different areas means that specific land and people belonging to them were not related to their position. It was rather that influential local *ponggawa* were appointed to the position. There seems to have been a pattern whereby a powerful local *ponggawa* from important pepper-producing areas became the official in charge of the promotion of pepper cultivation, and he was later appointed Prime Minister. Knowledge of and experience in the promotion of pepper cultivation were highly valued. In fact, the VOC commander Faure at Banten accepted Kyai Aria Tisnanagara, recommended by the sultan, as Prime Minister because he was very familiar with pepper cultivation.[66] Seated in these high positions, influential *ponggawa* would have further augmented their authority and income.

In spite of the steady increase in pepper production, however, VOC authorities in Banten, Batavia, and Amsterdam had doubted the effectiveness of pepper production promotion policy since 1777, because production remained less than expected.[67] Inspections in following years discovered problems, such as the inclusion of pebbles among harvested pepper seeds, lack of labor and inaccuracies (among other things) in inspection reports.[68] In order to deal with these problems, the inspection in 1789 was conducted in an extraordinarily serious manner by two newly appointed VOC officials. This inspection revealed that cultivators generally disliked growing pepper, and a number of them had fled their kampongs, deserting the pepper gardens. Production had been stagnating partly because of bad weather such as heat and drought, but more seriously because of cultivators' unwillingness. Kampong chiefs had also reported much larger numbers of pepper vines in previous inspections than existed in reality. They falsified numbers, sometimes by inserting tips of chopped vines in the ground, or by bribing local officials (*panlako*) sent by Dutch investigators.[69] The fact that since 1777 Dutch investigators had visited only the northern parts of the hinterlands, sending *panlako* to other areas for investigation, made these practices easier.[70]

---

66 VOC 3093: 19–21, Commander Hugo Pieter Faure in Banten to Batavia, 4 August 1763.

67 VOC 338, Patriase Missiven, 8 October 1777.

68 VOC 3503: 1593v–1594v., Generale Missiven, 31 December; MCP 4: 75–76, report by J. de Rovere van Breugel, 30 November 1786; VOC 3762: 26–27, Commander W.C. Engert to Batavia, 5 June 1787.

69 ADB 27: 50–51, pepper cultivation report, J. v.d. Boogaart and F. Chambon, Banten, 7 August 1789; ibid.: 56–57, 8 August 1789; ibid.: 85–86, 28 August 1789; ADB 30: 212r.–214r., pepper cultivation report, J. v.d. Boogaart and F. Chambon, Banten, 20 November 1789.

70 MCP 4: 187–188, report by J. de Rovere van Breugel, 5 May 1788.

The main reason for dissatisfaction among pepper cultivators was the low payment by the *ponggawa*.[71] They considered 7.5 Spanish Reals per bahar proper payment for their pepper. However investigators witnessed only one case where cultivators received this payment in 1789.[72] In other cases, cultivators received 6 to 6.5 Spanish Reals.[73] They complained strongly about low payments, and many fled their village in order to avoid pepper cultivation.[74]

This shows how eager ordinary cultivators were to gain cash income, and how sensitive they were to differences in payment. This is interesting, as prior to the introduction of pepper cultivation they had few opportunities for cash income. The cultivation of pepper and nutmeg, the only cash crops grown in the Banten hinterland in the pre-1763 period, was short-lived and limited to small areas. It was therefore only during the period of pepper cultivation promotion from the mid-1760s to 1790 that ordinary cultivators become eager for cash income.

Eagerness for cash income among ordinary cultivators was also obvious in their attempts to cultivate coffee, another important cash crop in eighteenth-century Java. In 1789, Dutch pepper investigators discovered 200 coffee trees grown in Pandeglang in the Karang South area, and a small number of coffee trees in some other places, such as Somang. In each place, they immediately ordered kampong chiefs to stop cultivation.[75] During the following year's investigation, however, 4,000 coffee trees were discovered between Cangoang and Passir Ginteng in the Karang South area. Having seen these trees, investigators concluded that coffee was not causing damage to pepper cultivation.[76] Coffee cultivation was probably a cultivator's spontaneous venture, as no information about any *ponggawa*'s enforcement appeared in inspection reports.[77]

71 ADB 27: 10–11, pepper cultivation report, J. v.d. Boogaart and F. Chambon, Banten, 27 July 1789; ibid.: 24–25, 30 July 1789; ibid.: 62–63, 10 August 1789.

72 ADB 27: 42, pepper cultivation report, J. v.d. Boogaart and F. Chambon, Banten, 3 August 1789.

73 ADB 27: 26–27, pepper cultivation report, J. v.d. Boogaart and F. Chambon, Banten, 1789; Ibid.: 43–44, 3 August 1789; ibid.: 116–118, 7 September 1789.

74 ADB 30: 217r.–218r., pepper cultivation report, J. v.d. Boogaart and F. Chambon, Banten, 20 November 1789.

75 ADB 27: 16, pepper cultivation report, J. v.d. Boogaart and F. Chambon, Banten, 28 July 1789; ibid.: 116–118, 7 September 1789.

76 ADB 30: no pagination, pepper cultivation report, J. v.d. Boogaart and F. Chambon, Banten, 11 November 1790.

77 This is a strong indication of cultivators' spontaneous coffee cultivation, because if their *ponggawa* forced them to do anything other than pepper cultivation, cultivators always

The VOC authorities, however, were not keen to promote coffee cultivation in the Banten hinterlands. The commander of the VOC factory at Kota Banten sent a sample of coffee grown there to Company executives in Amsterdam in 1791, probably in order to discuss the possibility of promoting its production for VOC trade. They replied that they would not recommend coffee cultivation in Banten because it would be difficult to promote it in addition to pepper.[78] Although detailed information about the hinterlands dies out after 1790, people seem to have continued cultivating coffee in spite of Dutch indifference, because in 1801, 130 pounds of coffee were delivered from the hinterlands.[79] As Dutch control on trade was weak and many foreign traders were looking for business opportunities around Banten at the turn of the nineteenth century (as I discuss later), it would be rather easy for cultivators to find non-Dutch buyers to bid a better price for produce. Coffee trees were probably sent from the neighboring Priangan region, where the VOC had strongly promoted coffee cultivation since the early eighteenth century. The small amount of export may not have strongly influenced overall trade in Java, but the interesting thing is that ordinary cultivators attempted to start cash-crop cultivation on their own initiative. This case shows that ordinary cultivators in the Banten highlands were becoming more market-oriented.

The market-oriented tendency of Banten cultivators is also clear in their choice of destination when fleeing kampongs. The most popular destination was Grending, upstream on the Sadane River. Investigators of pepper cultivation heard during their survey in 1789 that thousands of cultivators had migrated to Grending in recent years, because they could easily find a means of livelihood there.[80] This means of livelihood was probably first related to woodcutting, because Grending was one place that supplied firewood to sugar mills around the Sadane River.[81] An opportunity to obtain wages was an important factor behind migration to Grending.

---

complained about it to the pepper investigators, in order to make an excuse for their poor results of pepper cultivation.

78 VOC 343: s 400, Patriase Missiven, 7 December 1791; ibid.: s 385, 26 November 1792.

79 The coffee was exported to Batavia at 6 Rijksdaalders per picol. ADB 34: 19, Commander F.H. Beijnon to Batavia, 8 January 1801.

80 ADB 27: 167–169, pepper cultivation report, J. v.d. Boogaart and F. Chambon, Banten, 20 November 1789; ADB 30: 218r–219r, pepper cultivation report, J. v.d. Boogaart and F. Chambon, Banten, 20 November 1789.

81 Andries Teisseire, "Verhandeling over den tegenwoordigen staat der zuikermolens omstreeks de stadt Batavia, benevens de middelen tot derzelver herstel, en eenige

Grending had been a contested place, over which no authorities were clearly and stably established. In the treaty in 1747, the sultan had agreed to cede this area to the VOC. However, some members of the local *ponggawa* were not satisfied with this agreement, and they created trouble by, for example, forcibly relocating people from Grending to their lands. As a result, the VOC banished the native chiefs appointed by these local elites, and instead appointed a Dutch civil person as chief of Grending in 1768.[82] This solution, however, does not seem to have strengthened Dutch control over the area. Under a complicated and conflicting relationship between Dutch authorities and the local *ponggawa*, Grending became a place where no one exerted effective control.

Grending was developing into a brisk trade center, which gave opportunities for increasingly market-oriented people in Banten to obtain commercial items with their money. Grending had become a center of trade conducted between Batavia, Jakarta's upland region (*Jakatrase Bovenlanden*) and Banten. A number of Batavian Chinese and those from Jakarta's upland brought trade items such as textiles and household items to sell to customers from the Banten hinterlands. In return, those from Banten sold natural products such as kapok, buffalos, goats and leather.[83] Traders from Grending also came to the hinterlands of Banten, bought the pepper produced there, in all likelihood to sell in Grending or other places for outside markets.[84] Development of trade in Grending would have helped people in the Banten hinterlands become increasingly involved in the monetary economy.

In the face of outflow of their people, many *ponggawa* abandoned pepper cultivation entirely. Pepper production thus dropped after 1790. Instead, in order to maintain income and influence, many of them initiated wet rice cultivation. The first information on starting rice cultivation dates to 1768,[85] and Dutch

---

verdere daar toe betrekkelyke aanmerkingen," *Verhandelingen van de Bataviaasch Genootschap van Kunsten en Wetenschappen* (hereafter VBG), 5 (1790), pp. 206–209.

82 ADB 25: 3–7, Willem Hendrik van Ossenberch in Banten, to Batavia, 2 July 1768; VOC 3221: 2841r–2841v, Generale Missiven, 31 December 1768.

83 HRB 1005: 10, report by J. de Rovere van Breugel, Banten, no date, 1783; ADB 30: 253r–254r, pepper cultivation report, J. v.d. Boogaart and F. Chambon, Banten, 20 November 1789; ADB 31: 368–369, Commander F.H. Beijnon in Banten to Batavia, 23 September 1793.

84 ADB 27: 185, pepper cultivation report, J. v.d. Boogaart and F. Chambon, Banten, 20 November 1789.

85 VOC 3248: no pagination, pepper cultivation report, J. Benjamin Koehl to Commander J. Reijnouts in Banten, 21 July 1768.

sources frequently mentioned it in 1789.[86] In Sekong in the Karang South area, for example, the *ponggawa* forced his people to develop 120 morgen of wet rice fields.[87] Inspection reports of 1789 concluded that forced labor in rice fields in many places in the hinterlands kept cultivators away from pepper gardens.[88]

The most notable case of the development of rice cultivation is one promoted by Yuda Nagara in Caringin. Yuda Nagara, also called Pangeran of Caringin, was the most powerful *ponggawa* in the Karang Southwest area. In 1792 he reportedly mobilized 300 people to dig canals and to open new rice fields, and forcibly placed sixty to ninety people to maintain the fields. He forced people to work without payment, and imposed fines on those who neglected work. Using money collected from his people, he bought laborers' necessities and two cannons for protection from pirates. As a result of his tyranny, many people fled to other areas, deserting thirty-one pepper gardens. A Dutch official who investigated Caringin concluded that Yuda Nagara should be dismissed, although there is no information that this suggestion was put into practice.[89] Interestingly, Yuda Nagara established a monopoly on rice produced on his lands, and sold it to the outside market via the ports under his influence, in defiance of Dutch trade control. The elite in the hinterlands of Banten were now also strongly market-oriented.

Sugar Production in the Sadane River Area

Sugar production developed in Banten in the mid-eighteenth century on a much larger scale than before,[90] with the result that the center of production in the *ommelanden* of Batavia, which had produced most of the sugar in Java during the seventeenth and eighteenth centuries, gradually shifted

86 ADB 27: 34, pepper cultivation report, J. v.d. Boogaart and F. Chambon, Banten, 1 August 1789.

87 Morgen is a measure of the size of a rice field. One morgen is 15 x 6 fathoms (1 fathom is approximately 1.8 meters). ADB 27: 28–29, pepper cultivation report, J. v.d. Boogaart and F. Chambon, Banten, 31 July 1789.

88 ADB 27: 175–176, pepper cultivation report, J. v.d. Boogaart and F. Chambon, Banten, 20 November 1789; ADB 30: 233r.–234r., pepper cultivation report, J. v.d. Boogaart and F. Chambon, Banten, 20 November 1789.

89 ADB 30: 122–126, pepper cultivation report, J. v.d. Boogaart and F. Chambon, Banten, 22 October 1792; CZOHB 61: 1351r–1351v, Generale Missiven, 31 January 1794.

90 Sugar production had been attempted in the northeast coast of Banten in the early seventeenth century and the early eighteenth century, but these attempts ended within short periods. Talens, *Een feodale samenleving*, pp. 76–82.

westward.[91] The most important reason for this shift was an increasing shortage of the firewood necessary to refine sugar.[92] In search of firewood, the sugar industry had crossed the *ommelanden*-Banten border before 1747,[93] and the Banten Sultanate had become the sole provider of firewood before 1785.[94] Ample forest resources in East Banten allowed sugar cultivation to survive only in the Sadane River area (West *ommelanden* and East Banten) in the late eighteenth century. By this time sugar production was predominantly in the hands of Chinese entrepreneurs.[95]

Chinese sugar entrepreneurs were always faced with the difficulty of finding laborers. Natives of the *ommelanden* were notorious for their unwillingness to carry out the hard, unpleasant work in the sugar industry. Therefore sugar entrepreneurs recruited Chinese and Javanese laborers for sugar mills and

91 Previous studies tend to ignore the sugar production in the *ommelanden* of Batavia after the Chinese Massacre in 1740. They seem to have considered that the Massacre, which dramatically reduced the number of the Chinese population in Batavia and its vicinity, brought an end to the industry. Kristof Glamann, *Dutch-Asiatic Trade 1620–1740* (The Hague: Martinus Nijhoff, 1958), pp. 158–165; Leonard Blussé, *Strange Company: Chinese Settlers, Mestizo Women and the Dutch in VOC Batavia* (Dordrecht: Foris, 1986), pp. 91–93. More recently, however, Peter Boomgaard and myself argue that the sugar production in Java was neither negligible nor dying out in the late eighteenth century. Peter Boomgaard, "Java's Agricultural Production, 1775–1875," in Angus Maddison and Gé Prince (eds.), *Economic Growth in Indonesia, 1820–1940* (Dordrecht: Foris, 1989), pp. 99, 119; Ota *Changes of Regime*, pp. 132–135.

92 Starting in 1710, the VOC was worrying that too many sugar mills would soon destroy the remaining forests, and the VOC government at Batavia repeatedly attempted to restrict the number of sugar mills. Jan Hooyman, "Verhandeling over den tegenwoordigen staat van den land-bouw, in de Ommelanden van Batavia," *VBG*, 1 (1779), p. 238; Hooyman, "Verhandeling over den tegenwoordigen staat," pp. 238–239; N.P. van den Berg, "De suikerindustrie op Java onder het bestuur van de Oost-Indische Compagnie," in N.P. van den Berg (ed.), *Uit de dagen der Compagnie: geschiedkundige schetsen* (Haarlem: H.D. Tjeenk Willing & Zoon, 1904), p. 329.

93 *Opkomst*, X, p. 122, Director General Jacob Mossel in Banten to Batavia, 21 February 1747. The sultan of Banten sold firewood to sugar entrepreneurs, or leased the land with rights of logging at the latest since the 1760s. HRB 1004: 329–330, report by Commander J. Reijnouts, Banten to Batavia 2 July 1766. VOC 3767: 1153v, Genrerale Missiven, 29 December 1787.

94 Teisseire, "Verhandeling [...] omstreeks de stadt Batavia," pp. 122, 135–138.

95 Although the VOC government in Batavia attempted to promote the sugar industry by inviting Dutch entrepreneurs after the Chinese Massacre in 1740, they soon sold their rights to Chinese entrepreneurs because they hated unfavourable conditions such as limitation in inheritance and high tax after exemption for five years. F. de Haan, *Priangan: De Preanger-regentschappen onder het Nederlandsch bestuur tot 1811* (Batavia: G. Kolff, 1910–12), vol. I, pp. 267–271; ibid., vol. IV, p. 101.

fields. Unskilled Chinese laborers were shipped every year by Amoy junks, which carried at least 12,000 to 13,000 Chinese coolies. Chinese workers were considered suitable for heavy work because of their diligence, and it was considered totally impossible to conduct sugar cultivation without them. Sugar mill owners also recruited Javanese workers every year from Cirebon, Tagal and other densely populated regions, although recruitment was difficult because local chiefs (*bupati*) often opposed the outflow of their manpower.[96] Skilled laborers were almost all Chinese, and they probably moved from other parts of the *ommelanden*, as sugar production shifted westward.

In contrast to nineteenth-century sugar cultivation in Central Java, which often used existing rice fields to plant sugarcane, sugarcanes were usually planted in newly opened fields in the eighteenth-century Sadane River area. The sugar produced was sold only to the VOC at fixed prices.[97]

The sugar industry was not an enterprise consisting solely of sugar production. In fact, sugar mill owners gained considerable benefit from the management of stalls (*warung*) attached to their mills. The *warung* sold opium and other necessities to laborers, in exchange for tokens distributed in advance. Sugar laborers needed opium as refreshment after hard work. According to the Dutch entrepreneur Andries Teisseire, in the 1750s a sugar entrepreneur gained 900 Rijksdaalders of profit in one season, out of which 300 Rijksdaalders came from sales of opium at his *warung*. For sugar entrepreneurs, opium was a convenient tool to keep laborers in the sugar mills. They were obliged to buy opium exclusively from the *Amfioen Societeit*, an organization consisting of VOC officials.[98]

This is how sugar production in the Ci Sadane region was a VOC-controlled industry, through its exclusive purchase of sugar and exclusive provision of opium, until around the 1770s. Sugar mill owners also monopolized provision of opium and other necessities for their laborers. This monopolistic system began to collapse in the 1780s.

Development of the Borderland Society

In the 1780s, the sugar industry in the Sadane River area in general experienced crisis. Teisseire reported in 1790 that costs to maintain the industry, such as rice

96 Hooyman, "Verhandeling [...] in de Ommelanden van Batavia," pp. 215–216.

97 The VOC bought the sugar at 4.5 Rijksdaalders per picol for the first grade product, and 4.25 Rijksdaalders for the second grade. Hooyman, "Verhandeling [...] in de Ommelanden van Batavia," p. 210; Teisseire, "Verhandeling [...] omstreeks de stadt Batavia," pp. 152–153.

98 Teisseire, "Verhandeling [...] omstreeks de stadt Batavia," pp. 81, 126–127, 148–152, 176–178.

and firewood, rose generally and increasingly burdened mill owners. He desperately claimed that if the VOC would not raise its purchase price, the industry would not survive.[99]

Another important factor behind the crisis was the decline in sales at their *warung*. The price of opium provided by the *Amfioen Societeit* rose toward 1790.[100] This price increase was most likely related to the stabilization of British control in Bengal. As the British strengthened their control on the opium trade during the 1780s, it became increasingly difficult for the Dutch to procure opium directly from producers, and they had to buy it from the British at much higher prices.[101] *Warung*, however, could not raise their selling prices, because sugar laborers now frequented *warung* in the upland (*bovenlanden*), which were increasing in number, in order to buy opium and other commodities as cheaply as possible.[102]

The upland of the Sadane River area was Grending. As discussed earlier, Grending developed into a commercial center by the end of the 1780s, and opium was one of the most important items traded there. Chinese traders based in Batavia brought opium from Tangerang via Grending to Banten.[103] The opium brought to Banten would have been sold largely in sugar mills, considering their strong demand for cheap opium. This 'clandestine' opium was cheaper than that obtained through the official channels. The trade of opium and other necessities in Grending provided commodities to the *warung* there.

Both Banten and Dutch authorities kept a wary eye on the trade in Grending. First of all, opium was an item under VOC monopoly. In addition, the Dutch had attempted to concentrate Banten's trade with Batavia in a few authorized ports in Kota Banten, where Dutch officials checked trade items.[104] 'Unauthorized' trade in Grending meant a reduction in the sultan's tax revenue

---

99 The current purchase prices of 4.5 and 4.25 Rijksdaalders per picol for the first and the second grades of sugar, while Tesseire suggested they should be 5 and 4.75 Rijksdaalders respectively. Teisseire, "Verhandeling [...] omstreeks de stadt Batavia," pp. 152–153.

100 Teisseire, "Verhandeling [...] omstreeks de stadt Batavia," pp. 148–151.

101 Carl A. Trocki, *Opium, Empire and the Global Political Economy: A study of the Asian Opium Trade 1750–1950* (London and New York: Routledge, 1990), p. 54.

102 Teisseire, "Verhandeling [...] omstreeks de stadt Batavia," pp. 148–151, 177–178.

103 The original text states that opium was brought via the Jakarta's [upland] border to Banten. This route passes through Grending. HRB 1005: 10, report by J. de Rovere van Breugel, Banten, no date, 1783.

104 The result was recorded in the "list of incoming and outgoing ships" included in the reports and letters sent to Batavia. For the details of this series of lists, see also Knaap, *Shallow Waters*.

in authorized ports, and a break in VOC trade control. During a pepper cultivation inspection in 1789, Dutch inspectors attempted to send local officials to Grending in order to obtain more information, but they refused to go because they believed it was unhealthy there and they wouldn't be able to return.[105] It is not clear in what sense Grending was 'unhealthy', although it was an area outside state control, and local officials might therefore have thought it dangerous. There are no sources reporting that the sultanate or VOC took effective measures to control Grending during the eighteenth century. Grending continued to develop into the nineteenth century, and in 1808 it was considered a well populated and fertile place.[106]

In addition to Grending in the upland, a borderland society also developed in the coastal part of the Sadane River area and the northeast coast in Banten. Chinese kampongs had developed there from the mid-eighteenth century; first in relation to the sugar industry.[107] Toward the end of the eighteenth century, however, these Chinese kampongs became increasingly involved in 'clandestine' trade. Chinese kampongs such as Kramat, Tanjung Kait, Karang Serang and Ketapan became pivotal points of the 'smuggling' network centered on Tanara, a port town on the northeast coast of Banten. Tanara, also populated with a number of Chinese merchants, connected itself to the sugar mills in the above-mentioned Chinese kampongs and also to Grending through river and land routes. Tanara also established trade relations through sea routes with Batavia, and with islands off the coast.[108] Some islands in the Banten Bay and off the coast of the Ci Sadane area, such as Onrust, Pulau Panjang and Pulau Seribu, were important places for Bugis, Malay, Chinese and other Asian 'pirates' and 'smugglers' to trade commodities in the late eighteenth century. These groups of people brought to these islands pepper and other products such as rattan and birds' nests, which they obtained, sometimes forcibly, from Lampung, in defiance of the Dutch and the Banten sultan's monopoly. They sold these products to Chinese junk traders and British traders from Batavia, Malay Peninsula and India, and in exchange they obtained opium, ammunition and

---

105 ADB 27: 167–169, pepper cultivation report, J. v.d. Boogaart and F. Chambon, Banten, 20 November 1789.

106 For this reason the *ponggawa* Raden Ganya attempted to become the ruler (*regent*) there. MCP 58: 61–62, 29 January 1808.

107 Teisseire, "Beschryving," pp. 98–99. Commité tot de Zaken van de Oost-Indischen Handel en Bezittingen, Nationaal Archief, The Hague (hereafter CZOHB) 120: 14, Commander F.H. Beijnon in Banten to Batavia, 10 January 1795.

108 ADB 27: 185–186, pepper cultivation report, J. v.d. Boogaart and F. Chambon, Banten, 20 November 1789.

other commodities.[109] VOC officials discovered that Chinese sugar mill owners purchased opium there, sometimes from British traders.[110] Cheaper opium brought through these channels must have met strong demand in sugar mills.

This 'clandestine' trade in and around the Sadane River region was part of the interregional trade pattern that had been emerging in the Melaka-Sunda Strait region. Since the 1760s, the collection of Southeast Asian products for the China market, such as tin, pepper and edible maritime products, had become increasingly important for European and Chinese traders because of the growing Chinese economy and European interests in Chinese tea. British and Chinese traders purchased these products in exchange for, respectively, Indian opium and textiles and various Chinese items, while Bugis, Malay, Iranun, and other Asian traders collected Southeast Asian products, sometimes in a forcible manner, from various parts of the Archipelago. Riau, south of Singapore and capital of the Johor Kingdom, emerged as a center for these traders to exchange items. However, after the Dutch conquered Riau in 1784, the trade center dispersed into several smaller bases such as Terengganu, Siak, Bangka and Belitung. Asian traders based in these places collected Southeast Asian commodities for the Chinese market in the Melaka-Sunda Strait region and other places, and sold them to Chinese and British traders.[111] The Sadane River area became part of this trade pattern, and was thereby involved in the growing India-Sino-Southeast Asian trade system.

Local and Dutch authorities were on watch for Chinese sugar kampongs and their trade activities in the coastal areas. In 1772, the Chinese Captain in Kota Banten requested that the commander of the VOC Banten factory allow Chinese to live only in Banten, Tanara, and several sugar factories, and not in other places.[112] The Chinese Captain, nominated within the Chinese community and admitted by the VOC commander, was supposed to preside over social and economic issues in the Chinese community in the capital, which

---

109 VOC 3475: 1723v–1724r, Generale Missiven, 31 December 1777.

110 HRB 1005: 11, report by J. de Rovere van Breugel, Banten, no date, 1783.

111 For the trade pattern centered on Riau in the 1760s–1784 period, see Carl A. Trocki, *Prince of Pirates: The Temenggongs and the Development of Johor and Singapore 1784–1885* (Singapore: Singapore University Press, 1979); Reinout Vos, *Gentle Janus, Merchant Prince: The VOC and the Tightrope of Diplomacy in the Malay World, 1740–1800* (Leiden: KITLV, 1993); Dianne Lewis, *Jan Compagnie in the Straits of Malacca 1641–1795* (Athens, Ohio: Ohio University Center for International Studies, 1995). For the trade in the Malacca Strait region after 1784, see Ota, *Changes of Regime.*

112 VOC 3363: 9–10, Captain lieutenant of the Chinese, Lim Genko and Ong Tanko in Banten to Batavia, 7 September 1772.

was basically a community of registered *peranakan* (long-settled) Chinese. However, he did not have power over newly-emerged Chinese immigrant communities in coastal areas, and he was afraid that those communities would expand further and erode *peranakan* privileges. The Batavian government also attempted to check the expansion of new Chinese communities and their illicit trade. It promulgated an order in 1794, that apart from sugar mills in Karang Serang and Kramat, no Chinese should be allowed to live within two hours of the coast, because the Dutch strongly suspected that coastal Chinese communities were involved in clandestine trade. It was the sultan who was supposed to put this order into practice.[113] There is, however, no source establishing that this order was actually implemented or had effectively curbed 'smuggling'. In 1795, the commander of the VOC Banten factory requested that the sultan appoint a more competent chief to maintain peace and order on lands lent out to Batavian citizens; that is, most typically, sugar kampongs in the Sadane River area.[114] These chains of requests show that no one could exert effective authority over new Chinese communities.

In contrast to the development of the Sadane River area, the old economic centers Batavia and Kota Banten, fell into decline in the second half of the eighteenth century. The environment of Batavia increasingly deteriorated and the city was depopulated after 1740.[115] In Kota Banten, the Banten River, which connected the coastal port and upland areas, was heavily silted, and as a result the port became inaccessible for modest-sized ships during the 1770s.[116] Trade with Lampung declined after the 1770s, because its pepper transport was disrupted by increasing pirate attacks, and a part of Lampung pepper was sold to non-Dutch buyers. The sultan attempted to compensate for his declining income, partly by farming out rights of taxation on various commodities and commercial activities to a limited number of authorized Chinese merchants. However, this policy resulted instead only in choking an economy that was already in decline. In fact, the Chinese population in Kota Banten and Tanara declined remarkably in the late 1770s.[117] Some Chinese who left Kota Banten might have joined growing trade in the Sadane River area.

113 CZOHB 120: 13–14, Commander F.H. Beijnon in Banten to Batavia, 10 January 1795.

114 CZOHB 120: 13–14, Commander F.H. Beijnon in Banten to Batavia, 10 January 1795.

115 Blussé, *Strange Company*; Remco Raben, "Batavia and Colombo: The Ethnic and Spatial Order of Two Colonial Cities 1600–1800" (Ph.D. Dissertation, Leiden University, 1996).

116 J.D.R.V.B. (J. de Rovere van Breugel), "Bedenkingen over den Staat van Bantam," *BKI*, new series, 1 (1856), p. 130.

117 J.D.R.V.B., "Bedenkingen," pp. 122–125.

Conclusion

Until the early 1760s, the hinterlands of Banten were economically important neither for the state center nor for the outer world, because of their ecologically determined small population and low production. Pepper cultivation and the much shorter-lived nutmeg cultivation, the only two cash crops grown there, had died out by then.

The Dutch policy to promote pepper cultivation drastically changed this situation. The VOC strongly intervened in Banten hinterlands, and local *ponggawa* elites and ordinary cultivators obtained cash income. *Ponggawa* came to exert stronger influence on followers because pepper production made cultivators settle in one place for a much longer time than before. Powerful *ponggawa* took people and kampongs from weak *ponggawa*, in order to increase pepper cultivation effectively in geographically concentrated places.

The impact of cash income from pepper cultivation was enormous. Because of eagerness to gain income, ordinary cultivators withdrew from unprofitable pepper cultivation, and some of them attempted coffee cultivation while others migrated to Grending to earn wages. Some *ponggawa* started wet rice cultivation to sell the produce in outside markets. They became increasingly market-oriented.

The sugar industry brought another type of dynamism to the Sadane River area, the eastern edge of the Banten hinterlands. Demand for Chinese labor in the industry and the migration of Sundanese pepper cultivators from other parts of the Banten hinterlands created migrant communities. When the sugar industry experienced general crisis and the VOC increased opium prices, these migrant communities created 'clandestine' trade networks dealing in opium and other household items with Chinese traders from Batavia, Southeast Asian traders from various places in the Melaka-Sunda Strait region, and British traders from India and elsewhere. Coffee and pepper brought from the Banten hinterlands to Grending were also sold to outside markets, probably at least partly through these outside traders. This is how the Ci Sadane area developed into a borderland society, entailing multiple ethnicities and transborder trade.

Growing activities of outside traders were closely related to the world economy. As India-Sino-Southeast Asian trade thrived, stimulated by the growing Chinese economy and European interest in Chinese tea, Indian opium was circulated in Southeast Asia in large quantities, and Chinese and British traders attempted to purchase pepper and other Southeast Asian products for the Chinese market. The demand for coffee was growing in European markets.

The hinterlands of Banten responded to these developments in the world economy. Under weakening central control, the hinterlands of Banten became increasingly connected to the world economy through contacts with the outside traders. People's profit maximization behavior meant that the Banten hinterlands became increasingly market-oriented, multiethnic and more strongly involved in transborder trade.

CHAPTER 8

Hinterlands and Port Cities in Southeast Asia's Economic Development in the Eighteenth Century

The Case of Tin Production and its Export Trade

Ryuto Shimada

Introduction

Joseph A. Schumpeter, a well-known twentieth-century economist, pointed out five conditions that lead to economic development: that is, (1) the introduction of a new good; (2) the introduction of a new method of production; (3) the opening of a new market; (4) the conquest of a new source of supply of raw materials or half-manufactured goods; and (5) the carrying out of the new organization of any industry.[1] Similarly to other parts of the world, some of these conditions emerged in Southeast Asia during the early modern period. Some of these conditions can be easily found historically by performing research using an analytical framework that investigates the connections between a port and its hinterland in an economy. It is argued that the use of this specific analytical framework on the economic functions of ports and hinterlands should contribute significantly toward making the theory and the history of economic development in Southeast Asia much more sophisticated.

This is because the region provided several sorts of primary products to other regions on a large scale, and such exports formed a significant economic basis not only for the people engaged in trading business at port towns but also for ordinary producers in the hinterlands. Reacting to large demand for primary products from the outside, each local economic system developed in Southeast Asia, where local societies exported specific primary products while importing necessary items such as foodstuffs and clothes through port towns. In this sense, each port city can be regarded as a centre for each local economy in Southeast Asia. Moreover, they were also important places for political decision-making, as shown by the fact that local kings and sultans usually resided in such port cities. Although Ayutthaya and Palembang are typical examples of such economically and politically important port cities in Southeast Asia, there were other types of port cities. Some ports were relatively large and

1 Joseph A. Schumpeter, *The Theory of Economic Development* (Cambridge, Massachusetts: Harvard University Press, 1934), p. 66.

© KONINKLIJKE BRILL NV, LEIDEN, 2015 | DOI 10.1163/9789004283909_010

visited by Europeans traders, such as the Dutch East India Company [*Verenigde Oostindische Compagnie*: VOC] (1602–1799), and some ports were smaller but used by many indigenous traders for trading business. In addition, ports were connected multilaterally with each other and formed a large trading network as a whole.

A general and comparative survey of the network between several ports, therefore, would be beneficial to a fuller understanding of the function of ports and hinterlands. It should be emphasized that over the eighteenth century dynamic changes occurred in all of the economies of Asia, and not only in the economy of Southeast Asia, regarding the intensification of their contacts and connections with the global economy, which were to grow even more intensely in the nineteenth century. One of the most important elements in Asian economic development in the eighteenth century was the emergence of the Chinese economic influence in Southeast Asia. Based on detailed studies on the economy of Java, especially that of Batavia, as well as the trading activities of Chinese merchants, Leonard Blussé has proposed calling this century of expansion of Chinese economic activities in the South China Sea region (c.1740–c.1840) 'the Chinese century'.[2] In addition to Blussé's hypothesis, Carl A. Trocki has offered a general survey of Chinese expansion in the economy of Southeast Asia in terms of trading and migration by combining several cases studies.[3] Taking into consideration the geographical condition of Southeast Asia, which is located between two historically great economic powers, India and China, an examination of Southeast Asia's economic links with outside economies, from the point of view of investigating trading activities as well as economic changes in the hinterland, is clearly a significant topic.

By examining tin mining and production in Southeast Asia and its export trade in this paper (See Map 8.1), I propose not only to investigate the general functions of economic links between ports and hinterlands but also to examine the five conditions for economic development that were formulated by Schumpeter. For this purpose, this paper will focus on (1) the changes in the intra-Asian tin trade and the general global trade between Asia and Europe, especially based on the trading activities of the VOC, which was the most important trader in tin in Asian waters in terms of volume, and (2) a comparative analysis of tin

2 Leonard Blussé, 'Chinese Century: The Eighteenth Century in the China Sea Region', *Archipel*, 58 (1999), pp. 107–129.

3 Carl A. Trocki, 'Chinese Pioneering in Eighteenth-Century Southeast Asia', in Anthony Reid (ed.), *The Last Stand of Asian Autonomies: Responses to Modernity in the Diverse States of Southeast Asia and Korea, 1750–1900* (Houndmills and London: Macmillan Press, 1997), pp. 83–101.

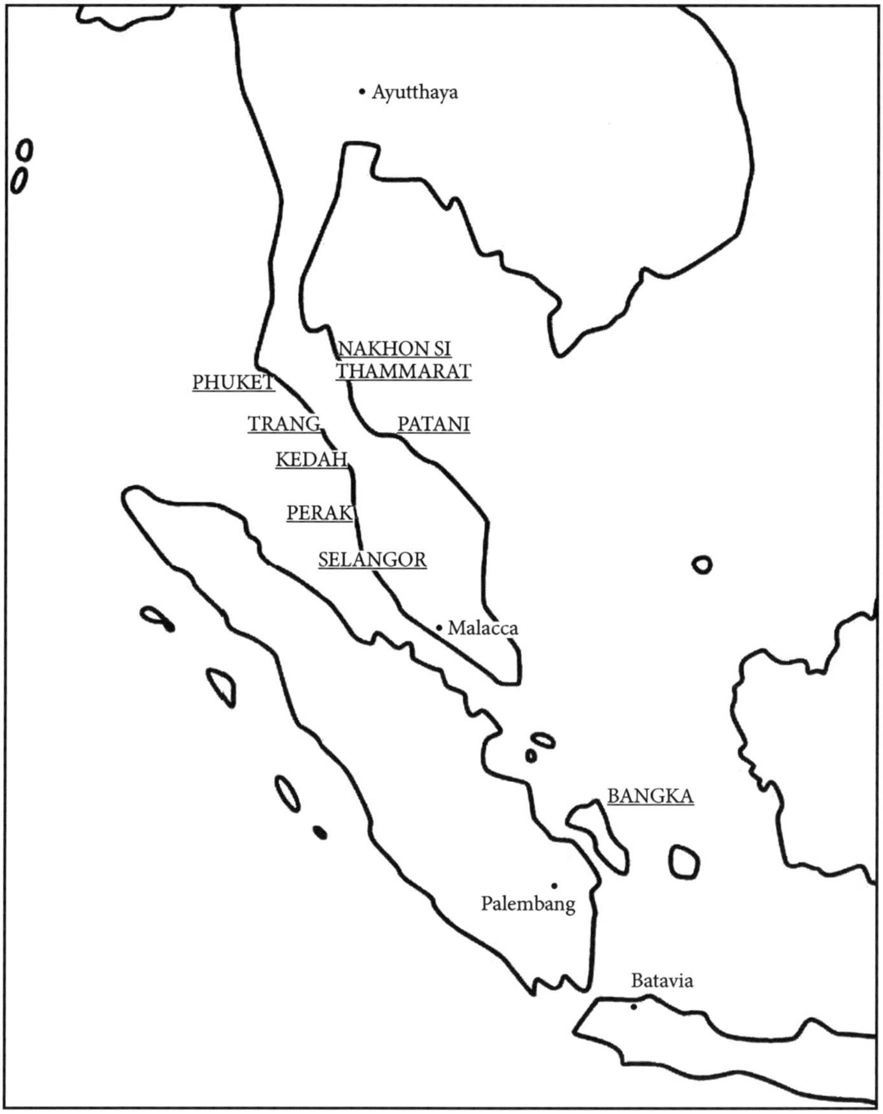

MAP 8.1 *Tin deposits in Southeast Asia in the Eighteenth Century*

production in several areas in Southeast Asia, which sheds light on the increasing role and importance of the Chinese in tin production, in particular.

VOC archival records, together with several previous studies, were consulted for this essay. The archival research included the examination of specific collections (*Archief van de Boekhouder Generaal te Batavia* (BGB) and *Archief van*

Nederlandse Factorij te Japan (NFJ), besides the regular collection of the VOC *Archief van de Verenigde Oostindische Compagnie* (VOC), all of which are preserved in the National Archives of the Netherlands (NA). It should be stressed that the study of ports and hinterlands in Southeast Asia during the early modern period are hampered in general by the relative absence of sufficient sources and records, except for specific areas in the case of the Company under strict VOC control, such as the Spice Islands and eighteenth-century Java. Company officials did not, in fact, personally visit the tin mines mentioned in this study, although they collected information on tin production from indigenous partners over the eighteenth century. While the VOC records are fragmentary and elusive, they do provide as accurate a general picture as we are likely to find of tin production in Southeast Asia in the eighteenth century, when large-scale change in the global economy was imminent.

Tin: Demand and Markets

Tin is a soft, faintly bluish-white, lustrous, low-melting, crystalline metallic element that is malleable and ductile, which was commonly used in Asia and partially in Europe in the early modern period to plate copper products. It was also used as an alloy with copper to produce bronze and as an alloy with lead to produce pewter. The respective alloys incorporating this metal were used to produce a variety of goods, such as household utensils, religious statues and cannons. There were additional demands and uses for tin in East Asia. In China, for example, people used paper-thin tin as sacrifice money when visiting temples, where it was burned as an offering for religious ceremonial purposes.[4] More significantly, during the Qing Dynasty from 1753 to 1793, tin was added to brass, an alloy of copper and zinc, in the production of copper coins in China. Although only an extremely small percentage was added, it nevertheless represented significant quantities of the metal annually.

From the seventeenth century to the first half of the eighteenth century, the most important sales or end-markets for tin from Southeast Asia for the VOC were in India, Persia, Mocha and Europe (See Table 8.2). In the eighteenth century, Qing monetary policy struggled to supply sufficient quantities of copper and zinc to mint the brass or 'copper' coin needed, due to the rapid expansion and growth of the Chinese economy and the ubiquitous use of 'copper'

4 Els M. Jacobs, *Merchant in Asia: The Trade of the Dutch East India Company during the Eighteenth Century* (Leiden: CNWS Publications, 2006), p. 201.

TABLE 8.1 *VOC deliveries of Tin to Batavia, 1711–1713 and 1751–1753*

1. 1711/12–1712/13			2. 1751/52–1752/53		
from	**Dutch lbs.**	**%**	**from**	**Dutch lbs.**	**%**
Siam	170,400	76	Siam	80,938	7
Malacca	52,500	22	Malacca	441,852	32
Palembang	0	0	Palembang	1,057,727	62
Ceylon	4,000	2	total	1,580,517	100
Total	226,900	100			

SOURCE: ELS M. JACOBS, *MERCHANT IN ASIA: THE TRADE OF THE DUTCH EAST INDIA COMPANY DURING THE EIGHTEENTH CENTURY* (LEIDEN: CNWS PUBLICATIONS, 2006), PP. 350, 368–369.

TABLE 8.2 *VOC exports of Tin from Batavia to Intra-Asian and European markets, 1711–1713 and 1771–1773*

1. 1711/12–1712/13			2. 1771/72–1772/73		
to	**Dutch lbs.**	**%**	**to**	**Dutch lbs.**	**%**
Persia	32,800	11	Coromandel	10,000	0.4
Mocha	17,600	6	Japan	25,600	4
Surat	21,600	7	Canton	552,800	86
Malabar	11,200	4	Cheribon	900	0.1
Ceylon	18,000	6	The Netherlands	65,000	10
Coromandel	30,400	10	total	646,700	100
Bengal	30,400	10			
The Netherlands	148,400	48			
total	310,400	100			

SOURCE: ELS M. JACOBS, *MERCHANT IN ASIA: THE TRADE OF THE DUTCH EAST INDIA COMPANY DURING THE EIGHTEENTH CENTURY* (LEIDEN: CNWS PUBLICATIONS, 2006), PP. 350, 368–369.

coin as currency in small-denomination transactions. Hence the addition of tin to brass in minting Chinese 'copper' coins.[5]

5 Mary F. Somers Heidhues, *Bangka Tin and Mentok Pepper: Chinese Settlement on an Indonesian Island* (Singapore: Institute of Southeast Asian Studies, 1992), p. 3.

Furthermore, according to Paul A. van Dyke, the growth of the Canton trade throughout the eighteenth century brought about increasing Chinese demand for tin. Huge amounts of Chinese tea were exported from Canton by European traders such as the VOC and English East India Company, and tin was used in packaging tea for export.[6]

Faced with these changes in the market and the resulting demand for tin, different sets of traders, including the VOC in particular, supplied large quantities of Southeast Asian tin to China. The proceeds of the VOC sales of tin from Bangka in China were used by the Company to purchase tea for export to Europe. This exchange of tin and tea began in the 1730s. From the mid-eighteenth century onwards, China was the most important end-market for Southeast Asian tin for the VOC (See Table 8.2), although China's annual imports were to decline toward the end of the century, as demonstrated in Figure 8.1. It was only in 1789 that the English East India Company (EIC) began exporting tin from Cornwall in southwest England to China, and in similar fashion the EIC used the proceeds of these sales to purchase tea in Canton for export to Europe.[7] The expanding regional demand for tin and its links with the emerging global demand for tea inevitably had several important effects on tin production in Southeast Asia.

In addition to China, Japan also emerged as a new consumer end-market for Southeast Asian tin in the second half of the eighteenth century. Due to economic growth in the eighteenth century, there was increased demand for copper and copper coins that were used for small transactions, resulting in a shortage of materials for their production, which created an opportunity for tin to be imported and incorporated in the production of 'copper' coins.[8] Like China, Japan's demand for foreign tin for the production of coinage arose in the second half of the eighteenth century. In fact, Japan imported tin from the VOC annually from 1764 onward, although the volumes of imports were much smaller than those of China (See Figure 8.1 and Table 8.3).

---

6 Paul A. van Dyke, *The Canton Trade: Life and Enterprise on the China Coast, 1700–1845* (Hong Kong: Hong Kong University Press, 2005), p. 148.

7 William Milburn, *Oriental Commerce: Containing a Geographical Description of the Principal Places in the East Indies, China, and Japan* (London: Black, Parry, & Co., 1813), vol. 2, p. 314; H.V. Bowen, 'Sinews of Trade and Empire: The Supply of Commodity Exports to the East India Company during the Late Eighteenth Century', *Economic History Review*, second series, 55, 3 (2002), pp. 473, 475.

8 Teijiro Yamawaki, *Nagasaki no Oranda Shōkan: Sekai no naka no Sakoku Nihon* [The Dutch Establishment in Nagasaki: Secluded Japan in the World] (Tokyo: Chūō Kōronsha, 1980), pp. 86–87.

FIGURE 8.1 *VOC exports of Southeast Asian Tin to China (Canton), 1763–1793 (quantities in Dutch pounds).*
SOURCE: YONG LIU, *THE DUTCH EAST INDIA COMPANY'S TEA TRADE WITH CHINA, 1757–1781* (LEIDEN AND BOSTON: BRILL ACADEMIC PUBLISHERS, 2007), PP. 178–203.

Tin Mines

During the early modern period, tin was mined and produced in Asia in Southeastern China and Southeast Asia. Tin mines and tin production in China were located in the province of Yunnan and developed alongside the rapid expansion in copper mining and production in this province throughout the eighteenth century. The tin production and output from these mines, however, was absorbed in the domestic Chinese market and not exported.

Mineral deposits of tin in Southeast Asia, on the other hand, were relatively abundant and accessible, permitting the development of major mines and sites that produced huge amounts of this metal for export in Siam (present-day Thailand), Malay states (currently Malaysia) and the island of Bangka (located east of Sumatra and northeast of the sultanate of Palembang, which claimed the island). As seen in Table 8.1, the VOC purchased and exported Southeast Asian tin from different ports at different locations in the region over the period. It is generally held that Chinese laborers were introduced in tin production in Southeast Asia in the eighteenth century, as was the case in the trade, retail and agriculture sectors. However, as shown later, this change in the organization of tin production occurred very slowly. Chinese laborers were introduced in some areas and not others, although the mining areas that did introduce Chinese laborers succeeded in rapidly expanding tin production on a large scale.

TABLE 8.3 *VOC and Dutch exports of Southeast Asian Tin to Japan, 1740–1800 (quantities in Dutch pounds)*

Year	Dutch lbs.	Year	Dutch lbs.	Year	Dutch lbs.
1740	0	1760	0	1780	150,000
1741	0	1761	0	1781	160,000
1742	40,000	1762	0	1782	no ship
1743	0	1763	0	1783	250,000
1744	?	1764	50,000	1784	50,000
1745	0	1765	84,000	1785	150,000
1746	75,000	1766	50,000	1786	200,000
1747	0	1767	50,000	1787	140,000
1748	0	1768	?	1788	200,000
1749	0	1769	?	1789	25,000
1750	0	1770	?	1790	50,000
1751	100,000	1771	?	1791	no ship
1752	0	1772	?	1792	40,000
1753	126,000	1773	50,000	1793	40,000
1754	0	1774	80,000	1794	30,000
1755	0	1775	60,000	1795	49,485
1756	0	1776	100,000	1796	no ship
1757	0	1777	100,000	1797	37,500
1758	0	1778	160,000	1798	30,282
1759	0	1779	100,000	1799	20,000
				1800	30,000

SOURCES: NA: NFJ 912 TO NFJ 966.

Tin Production in Siam

In the seventeenth century, Siam was already known as one of the leading exporters of tin in Asia. There were multiple tin mining areas in Siam, two of which were located south of the isthmus of Kra facing the Andaman Sea in the Bay of Bengal. There was one on the island of Phuket (*Ujong Salang* or Junk Ceylon), another still further south at Trang, close to the tin mining areas in Kedah, and a third and fourth, the more important and productive mines, at Ligor (*Nakhon Si Thammarat*) and Patani, facing the Gulf of Thailand and the South China Sea on the northeast coast of the Malay Peninsula.

Tin had been mined by Chinese settlers in Phuket since the early eighteenth century, if not before. Alexander Hamilton, a European private trader, reported that the governors of the island were generally Chinese who, having bought their positions at the court of Siam, oppressed the people to reimburse their costs.[9] According to a Western report from 1779, the tin mining and smelting industry on the island was conducted by numerous Chinese laborers and merchants, who resided at the port town of Tharuea on the island.[10] Besides tin production on Phuket, there were mines on the Siamese coast of the Malay Peninsula facing the Andaman Sea in the Bay of Bengal at Trang, for example, which were close to mining areas in Kedah.[11]

The more important tin mining areas in Siam were located at Ligor and Patani, both on the northeast coast of the Malay Peninsula. These cities were typical small port towns. Ligor was ruled by Siamese governors appointed by the king of Ayutthaya, and Patani was the capital of a Malay state, which was under the indirect rule of the king of Ayutthaya at the time. Both port towns were located along rivers with good connections to the hinterlands, and Chinese merchants resided in these ports for international trading business. Tin ingots were transported from upstream districts, where tin was collected and smelted by a local but specific class of people (*phrai suai*). *Phrai* is the Thai lower social status of the populace and *suai* is the term used for the obligation imposed on this group by royal authorities to deliver their production as a material tax. *Phrai* had to produce tin and deliver it to a location fixed by the royal authorities. Once tin was collected in Ligor, part of it was sent to Ayutthaya and the rest was sold to foreign traders visiting Ligor. The governor of Ligor had to send an annual amount of tin equal to one-fourth picul (1 picul = ca. 60 kg) per person registered in the province. The king of Ayutthaya sold the tin collected from the kingdom to foreign traders. In the seventeenth century, Siam was an important supplier of tin in Southeast Asia, but the tin production around Ligor declined during the eighteenth century. Especially in the 1710s, there was a severe decline due to the oppression of local officials, the outbreak of epidemics and the big storm of 1711.[12]

---

9 Alexander Hamilton, *A New Account of the East-Indies* (London: A. Bettesworth and C. Hitch, 2nd edn. 1739), vol. 2, p. 69.

10 G. William Skinner, *Chinese Society in Thailand: An Analytical History* (Ithaca: Cornell University Press, 1957), p. 2.

11 John Anderson, *Political and Commercial Considerations relative to the Malayan Peninsula and the British Settlements in the Straits of Malacca* (Prince of Wales Island: William Cox, 1824), pp. 140–141.

12 Supaporn Ariyasajsiskul, 'The So-called Tin Monopoly in Ligor: The Limits of VOC Power vis à vis a Southern Thai Trading Polity', *Itinerario: International Journal of the History of European Expansion and Global Interaction*, 28, 3 (2004), pp. 89–98.

Patani was also a collection centre for tin from the hinterland. This port town was one of the best transit ports in Southeast Asia, and prospered at the beginning of the sixteenth century. In this port town, Chinese commodities were available for Muslim and European merchants. However, in terms of international trade, Patani probably declined throughout the seventeenth century, particularly following the attack of Ayutthayan troops in 1688.[13]

The VOC had its main trading post in Siam at Ayutthaya and a sub-post at Ligor, and it purchased Siamese tin at both these locations. In Ayutthaya, the king was the sole supplier of tin, which was sent from mines in the country. The Dutch purchased and exported Siamese tin to India, Persia and Europe, as shown in Figure 8.2. Yet faced with the decline of tin production during the first half of the eighteenth century and the emergence of competition and rivalry from Chinese traders concerning this item, which they were exporting to China, the VOC lost its position and diminished its involvement in the Siamese tin trade.

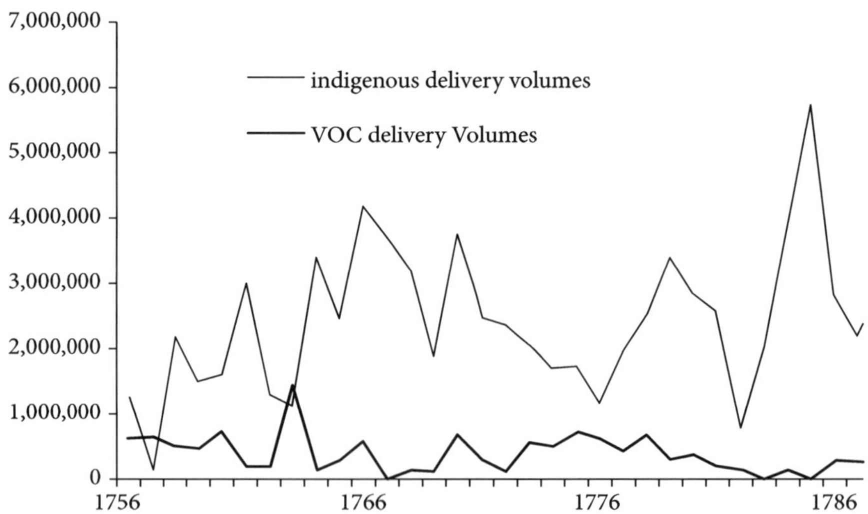

FIGURE 8.2 *Indigenous and VOC deliveries of Bangka tin to Batavia, 1756–1789 (Quantities in Dutch pounds).*
SOURCE: NA: VOC 3821: 793.

13 George Vinal Smith, *The Dutch in Seventeenth-Century Thailand* (DeKalb: Center for Southeast Asian Studies, Northern Illinois University, 1977), pp. 8, 44–45.

Tin Production at Bangka

An examination of tin production on the island of Bangka provides important information on the migration of the Chinese and their role in economic development. Tin production on Bangka began in the early decades of the eighteenth century. One legend reports that tin was discovered on Bangka in 1710 when a house burned down and the heat of the fire produced tin, although it is currently considered that the island produced tin on a small scale before that date.[14]

Politically, the island of Bangka was under the rule of the sultan of Palembang in the early modern period. In the seventeenth century, the court of Palembang had prospered from pepper cultivation and its export. But at the beginning of the eighteenth century, Palembang's economy began to suffer from unfavorable conditions in the world market for pepper, in which prices were declining. Because of declining income from pepper, the sultan became interested and involved in developing the island of Bangka's potential for tin production.

Sites for the easy extraction and mining of tin ore deposits on Bangka were developed relatively quickly, especially in the north and northeast of the island, where deposits were close to the surface. Jebus in the northern district as well as Belinyu, Sungailiat, Marawang and Boturusa in the northeast district were important places for tin mining and smelting. The sultan of Palembang appointed a governor, who resided at Mentok, one of Bangka's major ports, which faces the strait of Bangka and the island of Sumatra, to manage the exploitation of tin production on the island. Initially, Malay miners from Minangkabau (West Sumatra), Riau, Pontianak (West Kalimantan) and Java were engaged to produce tin on the island. However, in order to increase production, groups of Chinese miners, who were perceived as possessing superior mining and smelting techniques and also as being relatively indigenous as groups, were introduced in the middle of the eighteenth century. These Chinese laborers came not only from the surrounding islands but also directly from mainland China. The introduction of Chinese laborers was successful in terms of increasing the volume of tin produced. As the sultan of Palembang received huge amounts of tin from mines on Bangka worked by Chinese miners, he freed the indigenous people on the island in 1770 from supplying tin to the sultanate as tribute.[15]

In addition to the role and the involvement of the governor at Mentok, several *tiko*s emerged and took important roles in providing capital for tin production on Bangka. These *tiko*s, who were partly of Chinese descent,

14 Somers Heidhues, *Bangka Tin and Mentok Pepper*, p. 3.

15 Somers Heidhues, *Bangka Tin and Mentok Pepper*, p. 8.

resided in Palembang and were also responsible for preventing smuggling and for deliveries of tin from the island to Palembang. Representatives of the *tikos* on Bangka formed *congsees* (*kongsi*) to manage the tin mining districts.[16]

The administration of the mines on the island was in the hands of the masters of the mines, who organized their own groups of laborers to mine and produce the metal. In the latter half of the eighteenth century, most of the masters of the mines were of Chinese origin and they organized groups of Chinese laborers by providing them with basic essentials like foodstuffs, clothes and even opium. Chinese residents on the island numbered 6,460 in 1783 and the total population was 15,370 (apart from Chinese people, there were 7,400 Bangkans and 1,510 Malay and Bugis).[17] In 1823, Chinese miners and their families numbered 4,311 (including 2,601 male Chinese), with the Chinese in towns numbering 2,798, while there were 5,274 Malay people and 5,312 indigenous people (*Orang Gunong*), which meant that the total population of the island was 17,861.[18]

Since the VOC had not established a monopolist position in the tin trade in any one region in Southeast Asia and it became clear to the Company by the 1740s that there was an increasing demand for Southeast Asian tin in China, it therefore entered into large-scale engagement with Palembang for tin from Bangka. When the Bugis began to rival the Company for supplies of the metal in the mid-eighteenth century, supplies of tin from Bangka became even more important to the VOC and to their commercial strategies regarding Bangka and the tin trade.

Like the method of pepper delivery to Batavia, which was established over the course of the seventeenth century, once tin was brought to Palembang from Bangka, part of it was sold to the VOC and part was to ensure that the rest of the Bangka tin was sent by ships under the aegis of the sultan of Palembang to Batavia.[19] Under this arrangement, the quantities of Bangka tin exported from Palembang in ships under the aegis of the sultan to the Company in Batavia were greater than the quantities carried in the Company's ships.

By the middle of the eighteenth century, the Company's trade in tin primarily from Bangka had become highly profitable. In addition to Bangka being the

16 Somers Heidhues, *Bangka Tin and Mentok Pepper*, pp. 15–18.

17 NA: VOC 3867: 900–903; J.A. Schuurman, 'Historische schets van de tinwinning op Banka', Hoofdstuk I, *Jaarboek van het Mijnwezen in Nederlandsch Oost-Indië* (1898), Vervolg, 17–19.

18 Ph. Fr. von Siebold, *Nippon: Archiv zur beschreibung von Japan* (Leiden: Siebold, 1832), vol. 1, p. 24.

19 Jacobs, *Merchant in Asia*, p. 215.

TABLE 8.4 *Indigenous and VOC purchases and deliveries of Tin from Bangka, Siam and Malacca, 1758/59 (Quantities in Dutch pounds, values in guilders, and prices in guilders per 100 Dutch pounds)*

Bangka tin

	Place for purchase	**Deliverer to Batavia**	**Volume [Dutch lbs.]**	**Value [fl.]**	**Price per 100 Dutch lbs. [fl.]**
3-Oct	Palembang	VOC	106,250	25,664	24.2
26-Oct	Palembang	VOC	129,500	33,200	25.6
28-Feb	Batavia	indigenous	3,125	900	28.8
31-Mar	Batavia	indigenous	510,264	146,956	28.8
30-Apr	Batavia	indigenous	93,332	26,880	28.8
31-May	Batavia	indigenous	245,414	70,679	28.8
30-Jun	Batavia	indigenous	416,856	120,054	28.8
31-Jul	Batavia	indigenous	128,218	36,927	28.8
13-Aug	Palembang	VOC	75,000	19,248	25.7
31-Aug	Batavia	indigenous	254,335	75,622	29.7
total			1,962,294	556,129	28.3

Siamese tin

	Place for purchase	**Deliverer to Batavia**	**Volume [Dutch lbs.]**	**Value [fl.]**	**Price per 100 Dutch lbs. [fl.]**
6-Apr	Siam	VOC	30,736	11,718	38.1
total			30,736	11,718	38.1

Malacca tin

	Place for purchase	**Deliverer to Batavia**	**Volume [Dutch lbs.]**	**Value [fl.]**	**Price per 100 Dutch lbs. [fl.]**
21-Apr	Malacca	VOC	189,950	63,709	33.5
total			189,950	63,709	33.5

SOURCE: NA: BGB 10676: 131.

Company's largest supply source, the prices of tin from Bangka were lower than those from Malacca and Siam. Table 8.4 shows the prices paid for tin by the VOC at Batavia in 1758/59 from all of the above sources and confirms that the lowest price paid for tin by the Company was from Bangka. In this year, the Company's cost price for tin from Bangka was 28.3 guilders per 100 Dutch pounds (1 Dutch pound = approx. 0.494 kg), while tin from Siam cost 38.1 guilders and from Malacca 33.5 guilders. In addition to being competitively priced, Bangka was also the predominant source of tin supplies to the Company by volume. Approximately two million Dutch pounds of tin was imported from Bangka through Palembang, while about 30,000 Dutch pounds of tin came from Siam and around 190,000 Dutch pounds from Malacca. It is clear that by this year Bangka had become the single most important source of supplies of Southeast Asian tin for the VOC.

Tin Production in Malay States

The river-mouth ports of Kedah, Perak and Selangor, under the control of the respective sultans in those Malay states, were the major places for collecting tin that had been produced in the mountains and transported down-river to those ports, to be sold and exported abroad. The most important Malay state port to export tin in the early eighteenth century in terms of volume was Perak. According to Dianne Lewis, mining and smelting was conducted by local Malay laborers, since the Dutch records do not mention Chinese miners until the 1770s.[20] This situation was quite different from that of other sectors in the economy of the Malay states, such as international trade and agriculture, since significant numbers of Chinese migrants had been active in those sectors at a much earlier date in the Malay Peninsula.

Prior to the 1770s, tin mining in Perak, as in all the other Malay states, was conducted only by Malay miners. Perak, however, was the first Malay state to introduce Chinese miners to produce tin. The sultan of Perak granted permission to the Chinese living in Perak to develop tin mines in the mountain districts in 1776. There is some evidence to suggest that the Company was favorably inclined toward, or actually proposed the introduction of Chinese laborers in Perak to produce tin, based on the VOC's observation of the successful experience with Chinese labor in tin production on Bangka. Under the control of the sultan, the head of the Chinese, or Kaptain Cina, was responsible for

20 Dianne Lewis, 'The Tin Trade in the Malay Peninsula during the Eighteenth Century', *New Zealand Journal of History*, 3, 1, (1969), p. 55.

introducing Chinese laborers in Perak from Malacca with the support of the VOC. Afterwards, new mines were developed in Kinta and Sungkai as well as in the more mountainous area of Ulu Perak and Kuala Kangsar.[21]

Malacca was the major trading center for tin produced on the side of the Malay Peninsula facing the straits of Malacca and the Indian Ocean. Tin produced in mountainous hinterland districts was delivered to the river-mouth ports of Kedah and Perak, which were the capital cities of those Malay states. According to contracts between the VOC and the rulers of those states, the Company purchased a significant portion of the quantities of tin available at fixed prices. By virtue of the tin contracts between the VOC and the respective rulers of Kedah and Perak in 1678, for example, the Company secured half the total quantity of tin available.[22] The Company had established trading posts at each of these states' port cities, which co-ordinated the tin contracts and arranged the transfer of the metal to Malacca. Under these arrangements, the sultans of each of the states were free to market the remaining quantities of tin not contracted and sold to the VOC, and they sold this tin to other merchants, such as the Bugis, Chinese junk and British country traders. Some of this tin was exported to Aceh, as well as to India and China. Bugis traders also handled tin produced in Selangor, when their political power increased in the eighteenth century.

It is inaccurate to assume that the smuggling and trading of tin from Bangka caused major problems for the VOC, although the Company devoted considerable energy and effort to expelling smugglers and creating a monopoly over tin supplied from the island in the second half of the eighteenth century. One of the reasons for the VOC's relative indifference to the smuggling of tin from Bangka was that, by this time, the Company was observing adverse and distressed regional market conditions due to the overproduction and oversupply of Southeast Asian tin, which led, as demonstrated in Table 8.5, to the VOC selling tin in Malacca in the 1770s and 1780s.

Conclusion

One of the significant points in the economic history of Southeast Asia was its location between two Asian economic powers, namely India and China. At times, Southeast Asia's trade was oriented toward China, and at others there were shifts in its orientation in the other direction. A historical survey of tin

21 Barbara Watson Andaya, *Perak: The Abode of Grave: A Study of an Eighteenth Century Malay State* (Selangor: Oxford University Press, 1979), pp. 337–338.

22 Lewis, 'The Tin Trade in the Malay Peninsula', pp. 56–57.

TABLE 8.5 *VOC imports of Tin from Perak and other locations and VOC sales of Tin at Malacca, 1766–1788 (Quantities in Dutch pounds)*

	Imports			Sales
	Perak's tin	other tin	total	
1766/67	?	?	471,727	0
1767/68	?	?	359,926	0
1768/69	?	?	470,657	0
1769/70	?	?	443,465	0
1770/71	?	?	760,096	0
1771/72	?	?	610,423	101,950
1772/73	?	?	?	235,625
1773/74	?	?	?	540,150
1774/75	495,696	0	495,696	399,477
1775/76	?	?	495,373	281,359
1776/77	388,801	33,804	422,605	83,588
1777/78	386,642	7,869	394,511	0
1778/79	?	?	477,892	0
1779/80	?	?	551,795	0
1780/81	?	?	539,217	0
1781/82	?	?	117,568	26,787
1782/83	?	?	?	22,527
1783/84	?	?	166,589	153,365
1784/85	?	?	351,205	308,749
1785/86	?	?	624,720	301,439
1786/87	?	?	467,279	555,357
1787/88	?	?	111,783	77,530

SOURCES: NA: VOC 3245, 3274, 3304, 3334, 3360, 3386, 3443, 3467, 3495, 3554, 3582, 3599, 3625, 3650, 3702, 3734, 3812, 3940, 3961; NA: BGB 10797.

production and export trade in Southeast Asia demonstrates, and provides us with an important lesson about this specific character of this region.

Tin was produced in the so-called Malay world from Phuket through the Malay Peninsula to the island of Bangka, in the early modern period. Southeast Asian tin was imported mainly into the western part of Asia and Europe in the seventeenth century and early years of the eighteenth century. This situation suggests that the Malay economy had a western orientation at the time. Under these geographical conditions, tin mines in Southeast Asia were operated in hinterlands and systematically organized at maritime ports. Tin ore was mined and smelted mainly by local people in mountainous districts and the metal was transported to port cities, generally located on rivers (in the case of Bangka it was transported by ship from Mentok to Palembang). At this point in time, tin was shipped partly as tribute and partly as a commodity. In exchange for tin from mines as a commodity, necessities of life were sent upstream to mines. Once tin was collected in port cities, it was sold to maritime traders for export. These traders brought basic essentials like rice and cloth to the port cities, where such items were not produced. This whole system between mines and ports was controlled by the local indigenous authorities, while Chinese merchants engaged in supporting the system's actual business in some areas. In this way, the systematic connections between port and hinterland contributed to the production and export of tin.

Nevertheless, with the emergence and the strength of Chinese economic activities in Asia and the world economy in the first half of the eighteenth century, the situation largely changed. Although Schumpeter's first condition (the introduction of a new good) does not apply, the economic changes in the case of Southeast Asian tin production and export trade in the eighteenth century can be explained and summarized as having followed his other four conditions for bringing about economic development.

Firstly, Chinese demand for tin rose in the eighteenth century due to the development of the domestic economy (i.e. the condition of 'the opening of new market'). Tin was a necessary item not only for the production of household utensils and cannons, as seen elsewhere in Asia, but also for religious use and for minting coins in order to meet the growing demand for small denomination currency for ordinary people in China (large volumes of tin supply from Southeast Asia can be regarded as a form of the condition of 'the conquest of a new source of supply of raw materials' for the Chinese economy).

Secondly, increasing demand for tea from China in the European market and the development of the tea export trade at Canton provoked European traders to find commodities that were in demand and could be sold to produce an adequate supply of money to pay for their purchases and exports of Chinese tea. Although silver could be such item, it was clear that the more tea European traders purchased and exported, the more silver they had to take out of Europe. A partial alternative to silver for the VOC was Southeast Asian tin, which became one of the best merchandises they employed and sold in China to fund their purchases of tea at Canton.

And thirdly, when faced with growing demand for tin from China, the owners and operators of tin mines in Southeast Asia attempted to meet this demand, increasing their production by accepting groups of Chinese laborers with better mining and smelting skills (i.e. the condition of 'the introduction of a new method of production'). After the Qing dynasty was firmly established and had political control in China, it gradually relinquished its ban and control on maritime activities from the late seventeenth century onwards. The result of this Qing policy enabled Chinese people to trade as well as to migrate to Southeast Asia. Moreover, the VOC on Java and elsewhere also supported the introduction of Chinese laborers (i.e. a form of the condition of 'the carrying out of a new organization'). However, the introduction of Chinese labor in tin production in Southeast Asia was not as smooth as that in other sectors of the region's economy. It might therefore be concluded that Chinese overseas expansion in the eighteenth century suggests that Chinese economic growth in this century demonstrates a tendency toward external economic expansion. This type of expansion required not only the existence of large-scale international trade but also the interest and capability of relatively large populations to participate in large-scale emigration. Based upon the existence of the above conditions and external background, the economy of Southeast Asia was developed under the influences brought about by its port cities and hinterlands.

CHAPTER 9

Trade and Crisis

China's Hinterlands in the Eighteenth Century

Ei Murakami

Introduction

This chapter examines the relationship between the eighteenth-century expansion of the inland hinterlands of China, led by the expansion of trade during the eighteenth century, and China's nineteenth-century crisis. It also studies political, social, and economic institutions in relation to this crisis.

After Wong compared China to Western Europe without regarding the West as the standard,[1] China became the main subject in comparative economic history. Pomeranz also compared the core regions of northwestern Europe with China and concluded that the great divergence between these areas was caused by access to coal and New World resources.[2] Several economic historians subsequently compared Asian countries, such as China, India and Japan, with northwestern Europe with regard to various economic indicators.[3]

If the particular combination of economic changes that created industrial capitalism in Europe was historically special,[4] however, it is insufficient to compare only economic indicators during the eighteenth and nineteenth centuries. It is quite natural that a great divergence occurred between industrializing Western Europe and East Asian countries during the first half of the nineteenth century, because East Asian countries restricted citizen contact with Western people before this time. Hence there was little chance to introduce Western industrial capitalism until the mid-nineteenth century. It is important also to consider why individual East Asian countries developed differently when they tried to introduce industry. For example, there was no great

1 R. Bin Wong, *China Transformed: Historical Change and the Limits of European Experience*, (Ithaca and London: Cornel University Press, 1997).

2 Kenneth Pomeranz, *The Great Divergence: China, Europe, and the Making of the Modern World Economy* (Princeton and Oxford: Princeton University Press, 2000).

3 R.C. Allen, J.-P. Bassion, D. Ma, C. Moll-Murata and J.L. v. Zanden, "Wages, Prices and Living Standards in China, 1738: In Comparison with Europe, Japan and India" (Department of Economics Discussion Paper Series, No. 316. University of Oxford, 2007); Osamu Saito, *Hikaku kēzai hattenron: Rekishiteki apurōchi* [*A Comparative Study of Economic Development: A Historical Approach*] (Tokyo: Iwanami Shoten, 2008).

4 Wong, *China Transformed*, p. 58.

© KONINKLIJKE BRILL NV, LEIDEN, 2015 | DOI 10.1163/9789004283909_011

difference in living standards between China and Japan until the end of the nineteenth century.[5] Furthermore, coal reserves in China were much greater than in Japan and access to coal mines in China became easier with the development of railway technology. Therefore, access to coal and colonies cannot explain development differences between core regions of China and Japan.

The reason for the divergence between China's development and that of Japan may be found through examining the histories of both countries after the mid-nineteenth century. The difference in roles of governments has been regarded as one significant factor. However, the problems of China's Qing government, which tried to suppress rebellions and re-establish order, were quite different from those of Japan's Meiji government, which was established after the overthrow of the existing order (Tokugawa Shogunate) and tried to modernize the country. The difference in the problems reflects the history of each country before the mid-nineteenth century.

When we consider the divergence, therefore, we need to compare the differences between the two countries from the eighteenth century to the mid-nineteenth century. A major difference between China and Japan during this period was population growth. The population of Japan, which was about 12 million in 1600, increased significantly during the seventeenth century owing to the expansion of cultivated land and the increase in stability of rice farming, reaching 32 million in 1730. Although Japanese economic development continued and productivity per person increased, the population then stagnated until the mid-nineteenth century.[6] On the other hand, the estimated population of China increased continually from the eighteenth century to the mid-nineteenth century, from 160 million in 1679 to 312 million in 1776, to 382 million in 1820, and to 436 million in 1851.[7]

China had a vast undeveloped territory that could soak up huge numbers of people. Japan's expansion of cultivated land ended during the seventeenth century, however, and little new land was available from that time onward, which is why the Japanese population stagnated.

5 Dates provided by Allen for China are not very reliable. However, they show that there was no great difference between the developed areas of China and Japan until the end of the 19th century. Allen, "Wages, Prices and Living Standards."

6 Akira Hayami and Matao Miyamoto, "Gaisetsu, 17–18sēki [Overview: The 17th and 18th century]," in Akira Hayami and Matao Miyamoto (eds.), *Kēzai shakai no sēritsu* [*The Establishment of an Economic Society*] (Tokyo: Kōbundō, 1988), pp. 42–63.

7 Shuji Cao, *Zhongguo renkou shi* [*A history of Chinese Population*]; *Vol. 5. Qing shiqi* [*The Qing period*] (Shanghai: Fudan Daxue Chubanshe, 2001), pp. 831–834.

This chapter focuses on the mountainous inland areas of China that were newly opened by immigrants during the eighteenth century. The rebellions from the late eighteenth century to the mid-nineteenth century broke out mainly in these areas and were another major factor that distinguished the history of China from that of Japan.

Chinese and Japanese foreign maritime trade during the eighteenth century also differed significantly. Owing to restrictions by the Tokugawa Shogunate, which feared an outflow of precious metals, Japanese foreign trade in Nagasaki declined from the late seventeenth century. Foreign maritime trade in China began to grow again in the late seventeenth century, and trade in Guangzhou (Canton) developed rapidly during the second half of the eighteenth century. At the same time, China's domestic trade also made rapid gains.

The expansion of Chinese trade was closely connected to newly developed inland areas regarded as hinterlands in terms of foreign and domestic trade. This study aims to relate trade expansion with the crisis in the hinterlands from a standpoint of political, social and economic institutions that enrolled in China.

Firstly, we will consider the Ming-Qing transition and the features of the Qing system. Secondly, we will analyze the development of trade and the population expansion into the hinterlands from the late seventeenth century to the late eighteenth century. Thirdly, we will focus on the problems that developed in the hinterlands. And finally, we will consider the fluctuation of trade and the disasters in these remote areas from the late eighteenth century to the mid-nineteenth century.

The Ming-Qing Transition and the Establishment of the Qing System

Western scholars call the Ming and Qing periods the 'late imperial period'. However, we should not forget that the sixteenth to seventeenth centuries, when the Ming-Qing transition occurred, was a turning point in global history. Furthermore, the Qing dynasty's nature was completely different from that of the Ming dynasty.

The Ming dynasty, which arose from rebellions in the mid-fourteenth century, was established by a group of poor peasants in Western Anhui led by Zhu Yuanzhang, himself from a poor peasant family. After becoming emperor in 1368, Zhu adopted tight economic policies that protected peasants and suppressed millionaires and large landholders. With regard to foreign trade, he banned private trade and permitted only tribute trade. He organized descent groups whose members engaged in particular jobs. He also carried out large-scale population and land surveys and tried to keep order by introducing the Lijia system – composed of Li (100 households) and Jia (10 households) – based on these surveys. This early Ming system was 'rigid' and unable to cope with the mobilization of money and people.[8]

The Ming dynasty could not maintain this system. Because of increased social mobility owing to economic development, social frameworks such as the Lijia became systems in name only. The collapse of the early Ming system was caused by the lack of silver at home (excepting the northern provinces) and the development of foreign maritime trade led by this silver shortage, during the first half of the sixteenth century. Confronted by Mongols, the Ming dynasty deployed a huge army in the northern provinces, and consequently conveyed much silver to the north to purchase military supplies. As a result, silver was lacking in other parts of the empire. Because the custom of paying taxes in silver was spreading, the silver shortage caused the tax burden to become heavier and the number of people who did not pay taxes increased.[9]

Military lords actively developed Japanese silver mines, however, and new purification technology was introduced from Korea. Japan needed Chinese goods such as silks, and there was no central government to control trade prior to unification in Japan. Hence exports of Japanese silver to China were expected. The Ming dynasty adopted a maritime ban, however, and tribute trade from Japan was strictly restricted after the violent conflict between embassies of Japanese lords in Ningpo in 1523. Hence the emergence of *Wokou* ('Japanese pirates'), who were mainly organized by Chinese people and earned silver by exporting Chinese goods to Japan. Faced with rampant 'Japanese pirates', the Ming dynasty suppressed them and relaxed its maritime ban in 1567 in Haizheng county, Southern Fujian, by officially admitting private maritime trade. Furthermore, the dynasty concluded a peace treaty with the Mongols in 1571 and began trading with them at the border.[10]

The inflow of silver from Japan and the New World increased as tensions relaxed with the development of trade with European merchants, including

8 Mio Kishimoto, "Sinchō to Ūrashia [The Qing Dynasty and Eurasia]," in Rekishigaku Kenkyūkai (ed.), *Kindaisekai heno michi: Henyō to masatsu* [*Roads to the Modern World: Changes and Frictions*] (Tokyo: Tokyo Daigaku Shuppankai, 1995), pp. 15–16; Mio Kishimoto and Hiroshi Miyajima, *Minshin to Richō no jidai* [*The Age of Ming-Qing Dynasties and Li Dynasty*] (Tokyo: Chuōkōron Sha, 1998), pp. 19–28.

9 Kishimoto, *Minshin to Richō no jidai*, pp. 152–156.

10 Kishimoto, *Minshin to Richō no jidai*, pp. 156–162.

the Portuguese. The inflow of silver did not solve poverty in rural areas, though it did bring prosperity to cities. Civil and military officials involved in taxation, as well as merchants who procured military supplies, increased the stores of silver only in the cities where they lived.[11] Rebellions broke out in depressed inland rural areas in the 1620s, and then spread due to famine during the late 1630s. This toppled the Ming dynasty in 1644.[12]

As trade developed, business boomed in marginal areas such as Northeast China, Liaodong, and the southeast coast. In Liaodong, the inflow of military funds and the trade in sable and ginseng caused business to boom.

Through this boom, the Jurchens expanded power. Nurhaci, one of the leaders of the Jurchens, unified the Jurchens and established 'Later Jin' in 1616. Hung Taiji, who succeeded Nurhaci, established the Qing dynasty in 1636. Bolstered by the vigor of China-Japan trade, Zheng Jilong expanded power and ruled trade along the southeastern Chinese coast during the 1630s. The Ming rule fell into disorganization, due to growing power in marginal areas. After the Ming dynasty fell to the peasant rebellion of Li Zicheng in 1644, the Qing army entered and began to rule China proper. Finally, in 1683, the Qing subdued the Zheng family based in Taiwan, and established order in China proper.[13] The Qing dynasty intended to be a multi-ethnic nation, since it established and developed power based on mercantile activity in Liaodong. Its nature was therefore quite different from that of the Ming dynasty established by Han Chinese peasants.

The Qing dynasty established a system that differed radically from the Ming system. The Qing system was based on the Eight Banners, which were status groups, rather than on Han Chinese officials chosen by imperial examination. Initially, the Eight Banners were composed only of Manchus (Jurchen), but later they also included Mongols and Han Chinese. Banner officials dominated

11 Kishimoto, "Sinchō to Yūrashia," pp. 18–19.

12 The influence of the inflow of silver during the first half of the 17th century has been discussed in relation to the Ming-Qing transition. Dennnis O. Flynn and Arturo Giráldez, "Cycles of Silver: Global Economic Unity through the Mid-Eighteenth Century," *Journal of World History*, 13, 2 (2002), p. 405; William S. Atwell, "Another Look at Silver Imports into China, ca. 1635–1644," *Journal of World History*, 16, 4 (2005), pp. 467–483. However, one significant problem is that the inflow of silver did not influence poverty in rural areas. Therefore, we should connect this discussion with the market structure of China.

13 Shigeki Iwai, "Jyūroku Jyūnana sēki no Chūgoku henkyō shakai [The Society at the Northern Frontier in the Late Ming Period]," in Kazuko Ono (ed.), *Minmatsu Shinsyo no shakai to bunka* [*Society and Culture in the Late Ming and the Early Qing Period*] (Kyoto: Kyoto Daigaku Jinbunkagaku Kenkyūjyo, 1996), pp. 625–659; Kishimoto, *Minshin to Richō no jidai*, pp. 150–168, 207–214.

the high ranks and important posts of the entire empire. Han Chinese officials selected by imperial examination could not leave for areas outside China proper, however, so they had far fewer opportunities to become officials than other Banner officials.[14] This rule allowed the Qing dynasty to reduce the influence of Han Chinese officials and to adopt flexible policies that were completely different to those of the Ming dynasty.

The flexibility of the Qing dynasty can be observed in the changed foreign relations. It is inaccurate to describe Qing's foreign relations as a 'tribute system' or a 'tribute trade system'. Iwai regards the Ming-Qing transition as a change from a tribute system to a regulated border trade (*hushi*) system. The Ming dynasty carried out tribute with centripetal force to imperial authority. The Qing dynasty, on the other hand, adopted a regulated border trade system that marginalized foreign affairs and focused on business. Expansion of this system increased trade among East Asian countries and deepened mutual interdependence. It also separated the Celestial Empire from foreign countries and reduced friction, engendering East Asian prosperity and peace during the eighteenth century.[15]

Qing maritime trade policy clearly illustrated the transition in foreign relations. After the Zheng family surrendered, the Qing government lifted the maritime ban, admitted private maritime trade and established maritime customs offices in four provinces along the coast. These offices eventually supervised and controlled the whole of maritime trade, including tribute trade, trade by Chinese private merchants, and trade with Western countries. Each maritime customs office appointed brokers (*yahang*) who were contracted to monitor trade and collect taxes. The same system was adopted in Canton, and brokers (*hong* merchants) along with Macao pilots, compradors and linguists were contracted to handle trade control.[16]

The Qing government set up some rules to control trade. With regard to the embarkation of merchant ships, ship owners obtained permission for

14 Kiyohiko Sugiyama, "Daishin tēkoku to hakkisei: Manshu ōcho toshiteno kokusē shiron [The Structure of Qing Imperial Rule as seen from the Eight Banner System]," *Chūgoku Shigaku*, 18, (2008), pp. 159–180.

15 Shigeki Iwai, "Shindai no goshi to 'chinmoku gaikō' [Silent Diplomacy and Trade in the Qing Era]," in Susumu Fuma (ed.), *Chūgoku higashi ajia gaikō koryūshi* [*The History of Chinese Diplomacy and Cultural Exchange in East Asia*] (Kyoto: Kyōto Daigaku Gakujyutsu Shuppankai, 2007), pp. 354–382.

16 Takashi Okamoto, *Kindai Chūgoku to Kaikan* [*China and Maritime Customs System in Modern TImes*] (Nagoya: Nagoya Daigaku Shuppankai, 1999), pp. 60–94; Paul A. van Dyke, *The Canton Trade: Life and Enterprise on the China Coast, 1700–1845* (Hong Kong: Hong Kong University Press, 2005), pp. 7–91.

clearance after submitting a list of people on board and a cargo manifest to the maritime customs office through a broker.[17] Brokers were required to report the number of weapons carried aboard ships.[18] Therefore, when merchant ships departed or entered, brokers guaranteed compliance regardless of whether trade was domestic or foreign. So the Qing trade control system relied on brokers, and very flexible ones too. Since the government did not control total trade volumes as Japan did, its trade was freer than that of Japan and other East Asian countries (such as Korea and Ryukyu) during the eighteenth century.

With regard to policy related to rural areas, the Qing government did not try to reorganize the Lijia system, which bound peasants to land. The Qing government tried to establish land books, which acted as evidence for tax ledgers during the early Qing period. However, it gave up this idea owing to resistance by local elites.[19] As a result, private contractual groups composed of local elites, landholders and rice merchants became the tax collectors.[20] This is quite different from the Ming government system, which tried to suppress large landholders and take over their lands.

Hence the Qing system, which entrusted services to local agents, was much more flexible than the system of the Ming dynasty, and it could respond to the mobility of society. This can be seen in the simplification of taxation, achieved by introducing the *Didingyin* system, and through the disbanding of descent job groups.[21] Under this relaxed rule, trade developed and hinterlands expanded in population and commerce.

---

17 Kai Zhou, *Xiamen zhi* [*Gazetteer of Amoy*] (Taipei: Taiwansheng Wenxian Weiyuanhui, 1993 [1839]). pp. 168–169; Taiwan Yinghang Jingji Yanjiushi (ed.), *Fujian Shengli* [*Statutes of the Province of Fujian*] (Taipei: Taiwansheng Wenxian Weiyuanhui, 1997[1768]), pp. 614–616; Akira Matsuura, *Shindai Kaigai Bōekishi no Kenkyū* [*Foreign Trade during the Qing Period*], (Kyoto: Hōyū Shoten, 2002), pp. 585–587.

18 Lu Tuo et al. (eds.), *Qinding Daqing huidian shili* [*Imperially Commissioned Institutes and Precedents of the Great Qing*] (Beijing: [s.n.], 1818; reprint, Taipei: Wenhai Chubanshe, 1992), vol. 507.

19 Gensyō Nishimura, "Shinsho no tochi jyōryō ni tsuite: Tochidaichō to kakushida wo meguru koka to kyōshin no taikō kankē wo kijiku to shite [Early Qing Land Surveys]," *Tōyōshi Kenkyū*, 33, 4 (1974), pp. 102–142.

20 Gensyō Nishimura, "Shinsho no hōran: Shichō taisē no kakuritsu, kaikin kara ukeoi chōzēsei he [Pao-lan in the Early Qing: The Structural Formation of a Tax System in which the Right to Collect Taxes privately was usurped; from the Lifting of the Ban to the Contract Tax System]," *Tōyōshi Kenkyū*, 35, 4 (1976), pp. 114–165.

21 Kishimoto, "Sinchō to Yūrashia," pp. 23–26.

The Development of Trade and the Expansion of Hinterlands

After the establishment of Qing rule in the late seventeenth century, China proper enjoyed one hundred years of peace and economic boom. This boom was supported by the development of foreign maritime trade under relaxed Qing rule. As already observed, trade with Japan declined because the Tokugawa Shogunate restricted the number of Chinese ships permitted in Nagasaki and also limited trade values. On the other hand, trade with Southeast Asia by Chinese junks flourished in Amoy during the first half of the eighteenth century. During the second half of the eighteenth century, trade in Guangzhou, where Western ships could trade, expanded rapidly. Through this expansion, silver flowed consistently into China, which brought economic boom not only to cities, but also to rural areas.[22]

Economic boom in rural areas was caused partly by the reduction of peasant tax burdens. Reductions in the military budget due to the disappearance of the military threat from the north led to the Qing government introducing the *Didingyin* system and abolishing the poll tax. Reasonable taxes were therefore collected from the peasants and the tax burden was reduced relative to the Ming period.[23]

Accompanying the economic boom, domestic long-distance trade developed in addition to foreign maritime trade. In coastal areas, raw cotton and cotton cloth produced in the Lower Yangzi Region was exchanged for sugar from Fujian and Guangdong, and for beans and bean cakes from Northeast and North China. Fujian and Guangdong deep-draft ships moved along the entire coast from Northeast to South China, while flat-bottomed sand junks (*shachuan*) connected Northeast and North China to the Lower Yangzi Region. As for the scale of this trade, more than 160 Fujian and Guangdong ships docked in Tianjin and 3,500 sand junks were at work by the time of the Opium War.[24]

---

22 Mio Kishimoto, *Shindai Chūgoku no bukka to kēzai hendō* [*Price and Economic Fluctuation in Qing China*] (Tokyo: Kenbun Shuppan, 1997), pp. 176–205. Economic boom in rural areas was also caused by high grain prices owing to population growth. Population growth was sustained by crops of American origin. Hence the emphasis on American plants by Flynn and Giráldez. Dennnis O. Flynn and Arturo Giráldez, "Born Again: Globalization's Sixteenth Century Origins (Asian/Global Versus European Dynamics)," *Pacific Economic Review*, 13, 3 (2008), p. 374.

23 Makoto Ueda, *Chūgoku no rekishi 9, Umi to tēkoku: Minshin jidai* [*A History of China 9, Sea and Empire, Ming-Qing Period*] (Tokyo: Kōdansha, 2005), pp. 411–412.

24 Masanori Kosaka, "Shindai zenki no engan bōeki ni kansuru ichikōsatsu: Toku ni Yōzē nenkan Fukken Tensin kan ni okonawareteita mono ni tsuite [Coastal Trade during the First Half of the Qing Period: With Special Reference to Fujian/Tianjin Trade during the

According to these figures, if the average tonnage of sand junks was 100 tons, the total weight of the freight would have been 350,000 tons. If we assume that during half of the voyage to the north a ship was empty and that each ship made three round trips, they carried a total of 1,350,000 tons. Adding the tonnage of Fujian and Guangdong ships to this figure, annual trade in Shanghai could have reached over 1,700,000 tons.[25] This figure shows that Shanghai trade was already highly developed before it became a treaty port. The situation was quite similar in Tianjin, where many sand junks and Fujian/Guangdong ships entered.

In addition to coastal trade, large-scale trade was carried out along the Yangzi River. In the latter part of the eighteenth century, rice trade along the Yangzi River to the delta was probably between 15 million and 20 million *dan* annually (between about 900,000 tons and about 1,200,000 tons).[26] Therefore, total domestic long-distance trade was vast.

Long-distance trade was carried out by traveling merchants and brokers, who connected traveling merchants with native merchants. Although the scale of traveling merchants and brokers was small,[27] they nevertheless accounted for a vast percentage of the total distribution.

As mentioned above, the economic boom allowed the Chinese population to double during the eighteenth century. The increased population was absorbed in Sichuan, where the population had decreased during the

---

Yongzheng Period]," *Bunka*, 35 (1971); Akira Matsuura, "Shindai ni okeru engan bōeki ni tsuite: Hansen to shōhin ryūtsū [Coastal Trade during the Qing Period: Sailing Ships and Commodity Circulation]," in Kazuko Ono (ed.), *Minshin jidai no sēji to shakai* [Politics and Society in the Ming-Qing Period] (Kyoto: Kyoto Daigaku Jinbunkagaku Kenkyūjyo, 1983); Michiaki Miyata, "Jyūkyūsēki kohanki Chūgoku enganbu no shijyōkōzō: 'Hanshokuminchika' ni kansuru ichi shiten [Market Structure in the Coastal Area of China during the Second Half of the 19th Century: A Perspective on Semi-Colonisation]," *Rekishigaku Kenkyū*, 550 (1986); Akira Matsuura, "Shidai Fukken no kaisengyō ni tsuite [Trade among Seagoing Ships in Fujian during the Qing Period]," *Toyōshi Kenkyū*, 47, 3 (1988); Akira Matsuura, *Shidai Sasen kōungyōshi no kenkyū* [*The History of the Sand Ships Shipping Business during the Qing Period*] (Osaka: Kansai Daigaku shuppanbu, 2004).

25 Tan Xu, "Qingdai qianqi de yanhai moayi yu Shanghai de jueqi [The coastal trade and the rise of Shanghai during the early Qing period]," *Chengshishi yanjiu*, 15/16 (1998), pp. 50–51.

26 Yejian Wang, "Secular Trends of Rice Prices in the Yangzi Delta, 1638–1935," in *Qingdai jinjishi lunwenji* [*Collected Essays in the Economic History of Qing China*], vol. 3 (Banqiao: Daoxiang Chubanshe, 2003), p. 287.

27 The scale of traveling merchants and brokers was also much smaller than brokers in Japanese rural areas in the same period. Keiji Adachi, *Sensē kokka shiron: chūgokushi kara Sekaishi he* [*An Historical Theory on Autocratic State: From Chinese history to World History*] (Tokyo: Kashiwa Shobō, 1998), pp. 197–198.

Ming–Qing transition, in newly developed areas such as Taiwan and Northeast China, in minority areas such as the western part of Hunan and Hubei, Guizhou and Yuninan, and in mountain regions such as Southern Shaanxi, Northern Jiangxi, Zhejiang and Southern Anhui. The Sichuan population reached about 10 million in 1776, with immigrants and their descendents accounting for 60 to 70%. In Southern Shaanxi, immigrants and their descendants may have reached 3 million.[28] This large-scale migration was enabled by Qing policy that promoted emigration and relaxed control over peasants.

These migrations contributed to the expansion of foreign and domestic trade, as well as the activities of traveling merchants. In inland areas, immigration into Sichuan was related to commerce, because immigrants saved funds to purchase land for cultivation. Their new lives reflected their origins, and they shared with local residents methods of cultivating tobacco and sugar cane and of sugar manufacturing, which promoted economic development in Sichuan. Development of large-scale farms, salt wells, and coal mines was accomplished by organizing immigrant laborers.[29]

In the mountainous regions of Southern Shaanxi, development was also carried out by immigrants. Beginning in the mid-eighteenth century, many mills called '*chang*' were established in deep mountain areas with the capital of traveling merchants. At wood mills, trees were logged, and at iron mills, iron manufacturing was accomplished using charcoal. The number of immigrant laborers working at large wood mills reached 3,000 to 5,000, and large iron mills employed approximately 2,000 to 3,000.[30] Wood and iron produced in these mills was brought to market areas via the Han and Yangzi rivers.

As already observed, under the flexible Qing rules, the development of foreign trade caused an economic boom and occasioned development of domestic trade with the hinterlands, where augmented population resided. Because crops of American origin such as corn and tobacco were cultivated in developing mountainous areas, it could be said that this change was an aspect of globalization that began in the sixteenth century and expanded throughout the

28 Shuji Cao, *Zhongguo yimin shi* [*A history of Chinese Migration*]*; Vol. 6. Qing Minguo shiqi* [*The Qing and Republican Period*] (Fuzhou: Fujian Renmin Chubanshe, 1997), pp. 68–411, 473–504.

29 Noriko Mori, "Shindai Sisen no imin kēzai [The Immigrant Economy of Sichuan in Qing Dynasty]," *Tōyōshi Kenkyū*, 45, 4 (1986), pp. 141–164.

30 Makoto Ueda, "Chūgoku ni okeru sētai shisutemu to sanku kēzai: Shinrē sanmyaku no jirē kara [Environmental System in China and the Economy in the Mountainous Areas: An Example of the Qinling Mountains]," in Yūzō Mizoguchi et. al. (eds.), *Ajia kara kanngaeru 6 Chōki shakai hendō* [*Reconsiderations from Asia 6: Long-term social change*] (Tokyo: Tokyo Daigaku Shuppankai, 1994), pp. 114–120.

eighteenth century (Flynn and Giráldez, 2008),[31] but was this development of the hinterlands sustainable?

Problems in the Hinterlands

Lu Kun, Governor of Shaanxi, investigated the mountain regions of Southern Shaanxi in 1823, and observed that there were no wood or iron mills, although some small-scale mills with around 10 laborers remained. *Chang*, which had previously organized immigrants, had already declined.[32]

Decline occurred because immigrant land management in mountain regions was predatory. In the Qingling Mountains in Southern Shaanxi, for example, development was extended by propertied immigrants for the purpose of providing food for proletarian laborers who worked at the mills. At first, immigrants called 'shed people' (*pengmin*) borrowed cultivation rights from legal landowners. They adopted 'plunder-like' farming to quickly recover sums paid for the right to cultivate. First, immigrants cut trees and cross logs. A mushroom called 'tree ears' grew on logs and immigrants made a profit by selling tree ears for three years. After the land had been cleared, immigrants also started to cultivate corn. However, labor-intensive cultivation on slope areas without allowing for fallow periods led to severe soil erosion. As a result, cultivation in these areas was impossible after three to four years. Immigrants then abandoned barren lands, moved deeper into mountains, and carried out plunder-like production in new areas. Further forest destruction was caused by cutting trees for wood mills and large-scale consumption of charcoal by iron mills. This led to a decline in water retention in the soil and negative effects on corn cultivation in low-lying areas. This kind of mountain economy thus eventually destroyed as much as it developed,[33] and reached its limit in Southern Shaanxi about 1785 and in Northeastern Sichuan around 1798, which decreased the influx of immigrants.[34]

To stop deforestation and to maintain sustainable development, it was crucial to develop coal as an energy source. Although coal mines were developed by investing capital from officials, merchants and landowners, these mines depended upon seasonal peasant labor. As mine owners did not invest

---

31 Flynn and Giráldez, "Born Again."

32 Ueda, "Chūgoku ni okeru sētai shisutemu," p. 126.

33 Ibid., pp. 121–126.

34 Masaru Yamada, *Ijūmin no chitsujo* [*The Order of the Immigrants*] (Nagoya: Nagoya Daigaku Shuppankai, 1995), p. 27.

in technology, they rationalized methods so as to maximize profits through minimization of short-term investments. This meant that they abandoned mines when they began to flood. Abandoned mines increased in number and the price of coal rose, so coal mining did not function economically.[35] China's energy problem could therefore not be solved by coal mining.

Although China maintained sustainable development in core regions, it could not achieve this in the hinterlands through trade with core regions.[36] We should also note that this mountain region economy was vulnerable because it depended on exports readily influenced by any economic shifts.[37] In brief, the development of trade led to the expansion of an economically and environmentally unsustainable and socially unstable hinterland that depended on this trade.

Was it possible to stabilize this kind of economically unviable society? A vital role in this goal was played by clans (*zongzu*), groups based on quasi-blood relationships. In Xiunin county, Anhui province, development in the mountains was carried out by clans who had come there during Sui and Tang periods. In this area, clans controlling the shed people were mostly diligent, and consequently environmental destruction was contained.[38]

In Yunyan county, Sichuan province, however, the severe natural and social environment promoted the social integration of immigrants, so new clans were formed by landowners who occupied the area's narrow lowlands. As they controlled the distribution of commodities and obtained titles by imperial examination, they not only dominated the population as economic and political elites, but also acted as cultural elites in that they could form clans. By contrast, people who lived in mountainous areas and were economically

---

35 Yoichi Miyazaki, "Shinchō zenki no sekitangyō: Kenryūki no tankō sēsaku to kēei [Coal Mining during the Early Qing Period: Policy and Management of Coal Mining during the Qianlong Period]," *Shigaku Zasshi*, 100, 8 (1991), pp. 36–60.

36 Pomeranz compared forest coverage in the core region of Western Europe with that of Lingnan to compare regional resource depletion. Pomeranz, *The Great Divergence*, pp. 225–239. However, Lingnan is not appropriate for comparison with Western Europe, because this area was mainly developed after the 18th century. The paper he used does not show any evidence of this forest cover rate. Daxie Ling, "Wo guo senlin ziyuan de bianqian [Changes in the Forest Resources of our Country]," *Zhongguo nongshi*, 3, 2 (1983), pp. 34–35. Therefore, we should use these data carefully.

37 Kishimoto, *Minshin to Richō no jidai*, pp. 402–403.

38 Yuko Shibuya, "Shindai Kyūneiken ni okeru hōminzō [Shed People in Xiuning, Huizhou Prefecture in the Qing Period]," in Eishi Yamamoto (ed.), *Dentō Chūgoku no Chīkizō* [*Images of Regions in Traditional China*] (Tokyo: Keiogizyuku Daigaku Shuppankai, 2000), pp. 211–250.

suppressed by immigrant landholders could not form clans, and conflict eventually arose between these two groups.[39] This type of clan formation, therefore, did not contribute to social stability.

Similar conflict between elites and non-elites in immigrant society was seen in Guangxi, where influential Han-Chinese commercial immigrants established an economic foundation by accumulating land and cultivating rice, which was exported to Guangdong under protection of the local government. They maintained and enforced a political network with local officials and gained political voice by forming clans and by monopolizing elites chosen by imperial examination. Through this process, they formed a ruling group, the *keji* elite.

When attempting to gain status through imperial examination, a guarantor was required to assure proper status. Emerging Han-Chinese clans, Hakka immigrants, Zhuang people and lower class Han-Chinese immigrants could not obtain guarantors, however, and were thus prevented from forming elite groups. They were therefore opposed to these elite groups.[40]

Elite groups tried to defend the status quo in the hinterlands, while non-elite groups that formed were not allowed to join elite groups, hence friction between the two groups became serious. Because most hinterlands developed very quickly, clans established later were not annexed to those established earlier. The pace of population growth and immigration during the eighteenth century was too fast to allow assimilation.

Since the policy of *gaituguiliu* (literally 'replace the local ruler, return to central rule') promoted the immigration of Han-Chinese people into minority areas in southwestern China, this led to friction between local minorities and the Han-Chinese. In Yunnan, Guangxi and Sichuan, where the system of local rulers (*tusi*) continued, Han-Chinese immigrants provided high-cost loans to local rulers, making rulers dependent upon immigrants, who then acquired their lands. In Guangxi, tax payments from Zhuan people were supplied by the Han-Chinese, which made the Zhuan into tenants of Han-Chinese landowners, causing land-related conflicts.[41]

---

39 Yamada, *Ijyūmin no chitsujo*, pp. 24–99, 128–160.

40 Hideaki Kikuchi, *Kōsei imin shakai to Taihē Tengoku* [*The Immigrant Society in Guanxi and Taiping*] (Tokyo: Fūkyōsha, 1998).

41 Sēichi Inada, "Taihē tengokuki no Chiwan zoku hanran to sono haikē: Kōsēshō Ōshū/Ēijyunken no bāi [The Rebellion of Zhuang People and its Background during the Taiping Period: Cases in Heng Prefecture and Yonchun County)," *Shirin*, 71, 1 (1988), pp. 16–21; Fusaji Takeuchi, "Sēnan syōsūmizoku: Doshisēdo to sono hōkai katē wo megutte [Minorities in Southwestern China: With regard to the Collapse of the Tusi System]," in

When local social institutions could not stabilize society, the Qing governance system became more important. Although the Qing ruled a vast empire, its government was extremely small, as demonstrated by its fiscal system. With regard to Qing government central finances, the statutory section lacked flexibility, and real revenues decreased substantially during the eighteenth century owing to inflation. During this period, there was no dramatic increase in the number of statutory officials and soldiers. Population growth during this period, on the other hand, caused an inevitable increase in the number of Yamen clerks and runners required to provide local non-statutory finance and local governmental administrative and security services. Local government responded by expanding non-statutory finance based on surtaxes and additional taxes.[42]

Under this fiscal system, the range of services offered directly by local officials was limited, so there was an expansion in the services of commissioned agents. As for land taxes, elites who commissioned tax payments expanded their appropriations, although the principle of direct tax payments by landowners was established.[43] With regard to taxation on commerce, brokers' taxes and various commercial taxes, transaction taxes at points of sale, and taxes on special commodities were mainly collected by brokers.[44] As noted previously, brokers also collected taxes on maritime trade. Furthermore, the most important service local officials controlled, besides tax collection, was the lawsuit system which depended on *sonshi*, who were agents of a lawsuit. Although *sonshi* were officially banned by the government, their activities expanded during the Qing period.[45]

Masao Mori et al. (eds.), *Minshin Jidai no kihon mondai* [*The Fundamental Issues during the Ming Qing Period*] (Tokyo: Kyūko Shoin, 1997b), pp. 584–597.

42 Shigeki Iwai, *Chūgoku kinsei zaisēshi no kenkyū* [*A Study of Fiscal System in Early Modern China*] (Kyōto: Kyōto Daigaku Gakujyutsu Shuppankai, 2004), pp. 26–79.

43 Eishi Yamamoto, *Shindai Chūgoku no chīki shihai* [*The Regional Governance in the Qing Dynasty*] (Tokyo: Keiō Daigaku Shuppankai, 2007), pp. 79–106.

44 Susumu Yamamoto, *Kan Bokkai kōekiken no kēsē to henyō: Shinmatsu minkokuki kahoku tōhokuno sijyōkoōzō* [*The Formation and Changes of the Trade Zone around Bohai: The Market Structure of North China and Northeast China during Late Qing and Early Republican Period*] (Tokyo: Tōhō Soten, 2009), pp. 7–33. Owing to the reform during the mid-Qing period, various taxes were not collected by brokers in the Lower Yangzi region. However, the practice was continued in northern China. Ibid., pp. 28–30.

45 Susumu Fuma, "Minshin jidai no shōshi to soshō sēdo [Songshi and Litigation System during the Ming and Qing Period]," in Iku Umehara (ed.), *Chūgoku kinsē no hōsē to shakai* [*Law system and society in China during the Early Modern Period*] (Kyoto: Kyoto Daigaku Jinbunkagaku Kenkyūjyo, 1993), pp. 437–475.

This system succeeded in controlling the number of legal officials and in reducing the costs of administration. However, it also reduced the system's capacity to cope with local affairs. Local officials could deal with only a few of the vast number of letters of complaint written by *songshi*.[46] Entrusting these services to local elites strengthened their power and made it possible for them to suppress opponents. When it came to collecting unofficial taxes, privileged people such as local elites tended to be exempt from collection. This unequal tax collection system was the primary cause of rampant corruption during the late Qing period.[47]

The authority of the Qing government was weak, and rightly so, since it was dependent upon various agents. Qing officials recognized the deforestation problem and made major efforts to prevent it, but the speed of deforestation was too fast to halt,[48] and cutting and selling trees was more attractive to local people than protecting them.[49] Officials also failed to prevent the flow of Han-Chinese immigrants into minority areas. The development of the hinterlands thus proceeded without control from political and social institutions. This development began to reach its limits around the late eighteenth century.

Disasters in the Hinterlands

Beginning at the end of the eighteenth century, large-scale rebellions broke out in the hinterlands, including the mountainous areas and Taiwan. The largest was the White Lotus Rebellion, which took place in mountainous areas where three provinces (Hubei, Sichuan and Shaanxi) come together. Non-elites, who were politically, economically and culturally less powerful than local elites, such as immigrant landholders, were attracted to the White Lotus group because they wanted to challenge the existing social order. This led to rebellion in 1797.[50] The Qing standing army was useless in suppressing this rebellion, so local Qing officials ordered local elites to organize militias (*tuanlian*) to defend each village. Such local defenses and activities of braves

---

46 Fuma, "Minshin jidai no shōshi," p. 472.

47 Iwai, *Chūgoku kinsei zaisēshi*, pp. 57–62.

48 Yoichi Miyazaki, "Minshin jidai, shinrin sigen sēsaku no suii: Chūgoku ni okeru kankyō ninshiki no hensen [The Policies of Forest Resources during the Ming Qing Period: A Change of Environmental Recognition in China]," *Tōyōshi Ronshū*, 23 (1994), pp. 19–35.

49 Mark Elvin, *The Retreat of the Elephants: An Environmental History of China* (New Haven and London: Yale University Press, 2004), pp. 82–85.

50 Yamada, *Ijūmin no chitsujo*, pp. 155–186.

(*xiangyong*) allowed the Qing government to suppress the rebellion by 1807.[51] Rebellions at the turn of the century were thus suppressed partly due to the activities of local elites. Although these rebellions were affected by the financial difficulties of the Qing government, the influence of these rebellions upon the overall Chinese economy was small, because rebellions were limited to the mountainous areas and Taiwan.

Population growth continued, however, even after these rebellions. In Guizhou, the rebellion of the Buyei people broke out in 1795, owing to hostility toward the encroachment of the Han-Chinese immigrants and their acquisition of land. After the rebellion, immigration started again.[52] In Dayao county and the Yongbei sub-prefecture in Yunnan, the rebellion of the Lisu people broke out in 1820 because Han-Chinese traveling merchants developed a mushroom-growing business in the mountains, and their deforestation of mountains deprived the Lisu people of their livelihood.[53] Furthermore, increased immigration into western Yunnan led to severe competition, which led to intensified Han-Chinese and Muslim unions and deepened conflicts between these two groups.[54] Problems thus became more serious in inland areas during the early nineteenth century.

While tensions increased in the hinterlands, economic conditions worsened throughout China. First, declining temperatures reduced agricultural production during the first half of the nineteenth century. In Guangdong, for example, the resulting decrease in the supply of rice led to rising prices.[55] Economic depression in core regions also influenced economies in the hinterlands.

Economic conditions in the hinterlands also deteriorated due to fluctuating foreign trade. In Amoy, the trade control system run by brokers collapsed

51 Philip A. Khun, *Rebellion and its Enemies in late Imperial China: Militarization and Social Structure, 1796–1864* (Cambridge, Massachusetts: Harvard University Press, 1970), pp. 37–50.

52 Fusaji Takeuchi, "Shinmatsu Doshi shisutemu no kaitai to minzoku mondai: Kishū sēnan Pui zoku chiku wo chūshinni [The End of Tu-Si System and Inter-Communal Relations in South Western Guizhou during the Qing Period]," *Rekishigaku Kenkyū*, 700 (1997a), pp. 3–6.

53 Takeuchi, "Sēnan syōsūmizoku," pp. 600–601.

54 Junichiro Ando, "Shindai Kakē/Doko nenkan no Unnanshō sēbu ni okeru kankai tairitsu: 'Unnan kaiminkikgi' no haikeini kansuru ichi kōsatsu [Ethnic Confulict between Han-Chinese and Muslims in Mid-19th Century Yunnan: An Inquiry into the Cause of the Yunnan Muslim Uprising]," *Shigaku Zasshi*, 111, 8 (2002), pp. 46–65.

55 Robert B. Marks, *Tigers, Rice, Silk, & Silt: Environment and Economy in Late Imperial South China* (New York: Cambridge University Press, 1998), pp. 217–218.

during the early nineteenth century because Fujian merchants left Amoy to trade in Guangzhou and small ports in southern Fujian and Southeast Asia, where they earned higher profits and evaded the high taxes of Amoy.[56] During rapid trade growth in Canton, Hong merchants who were unable to obtain sufficient capital went into bankruptcy. The trade control system in Guangzhou, which depended on brokers, was therefore reduced to being a front.[57]

Expansion of the opium trade also took place at this time, as foreign maritime traders left Guangzhou in favor of Lintin, at the mouth of the Pearl River, and for small ports on the southeastern coast of China. The Qing government regarded opium imports as the cause of silver outflow and tried to control this trade through brokers. This led to an increase in small-scale transactions that evaded the brokers, however, and the Qing trade control system collapsed entirely.[58] The Qing government failed to control the outflow of silver,[59] which Lin claims led to economic depression throughout China.[60]

Why did the outflow of silver cause such a nationwide depression? This was due to the market structure in China. Kishimoto describes the market structure from the sixteenth to the eighteenth century as a 'chains of ponds' model. In this metaphor, numerous shallow ponds (local markets) are connected to

56 Ei Murakami, *Umi no Kindai Chūgoku: Fukkenjin no katsudō to Igirisu/Shinchō* [Maritime History of Modern China: Local Fujian actors and British and Chinese Empires] (Nagoya: Nagoya Daigaku Shuppankai, 2013), pp. 32–37.

57 Okamoto, *Kindai Chūgoku to Kaikan*, pp. 95–107.

58 Murakami, *Umi no Kindai Chūgoku*, pp. 61–84.

59 Global depression, decrease in silver production, decrease in silver coin exports from the United States, and fragmentation of coinage and seigniorage across post-independence Spanish America have recently been noted as reasons for this outflow of silver, and it has been stressed that the opium trade was not the only reason. Man Houng Lin, *China Upside Down: Currency, Society, and Ideologies, 1808–1856* (Cambridge, Massachusetts: Harvard University Asia Centre, 2006), pp. 72–114; Richard von Glahn, "Foreign Silver Coins in the Market Culture of Nineteenth Century China," *International Journal of Asian Studies*, 4, 2 (2007), pp. 61–62; Alejandra Irigoin, "The End of a Silver Era: The Consequences of the Breakdown of the Spanish Peso Standard in China and the United States, 1780s–1850s," *Journal of World History*, 20, 2 (2009), pp. 222–239). However, the outflow would not have been so momentous if the Qing empire had succeeded in suppressing the opium trade and recovering trade control.

60 Lin, *China Upside Down*, pp. 115–143. Lin estimated that silver outflow started in 1808. Ibid., pp. 74–87. However this estimation is based on miscalculation. Silver outflow started in the 1820s. Mio Kishimoto, "New Studies on Statecraft in Mid-and Late-Qing China: Qing Intellectuals and Their Debates on Economic Policies," *International Journal of Asian Studies*, 6, 1 (2009), pp. 93–95). Therefore, if Lin's claim is true, the depression started after the 1820s.

one another by channels. Because of shallowness, the ponds are vulnerable to changes in external economic conditions. An excessively small flow of money could easily dry up these ponds, thus paralyzing local economies.[61] Depression caused by the outflow of silver on a national scale thus affected remote inland areas.

During the mid-nineteenth century depression, long-fomenting rebellions broke out. In Guangxi, non-elites were attracted by a religious group called *Baishangdihui* (Society of God worshippers) that led the Taiping Rebellion in 1851. In 1856, Muslims rebelled in Yunnan, while other minorities in Southwest China also protested during this period. Rebellions that broke out in the hinterlands spread to involve many people who had lost jobs.

Why did so many people join these rebellions? Although China suffered depression, why didn't developing foreign trade help solve the unemployment problem? First, we should note that the reach of foreign maritime trade into the hinterlands was concentrated. Principal export goods such as tea, silk, and porcelain were mainly produced in specific regions in Guangdong, Fujian, Zhejiang, Jiangsu and Jiangxi. Furthermore, foreign trade could not contribute significantly to stimulating the economy, because of the outflow of silver. China had an economic structure that was vulnerable to fluctuations in foreign maritime trade.

During the mid-nineteenth century, the numbers of jobless people increased in both the hinterlands and core regions, with no social institutions to control them effectively. The power of local government was extremely limited. When rebellions broke out, jobless people therefore joined rebellious groups, forming an army of rebels that rushed into the core regions of the province and the country. Developments within the hinterlands finally shook the entire nation of China.

Conclusion

Expansion of trade under the loose rule of the Qing led to immigration, population expansion and development of the hinterlands. However, it also led to a

---

61 Kishimoto, *Shindai Chūgoku*, pp. 206–207. Von Glahn and Flynn/Giráldez emphasize 'inventory demand' as determining inflows and outflows of silver. Richard von Glahn, *Fountain of Fortune, Money and Monetary Policy in China, 1000–1700* (Berkeley: University of California Press, 1996), pp. 237–245; Flynn and Giráldez, "Born Again," p. 378. Based on this theory, however, it is quite difficult to explain the silver outflow from China during the first half of the 19th century. Although Von Glahn and Irigoin try to explain this outflow,

mid-nineteenth century disaster, because economic development in the hinterlands was unsustainable, and political, social and economic institutions were incapable of responding to this change.

This situation differed fundamentally from the situation in Japan, which maintained sustainable development with solid political and social institutions that prevented the outbreak of large-scale rebellions during the heavy farming period of the 1630s and 1830s. This allowed Japan to maintain sustainable development during the eighteenth century and to minimize casualties during political changes of the mid-nineteenth century.

Different institutions in China and Japan led to different processes of history in each country. We should therefore devote more effort to the analysis of hinterlands and the institutions that surrounded them, rather than merely comparing core regions of China with core regions of Western Europe.

The reorganization of institutions started after the mid-nineteenth century. Before the outbreak of the Taiping rebellion, Britain defeated China and opened treaty ports. After the mid-1850s, the Qing local government introduced a foreign inspector into the system of taxation for maritime customs, which enabled the Qing central government to secure revenues from maritime trade. Furthermore, provincial governments were allowed to tax the commercial sector in order to suppress rebellions, which was something that had not been done effectively before. This institutional change enabled the Qing government to cope with an expanding economy. Although this fiscal change led to the rise of influential Han-Chinese officials, who took the place of Banner officials, and brought about political decentralization based on fiscal decentralization, the Qing government succeeded in suppressing rebellions and order was restored. From the mid-1850s, China's foreign trade began to increase under a stable treaty ports system. With the development of treaty ports and the hinterlands, China was integrated into the world economy by the late nineteenth century.

Hinterland access to treaty ports was limited, however, partly due to delays in the development of infrastructure. Regions that could not access this trade were left behind economically. Hence the continued expansion in disparity between coastal areas (treaty ports and their hinterlands), which sustained economic development and absorbed capital, and less connected inland areas. This conflict led to the victory of the Communist Party over the Nationalist

---

they have not offered a persuasive explanation for this period (especially after the 1820s) when the whole of China suffered from a silver shortage. Von Glahn, "Foreign Silver Coins"; Irigoin, "The End of a Silver Era."

Party in the mid-20th century, which in turn led to China's withdrawal from the world economy once again.

China has recently experienced rapid economic growth. Whether China can remain stable, unlike certain times in the past, depends upon growth in inland areas and upon changes in the political, social and economic institutions needed to accompany social and economic changes.

Bibliography

Adachi, Keiji, *Sensē kokka shiron: chūgokushi kara Sekaishi he* [An Historical Theory on Autocratic State: From Chinese History to World History] (Tokyo: Kashiwa Shobō, 1998).

Adelman, Jeremy, and Stephen Aron, "From Borderlands to Borders: Empires, Nation-States, and the Peoples in between in North American History." *American Historical Review* 10:3–4 (1999).

Alam, Muzaffar and Sanjay Subrahmanyam, *Indo-Persian Travels in the Age of Discoveries, 1400–1800* (Cambridge: Cambridge University Press, 2007).

Alavi, Seema (ed.), *The Eighteenth Century in India: Debates in Indian History and Society* (Delhi: Oxford University Press, 2002).

Ali Mohammad Khan, *Mirat-i Ahmadi*, 2 vols. (Baroda: Oriental Institute, 1928).

Allen, R.C., Bassion, J.-P., Ma, D., Moll-Murata, C., and Van Zanden, J.L., "Wages, Prices and Living Standards in China, 1738: In Comparison with Europe, Japan and India" (Department of Economics Discussion Paper Series, No. 316, University of Oxford, 2007).

Andaya, Barbara Watson, *Perak: The Abode of Grave: A Study of an Eighteenth Century Malay State* (Selangor: Oxford University Press, 1979).

Anderson, Clare, *Convicts in the Indian Ocean: Transportation from South Asia to Mauritius, 1815–53* (London: Macmillan Press Ltd., 2000).

Anderson, John, *Political and Commercial Considerations Relative to the Malayan Peninsula and the British Settlements in the Straits of Malacca* (Prince of Wales Island: William Cox, 1824).

Ando, Junichiro, "Shindai Kakē/Doko nenkan no Unnanshō sēbu ni okeru kankai tair-itsu: "Unnan kaiminkikgi" no haikeini kansuru ichi kōsatsu [Ethnic Conflict between Han-Chinese and Muslims in Mid-19th Century Yunnan: An Inquiry into the Cause of the Yunnan Muslim Uprising]." *Shigaku Zasshi*, 111: 8 (2002).

Anon, *Tōban Kamotsu-Chō* [唐蛮貨物帳] [the Cargo List of Chinese and European Ships]. 2 vols. (Tokyo: Naikaku bunko, 1970).

Appadurai, Arjun, "Right and Left Hand Castes in South India." *Indian Economic and Social History Review*, 11:2–3 (1974).

———, "Commodities and the Politics of Value." In Arjun Appadurai (ed.), *The Social Life of Things: Commodities in Cultural Perspective* (Cambridge; New York: Cambridge University Press, 1986).

Arasaratnam, S., "Weavers, Merchants and Company: The Handloom Industry in South-eastern India 1750–1790." In S. Subrahmanyam (ed.), *Merchants, Markets and the State in Early Modern India* (Delhi: Oxford University Press, 1990).

——, *Maritime Commerce and English Power: Southeast India 1750–1800* (New Delhi: Sterling Publishers Private Ltd., 1996).

Ariyasajsiskul, Supaporn, "The So-Called Tin Monopoly in Ligor: The Limits of VOC Power vis à vis a Southern Thai Trading Polity." *Itinerario*, 28:3 (2004).

Árnason, Jóhann Páll, *Civilizations in Dispute: Historical Questions and Theoretical Traditions* (Leiden; Boston: Brill, 2003).

Aslanian, Sebouh, "Social Capital, 'Trust' and the Role of Networks in Julfan Trade: Informal and Semi-Informal Institutions at Work." *Journal of Global History*, 1 (2006).

——, "The Circulation of Men and Credit: The Role of the *Commenda* and the Family Firm in Julfan Society." *Journal of the Economic and Social History of the Orient*, 50: 2–3 (2007).

Atwell, William S., "Another Look at Silver Imports into China, ca. 1635–1644." *Journal of World History*, 16:4 (2005).

Baghdiantz McCabe, Ina, "Global trading ambitions in diaspora: the Armenians and their Eurasian silk trade, 1530–1750." In Ina Baghdiantz McCabe, Gelina Harlaftis, and Ioanna Pepelasis Minoglou, (eds.), *Diaspora Entrepreneurial Networks: Four Centuries of History* (Oxford and New York: Berg, 2005).

Baghdiantz-McCabe, Ina, *The Shah's Silk for Europe's Silver: The Eurasian Trade of the Julfa Armenians in Safavid Iran and India, 1530–1750* (Atlanta: Scholars Press, 1999).

Bajaj, J.K. and Srinivas, M.D., "Indian Economy and Polity in the Eighteenth Century: The Chengalpattu Survey: 1767–74." In *Indian Economy and Polity* (Madras: Centre for Policy Study, 1995).

Banga, Indu (ed.), *Ports and Their Hinterlands in India, 1700–1950* (New Delhi: Manohar Publications, 1992).

Barbier, Edward B., *Scarcity and Frontiers: How Economies Have Developed through Natural Resource Exploitation* (Cambridge; New York: Cambridge University Press, 2011).

Basten, J., *The Changing Balance of the Early Southeast Asian Pepper Trade* (Kuala Lumpur: Department of History, University of Malaya, 1960).

Basu, Dilip K. (ed.), *The Rise and Growth of the Colonial Port Cities in Asia* (Lanham: University Press of America, 1985).

Bayly, C.A., "Inland Port Cities in North India: Calcutta and the Gangetic Plains, 1780–1900." In Dilip K. Basu (ed.), *The Rise and Growth of the Colonial Port Cities in Asia* (Lanham: University Press of America, 1985).

——, *Imperial Meridian: The British Empire and the World, 1780–1830* (Harlow: Longman, 1989).

Beck, B.E.F., *Peasant Society in Konk: A Study of Right and Left Sub-castes in South India* (Vancouver: University of British Columbia Press, 1972).

Bello, David Anthony, *Opium and the Limits of Empire: Drug Prohibition in the Chinese Interior, 1729–1850* (Cambridge, Mass.: Harvard University Asia Center/Harvard University Press, 2005).

Bhadra, Gautam, "Social Groups and Relations in the Town of Murshidabad, 1765–1793." *Indian Historical Review*, 2:2 (1976).

Bhattacharya, B., "Between Fact and Fiction: *Khoja* Gregory Alias Gurgin Khan, the "Evil Genius" of Mir Qasim." In J.J.L. Gommans and Om Prakash (eds.) *Circumambulations in South Asian History: Essays in Honour of Prof. D.H.A. Kolff* (Leiden: Brill, 2003).

——, "Armenian European Relationship in India, 1500–1800: No Armenian Foundation for European Empire?" *Journal of the Economic and Social History of the Orient*, 48:2 (2005).

——, "The 'Book of Will' of Petrus Woskan (1680–1751): Some Insights into the Global Commercial Network of the Armenians in the Indian Ocean." *Journal of the Economic and Social History of the Orient*, 51:1 (2008).

Bhattacharya, Susmita, "The Armenians of Calcutta." In Himadri Banerjee et al. (eds.), *Calcutta Mosaic: Essay and Interviews on the Minority Communities of Calcutta* (New Delhi: Anthem Press, 2009).

Blussé, Leonard, "Chinese Century: The Eighteenth Century in the China Sea Region." *Archipel*, 58 (1999).

Blusse, Leonard, and F.S. Gaastra (eds.), *On the Eighteenth Century as a Category of Asian History: Van Leur in Retrospect* (Aldershot and Brookfield: Ashgate, 1998).

Blussé, Leonard et al. (eds.), *De Dagregisters van het Kasteel Zeelandia, Taiwan, 1629–1662*. 4 vols. (s-Gravenhage: M. Nijhoff, 1986–2000).

Blussé, Leonard, *Strange Company: Chinese Settlers, Mestizo Women and the Dutch in VOC Batavia* (Dordrecht: Foris, 1986).

Bolts, Willem, *Considerations on Indian Affairs* (London: s.n., 1772).

Boomgaard, Peter, "Java's Agricultural Production, 1775–1875." In Angus Maddison and Gé Prince (eds.), *Economic Growth in Indonesia, 1820–1940* (Dordrecht: Foris, 1989).

Boontharm, Dinar, "The Sultanate of Banten AD 1750–1808: A Social and Cultural History" (Ph.D. Dissertation, University of Hull, 2003).

Bowen, H.V., "Sinews of Trade and Empire: The Supply of Commodity Exports to the East India Company during the Late Eighteenth Century." *Economic History Review*, second series, 55:3 (2002).

Braddell, T., *Statistics of the Population, Commerce, Agriculture, Revenue and Government Establishments of the British Settlements in the Straits of Malacca* (Pinang: Gazette Printing Office, 1861).

Brandes, J.L.A., "Nog eenige Javaansche piagem's uit het mohammedaansche tijdvak, afkomstig van Mataram, Banten en Palembang." *Tijdschrift voor Indische Taal-, Land- en Volkenkunde*, 32; 34; 35; 37; 42 (1889–1900).

Brennig, Joseph J., "Textile Producers and Production in Late Seventeenth Century Coromandel." *Indian Economic and Social History Review*, 23 (1986).

Broeze, F. (ed.), *Brides of sea: Port Cities of Asia from the 16th–20th Centuries* (New South Wales: University Press, 1989).

—— (ed.), *Gateways of Asia: Port Cities of Asia in the 13th–20th Centuries* (London; New York: Kegan Paul International, 1997).

Cain, P.J., and Hopkins, A.G., *British Imperialism, 1688–2000* (Harlow: Pearson Education, 2nd ed. 2002).

——, *Calendar of Persian Correspondence: Being Letters, referring mainly to Affairs in Bengal, which passed between some of the Company's Servants and Indian Rulers and Notables*, vol. 1, 1759–1767 (Calcutta: Government of India Press, 1911).

Cao, Shuji, *Zhongguo yimin shi* [A history of Chinese Migration]*; Vol. 6. Qing Minguo shiqi* [The Qing and Republican Period] (Fuzhou: Fujian Renmin Chubanshe, 1997).

——, *Zhongguo renkou shi* [A history of Chinese Population]*; Vol. 5. Qing shiqi* [The Qing period] (Shanghai: Fudan Daxue Chubanshe, 2001).

Carré, Abbé, *The Travels of Abbé Carré in India and the Near East, 1672 to 1674*, ed. Charles Fowcett, trans. Lady Fawcett, 3 vols. (London: the Hakluyt Society, 1947–8).

Cartier, Carolyn, "Origins and Evolution of a Geographical Idea: The Macroregion in China." *Modern China* 28:1 (2002).

Cauwenberghe, E. Van (ed.), *Precious Metals, Coinage and the Changes of Monetary Structures in Latin America, Europe and Asia* (Leuven: Leuven University Press, 1989).

Chaliha, Jaya and Bunny Gupta, "The Armenians in Calcutta." In S. Chaudhuri (ed.) *Calcutta: the Living City; Vol. 1. The Past* (Calcutta: OUP, 1990).

Chapelle, Howard Irving, *The Search for Speed under Sail, 1700–1855* (New York: Norton, 1967).

Chatterjee, Kumkum, *Merchants, Politics and Society in Early Modern India: Bihar, 1733–1820* (Leiden: Brill, 1996).

Chaudhuri, K.N., "Some Reflections on the Town and Country in Mughal India." *Modern Asian Studies*, 12:1 (1978).

——, "The Structure of Indian Textile Industry in the Seventeenth and Eighteenth Centuries." *Indian Economic and Social History Review*, 11:2–3 (1974).

Chaudhury, Sushil, "Merchants, Companies and Rulers: Bengal in the Eighteenth Century." *Journal of the Economic and Social History of the Orient*, 31:1 (1988).

——, "International Trade in Bengal Silk and the Comparative Role of Asians and Europeans, circa. 1700–1757." *Modern Asian Studies*, 29:2 (1995a).

——, *From Prosperity to Decline: Eighteenth Century Bengal* (Delhi: Manohar, 1995b).

Chen, Hailian, "Zinc for Coin and Brass: Bureaucrats, Merchants, and Laborers in Qing China, c.1684–1835." Ph.D. dissertation, Eberhard Karls Universität Tübingen, 2014 forthcoming.

Chen, Hailian, and George Bryan Souza, "Zinc in Ming and Early Qing China, ca. 1400 – ca. 1680s." In Theobald, Ulrich, et al. (eds), *Sino-Japanese Trade, Commodity Chains, Regional Economies and the Environment: Monies, Markets and Finance in China and East Asia, April 2010 Conference Proceedinga* (Leiden: Brill, forthcoming).

Chowdhury, Benoy, *Growth of Commercial Agriculture in Bengal (1757–1900)*, vol. 1 (Calcutta: Indian Studies Past & Present, 1964).

Christaller, Walter. *Central Places in Southern Germany*. Trans. Carlisle W. Baskin (Englewood Cliffs, N.J.: Prentice-Hall, 1966).

City Council of Georgetown, *Penang Past and Present 1786–1963: A Historical Account of the City of Georgetown since 1786* (Malaysia: Ganesh Printing Works, 1966).

Cleef, Eugene van, "Hinterland and Umland." *Geographical Review* 31:2 (1941).

Colenbrander, H.T. et al. (eds.), *Daghregister Gehouden int Casteel Batavia vant Passerende daer ter Plaetse als over Geheel Nederlandts-India*. 31 vols. ('s-Gravenhage; Batavia: Martinus Nijhoff; Landsdrukkerii, 1887–1931).

Colombijn, Freek, "Foreign Influence on the State of Banten, 1596–1682." *Indonesian Circle*, 50 (1987).

Coolhaas, Willem Philippus et al. (eds.), *Generale Missiven van Gouverneurs-General en Raden aan Heren XVII der Verenigde Oostindische Compagnie*. 14 vols. ('s-Gravenhage: M. Nijhoff, 1960–2008).

Cowan, C.D., "Early Penang and the Rise of Singapore, 1805–1832." *Journal of the Malayan Branch of the Royal Asiatic Society*, 23:2 (1950).

Crawfurd, John, *Journal of an Embassy to the Courts of Siam and Cochin China* (London: Henry Colburn, 1st ed., 1828; reprint, London: Oxford University Press, 1967).

Crosby Jr., Alfred W., *Ecological Imperialism : The Biological Expansion of Europe, 900–1900* (Cambridge; New York: Cambridge University Press, 1986).

Dale, S.F., *Indian Merchants and Eurasian Trade, 1600–1750* (Delhi: Foundation Books, 1994).

Dam, Pieter van, [Frederik Willem Stapel and Carel Wessel Theodorus van Boetzelaer van Asperen en Dubbeldam, eds.] *Beschrijvinge van de Oostindische Compagnie*. 7 vols. ('s-Gravenhage: Nijhoff, 1927–1954).

Daniels, Christian, *Science and Civilisation in China, Vol. 6. Biology and Biological Technology. Pt. 3. Agro-industries and Forestry: Sugarcane Technology* (Cambridge; New York: Cambridge University Press, 1996).

Das Gupta, Ashin, *Indian Merchants and the Decline of Surat, 1700–1750* (Wiesbaden: Frans Steiner, 1979).

De Haan, F., *De Opkomst van het Nederlandsche gezag in Oost-Indië, Verzameling van onuitgegeven stukken uit het Oud-Koloniaal Archief*, ed. J.K.I. de Jonge, 18 vols. (Amsterdam and The Hague: Martinus Nijhoff, 1862–1909).

——, *Priangan: De Preanger-regentschappen onder het Nederlandsch bestuur tot 1811*, 4 vols. (Batavia: G. Kolff, 1910–1912).

De Vries, Jan, "Connecting Europe and Asia: A Quantitative Analysis of the Cape-Route Trade, 1497–1795." In Flynn, Dennis O., Arturo Giráldez and Richard Von Glahn (eds.), *Global Connections and Monetary History, 1470–1800* (Burlington, VT Ashgate, 2003).

——, *The Industrious Revolution: Consumer Behavior and the Household Economy, 1650 to the Present* (Cambridge; New York Cambridge University Press, 2008).

——, "The Limits of Globalization in the Early Modern World." *The Economic History Review* 63:3 (2010).

Deloche, Jean, *Transport and Communications in India prior to Steam Locomotion*, 2 vols., trans. James Walker (Delhi: Oxford University Press, 1993–94).

Doherty, Kerry W., and D.O. Flynn, "A Microeconomic Quantity Theory of Money and the Price Revolution." In *Precious Metals, Coinage and the Changing Structures in Latin America, Europe and Asia*, edited by E. Van Cauwenberghe, 185–208 (Leuven: University of Leuven Press, 1989). Reprinted in Dennis O. Flynn, *World Silver and Monetary History in the 16th and 17th Centuries*, (Variorum: Aldershot, 1996).

Eaton, Richard, *Eindresumé van het bij Gouvernementsbesluit dd. 10 Juni 1867 No. 2 bevolen onderzoek naar de rechten van den inlander op den grond op Java en Madoera*, ed. Willem Bernardus Bergsma (Batavia: Ernst, 1876–1896).

——, *The Rise of Islam and the Bengal Frontier, 1204–1760* (Berkeley: University of California Press, 1993).

Elvin, Mark, *The Retreat of the Elephants: An Environmental History of China* (New Haven and London: Yale University Press, 2004).

Elvin, Mark, and Josephine Fox, "Marriages, Births, and Deaths in the Lower Yangzi Valley during the Later Eighteenth Century." In Clara Wing-chung Ho. *Windows on the Chinese World: Reflections by Five Historians* (Lanham: Lexington Books, 2009).

Esser, S.J., "Talen." In Koninklijk Nederlands Aardrijkskundige Genootschap (ed.), *Atlas van Tropisch Nederland* (Batavia: Reproductiebedrijf van den Topografische dienst in Nederlands Indië, 1938).

Floor, Willem, "The Decline of the Dutch East India Company in Bandar Abbas (1747–1759)." *Moyen Orient & Océan Indien*, 6 (1989).

Flynn, Dennis O., *A Price Theory of Monies: Evolving Lessons in Monetary History* (Wetteren: Moneta, 2009).

Flynn, Dennis O., "Link-Unit-of-Account versus Ratio-Unit-of-Account Moneys: Seventeenth-Century Dutch Mint Policy." In *Empires, Systems, and Maritime Networks: Reconstructing Supra-Regional Histories in Pre-19th Century Asia*. Working Paper Series 05 (Ritsumeikan Asia Pacific University, Beppu, Oita, Japan, 2011).

——, "East Asian Trade before/after 1590s Occupation of Korea: Modeling Imports and Exports in Global Context." *Asian Review of World Histories* 1:1 (2013).

Flynn, Dennis O. and Arturo Giráldez, "Cycles of Silver: Global Economic Unity through the Mid-Eighteenth Century." *Journal of World History*, 13, 2 (2002).

——, "Born Again: Globalizaion's Sixteenth Century Origins (Asian/ Global Versus European Dynamics)." *Pacific Economic Review* 13:3 (2008).

Flynn, Dennis O. and Marie A. Lee, "Link-Unit-of-Account versus Ratio-Unit-of-Account Moneys: Seventeenth-Century Dutch Mint Policy." In Jane Kate Leonard and Ulrich Theobald (eds.), *Small Currencies Matter: Trade and Transactions in Early Modern East Asian Economies: Third International Workshop of the Research Group 'Monies, Markets, and Finance in China and East Asia, 1600–1900', 1–3 October 2008* (Leiden: Brill, forthcoming).

Flynn, Dennis O., and Arturo Giráldez (eds.), *Metals and Monies in an Emerging Global Economy* (Aldershot, Hampshire, Great Britain; Brookfield, Vt.: Variorum, 1997).

——, *China and the Birth of Globalization in the 16th Century* (Farnham: Ashgate/ Variorum, 2010).

Friedman, Milton, *Price Theory* (Chicago: Aldine Publishing Company, 1976).

Fuma, Susumu, "Minshin jidai no shōshi to soshō sēdo [Songshi and Litigation System during the Ming and Qing Period]." In Iku Umehara (ed.), *Chūgoku kinsē no hōsē to shakai* [*Law system and society in China during the Early Modern Period*] (Kyoto: Kyoto Daigaku Jinbunkagaku Kenkyūjyo, 1993).

Ghosal, H.R., *Economic Transition in the Bengal Presidency (1793–1833)* (Calcutta: Firma K.L. Mukhopadhyay, 1950).

Ghougassian, V., *The Armenian Diocese of New Julfa in the Seventeenth Century* (Atlanta, GA: Scholars Press, 1998).

Glamann, Kristof, *Dutch-Asiatic Trade 1620–1740* (The Hague: Martinus Nijhoff, 1958).

Goitein, Shelomo D., and Mordechai Akiva Friedman, *India Traders of the Middle Ages: Documents from the Cairo Geniza ('India Book')* (Leiden: Brill, 2008).

Gommans, Jos J.L., *The Rise of the Indo-Afghan Empire, c. 1710–1780* (Leiden: Brill, 1995).

Grover, B.R., "An Integrated Pattern of Commercial Life in the Rural Society of North India during the Seventeenth and Eighteenth Centuries." In S. Subrahmanyam (ed.), *Money and Market in India, 1100–1700* (Delhi: Oxford University Press, 1994).

Guillot, Claude, "Libre entreprise contre économie dirigée: guerres civiles à Banten, 1580–1609." *Archipel*, 43 (1992).

——, *The Sultanate of Banten* (Jakarta: Gramedia, 1990).

Hamashita, Takeshi, *Hon Kon: Ajia no Nettowaku-Toshi* [Hong Kong: A Network-City of Asia] (Tokyo: Chikuma Shobo, 1996).

Hamilton, Alexander, *A New Account of the East-Indies* (London: A. Bettesworth and C. Hitch, 2nd edn. 1739).

Hasan, Farhat, *State and Locality in Mughal India: Power Relations in Western India, c. 1572–1730* (Cambridge: Cambridge University Press, 2004).

Hayami, Akira, and Miyamoto, Matao, "Gaisetsu, 17–18seiki [Overview: The 17th and 18th century]." In Akira Hayami and Matao Miyamoto (eds.), *Kēzai shakai no sēritsu* [The Establishment of an Economic Society] (Tokyo: Kōbundō, 1988).

Haynes, Douglas, "From Avoidance to Confrontation? A Contestatory History of Merchant-State Relations in Surat, 1600–1924." In Douglas Haynes and Gyan Prakash (eds.), *Contesting Power: Resistance and Everyday Social Relations in South Asia* (Delhi: Oxford University Press, 1991).

Herzig, Edmund, "The Armenian Merchants of New Julfa, Isfahan: A Study in Pre-modern Asian Trade" (D. Phil. Thesis, Oxford, 1991).
——, "The Family Firm in the Commercial Organisation of the Julfa Armenians." In J. Calmard (ed.), *Études Safavides*, (Paris: Institut Français de recherche en Iran, 1993).
Hill, S.C. (ed.), *Bengal in 1756–57: A Selection of Public and Private Papers dealing with the Affairs of the British in Bengal during the Reign of Siraj-uddaula*, 3 vols. (London: J. Murray, 1905).
Hirosue, M., *Tonan Ajia no Kousi Sekai* [Port Cities in Southeast Asia] (Tokyo: Iwanami Shoten, 2004).
Ho, Ping-Ti, *Studies on the Population of China, 1368–1953* (Cambridge, Mass.: Harvard University Press, 1959).
Hogendorn, Jan S., and Marion Johnson, *The Shell Money of the Slave Trade* (Cambridge; New York: Cambridge University Press, 1986).
Hooyman, Jan, "Verhandeling over den tegenwoordigen staat van den landbouw, in de Ommelanden van Batavia." *Verhandelingen van de Bataviaasch Genootschap van Kunsten en Wetenschappen*, 1 (1779).
Hopkins, Terence K., and Immanuel Maurice Wallerstein, "Commodity Chains in the World-Economy prior to 1800." *Review (Fernand Braudel Center)* 10:1 (1986).
Humme, H.C., "Javaansche Inscriptie." *Bijdragen tot de Taal-, Land- en Volkenkunde van Nederlandsch-Indië, tijdschrift van het Koninklijk Instituut voor de Taal-, Land- en Volkenkunde van Nederlandsch-Indië*, fourth series, 8 (1884).
Hunter, William, "Remarks on the Species of Pepper, which are found on Prince of Wales' Island." *Asiatick Research, or, Transactions of the Society*, 9 (1807).
Hussin, Nordin, *Trade and Society in the Straits of Malacca: Dutch Melaka and English Penang, 1780–1830* (Singapore: NUS Press, 2007).
Inada, Sēichi, "Taihē tengokuki no Chiwan zoku hanran to sono haikē: Kōsēshō Ōshū/Ēijyunken no baai [The Rebellion of Zhuang People and its Background during the Taiping Period: Cases in Heng Prefecture and Yonchun County)." *Shirin*, 71, 1 (1988).
Innes, Robert LeRoy, "The Door Ajar: Japan's Foreign Trade in the Seventeenth Century." Ph.D dissertation, University of Michigan, 1980.
Innis, Harold Adams, *Staples, Markets, and Cultural Change: Selected Essays* (Montreal: McGill-Queen's University Press, 1995).
Irigoin, Alejandra, "The End of a Silver Era: The Consequences of the Breakdown of the Spanish Peso Standard in China and the United States, 1780s–1850s." *Journal of World History*, 20:2 (2009).
Ishii, Yoneo, *The Junk Trade from Southeast Asia: Translations from the Tôsen Fusetsu-Gaki, 1674–1723* (Singapore: Institute of Southeast Asian Studies, 1998).
Iwai, Shigeki, "Jyūroku Jyūnana sēki no Chūgoku henkyō shakai [The Society at the Northern Frontier in the Late Ming Period]." In Kazuko Ono (ed.), *Minmatsu Sinsyo*

no shakai to bunka [Society and Culture in the Late Ming and the Early Qing Period] (Kyoto: Kyoto Daigaku Jinbunkagaku Kenkyūjyo, 1996).

——, *Chūgoku kinsei zaiseishi no kenkyū* [A Study of Fiscal System in Early Modern China] (Kyōto: Kyōto Daigaku Gakujyutsu Shuppankai, 2004).

——, "Shindai no goshi to "chinmoku gaikō" [Silent Diplomacy and Trade in the Qing Era]." In Susumu Fuma (ed.), *Chūgoku higashi ajia gaikō koryūshi* [The History of Chinese Diplomacy and Cultural Exchange in East Asia] (Kyoto: Kyōto Daigaku Gakujyutsu Shuppankai, 2007).

Jackson, James C., *Planters and Speculators: Chinese and European Agriculture Enterprise in Malaya, 1786–1921* (Kuala Lumpur: University of Malaya Press, 1968).

Jacobs, Els M., *Merchant in Asia: The Trade of the Dutch East India Company during the Eighteenth Century* (Leiden: CNWS, 2006).

Kathirithamby-Wells, J., "Banten: A West Indonesian Port and Polity during the Sixteenth and Seventeenth Centuries." In J. Kathirithamby-Wells and John Villiers (eds.), *The Southeast Asian Port and Polity: Rise and Demise* (Singapore: Singapore University Press, 1990).

Khachikian, Levon, "The Ledger of the Merchant Hovannes Joughayetsi." *Journal of the Asiatic Society of Bengal*, 4th series, 8 (1966).

Khan, Abdul Majed, *The Transition in Bengal, 1756–1775: A Study of Saiyid Muhammad Reza Khan* (Cambridge: Cambridge University Press, 1969).

Khun, Philip A., *Rebellion and Its Enemies in late Imperial China: Militarization and Social Structure, 1796–1864* (Cambridge, Massachusetts: Harvard University Press, 1970).

Kidwai, Atiya Habeeb, "Conceptual and Methodological Issues: Ports, Port Cities and Port-Hinterlands." In Indu Banga (ed.), *Ports and Their Hinterlands in India, 1700–1950* (Delhi: Manohar, 1992).

Kikuchi, Hideaki, *Kōsei imin shakai to Taihei Tengoku* [The Immigrant Society in Guanxi and Taiping] (Tokyo: Fūkyōsha, 1998).

Kishimoto, Mio, and Hiroshi Miyajima, *Minshin to Richo no jidai* [The Age of Ming-Qing Dynasties and Li Dynasty] (Tokyo: Chuōkōron Sha, 1998).

Kishimoto, Mio, "Sinchō to Ūrashia [The Qing Dynasty and Eurasia]." In Rekishigaku Kenkyūkai (ed.), *Kindaisekai heno michi: Henyō to masatsu* [Roads to the Modern World: Changes and Frictions] (Tokyo: Tokyo Daigaku Shuppankai, 1995).

——, *Shindai Chūgoku no bukka to kēzai hendō* [Price and Economic Fluctuation in Qing China] (Tokyo: Kenbun Shuppan, 1997).

——, "New Studies on Statecraft in Mid-and Late-Qing China: Qing Intellectuals and Their Debates on Economic Policies." *International Journal of Asian Studies*, 6:1 (2009).

Knaap, Gerrit J., *WatersShallow, Rising Tide: Shipping and Trade in Java around 1775* (Leiden: KITLV Press, 1996).

Kosaka, Masanori, "Shindai zenki no engan bōeki ni kansuru ichikōsatsu: Toku ni Yōzē nenkan Fukken Tensin kan ni okonawareteita mono ni tsuite [Coastal Trade during the First Half of the Qing Period: With Special Reference to Fujian/Tianjin Trade during the Yongzheng Period]." *Bunka*, 35 (1971).

Kuiters, Willem, *The British in Bengal 1756–1773: A Society in Transition Seen Through the Biography of a Rebel: William Bolts (1739–1808)* (Paris: Les Indes Savantes, 2002).

Kumar, Dharma, *Colonialism, Property and the State* (Delhi: Oxford University Press, 1998).

Kuroda, Akinobu, "Another Monetary Economy: The Case of Traditional China." In A.J.H. Latham and Heita Kawakatsu (eds.), *Asia Pacific Dynamism, 1550–2000* (London; New York: Routledge, 2000).

——, "Concurrent but Non-integrable Currency Circuits: Complementary Relationships among Monies in Modern China and Other Regions." *Financial History Review* 15:1 (2008).

Leith, George, *A Short Account of the Settlement, Produce and Commerce of Prince of Wales Island in the Straits of Malacca* (London: J. Booth, 1805).

Levi, Scott C., *The Indian Diaspora in Central Asia and its Trade, 1550–1900* (Leiden: Brill, 2002).

Lewis, Dianne, "The Tin Trade in the Malay Peninsula during the Eighteenth Century." *New Zealand Journal of History*, 3:1, (1969).

——, *Jan Compagnie in the Straits of Malacca 1641–1795* (Athens, Ohio: Ohio University Center for International Studies, 1995).

Lieberman, Victor B., *Strange Parallels: Southeast Asia in Global Context, c. 800–1830*, 2 vols. (Cambridge; New York: Cambridge University Press, 2003–2009).

Lin, Man Houng, *China Upside Down: Currency, Society, and Ideologies, 1808–1856* (Cambridge, Massachusetts: Harvard University Asia Centre, 2006).

Lin, Weisheng, *Luohanjiao: Qingdai Taiwan shehui yu fenlei jiedou* [Luohanjiao: Taiwanese Society and Clan Fight between the Different Origins during the Qing Period] (Taipei: Ziliawangbao Wenhua Chubanbu, 1993).

Ling, Daxie, "Wo guo senlin ziyuan de bianqian [Changes in the Forest Resources of our Country]." *Zhongguo nongshi*, 3:2 (1983).

Liu, Yong, *The Dutch East India Company's Tea Trade with China, 1757–1781* (Leiden and Boston: Brill Academic Publishers, 2007).

Lodewycksz, Willem, *De eerste schipvaart naar Oost-Indië onder Cornelis de Houtman, 1595–1597*, eds. G.P. Roufaer and J.W. IJzerman (The Hague: Martinus Nijhoff, 1915 [1598]).

Long, James, *Selections from Unpublished Records of the Government: For the Years 1748 to 1767 Inclusive Relating Mainly to the Social Condition of Bengal*, ed. Mahadev Saha (Calcutta: Firma KLM, 1973).

Love, H.D., *Vestiges of Old Madras, 1640–1800*, 4 vols. (London: Govt. of India, 1913).

Machado, Pedro, "Cloths of a New Fashion: Indian Ocean Networks of Exchange and Cloth Zones of Contact in Africa and India in the Eighteenth and Nineteenth Centuries." In Giorgio Riello and Tirthankar Roy (eds.), *How India Clothed the World: The World of South Asian Textiles, 1500–1850* (Leiden: Brill, 2009).

Maloni, Ruby, *Surat: Port of the Empire* (Mumbai: Himalaya Publishing House, 2003).

Mann, Charles C., *1493: Uncovering the New World Columbus Created* (New York: Knopf, 2011).

Manning, Catherine, *Fortunes a Faire: The French in Asian Trade, 1719–48* (Aldershot, UK: Variorum, 1996).

Margariti, Roxani E., *Aden and the Indian Ocean Trade: 150 Years in the Life of a Medieval Arab Port* (Chapel Hill: The University of North Carolina Press, 2007).

Markovits, Claude, *The Global World of Indian Merchants, 1750–1947: Traders of Sind from Bukhara to Panama* (Cambridge: Cambridge University Press, 2000).

Marks, Robert B., *Tigers, Rice, Silk, & Silt: Environment and Economy in Late Imperial South China* (New York: Cambridge University Press, 1998).

Marsden, William, *A History of Sumatra* (Kuala Lumpur: Oxford University Press, 1975 [1811]).

——, *East Indian Fortunes: The British in Bengal in the Eighteenth Century* (Oxford: Clarendon Press, 1976).

Marshall, P.J. (ed.), *The Eighteenth Century in Indian History: Evolution or Revolution?* (Delhi: Oxford University Press, 2003).

Martin, Francois, *Francois Martin Mémoires: Travels to Africa, Persia and India, 1664–1670*, ed. and trans. Aniruddha Ray (Calcutta: Subarnarekha, 1990).

Mason, Will Edwin, "The Neoclassical Dichotomization of Economic Theory." *Economic Inquiry* 12 (1974).

Matsuura, Akira, "Shindai ni okeru engan bōeki ni tsuite: Hansen to shōhin ryūtsū [Coastal Trade during the Qing Period: Sailing Ships and Commodity Circulation]." In Kazuko Ono (ed.), *Minshin jidai no sēji to shakai* [Politics and Society in the Ming-Qing Period] (Kyoto: Kyoto Daigaku Jinbunkagaku Kenkyūjyo, 1983).

——, "Shidai Fukken no kaisengyō ni tsuite [Trade among Seagoing Ships in Fujian during the Qing Period]." *Toyōshi Kenkyū*, 47, 3 (1988).

——, *Shindai Kaigai Bōekishi no Kenkyū [Foreign Trade during the Qing Period]*, (Kyoto: Hōyū Shoten, 2002).

——, *Shidai Sasen kōungyōshi no kenkyū* [The History of the Sand Ships Shipping Business during the Qing Period] (Osaka: Kansai Daigaku shuppanbu, 2004).

Matthee, Rudi, *The Politics of Trade in Safavid Iran: Silk for Silver, 1600–1730* (Cambridge: Cambridge University Press, 1999).

Mazumdar, Sucheta, *Sugar and Society in China: Peasants, Technology, and the World Market.* (Cambridge, Mass.: Harvard University Asia Center, 1998).

Meilink-Roelofsz, M.A.P., *Asian Trade and European Influence in the Indonesian Archipelago between 1500 and about 1630* (The Hague: Martinus Nijhoff, 1962).

Meinsma, J.J., "Eene proklamatie van een Sultan van Bantam." *Bijdragen tot de Taal-, Land- en Volkenkunde van Nederlandsch-Indië, tijdschrift van het Koninklijk Instituut voor de Taal-, Land- en Volkenkunde van Nederlandsch-Indië*, third series, 8 (1873).

Milburn, William, *Oriental Commerce: Containing a Geographical Description of the Principal Places in the East Indies, China, and Japan* (London: Black, Parry, & Co., 1813).

Mintz, Sidney Wilfred, *Sweetness and Power: The Place of Sugar in Modern History* (New York: Viking, 1985).

Miyata, Michiaki, "Jūkyūsēki kohanki Chūgoku enganbu no shijōkōzō: "Hanshokuminchika" ni kansuru ichi shiten [Market Structure in the Coastal Area of China during the Second Half of the 19th Century: A Perspective on Semi-colonisation]." *Rekishigaku Kenkyū*, 550 (1986).

Miyazaki, Yoichi, "Shinchō zenki no sekitangyō: Kenryūki no tankō sēsaku to kēei [Coal Mining during the Early Qing Period: Policy and Management of Coal Mining during the Qianlong Period]." *Shigaku Zasshi*, 100, 8 (1991).

——, "Minshin jidai, shinrin sigen sēsaku no suii: Chūgoku ni okeru kankyō ninshiki no hensen [The Policies of Forest Resources during the Ming Qing Period: A Change of Environmental Recognition in China]." *Toyoshi Ronshu* 23 (1994).

Mizushima, T., "Nattars in Pondicherry in Mid-Eighteenth Century." In *Proceedings of the International Conference-Seminar of Tamil Studies*, vol. 2 (Madras: Kalakshetra Publications Press, 1981).

——, *Nattar and the Socio-Economic Change in South India in the 18th–19th Centuries*, Study of Languages and Cultures of Asia and Africa, Monograph Series No. 19 (Tokyo: Institute for the Study of Language and Cultures in Asia and Africa, Tokyo University of Foreign Studies, 1986).

——, "From Mirasidar to Pattadar: South India in the Late Nineteenth Century." *Indian Economic and Social History Review*, 39:2–3 (2002).

——, "The Mirasi System as Social Grammar: State, Local Society, and Raiyat in Eighteenth-Nineteenth Century South India." In M. Kimura and A. Tanabe (eds.), *The State in India: Past and Present* (Delhi: Oxford University Press, 2006).

——, "Globaler Handel und binnenwirtschaftliche Entwicklung. Südindische Hafenstädte in der vorkolonialen Zeit." *Hamburger Wirtschafts-Chronik*, Neue Folge, Band 7 (2007/2008).

——, "Features of Economic Development in Early Modern India." In *Multiple Paths of Economic Development in Global History: Proceedings of the Symposium in Commemoration of the Executive Committee Meeting of the IEHA, November 8–9, 2008* (Kyoto and Osaka: Centre for Southeast Asian Studies, Kyoto University and the Graduate School of Letters, Osaka University, 2009).

Moosvi, Shireen, "The Gujarat Ports and Their Hinterland: The Economic Relationship." In Indu Banga (ed.), *Ports and Their Hinterlands in India, 1700–1950* (Delhi: Manohar, 1992).
Mori, Noriko, "Shindai Sisen no imin kēzai [The Immigrant Economy of Sichuan in Qing Dynasty]." *Tōyōshi Kenkyū*, 45, 4 (1986).
Mukherjee, Rudrangshu, and Lakshmi Subramanian (eds.), *Politics and Trade in the Indian Ocean World: Essays in Honour of Ashin Das Gupta* (Delhi; New York: Oxford University Press, 1998).
Murakami, Ei, "Binetsu enkaimin no katsudō to Shinchō: Jūkyū sēki zenhan no ahen bōeki katsudō wo chūsin ni [The Activities of the Local Populace in the Southern Fujian–Guangdong Coastal Areas and the Qing Dynasty, concentrating on their Opium Traffic during the Former Half of the 19th Century]" *Tōhō Gakuhō*, 75 (2003).
Nadri, Ghulam A., "Indigo Industry and Trade in Gujarat in the Seventeenth Century" (M.Phil. Dissertation, Aligarh Muslim University, 1996).
——, "Exploring the Gulf of Kachh: Regional Economy and Trade in the Eighteenth Century." *Journal of the Economic and Social History of the Orient*, 51, 3 (2008a).
——, "The Dutch Intra-Asian Trade in Sugar in the Eighteenth Century."." *International Journal of Maritime History*, 20, 1 (2008b).
——, *Eighteenth-Century Gujarat: The Dynamics of Its Political Economy, 1750–1800* (Leiden: Brill, 2009).
——, "Sailing in Hazardous Waters: Maritime Merchants of Gujarat in the Second half of the Eighteenth Century," in Prakash (ed.), *The Trading World of the Indian Ocean, 1500–1800* (New Delhi: Centre for Studies in Civilisations, 2012).
Nagazumi, Yōko (ed.), *Tōsen Yushutsunyūhin Sūryō Ichiran – 1637–1833 Nen Fukugen Tōsen Kamotsu Aratamechō, Kihan Nimotsu Kaiwatashichō* [唐船輸出入品数量一覧 : *1637~1833*年 復元唐船貨物改帳・帰帆荷物買渡帳] [Statistical Lists of Import–export Goods by Chinese Ships for the Years 1637–1833: Reconstruction of Tōsen Kamotsu Aratamechō (Control List of Chinese Cargo) and Kihan Nimotsu Kaiwatashichō (List of Japanese Goods Sold to Ships Returning to China) Using Dutch Records] (Tokyo: Sōbunsha, 1987).
Neild, Susan M., "Colonial Urbanism: The Development of Madras City in the Eighteenth and Nineteenth Centuries." *Modern Asian Studies*, 13, 2 (1979).
Newbold, T.J., with an introduction by C.M. Turnbull, *Political and Statistical Account of the British Settlements in the Straits of Malacca (1839)* (Oxford: Oxford University Press, 1971).
Nicholas, Stephen, and Shergold, Peter R., "Transportation as Global Migration." In Stephan Nicholas (ed.), *Convict Workers: Reinterpreting Australia's Past* (Cambridge: Cambridge University Press, 1988).
Nishimura, Gensyo, "Shinsho no tochi jyōryō ni tsuite: Tochidaichō to kakushida wo meguru koka to kyōshin no taikō kankē wo kijiku to shite [Early Qing Land Surveys]." *Tōyōshi Kenkyū*, 33, 4 (1974).

——, “Shinsho no hōran: Shichō taisē no kakuritsu, kaikin kara ukeoi chōzēsei he [Pao-lan in the Early Qing: The Structural Formation of a Tax System in which the Right to Collect Taxes privately was usurped; from the Lifting of the Ban to the Contract Tax System].” *Tōyōshi Kenkyū*, 35:4 (1976).

O’Rourke, Kevin, and Jeffrey G. Williamson, “Once More: When Did Globalization Begin?” *European Review of Economic History* 8 (2004).

Okamoto, Takashi, *Kindai Chūgoku to Kaikan* [China and Maritime Customs System in Modern TImes] (Nagoya: Nagoya Daigaku Shuppankai, 1999).

——, *Changes of Regime and Social Dynamics in West Java: Society, State, and the Outer World of Banten, 1750–1830* (Leiden; Boston: Brill, 2006).

——, “Orthodoxy and Reconciliation: Islamic Strategies in the Kingdom of Banten, c. 1520–1813.” In Ota Atsushi, Okamoto Masaaki, and Ahmad Suaedy (eds.), *Islam in Contention: Rethinking Islam and State in Indonesia* (Kyoto: CSEAS; Taipei: CAPAS; Jakarta: Wahid Institute, 2010).

Parthasarathi, Prasannan, *The Transition to a Colonial Economy: Weavers, Merchants and Kings in South India, 1720–1800* (Cambridge: Cambridge University Press, 2001).

——, “Historical Issues of Deindustrialization in Nineteenth-Century South India.” In Giorgio Riello and Tirthankar Roy (eds.), *How India Clothed the World: The World of South Asian Textiles, 1500–1850* (Leiden and Boston: Brill, 2009).

Pearson, Michael, *Pilgrimage to Mecca: The Indian Experience, 1500–1800* (Princeton: Markus Wiener, 1996).

——, *The Indian Ocean* (New York: Routledge, 2003).

Pigeaud, Theodore G.Th., “Afkondigingen van Bantamsche Soeltans voor Lampoeng.” *Djawa*, 9 (1929).

Pomeranz, K., *The Making of a Hinterland: State, Society, and Economy in Inland North China, 1853–1937* (Berkeley: University of California Press, 1993).

Pomeranz, Kenneth, *The Great Divergence: China, Europe, and the Making of the Modern World Economy* (Princeton; Oxford: Princeton University Press, 2000).

Prakash, Om, *The Dutch East India Company and the Economy of Bengal, 1630–1720* (Princeton: Princeton University Press, 1985).

——, *The New Cambridge History of India; Vol. 2. Part 5. European Commercial Enterprise in Pre-colonial India* (Cambridge: Cambridge University Press, 1998).

Raben, Remco, “Batavia and Colombo: The Ethnic and Spatial Order of Two Colonial Cities 1600–1800” (Ph.D. Dissertation, Leiden University, 1996).

Ramaswami, N.S., *The Founding of Madras* (New Delhi: Orient Longman, 1977).

Ray, Aniruddha, “Cambay and Its Hinterland: Early Eighteenth Century.” In Indu Banga (ed.), *Ports and Their Hinterlands in India, 1700–1950* (Delhi: Manohar, 1992).

Raychaudhuri, Tapan, and Irfan Habib (eds.), *The Cambridge Economic History of India; Vol. 1. c. 1200–c. 1750* (Cambridge: Cambridge University Press, 1982).

Reid, Anthony, *Southeast Asia in the Age of Commerce 1450–1680; Vol. 2. Expansion and Crisis* (New Haven and London: Yale University Press, 1993).

——, "Chinese Trade and Southeast Asian Economic Expansion in the Later Eighteenth and Nineteenth Centuries: An Overview." In Nola Cooke and Li Tana (eds.), *Water Frontier: Commerce and the Chinese in the Lower Mekong, 1750–1880* (Lanham: Rowman & Littlefield Publishers, 2004).

Reid, Anthony, and Fernando, Radin, "Shipping on Melaka and Singapore as an Index of Growth, 1760–1840." *South Asia*, 19 (1996).

Richards, J.F., "European City-States on the Coromandel Coast." In P.M. Joshi and M.A. Nayeem (eds.), *Studies in the Foreign Relations of India* (Hyderabad: State Archives, Government of Andhra Pradesh, 1975).

Richards, J.F., *The New Cambridge History of India; Vol. 1. Part 5. The Mughal Empire* (Cambridge: Cambridge University Press, 1993).

Riello, Giorgio, and Tirtankar Roy (eds.), *How India Clothed the World: The World of South Asian Textiles, 1500–1850* (Leiden: Brill, 2009).

Ross, Robert J., and Telkamp, Gerard J., "Introduction." In Robert J. Ross and Gerard J. Telkamp (eds.), *Colonial Cities* (Dordrecht: Martinus Nijhoff Publishers, 1985).

Russell, J., "Two Armenian Graffiti's from Ziârat, Pakistan." *Revue Etude Armeninnes*, 16 (1988–89).

Saito, Osamu, *Hikaku kēzai hattenron: Rekishiteki apurōchi [A Comparative Study of Economic Development: A Historical Approach]* (Tokyo: Iwanami Shoten, 2008).

Sandhu, Kernial Singh, *Indians in Malaya: Some Aspects of their Immigration and Settlement (1786–1957)* (Cambridge: Cambridge University Press, 1969).

SarDesai, D.R., *British Trade and Expansion in Southeast Asia, 1830–1914* (New Delhi: Allied, 1977).

Schumpeter, Joseph A., *The Theory of Economic Development* (Cambridge, Massachusetts: Harvard University Press, 1934).

Schuurman, J.A., "Historische schets van de tinwinning op Banka." Hoofdstuk I, *Jaarboek van het Mijnwezen in Nederlandsch Oost-Indië* (1898), Vervolg, 17–19.

Seth, Mesrovb, *Armenians in India: From the Earliest Times to the Present Day—A work of Original Research* (Delhi: Oxford Book House etc., reprint, 1983(1937)).

Shibuya, Yuko, "Shindai Kyūneiken ni okeru hōminzō [Shed People in Xiuning, Huizhou Prefecture in the Qing Period]." In Eishi Yamamoto (ed.), *Dentō Chūgoku no Chīkizō [Images of Regions in Traditional China]* (Tokyo: Keiogizyuku Daigaku Shuppankai, 2000).

Shimada, Ryuto, *The Intra-Asian Trade in Japanese Copper by the Dutch East India Company during the Eighteenth Century* (Leiden; Boston: Brill, 2006).

Sinha, N.K., *The Economic History of Bengal: From Plassey to the Permanent Settlement*, 3 vols. (Calcutta: Firma KLM, 1956–1970).

Sinha, Pradip, *Calcutta in Urban History* (Calcutta: Firma KLM, 1978).

Skinner, G. William, *Chinese Society in Thailand: An Analytical History* (Ithaca: Cornell University Press, 1957).
——, "Presidential Address: The Structure of Chinese History." *The Journal of Asian Studies* 44:2 (1985).
Slot, Ben, "At the Backdoor of the Levant: Anglo-Dutch Competition in the Persian Gulf, 1623–1766." In Hamilton Alastair (ed.), *Friends and Rivals in the East: Studies in Anglo-Dutch Relations in the Levant from the Seventeenth to the Early Nineteenth Century* (Leiden: Brill, 2000).
Smith, George Vinal, *The Dutch in Seventeenth-Century Thailand* (DeKalb: Center for Southeast Asian Studies, Northern Illinois University, 1977).
Somers Heidhues, Mary F., *Bangka Tin and Mentok Pepper: Chinese Settlement on an Indonesian Island* (Singapore: Institute of Southeast Asian Studies, 1992).
Souza, George Bryan, "Ballast Goods: Chinese Maritime Trade in Zinc and Sugar in the Seventeenth and Eighteenth Centuries." In Dietmar Rothermund and Roderick Ptak (eds.), *Emporia, Commodities and Entrepreneurs in Asian Maritime Trade, c.1400–1750* (Stuttgart: Steiner Verlag 1990).
——, "Country Trade and Chinese Alum: Raw Material Supply in Asia's Textile Production in the Seventeenth and Eighteenth Centuries." *Revista de Cultura* 11 (2004).
——, "The Portuguese Crown and Brazil: Tobacco Cultivation, the African Slave Trade, and the Atlantic and Global Economy c.1674 to 1776." *Revista da Cultura* 25 (2008).
——, "Cowries and Commerce: Mozambique, the Portuguese, and Afro-Asian-American Exchanges in the Emerging Global Economy." In *Monies for ordinary people: neither precious nor national* Institute of Oriental Culture, University of Tokyo, Tokyo, Japan, unpublished conference presentation 2009.
Steensgaard, Niels, "The Route through Quandahar: The Significance of the Overland Trade from India to the West in the Seventeenth Century." In Sushil Chaudhury and Michel Morineau (eds.), *Merchants, Companies and Trade: Europe and Asia in the Early Modern Era* (Cambridge: Cambridge University Press, 1999).
Stevens, F.G., "A Contribution to the Early History of Prince of Wales' Island." *Journal of the Malayan Branch of the Royal Asiatic Society*, 7 (1929).
Stockwell, A.J., "British Expansion and Rule in South-East Asia." In Wm. Roger Louis (editor-in-chief), *The Oxford History of the British Empire,* Vol. III: Andrew Porter (ed.), *The Nineteenth Century* (Oxford: Oxford University Press, 1999).
Subrahmanyam, Sanjay, "Iranians Abroad: Intra-Asian Elite Migration and Early Modern State Formation." *Journal of Asian Studies*, 51:2 (1992).
Subramanian, Lakshmi, "Capital and Crowd in a Declining Asian Port City: The Anglo-Bania Order and the Surat Riots of 1795." *Modern Asian Studies*, 19:2 (1985).

——, "Banias and the British: the Role of Indigenous Credit in the Process of Imperial Expansion in Western India in the Second Half of the Eighteenth Century." *Modern Asian Studies*, 21:3 (1987).

——, "The Eighteenth Century Social Order in Surat: A Reply and an Excursus on the Riots of 1788 and 1795." *Modern Asian Studies*, 25:2 (1991).

——, *Indigenous Capital and Imperial Expansion: Bombay, Surat and the West Coast* (Delhi: Oxford University Press, 1996).

Sugihara, Kaoru, *Ajiakan Boueki no Keisei to Kozo* [The Formation and Structure of Intra-Asian Trade] (Kyoto: Mineruva Shobo, 1996).

——, "Daishin tēkoku to hakkisei: Manshu ōcho toshiteno kokusē shiron [The Structure of Qing Imperial Rule as seen from the Eight Banner System]." *Chūgoku Shigaku*, 18 (2008).

——, "19 Seiki Zenhan no Ajia Koekiken: Tokeitekikousatu [Intra-Asian Trade in the First Half of the Nineteenth Century: A Statistic Inquiry]." In Naoto Kagotani and Kohei Wakimura (eds.), *Teikoku to Ajia Nettowaku, Choki no 19 Seiki* [Empire and Asian Network: The Long Nineteenth Century], (Kyoto: Sekai Shisosha, 2009).

Taeuber, Irene Barnes, *The Population of Japan* (Princeton: Princeton University Press, 1958).

Taiwan Yinghang Jingji Yanjiushi (ed.), *Fujian Shengli* [*Statutes of the Province of Fujian*] (Taipei: Taiwansheng Wenxian Weiyuanhui, 1997[1768]).

Takeuchi, Fusaji, "Sēnan syōsūmizoku: Doshisēdo to sono hōkai katē wo megutte [Minorities in Southwestern China: With regard to the Collapse of the Tusi System]." In Masao Mori et al. (eds.), *Minshin Jidai no kihon mondai* [*The Fundamental Issues during the Ming Qing Period*] (Tokyo: Kyūko Shoin, 1997a).

——, "Shinmatsu Doshi system no kaitai to minzoku mondai: Kishū sēnan Pui zoku chiku wo chūshinni [The End of Tu-Si System and Inter-Communal Relations in South Western Guizhou during the Qing Period]." *Rekishigaku Kenkyū*, 700 (1997b).

Talens, Johan, *Een feodale samenleving in koloniaal vaarwater: Staatvorming, koloniale expansie en economische onderontwikkeling in Banten, West-Java 1600–1750* (Hilversum: Verloren, 1999).

Teisseire, Andries, "Verhandeling over den tegenwoordigen staat der zuikermolens omstreeks de stadt Batavia, benevens de middelen tot derzelver herstel, en eenige verdere daar toe betrekkelyke aanmerkingen." *Verhandelingen van de Bataviaasch Genootschap van Kunsten en Wetenschappen*, 5 (1790).

Temple, R.C., "Side-lights on Omichund: An Echo of the Intrigues before Plassey." *Indian Antiquary*, (2nd series, 47) (1918).

——, *The Private Diary of Ananda Ranga Pillai*, trans. and eds. J.F. Price and K. Rangachari, 12 vols. (Madras: Government Press, 1904–1928; reprint, New Delhi: Asian Educational Services, 1985).

Topik, Steven C., and Allen Wells, "Commodity Chains in a Global Economy." In Emily S. Rosenberg (ed.), *A World Connecting, 1870–1945* (Cambridge, Mass.: Belknap Press of Harvard University Press, 2012).

Topik, Steven C., Carlos Marichal, and Zephyr L. Frank (eds.), *From Silver to Cocaine: Latin American Commodity Chains and the Building of the World Economy, 1500–2000* (Durham: Duke University Press, 2006).

Torri, Michelguglielmo, "Mughal Nobles, Indian Merchants and the Beginning of British Conquest in Western India: The Case of Surat, 1756–1759." *Modern Asian Studies*, 32:2 (1998).

Travers, Robert, "The Eighteenth Century in Indian History: A Review Essay." *Eighteenth-Century Studies* 40:3 (2007).

Tripathi, Amlesh, *Trade and Finance in the Bengal Presidency, 1793–1833* (Calcutta: Oxford University Press, revised edition, 1979).

Trocki, Carl A., *Prince of Pirates: The Temenggongs and the Development of Johor and Singapore 1784–1885* (Singapore: Singapore University Press, 1979).

——, "Chinese Pioneering in Eighteenth-Century Southeast Asia." In Anthony Reid (ed.), *The Last Stand of Asian Autonomies: Responses to Modernity in the Diverse States of Southeast Asia and Korea, 1750–1900* (Houndmills and London: Macmillan Press, 1997).

Tuo, Lu et al. (eds.), *Qinding Daqing huidian shili* [Imperially Commissioned Institutes and Precedents of the Great Qing] (Beijing: [s.n.], 1818; reprint, Taipei: Wenhai Chubanshe, 1992).

Ueda, Makoto, "Chūgoku ni okeru sētai shisutemu to sanku kēzai: Shinrē sanmyaku no jirē kara [Environmental System in China and the Economy in the Mountainous Areas: An Example of the Qinling Mountains]." In Yūzō Mizoguchi et al. (eds.), *Ajia kara kanngaeru 6 Chōki shakai hendō [Reconsiderations from Asia 6: Long-term social change]* (Tokyo: Tokyo Daigaku Shuppankai, 1994).

——, *Chūgoku no rekishi 9, Umi to tēkoku: Minshin jidai* [A History of China 9, Sea and Empire, Ming-Qing Period] (Tokyo: Kōdansha, 2005).

Unger, Richard W. (ed.), *Shipping and Economic Growth, 1350–1850*. (Leiden; Boston: Brill, 2011).

Van Breugel, J. de Rovere, "Bedenkingen over den Staat van Bantam." *Bijdragen tot de Taal-, Land- en Volkenkunde van Nederlandsch-Indië, tijdschrift van het Koninklijk Instituut voor de Taal-, Land- en Volkenkunde van Nederlandsch-Indië*, new series, 1 (1856).

Van den Berg, N.P., "De suikerindustrie op Java onder het bestuur van de Oost-Indische Compagnie." In N.P. van den Berg (ed.), *Uit de dagen der Compagnie: geschiedkundige schetsen* (Haarlem: H.D. Tjeenk Willing & Zoon, 1904).

Van der Tuuk, H.N., "Naar aanleiding van eene proclamatie van den Sultan van Bantam." *Tijdschrift voor Indische Taal-, Land- en Volkenkunde*, 23 (1876).

——, "Lampongsche pijagem's." *Tijdschrift voor Indische Taal-, Land- en Volkenkunde*, 29 (1884).

Van Dyke, Paul A., *The Canton Trade: Life and Enterprise on the China Coast, 1700–1845* (Hong Kong: Hong Kong University Press, 2005).

Van Santen, H.W., "De Verenigde Oost-Indische Compagnie in Gujarat en Hindustan, 1620–1660" (Ph.D. Dissertation, Leiden University, 1982).

Van Schendel, Willem, *Global Blue: Indigo and Espionage in Colonial Bengal* (Dhaka: University Press, 2006).

Vansittart, H., *A Narrative of the Transactions in Bengal 1760–1764*, eds. A.C. Banerjee and B.K. Ghosh (Kolkata: K.P. Bagchi, 1976).

Viallé, Cynthia, and Leonard Blussé (eds.), *The Deshima Dagregisters*. 12 vols. (Leiden: Institute for the History of European Expansion, 1986–2005).

Von Glahn, Richard, *Fountain of Fortune, Money and Monetary Policy in China, 1000–1700* (Berkeley: University of California Press, 1996).

——, "Foreign Silver Coins in the Market Culture of Nineteenth Century China." *International Journal of Asian Studies*, 4, 2 (2007).

Von Siebold, Ph. Fr., *Nippon: Archiv zur beschreibung von Japan* (Leiden: Verfasser, 1832).

Vos, Reinout, *Gentle Janus, Merchant Prince: The VOC and the Tightrope of Diplomacy in the Malay World, 1740–1800* (Leiden: KITLV, 1993).

Wallerstein, Immanuel Maurice, *The Modern World-System*. 4 vols (New York: Academic Press, 1974–2011).

Wang, Yejian, "Secular Trends of Rice Prices in the Yangzi Delta, 1638–1935." In *Qingdai jinjishi lunwenji* [Collected Essays in the Economic History of Qing China], vol. 3 (Banqiao: Daoxiang Chubanshe, 2003).

Webster, Anthony, "British Expansion in South-East Asia and the Role of Robert Farquhar, Lieutenant-Governor of Penang, 1804–5." *Journal of Imperial and Commonwealth History*, 23:1 (1995).

——, *Gentlemen Capitalists: British Imperialism in South East Asia 1770–1890* (London: Tauris Academic Studies, 1998).

——, *The Twilight of the East India Company: The Evolution of Anglo-Asian Commerce and Politics 1790–1860* (Woodbridge: Boydell Press, 2009).

Wendt, Ian C., "Four Centuries of Decline? Understanding the Changing Structure of the South Indian Textile Industry." In Giorgio Riello and Tirthankar Roy (eds.), *How India Clothed the World: The World of South Asian Textiles, 1500–1850* (Leiden and Boston: Brill, 2009).

Williams, Michael, *Communism, Religion, and Revolt in Banten* (Athens, Ohio: Ohio University Center for International Studies, 1990).

Wink, André, *Al-Hind: The Making of the Indo-Islamic World*, 3 vols. (Leiden: Brill, 2004).

Wong, R. Bin, *China Transformed: Historical Change and the Limits of European Experience* (Ithaca and London: Cornell University Press, 1997).

Xu, Tan, "Qingdai qianqi de yanhai moayi yu Shanghai de jueqi [The coastal trade and the rise of Shanghai during the early Qing period]." *Chengshishi yanjiu*, 15/16 (1998).

Yamada, Masaru, *Ijūmin no titsujo* [The Order of the Immigrants] (Nagoya: Nagoya Daigaku Shuppankai, 1995).

Yamamoto, Eishi, *Shindai Chūgoku no chīki shihai* [The Regional Governance in the Qing Dynasty] (Tokyo: Keiō Daigaku Shuppankai, 2007).

Yamamoto, Susumu, *Shindai no Sijyōkōzō to kēzai sēsaku* [Market Structure and Economic Policy during the Qing Period] (Nagoya: Nagoya Daigaku Shuppankai, 2002).

——, *Kan Bokkai kōekiken no kēsē to henyō: Shinmatsu minkokuki kahoku tōhokuno sijyōkoōzō* [The Formation and Changes of the Trade Zone around Bohai: The Market Structure of North China and Northeast China during Late Qing and Early Republican Period] (Tokyo: Tōhō Soten, 2009).

Yamawaki, Teijiro, *Nagasaki no Oranda Shōkan: Sekai no naka no Sakoku Nihon* [The Dutch Establishment in Nagasaki: Secluded Japan in the World] (Tokyo: Chūō Kōronsha, 1980).

Yang, Anand A., "Indian Convict Workers in Southeast Asia in the Late Eighteenth and Early Nineteenth Centuries." *Journal of World History*, 14:2 (2003).

Yim, Shui-Yuen, "Famine Relief Statistics as a Guide to the Population of Sixteenth-Century China: A Case-Study of Honan Province." *Ch'ing-shih wen-t'i* 3:9 (1978).

Zhou, Kai, *Xiamen zhi* [*Gazetteer of Amoy*] (Taipei: Taiwansheng Wenxian Weiyuanhui, 1993 [1839]).

Zhuang, Jifa, *Qingdai Tiandihui yanliu kao* [An Investigation of the Origin of Tiandihui during the Qing Period] (Taipei: National Palace Museum, 1981).

Index